MEDIA, MEMORY, AND THE FIRST WORLD WAR

McGill-Queen's Studies in the History of Ideas
Series Editor: Philip J. Cercone

1 Problems of Cartesianism
Edited by Thomas M.
Lennon, John M. Nicholas,
and John W. Davis

2 The Development of the Idea
of History in Antiquity
Gerald A. Press

3 Claude Buffier
and Thomas Reid:
Two Common-Sense
Philosophers
Louise Marcil-Lacoste

4 Schiller, Hegel, and Marx:
State, Society, and the
Aesthetic Ideal
of Ancient Greece
Philip J. Kain

5 John Case
and Aristotelianism
in Renaissance England
Charles B. Schmitt

6 Beyond Liberty
and Property:
The Process of Self-
Recognition in Eighteenth-
Century Political Thought
J.A.W. Gunn

7 John Toland: His Methods,
Manners, and Mind
Stephen H. Daniel

8 Coleridge and
the Inspired Word
Anthony John Harding

9 The Jena System, 1804–5:
Logic and Metaphysics
G.W.F. Hegel
Translation edited by
John W. Burbidge and
George di Giovanni
Introduction and notes
by H.S. Harris

10 Consent, Coercion,
and Limit:
The Medieval Origins
of Parliamentary Democracy
Arthur P. Monahan

11 Scottish Common Sense
in Germany, 1768–1800:
A Contribution to the
History of Critical
Philosophy
Manfred Kuehn

12 Paine and Cobbett:
The Transatlantic Connection
David A. Wilson

13 Descartes and the
Enlightenment
Peter A. Schouls

14 Greek Scepticism:
Anti-Realist Trends
in Ancient Thought
Leo Groarke

15 The Irony of Theology
and the Nature
of Religious Thought
Donald Wiebe

16 Form and Transformation:
A Study in the Philosophy
of Plotinus
Frederic M. Schroeder

17 From Personal Duties
towards Personal Rights:
Late Medieval and Early
Modern Political Thought,
1300–1650
Arthur P. Monahan

18 The Main Philosophical
Writings and the
Novel *Allwill*
Friedrich Heinrich Jacobi
Translated and edited by
George di Giovanni

19 Kierkegaard as Humanist:
Discovering My Self
Arnold B. Come

20 Durkheim, Morals
and Modernity
W. Watts Miller

21 The Career of Toleration:
John Locke, Jonas Proast,
and After
Richard Vernon

22 Dialectic of Love: Platonism
in Schiller's Aesthetics
David Pugh

23 History and Memory
in Ancient Greece
Gordon S. Shrimpton

24 Kierkegaard as Theologian:
Recovering My Self
Arnold B. Come

25 An Enlightenment Tory
in Victorian Scotland:
The Career of
Sir Archibald Alison
Michael Michie

26 The Road to Egdon Heath:
The Aesthetics of the Great
in Nature
Richard Bevis

27 Jena Romanticism and
Its Appropriation
of Jakob Böhme:
Theosophy – Hagiography –
Literature
Paolo Mayer

28 Enlightenment and
Community:
Lessing, Abbt, Herder,
and the Quest for
a German Public
Benjamin W. Redekop

29 Jacob Burckhardt and
the Crisis of Modernity
John R. Hinde

30 The Distant Relation:
Time and Identity in
Spanish-American Fiction
Eoin S. Thomson

31 Mr Simson's Knotty Case:
Divinity, Politics, and Due
Process in Early Eighteenth-
Century Scotland
Anne Skoczylas

32 Orthodoxy and
Enlightenment:
George Campbell in the
Eighteenth Century
Jeffrey M. Suderman

33 Contemplation and
Incarnation: The Theology
of Marie-Dominique Chenu
Christophe F. Potworowski

34 Democratic Legitimacy:
Plural Values
and Political Power
F.M. Barnard

35 Herder on Nationality,
Humanity, and History
F.M. Barnard

36 Labeling People: French
Scholars on Society, Race,
and Empire, 1815–1848
Martin S. Staum

37 The Subaltern Appeal
to Experience:
Self-Identity, Late Modernity,
and the Politics of Immediacy
Craig Ireland

38 The Invention of Journalism
Ethics: The Path to
Objectivity and Beyond
Stephen J.A. Ward

39 The Recovery of Wonder:
The New Freedom and
the Asceticism of Power
Kenneth L. Schmitz

40 Reason and Self-Enactment
in History and Politics:
Themes and Voices
of Modernity
F.M. Barnard

41 The More Moderate
Side of Joseph de Maistre:
Views on Political Liberty
and Political Economy
Cara Camcastle

42 Democratic Society
and Human Needs
Jeff Noonan

43 The Circle of Rights Expands:
Modern Political Thought
after the Reformation,
1521 (Luther) to 1762
(Rousseau)
Arthur P. Monahan

44 The Canadian Founding:
John Locke and Parliament
Janet Ajzenstat

45 Finding Freedom: Hegel's
Philosophy and the
Emancipation of Women
Sara MacDonald

46 When the French Tried to Be
British: Party, Opposition,
and the Quest for Civil
Disagreement, 1814–1848
J.A.W. Gunn

47 Under Conrad's Eyes
The Novel as Criticism
Michael John DiSanto

48 Media, Memory,
and the First World War
David Williams

49 An Aristotelian Account
of Induction
Creating Something
from Nothing
Louis Groarke

(*continued on page 322*)

Media, Memory,
and the First World War

DAVID WILLIAMS

McGill-Queen's University Press
Montreal & Kingston • London • Ithaca

© McGill-Queen's University Press 2009
ISBN 978-0-7735-3507-7 (cloth)
ISBN 978-0-7735-3907-5

Legal deposit second quarter 2009
Bibliothèque nationale du Québec

Printed in Canada on acid-free paper that is 100% ancient forest free
(100% post-consumer recycled), processed chlorine free

This book has been published with the help of a grant from the Canadian
Federation for the Humanities and Social Sciences, through the Aid to
Scholarly Publications Programme, using funds provided by the Social
Sciences and Humanities Research Council of Canada. Funding has also
been received from the Office of Research Services and the Faculty of Arts
of the University of Manitoba.

McGill-Queen's University Press acknowledges the support of the Canada
Council for the Arts for our publishing program. We also acknowledge
the financial support of the Government of Canada through the Book
Publishing Industry Development Program (BPIDP) for our publishing
activities.

Library and Archives Canada Cataloguing in Publication

Williams, David, 1945–
    Media, memory, and the First World War / David Williams.

    (McGill-Queen's studies in the history of ideas 48)
    Includes bibliographical references and index.
    ISBN 978-0-7735-3507-7 (bnd)
    ISBN 978-0-7735-3907-5 (pbk)

    1. World War, 1914–1918 – Motion pictures and the war.
    2. Memory – History. 3. War and literature. 4. Motion pictures
    and literature. 5. Literature, Modern – 20th century – History
    and criticism. I. Title. II. Series.

D522.23.W54 2009   791.43'658   C2008-907352-5

This book was typeset by Interscript in 10.5/13 Sabon.

In memory of

PTE J. MORRIS WILLIAMS, 6970

1st Infantry Battalion, Western Ontario
d. 22 April 1915 at the Second Battle of Ypres

Contents

Acknowledgments   xi

Introduction   3

PART ONE   MEMORY AND MEDIA

1   Modern Memory   17

2   Mediated Memory   33

PART TWO   CLASSICAL MEMORY: ORALITY AND LITERACY

3   Oral Memory and the Anger of Achilleus   53

4   Scripts of Empire: Remembering Virgil in *Barometer Rising*   72

PART THREE   THE END OF THE BOOK
AND THE BEGINNING OF CINEMA

5   Cinematic Memory in Owen, Remarque, and Harrison   103

6   "Spectral Images": The Double Vision of Siegfried Sassoon   138

PART FOUR   PHOTO / PLAY:
SEEING TIME AND (HEARING) RELATIVITY

7   Photographic Memory: "A Force of Interruption"
in *The Wars*   161

8   A Play of Light: Dramatizing Relativity in R. H. Thomson's
The Lost Boys   182

PART FIVE   VIRTUAL PRESENCES:
HISTORY IN THE ELECTRONIC AGE

9   Electronic Memory: "A New Homeric Mode" on History
    Television   205

10 Sound Bytes in the Archive and the Museum   237

    Conclusion   269

    Notes   285

    Works Cited   297

    Index   307

Acknowledgments

Once again, I begin by thanking friends and colleagues in the Indian Association for Canadian Studies, who made up the first audience for portions of this monograph. Dr Jameela Begum and Dr B. Hariharan of the University of Kerala invited me to address a large audience at the Institute for English Studies on 15 February 2007, many of whom offered helpful comments on the photography chapter. Two days later, Dr Roopkumar Balasingh, Head of English, who had written his Ph.D. thesis on my novels, welcomed my wife and me to Bishop Heber College, Tiruchirapalli, where a large crowd from three Tamil Nadu universities listened on a Saturday afternoon to the chapter on *The Lost Boys*.

I am most grateful as well to *Canadian Literature* for allowing me to reprint the photography essay, therein titled, "'A Force of Interruption': The Photography of History in Timothy Findley's *The Wars*," which appeared in *CL* 194 (Autumn 2007): 54–73.

Extracts from "Collected Letters" by Wilfrid Owen (1967) are reprinted by permission of Oxford University Press, Inc.

The generous leave policy of the University of Manitoba made it possible for me to do much of my research in France in 2007. In addition, Richard Sigurdson, Dean of Arts, Barbara Crutchley, Office of Research, and Joanne Keselman, Vice-President (Research), responded most generously to the Press's request for a subvention in aid of marketing.

I am deeply indebted to the two anonymous readers for MQUP and the Canadian Federation for the Humanities and Social Sciences for their generous comments, as well as for their stimulating suggestions.

Last, but not least, I acknowledge my friend and colleague, the noted historian Dr Gerald Friesen of the University of Manitoba, who not only introduced me to the work of Harold Innis but also encouraged me to work at the boundaries of our two disciplines.

MEDIA, MEMORY, AND THE FIRST WORLD WAR

Language has unmistakably made plain that memory is not an
instrument for exploring the past, but rather a medium.
            Walter Benjamin, "Excavation and Memory"

Introduction

Cinema makes a telling point of departure for the history of mass bereavement and healing that Jay Winter documents in *Sites of Memory, Sites of Mourning: The Great War in European Cultural History* (1995). Time and again, Winter is drawn back to Abel Gance's silent film *J'accuse* (1919), whose viewers, in "one of the great scenes of the early cinema," witness a murky cloud of soldiers rising from their graves and returning to judge the living, to see "if their sacrifices had been in vain ... The sight of the fallen so terrifies the townspeople that they immediately mend their ways, and the dead return to their graves, their mission fulfilled" (15). To Winter, this "return of the dead" expresses a powerful longing for "aesthetic redemption" (133), even as it leaves its indelible image of a great "cloud of grief" (17) hanging over Europe in the aftermath of 1914–1918. Gance's film and others like it compel Winter "to sketch," in complex and fascinating detail, "some of the ways in which Europeans imagined the postwar world as composed of survivors perched on a mountain of corpses."

The first context in which the cultural historian sets Gance's film is that of the pressing problem of battlefield clearances immediately after the war. Hundreds of thousands of unburied, misidentified, and missing men would prompt the French ministry of war to dream of cemeteries of national remembrance, whereas families were still hoping to bring bodies home to ancestral cemeteries throughout France. As Winter remarks, "The need to bring the dead home, to put the dead to rest, symbolically or physically, was pervasive" (28). And it is at this literal, very practical, level that "the return of the dead" is immediately relevant and resonant.

Put in the context of Gallic military history, Gance's film also reso-
nates with the powerful "nineteenth-century trope of the return of
the dead from the field of battle" (128), a figure based on a form of
popular piety that, in the wake of Waterloo, had been marketed
throughout France as *images d'Epinal*. After 1815, images of Napoleonic glory became fused with religious iconography. Soon after the
Battle of the Marne, this imagery was resurrected in lithographs such
as "Old-timers to the Rescue," where "the men of battles past" were
aligned "with the front-line soldiers of 1914" (129). Films like *J'accuse* thus "continued what *images d'Epinal* had begun: the sanitiza-
tion of the worst features of war and its presentation as a mythical or
romantic adventure" (132). Contrary to filmmakers such as Lewis
Milestone in *All Quiet on the Western Front* (1930), his adaptation
of Remarque's novel, Gance "was not a pacifist. He was a celebrant
of Gallic military virtues who drew on a distinctively French tradition
in the graphic arts" (141). Viewed in the historical context of this
early "twentieth-century revival of popular romanticism," the films
of Gance and others "show well the imprint of the experience of
mass death and mass bereavement on the cultural history of early
twentieth-century Europe" (142–3).

In prose fiction, too, as well as in memoirs and war poetry, "the return of the dead from the field of battle" (205) reveals a widespread
longing of Britons and Germans, as well as French, to make sense of
unimaginable losses. "Whatever form it took, this invocation of the
dead is an unmistakable sign of the commonality of European cultural life in this period" (227). Whether appearing in the apocalyptic
visual images of Otto Dix, Max Beckmann, Stanley Spencer, and
Georges Rouault (145–77), or in anti-war fiction such as Henri
Barbusse's *Le Feu* (1916), or in the war poems of Heinrich Lersch,
Anton Schnack, Wilfred Owen, and Guillaume Apollinaire (204–21),
the content of each form invariably suggests "the persistence of tradition," given how "these varied cultural forms carried messages about
mourning which were highly traditional in character" (225). Most
notably among the war poets in all three countries, "[t]heir 'modernism' was the product of a recasting of traditional language, not its rejection. They are the first in a long line of twentieth-century
romantics, who walk backwards into the future, struggling to understand the chaotic history of this century" (222).

Given his wide-angle lens, Winter is able to offer a broad view of
the means by which "the war gave a new lease of life to a number

of traditional languages expressed both conventionally and in unusual and modern forms" (18). Breadth helps to tone down the parochialism of period styles as much as of jingoistic nationalism, revealing in various media the "process of breathing life into the symbolic language of romantic, classical, and religious reference" (228). And yet this range of reference can also blind the cultural historian to what is most unsettling in Gance's *J'accuse,* which is its literal resurrection of the dead by technological means. Returning to Gance after a chapter on the spiritualist movement and the piteous hope it offered of communication with the dead, Winter remarks somewhat reductively, "The attractions of the silent cinema in this context are apparent. In the dark, to the accompaniment of appropriately spiritual music, millions could half dream of the war, its supernatural aura, and of the men who had fallen. Cinema was a kind of semi-private séance, bringing old images to millions through 'modern' technology" (138). In other words, the historian pays little attention to the medium itself, to the way film technology has made it possible to see "ghosts" at will, summoning apparitions by mechanical means to appear in forms that are at once both present and absent.

Restricting his focus to the traditional character of these "images," Winter thus fails to see cinema as anything more than "the most modern vehicle for the delivery to mass audiences of timeless images" (18). But something else is apparent the moment we change our focus from the image (content) to the medium (form): here, in the "return of the dead" sequences, the dead re-enter our time much as they were in their own time. Winter is aware that "many of the soldiers in earlier scenes of Gance's film had returned to the front in the last months of the war and had been killed. Gance himself noted that some of those playing the dead in his film soon became the dead. Representation and reality had become one" (15). But Winter's cultural history fails to take the logical next step: if the "representation" *is* the "reality," then the collapse of boundaries between the two implies the collapse of boundaries between past and present. Indeed, the past (both as "representation" and as "reality") is now able to invade the present in ways that seem to telescope the past *into* the present. Here and now, in the immediacy of the image as well as in the presentness of viewing, we confront a new tense in the grammar of existence, which we might call a past-progressive-present tense.

Unless the cultural historian takes account of how our temporal sense is altered in viewing cinema, he is unlikely to explain the appeal of Gance's film, why it "ascends to another level of art. It rises from conventional pieties to transcendental ones" (136). The peculiar force of "the return of the dead" in the film evidently derives from the fortunate coincidence of a literal *and* an allegorical truth: the dead, by "returning" on film, create a deep disturbance in our notions of temporality. If *J'accuse* still speaks a traditional language, it does so in the curiously troubling accents of modern cinema. And what it says is no longer really traditional, at least not in the sense meant by Winter.

In what appears to be a rather old debate between ancients and moderns, Paul Fussell had taken up the cause of the latter in *The Great War and Modern Memory* (1975). Yet he did so in ways that made a very few writers of the British officer class the heirs of a long tradition of English letters. A title such as *Sherston's Progress* (1936) allows Fussell to locate Siegfried Sassoon in the tradition of John Bunyan's *The Pilgrim's Progress*, while Robert Graves' *Goodbye to All That* is placed in a line dating back to Ben Jonson's "comedy of humours." And Wilfred Owen's poems take their place in a line of English pastoral and Romantic poets. Oddly, it is the "modernist" who claims that "[i]n 1914 there was virtually no cinema" (158), since the "more kinetic sense of cinema" belongs to "the experience of later wars, wars characterized by a new geographical remoteness, mobility, rapidity, complex technology, and ever-increasing incredibility" (221). A cinematic form of memory that is likely the defining characteristic of *modern* writers of the Great War is thus reserved for the Second World War in which Fussell himself had fought.

And yet, August 1914 is still *the* moment of historical rupture for him, dividing all that came before from all that would come after. Less a tear in the fabric of history than a steam iron flattening the "First" war into a series of later wars, however, Fussell's rupture creates a space for his countrymen in a war they almost missed. At the end of his second chapter, for example, he telegraphs his parochial view: "The idea of endless war as an inevitable condition of modern life would seem to have become seriously available to the imagination around 1916. Events, never far behindhand in fleshing out the nightmares of imagination, obliged with the Spanish War, the Second World War, the Greek War, the Korean War, the Arab-Israeli War, and the Vietnam War." Fussell's genealogy of war as the real pedigree of modernity concludes with "this headline from the *New York Times* for September 1, 1972: U. S. AIDES IN VIETNAM / SEE AN UNENDING WAR" (74).

In reducing eight wars to one, Fussell creates a fiction of "modernity" that can include his nation – long missing in action in the Great War – but that will also exclude what is most "modern" in his British authors. In adopting this voice of prophecy in the telling of "history," Fussell thus ignores the fact that memory is also a medium, one designed to carry us back to the past, not back to the future. In limiting his choice of texts, he further fails to put the British officer class in its proper context of empire. Finally, in limiting "modern memory" to a few books while excluding other media, he ignores the context of his own moment of writing – the first televised war – as much as he avoids the broader implications of the first war on film. What I am claiming in this study is that film, as Jay Winter rightly intuited, had made the Great War a powerful zone of memory, albeit a modern, not a traditional, one. At the same time, I claim that "modern memory" is both larger and other than Fussell's "modern" mode of irony, since it is ultimately defined by a filmic epistemology that silently underwrote the undisputed classics of the Great War.

In my first, fifth, and sixth chapters, I show how this cinematic epistemology first opened a chasm between "modern" and traditional ways of seeing, and how these new perceptual frameworks, developed in the two decades *before* 1914, are evident in writers that Fussell called "modern" but quickly reduced to the traditional category nonetheless. Moreover, the German Remarque (whose work Fussell dismisses as "Gothic") depended on precisely the same perceptual frameworks that appear in the work of Owen and Sassoon. In a Canadian "classic" probably unknown to Fussell, *Generals Die in Bed* (1930) by the American-Canadian Charles Yale Harrison, a similar cinematic epistemology is at work. It is this common shift from a print epistemology to "filmic" ways of seeing that more clearly shows what is "new" in these works by writers on both sides of the conflict, from several different countries, and helps us to see what is truly "modern" in the Great War canon.

Basically, I argue that this "cinematic memory" of the Great War produced a new tense in the grammar of existence. Unlike the past-tense narration of novels in general, the verbal "cinema" of the

Great War classics worked to telescope past and present, thus allowing the past to *invade* the present with a force that erased ontological distinctions between them. One finds such new relations to temporality in the present-tense narration of *All Quiet* and *Generals*, where memories of the war are narrated in a present-progressive tense, and where the past likewise looms out of cinematic straight-cuts into the present-progressive tense of a verb without a "future." In other words, both the future and past cease to exist in these narratives; the present is all that remains in such forms of "filmic" memory, where the image appears with something approaching the visual immediacy of the filmic image, even in a verbal medium such as the novel.

In Owen's poetry, much as in Sassoon's fiction, the speakers tend to be haunted by "spectral images" from the past that invade the present with cinematic immediacy. In such temporal displacements, a series of ontological doublings occurs that also shows how filmic ways of seeing enable Sassoon to summon "ghosts" at will by mechanical means. Memory thus becomes "immediate" for his readers, who experience the simultaneity of present and past in their own presentness of "viewing." The invasive power of film is further redoubled by combatants' memories of the Western Front, where "total war" and cinema together have invaded the "distancing" medium of print.

In his "Critical History," *Nonfiction Film* (1992), Richard M. Barsam remarked a unique change that cinema had created in the grammar of perception: "Previously, paintings and photographs could only preserve a visual memory of movement. They function as the visual equivalent of the past tense; their single, static images are the remembrance of a moment in time and space" (6). The same thing is evidently true of the fixities of print, where the past tense is the "normal" tense of narrative, much as it is in the static pictorial arts. "Motion pictures," by contrast, "record memories, but they also provide a visual equivalent of the present tense, a representation of movement itself. Their kinetic images, which record temporal sequences and make space move, not only confirm the process of human vision, but also alter the spectator's psychological relationship to the visible world as projected on a screen" (6).

My notion of "cinematic memory" as a new tense in the grammar of perception is developed in this book's central chapters, which are devoted to the works of Owen, Remarque, Harrison, and

Sassoon. Contrary to McLuhan's non-reciprocal theory – that the content of new media is bound to be older media – the content of older media (e.g., print) is also likely – by an evolutionary law of adaptation to environment – to be a new medium such as film.[1] A reciprocal reading of the content of the form is premised on the fact that memory is itself a medium, albeit one that takes its character from the media environment in which it finds itself. We fail to understand memory if we do not see it as a medium of communication. Even as it physically mediates between centres in the brain (see pages 37–9), it also mediates psychologically between then and now – or forgetting and recall – as it mediates, in a metaphysical sense, between absence and presence. Indeed, memory is the primary medium of our experience of time, and yet we tend, like fish in water, to be perfectly oblivious to this intervening substance of our experience.

What follows in this book is no more than a selective history of memory, based on changes in the forms that memory has taken in several epochal shifts from one medium to another. The Great War spans one such era (at the end of this introduction I will explain my interest in it for its own sake). But, since that war coincided with the epochal shift from print to film as a dominant mode of communication, it should help us to rethink the curious history of memory offered by Frances A. Yates in *The Art of Memory,* one that had ended for her with the printing press. Yates's central insight is that memory has a history that is divisible into periods. For her, these periods can be classified in terms of "the mnemonic of *places* and *images* (*loci* and *imagines*)" that Cicero, in *De oratore,* had said was "used by the Roman rhetors" (2). In Quintilian's *Institutio oratoria,* we get a more detailed explanation "of the general principles" of the classical "mnemonic. The first step was to imprint on the memory a series of *loci* or places. The commonest, though not the only, type of mnemonic place system used was the architectural type" (3). The classical ideal of memory was thus indispensable in an oral culture, where one follows an ancient orator "moving in imagination through his memory building *whilst* he is making his speech, drawing from the memorised places the images he has placed on them."

By the Middle Ages, however, this idea of "artificial memory has moved over from rhetoric to ethics" (57), to such an extent that Thomas Aquinas seems to have "memorised his own *Summa*

through 'corporeal similitudes' disposed on places following the order of its parts," leading to the surprising possibility that "the abstract *Summa* might be corporealised in memory into something like
a Gothic cathedral full of images on its ordered places" (79). On the
other hand, sixteenth-century "Renaissance memory" was based on
the "memory theatre" of Giulio Camillo, for whom the "art of memory has become the instrument in the formation of a Magus, the
imaginative means through which the divine microcosm can reflect
the divine macrocosm, can grasp its meaning from above, from that
divine grade to which his *mens* belongs. The art of memory has become an occult art, a Hermetic secret" (157–8). Within a century,
however, the "printed book" began "destroying age-old memory
habits" (127). The "new science," claiming to "be able to solve all
questions concerning quantity," marks a final break of print culture
"from qualitative and symbolic use of number" (375).

Yates does not hide the fact that "[t]he art of memory is a clear
case of a marginal subject, not recognised as belonging to any of the
normal disciplines, having been omitted because it was no one's
business. And yet it has turned out to be, in a sense, everyone's business" (389). Nor does she shrink from the responsibility to make a
truly interdisciplinary study: "The history of the organisation of
memory touches at vital points on the history of religion and ethics,
of philosophy and psychology, of art and literature, of scientific
method" (389). And yet, as if she herself were trapped in the epistemology of print, she abandons her best insight by making print the
end term, a fixed mode of recall that rendered the ancient rules superfluous.[2] This failure to carry through on her own logic is surprising, given her sense that "oral memory" was already a form of
inscription: "The art of memory is like an inner writing. Those who
know the letters of the alphabet can write down what is dictated to
them and read out what they have written" (6). Why would the external writing of the printing press not supplement, rather than
abolish, this form of "inner writing," making it possible for an
eighteenth-century orator to visualize a page recalled in speech?

In our age of film and television, we need to think through this
idea that classical rhetors were "describing inner techniques" of an
ancient art of memory that had long depended "on visual impressions of almost incredible intensity. Cicero emphasises that
Simonides' invention of the art of memory rested, not only on his
discovery of the importance of order for memory, but also on the

discovery that the sense of sight is the strongest of all the senses" (4). In an age not just of film and television, but of new digital media, the historian of memory needs to ask as well how "visual impressions of almost incredible intensity" would affect the structure of memory by altering our sense of time, or even by altering our relation to reality in the simulation of virtual worlds. This is the burden of my own interdisciplinary approach.

At the same time, long-term changes in the structure of memory necessarily complicate the structure of this study, making it difficult, if not impossible, to offer a linear history of "the Great War and modern memory," let alone a history of memory along the lines of classical, medieval, and renaissance modes of remembering. For the breakpoint in a history of mediated memory is not – as Yates seems to think – print, but this "cinematic memory" of the Great War that was to change print itself. Later developments of "a new Homeric mode" on History Television, or of a new orality in *The Memory Project*, an Internet-based project founded by The Dominion Institute, have yet to be viewed in the context of the "old Homeric mode." The relevance of "oral memory" to the postmodern forms of "electronic memory" that emerge in this study is assumed. But Homer hardly fits in a book on "modern memory" any more than he fits in a book centred on a filmic "memory" of the Great War. Chapter 3, "Oral Memory and the Anger of Achilleus" takes a considerable risk of alienating the reader who expects a more immediate "memory" of the Great War.

One way to dampen this expectation is to stress how the Great War canon is but one element in a longer history of memory as a function of the changing technologies of memory. Any meaningful history of memory must start, as does Yates's *The Art of Memory,* with the ancient culture of oral memory. If Homer and the Trojan war seem alien to the project of understanding the Great War and "modern memory," they help nonetheless to understand another epochal shift from oral to written memory, a history treated at length in my *Imagined Nations* (2003), in three chapters comprising "Nations of the Book."

The present work is less concerned with the phenomenon of space (or the space of political community) than with the phenomenon of time, or with various forms of memory shaped by different media. The type of "oral memory" found in Homer is strikingly different from Virgil's "written memory" seven centuries later. Writing on papyrus, Virgil could sketch the blueprint of Roman empire in this revolutionary form of memory: "*Romane memento,*" father Anchises addresses his heirs and successors in the Underworld waiting to be born into the light: "Roman, remember." What they are enjoined to remember is the purpose of Roman "arts": to "impose the habit of peace" by "sparing the humble" and "battling down the proud." The written prophecy of Virgil is, of course, a self-fulfilling prophecy of Roman, not British, empire. But an important Virgilian novel of the Great War reminds us of the significance of this historical shift from oral to written memory, since it is the Virgilian discourse of empire that informs Hugh MacLennan's *Barometer Rising* (1941), a novel about the coming of the war to Canada in the 1917 Halifax explosion.

After two chapters on "Classical Memory," my doubled history of memory and media leaps from "classical" to modern, "cinematic" memory. Although a discussion of "photographic" memory would normally precede "cinematic" memory – the invention of photography in the 1820s antedating the invention of cinema in the 1890s – its placement is delayed for two reasons. In the first place, Timothy Findley's Great War novel, *The Wars* (1977), adopts the structure of "photographic memory" to distance the protagonist from his own time, before moving him (in implicit cinematic fashion) down the light rays into our era. Conversely, R. H. Thomson's play *The Lost Boys* (2001) turns photographs back into projected beams of light in order to stage Einstein's theory of relativity. This fourth section on Findley and Thomson is meant to expose underlying differences in these two forms of "photographic memory," grouping the printed image with more "objective" history and the light-borne image with more "modern" concepts of time.

Beyond this form of "modern memory" shaped by film, the last pair of chapters begins to explore several forms of "electronic memory" mediated through television, the Internet, and other digital media. Television, with its ideology of liveness, its participatory mystique, and its erosion of boundaries between producers and receivers, has been creating a new species of orality in programs such as Norm Christie's *For King and Empire* (2001), a staple every November on History Television. The use of sound in the Digital Archive of *The Memory Project* (Dominion Institute, 2003), and in interactive displays in the new Canadian War Museum in Ottawa also furthers the revival of oral forms of cultural memory. In a way

very distinct from the depiction of the Battle of the Somme in L'Historial de la Grande Guerre in Péronne, Canadian institutional media have extended the possibilities of oral memory in keeping with a
"museological revolution" that favours subjective experience over
object-centred displays. Tellingly, the Internet also enables the dead
to speak for themselves in ways that McCrae could not have imagined in "In Flanders Fields."

In this context, it may be apparent why the final term of my title,
The First World War, is so important for this history of memory.
For none of these changes in our mediated sense of temporality
changes the deeper truth of our human experience of time, which
Hayden White describes as our "apprehension of the relation of
'eternity' to 'death,' which is the content of the form of temporality
itself" (180). What White so powerfully identifies as the shared
concern of history and fiction is the fact that "their ultimate content
is the same: the structures of human time. Their shared form, narrative, is a function of this shared content. There is nothing more real
for human beings than the experience of temporality – and nothing
more fateful, either for individuals or for whole civilizations."

In the various forms of autobiographical fictions, historical fictions, and narrative histories that are the immediate subject of this
work, one is never far from the memory of an unprecedented cultural tragedy in the Great War. The scale of that war, as well as the
extent of suffering produced by it, still test our human ability to
make sense of it. Of course, this ability is likely our definitive "human effort to endow life with meaning." As White puts it with magisterial force, "This universal, human quest for meaning is carried
out in the awareness of the corrosive power of time, but it is also
made possible and given its distinctively human pathos by this very
awareness" (181).

Such a tragic awareness of time was expressed with nearly equal
force in the midst of the Great War by "Frances Stevenson, Lloyd
George's secretary and mistress who had lost her brother Paul in the
fighting" on the Somme, and who was moved by its cinematic representation in *The Battle of the Somme* (1916), the most popular
film in the history of British cinema: "It reminded me of what [her
brother] Paul's last hours were. I have often tried to imagine to myself what he went through, but now I know, and I shall never forget.
It was like going through a tragedy. I felt something of what the
Greeks must have felt when they went in their crowds to witness

those grand old plays – to be purged in their minds through pity and terror" (Hudson, online 1).

The truth of such works "resides not only in their fidelity to the facts of given individual or collective lives," as Hayden White says with reference to historical and fictional narratives (although not to film), "but also, and most importantly, in their faithfulness to that vision of human life informing the poetic genre of tragedy. In this respect, the symbolic content of narrative history, the content of its form, is the tragic vision itself." Indeed, it is this tragic vision of time that has made the Great War the definitive "theatre" of modern memory, the paramount reason why it still compels us to remember, and even re-member, the millions who perished in it. But if this "allegory of temporality" (White 181) explains *why* we remember the Great War, it is *how* we remember, and how media-derived memory is its ultimate referent, that shapes my reflections on "those allegories of temporality that we call narrative histories."

PART ONE

Memory and Media

I

Modern Memory

Anyone who writes today about the literature of the Great War owes a substantial debt to Paul Fussell, the founder of a discourse on war and modern memory that has evolved well beyond the literary text into other forms of cultural studies. I first read *The Great War and Modern Memory* (1975) in the early 1980s, when I was by choice and training still a professor of American literature. There, in my appalling ignorance, I encountered writers – none of the first rank, at least none of the "great" innovators – whose names, let alone works, I scarcely knew. Even at that date, I had to wonder why a writer named Siegfried Sassoon was on "our" side – which says as much about my provinciality as it does about the state of graduate English education in the 1960s.

Nonetheless, my rudimentary sense of modernity as a type of traumatic memory was shaped at that time by Fussell's response to an unparalleled cultural tragedy. He had fought in 1944–45 in France, and spoke of the Great War with all the passion of a fed-up infantryman: "Every war is ironic," he wrote, "because every war is worse than expected ... But the Great War was more ironic than any before or since. It was a hideous embarrassment to the prevailing Meliorist myth which had dominated the public consciousness for a century. It reversed the Idea of Progress" (7–8). In many respects, Fussell saw his war as an extension of that reversal and its ironic literature as merely another chapter "in the whole long history of human disillusion" (29). On such a premise his chapter structure will often build to a paradigmatic American text from the Second World War, such as in his first chapter's concluding discussion of Joseph Heller's *Catch-22*: "This 'primal scene,'" as Fussell terms it, "works because it is undeniably horrible, but its irony, its dynamics of hope abridged, is what makes it haunt the memory. It embodies the contemporary equivalent of the experience offered by the first day on the Somme, and like that archetypal original, it can stand as a virtual allegory of political and social cognition in our time" (35). Insofar as "our time" – evidently the time of Fussell's writing – is also the era of the Vietnam war, the Somme can then stand as the ironic paradigm for modern history. Indeed, "I am saying that there seems to be one dominating form of modern understanding, that it is essentially ironic; and that it originates largely in the application of mind and memory to the events of the Great War" (35).

Even to survey that cultural landscape before 1914 is to glimpse in an instant the unique character of modern literature: "Indeed, the literary scene is hard to imagine. There was no *Waste Land*, with its rats' alleys, dull canals, and dead men who have lost their bones; it would take four years of trench warfare to bring these to consciousness. There was no *Ulysses*, no *Mauberley*, no *Cantos*, no Kafka, no Proust, no Waugh, ... no 'Valley of Ashes' in *The Great Gatsby*" (23). Only in his evocative conclusion, however, does Fussell finally spell out the larger literary consequences of 1914–18. The following judgment, for example, illuminates in a flash the landscape of a whole era:

> Seen in its immediate postwar context, a work like *The Waste Land* appears much more profoundly a "memory of the war" than one had thought. Consider its archduke, its rats and canals and dead men, its focus on fear, its dusty trees, its conversation about demobilization, its spiritualist practitioners reminding us of those who preyed on relatives anxious to contact their dead boys, and not least its settings of blasted landscapes and ruins, suggestive of what Guy Chapman recalls as "the confluent acne of the waste land under the walls of Ypres." It was common to identify "the waste land" that modern life seemed to resemble with the battlefields of the war rather than with the landscape of Eliot's poem. (325–6)

If there is a single paragraph in the history of literary criticism that has more to say about the text as a product of its historical moment, I have not read it.

Two decades later, however, Fussell's methods and definitions had begun to feel far more limiting than invigorating. Jay Winter's *Sites of Memory, Sites of Mourning* (1995) offers an especially pertinent critique of Fussell's revival of the old quarrel between "ancients" and "moderns." As Winter notes in his wide-ranging discussion of the art and film and literature of the interwar years, all set in the still wider context of commemorative practices of British, French, and German communities, "The strength of what may be termed 'traditional' forms in social and cultural life, in art, poetry, and ritual, lay in their power to mediate bereavement. The cutting edge of 'modern memory,' its multi-faceted sense of dislocation, paradox, and the ironic, could express anger and despair, and did so in enduring ways; it was melancholic, but it could not heal" (5). Winter's reading of the "[c]ultural codes and languages of mourning" (117) very movingly shows how the process of cultural healing was deeply informed by the older language of tradition.

Another note of dissent may be heard in the title of a recent collection of essays, *The Literature of the Great War Reconsidered: Beyond Modern Memory* (2001). In their introduction, editors Patrick J. Quinn and Steven Trout point to a wider blurring in Great War scholarship of several dichotomies between combatant and civilian, male and female, and literary and non-literary representations of this conflict that "brought profound changes both to our understanding of the Great War as a cultural event and to our conception ... of what we mean by, and include in, the term 'war literature'" (1). A "far more complex, varied and contradictory assemblage of works confronts us" as we realize how very unrepresentative were a few British war texts that Fussell reimagined with such eloquence. For example, in an essay on the Canadian Billy Bishop's *Winged Warfare* (1918), Chris Hopkins reasons that a continuing cultural obsession with trench warfare is a form of "selective critical memory" that is productive of a selective "general collective memory" (14).

The exclusion of writings from the home front, as Debra Rae Cohen argues in another essay, likewise signals the more general privileging of combatant experience in Fussell's "modern memory." In Cohen's treatment of Stella Benson's war fiction, "the hegemonic system of exclusions that make the war possible" (39) is what stands fully exposed. Conversely, the fiction of May Sinclair, as Terry Phillips shows, cannot be "dismissed as simply sentimentalizing, romanticizing or glorifying war"; far more painfully, it deals with "the complexity of women's position in the war and provides evidence of the 'double-bind' in which women found themselves, blamed whether they supported or discouraged their menfolk" (66).

In his useful reading of British newspapers before the Great War, Glenn R. Wilkinson notes how non-literary writings, such as "spontaneously submitted" poetry, letters, diaries, memoirs, and short stories "can be used to ascertain the literary perception of warfare held by contemporaries" (24). Even so, his reading stops well short of explaining why "soldiers had come to be seen in the press as harbingers of civilization, due mostly to the perceived benefits of Western Imperialism and to the impression that soldiers represented order, justice and reason" (26). Here, the classical discourse of empire is never mentioned, a discourse that helps to show why writers schooled in the Virgilian art of "imposing the habit of peace" on "barbarian races" so often failed to examine their own assumptions. Indeed, few writings before the war, whether "low" or "high," could escape the shadow cast by Aeneas and the civilizing mission of Roman empire. If Wilkinson typically looks no further than the local and contemporary Kipling – and "the white man's burden" – to account for these pre-war attitudes, Fussell ignores both the contemporary *and* the classical discourses of empire. The Augustan *Aeneid* is never once mentioned in his reading of British war literature; indeed, his only reference to Virgil is to the "Second Eclogue" (278), dating from the late Republic, which he takes as a source for "The British Homoerotic Tradition" (279) and the pastoral poetry of Wilfred Owen.

Fussell's extremely narrow focus on the writings of a few middle-class, British soldiers further limits his notion of "modern memory," as Donna Coates demonstrates in a comparative essay on "Australian, New Zealand, and Canadian Women's Fictional Responses to the Great War." Here, a considerable difference emerges between Australian women writers, constrained by the national myth of "the Digger," or "bushman," to reproduce the dominant patriarchal discourse of the nation (118), and women writers from Canada and New Zealand, whose lack of a national myth enabled them to repudiate the "master narrative" of the heroic soldier (119–20). The idea that the lack of "a clearly defined national myth" in Canada freed women from having "to be 'myth-fits,'" enabling them rather "to shape their own cultural space" (136), is not only historically improbable but totally out of keeping with Jonathan Vance's study,

Death So Noble: Memory, Meaning, and the First World War (1997), his evocative and groundbreaking treatment of Canadian cultural memory in the interwar period. In fact, Vance's book "is about constructing a mythic version of the events of 1914–18 from a complex mixture of fact, wishful thinking, half-truth, and outright invention, and expressing that version in novel and play, in bronze and stone, in reunion and commemoration, in song and advertisement" (3). One of the cardinal points of Vance's approach is its salutary reminder that "value judgments based on literary merit are not borne out by the weight of evidence. On the contrary, if all Canadian accounts of the war are considered on equal terms, a very different picture emerges than [*sic*] the one discerned by Fussell" (90).

Vance carefully situates himself with "[r]ecent scholars such as Rosa Maria Bracco and David Englander [who] have begun to re-examine the cultural and philosophical legacy of the war, painting very different pictures than [*sic*] those sketched by Fussell and his intellectual heirs" (5). As Vance notes, Bracco and Englander "find conservatism and tradition persisting deep within interwar societies as a sort of bedrock of stability. Where Fussell identified the forces of change, they have emphasized continuity; in opposition to the shock of the new, they have found an old order that is much more resilient than *The Great War and Modern Memory* allowed." Like them, Vance employs "a methodology that treats all sources, regardless of their literary quality, on an equal footing." Instead of making aesthetic criteria the ground of "modern memory," he considers the social aims of cultural memory: "In remembering the war," for example, "Canadians were concerned first and foremost with utility: those four years had to have been of some use. The war had to be recalled in such a way that positive outcomes, beyond the defeat of German aggression, were clear. In short, the mythic version existed to fashion a usable past out of the Great War" (9).

Fussell, by contrast, is utterly contemptuous of cultural practices that do not fit his criteria. Reading John McCrae's "In Flanders Fields," he "finally see[s] – and with a shock – what the last six lines really are: they are a propaganda argument – words like *vicious* and *stupid* would not seem to go too far – against a negotiated peace" (250). While the last six lines of McCrae's rondeau might disappoint on aesthetic grounds, they do not seem "stupid" or shocking when read in the historical context. Canadian readers ought to be shocked instead by the historian's blatant failure to link the publication date "in *Punch* on December 6, 1915" (249), to the military situation in Flanders in the spring of 1915, when McCrae wrote the poem. Here, words like *vicious* and *stupid* could just as easily recoil on their user.

In fact, Lt-Colonel John McCrae wrote his oft-recited rondeau when "Second Ypres" was still in doubt, when the war could have ended, not in a negotiated peace, but in sudden victory for the Central Powers. On the night of 3 May 1915, the surgeon McCrae knelt to scribble a few lines on the banks of the Canal de l'Yser a few hundred yards north of Ypres, in defiance of the two-week-old artillery bombardment that only the day before had killed his friend and former medical student Lt Alexis Helmer. The informed reader might well experience a moral shock – registered in the "recruiting-poster rhetoric" (249) of "Take up our quarrel with the foe" – but it is shock expressed in traditional terms. Before gas masks, McCrae could hardly warn in 1915 of "Gas! GAS! Quick, boys! – An ecstasy of fumbling," as Owen was able to do in the era of the "box respirator"; nor would he have aesthetic justification to do so in an "oral" poem about voices speaking from beyond the grave. Rather, the moral shock comes from the moral outrage of fighting with gas; this tactic of "total war" goes against convention and conscience.

If gas warfare still elicited shock in Owen's "Dulce" (1917), when box respirators had become standard issue, consider the events of 22 April 1915, when a 3-metre-high wall of chlorine gas drifted over unsuspecting Canadian and French Algerian troops in a lung-scalding fog north of Ypres. "Take up our quarrel with the foe" in this setting is far closer to understatement than to recruiting-poster rhetoric, implying, if not claiming, the valour of an action that, at the instant of writing, was barely holding off a German breakthrough to the Channel ports and a disastrous end to the war. The shock of the new, announced in the ironic version of pastoral that Fussell does admire in McCrae's opening lines, is at this point still too fresh; it can only be absorbed in the last six lines by traditional means. But the cultural historian who hears no more in these half-choked words than "the rhetoric of Sir Henry Newbolt or Horatio Bottomley or the Little Mother" (250) is likely to mistake as well a Canadian for a British voice, in much the same way that he mistakes April 1915 as a missed opportunity for a "negotiated peace."

Not so provincial as to mistake Flanders "poppies as orange or yellow" (247) – as he expects his American readers, ignorant of the red paper poppies sold by the British and Canadian Legions each November, to do – Fussell fails nonetheless to picture the many crowds on this continent gathering at the cenotaph each November 11th, their lapels brightened by red poppies as they recite, "In Flanders fields the poppies blow, / Between the crosses, row on row." Had he envisioned this scene, Fussell could not have linked McCrae's words to "the vulgarities of 'Stand Up! Stand Up and Play the Game!'" (249).

I have not forgotten standing as a child in the 1950s at the cenotaph on Remembrance Day in Naicam, Saskatchewan, reciting McCrae's words as I pictured my grandfather's brother lying in a shallow trench filling with chlorine gas on the evening of 22 April 1915. My paternal great-uncle, in the High Diction of Kipling's phrase, was one of those "Known unto God," his body left nameless with his identity disk removed for purposes of notification. (A system of double identity disks had yet to be implemented to prevent this final indignity.) Recently, I visited the Menin Gate in Ypres to see his name, with 55,000 others, incised in the marble of that colossal monument, and felt again the immediacy of McCrae's words, "To you from failing hands we throw / The torch." But as a boy, I knew only that "the torch" had nearly been dropped on 24 April (one of the worst days of the war for Canadians) when 1,500 of our men (including my grandfather's other brother) were overrun and captured at St-Julien.[3] Until the end of the war, this paternal great-uncle was condemned to slave labour in a coal mine, at least until he volunteered to fix a McCormack reaper and was sent to work on a German farm, where he survived the war. But on the reeking ground of Ypres, the words of McCrae still weighed as heavily then as they do now in Canada each and every 11th of November: "If ye break faith with us who die / We shall not sleep, though poppies grow / In Flanders fields."

In myriad ways, the public forms of remembrance that Jonathan Vance documents in Canadian life from 1919–39 continue to evoke this sense "of sacrifice, redemption, salvation, and resurrection … The sheer size of loss experienced by the country demanded it. To abandon these ideals was to abandon oneself to despair; to embrace them more fervently than ever was to give meaning to the war" (72). Most tellingly, the local churchyard and town park were made sites for this "language of commemoration … dominated by the figures of Winged Victory and the rejoicing soldier, symbols of earthly triumph that constituted the single most important theme in war memorials erected by Canadians" (17). A cult of the service roll further kept in the public eye the names of those who had flocked to the colours, since the Honour Roll would be erected in churches across the land. "More importantly, the emphasis on naming the dead," both in the bronze tablets of local war memorials and in memorial volumes published by individual towns and villages, "was intended to insure that the identities of the fallen remained prominent in the public consciousness; if the names were forgotten, the memory of the sacrifice would inevitably slip away as well" (119).

Even the blood-soaked soil of the Western Front was transformed into a Holy Land for pilgrims in the thousands who attended the unveiling of Walter Allward's Vimy Monument in 1936. From this "new Mecca or Canterbury" (60), the pilgrims would then fan out to the nearby graveyards of Canadians and other imperial troops, as well as to hundreds of other "gardens of the dead" in Picardy and Flanders, which the Imperial War Graves Commission (later the Commonwealth War Graves Commission) had designed to be "so appealing that people would not insist on the repatriation of bodies" (64).

In other ways as well, Canadians were firmly bound together in this cult of remembrance. "In stark contrast to the judgment of history, Canada's memory declined to interpret the Great War as a technological nightmare of man-destroying machines; instead it was a contest between human beings in which technology played a secondary role to the gallantry and élan of the soldier" (142). Vance brings together a vast array of artworks in word, paint and glass to show how "[t]he modernity of machine-made warfare could be glossed over by linking the struggle to its precedents from the nation's past" (151). Even a national "railway history affirmed the strength of historical continuity by reminding readers that General Wolfe's fleet had stopped near Valcartier on its way to besiege Quebec" (173). Another popular way of giving the war meaning through visual media, an example of which is the stained glass in the memorial chapel at Ridley College in St. Catharines, Ontario, was to place the dead of the Great War within a larger pantheon of historical heroes: "La Vérendyre, Cartier, La Salle, Wolfe, Brock, and an infantryman of the CEF" were set side by side in historical sequence. "In each case, Canadian history was made manifestly linear and contiguous; the memorials confirmed that the events of 1914–18 entailed no break with the past" (151–2).

To impugn this heroic myth was to commit social heresy in the interwar years, as evidenced by the public reaction against Charles Yale Harrison's *Generals Die in Bed* (1930) for giving, in fictional form, an eyewitness account of Canadian troops looting Arras and murdering surrendering German soldiers in August 1918 at the Battle of Amiens. Even Harrison's title was scandalous, given the "sacrificial" deaths of "Major-General Malcolm Mercer, killed at Mount Sorrel in June 1916 while leading the 3d Division; and Major-General L. J. Lipsett, killed in September 1918 shortly after leaving the 3d Division" (Vance 194). Indeed, Lt-General Arthur Currie, the commander of the Canadian Corps in the decisive battles of the Last Hundred Days, said of Harrison's novel: "There is not a single line in it worth reading, nor a single incident worthy of record ... I have never read, nor do I hope ever to read, a meaner, nastier and more foul book" (194). Not long before the appearance of Harrison's novel, Currie had been forced to sue a regional newspaper, the Port Hope (Ontario) *Evening News,* which in June 1927 had defamed his record for ordering a "needless" attack on Mons, the Belgian city where the war began and where the last shot was fired. "When Sir Archibald Macdonell wondered 'why they should try to deprive Canada of the Glory he [Currie] won for her,' he was articulating a widely held belief that Hughes and Preston had gone beyond merely libelling the former commander of the Canadian Corps, to attacking everything that the corps achieved" (185).

In a broad sense, "the canon of antiwar literature became a battleground, rallying the defenders of Canada's war myth just as ... the Currie trial had done" (187). Books such as Harrison's *Generals Die in Bed,* Remarque's *All Quiet on the Western Front,* and Robert Graves' *Goodbye to All That* were especially offensive to Lt-General Currie

> and countless other Canadians for the same reason that they so impressed later critics; they universalized the experience of the trenches. Remarque's Paul Bäumer might have served in any army; he represented the suffering of millions of other soldiers from all nations, including Canada. This, of course, was precisely the objection. To many people, universalization was in fact defamation: these books tarred Canadian soldiers with the sins of others by claiming that, like all other soldiers, the men of the CEF had been brutalized and dehumanized by war. (191)

In a country that prided itself on having "won the war" against Germany, and even on having won its national independence from Britain by spearheading the Allied victory, this was the lowest blow of all – that the "victors" should be dragged down to the level of the vanquished, supposedly demoralized as badly as the "foe" they had beaten.

For all its strengths, a work such as Vance's *Death So Noble* risks perpetuating several regressive aspects of the public myth. For one thing, it fails to explain how a catastrophic war of nationalism is ennobled by the birth of yet another nationalism. Nor does it prevent the unfortunate impression that, in a "transformative" era of "modern" memory, Canada somehow regressed to being a cultural backwater, speaking a nineteenth-century language to describe a twentieth-century war. Indeed, there is little in Vance's defense of the myth to suggest that Canada was modernized at all in the forge of war. If Ypres and the Somme and Passchendaele "could take their places alongside the Charge of the Light Brigade, the relief of Batoche, and the Battle of Paardeberg" (94), perhaps "modern memory" is one more casualty of war that failed to return to these shores with some of its soldiers. Fussell's account, in spite of its limitations, is still more "modern" than this view, since it more accurately identifies a true crisis of modernity in Western civilization.

Nonetheless, a fatal contradiction undercuts Fussell's premise that modernity is itself a legacy of the Great War. The obsessive writings of his war-memoirists do not suggest any historical rupture or even discontinuity with the past – not, certainly, if these soldiers feel condemned to go "over the ground again" in an "act of memory conceived as an act of military reconnaissance" (260). As Fussell admits, "The act of fighting a war becomes something like an unwitting act of conservative memory, and even of elegy" (314). In that case, a better motive for remembrance would be to "keep faith with us who die" (McCrae). Yet "to be radically modern means to sever all links to the past" (Huyssen 250); this is the only way irony could ever be a hallmark of "modern memory," since it is more corroding than conserving of tradition. But how does one explain all those other modes of remembrance about which Fussell writes, from pastoral elegy to comedy?

Here is the literary crux of the problem. Adopting a critical method from Northrop Frye, Fussell sets up a sequence of forms in British war writings, from epic to romance and from "high" to "low" mimesis that, on the basis of a "seasonal" myth, ends in the ironic mode. Patently, Frye's system of genres is much less historical than it is proto-structuralist, isolating a sequence of generic functions outside of historical causation. Then to identify the emergence of an atemporal, ironic mode in literature with a manifestly *historical* cause – the Great War – is ultimately to confuse a synchronic method with a diachronic content. Fussell's whole attempt to yoke an ahistorical method to historical contingency finally slides into incoherence when he says that David Jones obeys the laws of "romance" in his *In Parenthesis* (1937), and that other important Great War memoirs conform to a similar pattern of medieval quest. Indeed, "[i]t is impossible not to be struck by the similarity between this conventional 'romance' pattern and the standard experience re-enacted and formalized in memoirs of the war" (130). How is this modern?

One is far more likely to feel the conservatism, and not the modernity, of "modern" British writers such as Edmund Blunden, whom Fussell regards as clinging to a pastoral mode in *Undertones of War* (254–69), or Robert Graves in *Goodbye to All That,* who clearly follows in the tradition of Ben Jonson and the "Comedy of Humors" (204). Even Fussell's Exhibit A for a new, ironic mode in literature – Sassoon's *The Memoirs of George Sherston* – retreats from irony to romance in the title to his trilogy's final volume, *Sherston's Progress.* Thus, in apparent disregard of his whole thesis, Fussell writes:

> It is odd and wonderful that front-line experience should ape the pattern of the one book everybody knew. Or to put it perhaps more accurately, front-line experience seemed to become available for interpretation when it was seen how closely parts of it resembled the action of *Pilgrim's Progress.* Sassoon took it for granted that his title *Sherston's Progress* will contribute significant shape to his episodic account of his passage through anxiety to arrive at his triumphant moment of relief as Rivers enters his hospital room. (138–9)

Did Sassoon really see George Sherston as a modern-day pilgrim, much like Bunyan's Christian, who arrives at the "Heavenly City" by way of Doubting Castle, the Slough of Despond, and the Valley of the Shadow of Death? If it is true that "the trilogy is elaborately structured to enact the ironic redemption of a shallow fox-hunting man by terrible events" (102), it must then follow that all these "terrible events" of the war have been reshaped by habits of mind more medieval than modern. The great caesura in Western history resulting from the Great War is then less real than apparent, at least if this presumptive continuity in form is true. In the end, Fussell virtually admits as much, conceding: "A corollary to the technical traditionalism of these memoirists is the kind of backward-looking [*sic*] typical of war itself – it is a profoundly conservative activity, after all – and of any lifelong imaginative obsession with it" (314). Vance, and Bracco and Englander, are then authorized by Fussell himself to "find conservatism and tradition persisting deep within interwar societies as a sort of bedrock of stability" (Vance 5).

A much better measure of modernity would be the industrial character of modern warfare that Fussell regards as making human beings into machines and opening a gulf between "two Britains," the one a safe pastoral retreat, the other a blighted zone of industrial killing. He recalls "the deep hatred of civilian England experienced by soldiers returning from leave" (86) as evidence of the combatant's hatred of the ignorant, uninitiated multitudes who shared nothing of the horror in holding to their customary way of life: "But even if those at home had wanted to know the realities of the war, they couldn't have without experiencing them: its conditions were too novel, its industrial ghastliness too unprecedented. The war would have been simply unbelievable" (87).

On this score, the British novelist Pat Barker has revised Sassoon's trilogy in the 1990s to suggest that the old divisions of class were more likely to be the cause of "two Britains," and that wartime industrialization was hardly a new experience for "Tommies" who could only imagine hunting foxes on the Downs. In *The Eye in the Door* (1993), for example, Barker's working-class character Billy Prior is crossing a patch of brick-fields on home-leave when he finds himself brooding about conditions in France:

> One of the ways in which he felt different from his brother officers, one of the many, was that *their* England was a pastoral place: fields, streams, wooded valleys, medieval churches surrounded by ancient elms. They couldn't grasp that for him, and for the vast majority of the men, the Front, with its mechanization, its reduction of the individual to a cog in a machine, its blasted landscape, was not a contrast with the life they'd known

at home, in Birmingham or Manchester or Glasgow or the Welsh pit villages, but a nightmarish culmination. (115–16)

Barker is doubtless right about these class divisions: industrial "modernity" was less a "memory" of war than a lived reality for most Britons for six decades before 1914.

A more telling index of modernity that Fussell fails to see is the new experience of temporality that differed profoundly from the pre-modern experience of time, but that did pre-date the Great War by almost two decades. This unique structure of temporality appears in a German war novel that Fussell mentions several times, but never discusses, since it does not fit his cultural frame: Erich Maria Remarque's *Im Westen nichts Neues* (1928), published in English as *All Quiet on the Western Front* in 1929. Remarkably, *All Quiet* heads Fussell's list of Great War memoirs appearing in that portentous year, including "the first performance of Sherriff's *Journey's End,* as well as Sassoon's *Memoirs of a Fox-Hunting Man,* Blunden's *Undertones of War,* Max Ploughman's *A Subaltern on the Somme,* and Hugh Quigley's *Passchendaele and the Somme*" (109). And yet Fussell himself sees nothing more in the German work than a fevered instance of the Gothic, rather than the modern, mind: "Chapter 4 of *All Quiet* enacts a mad and quite un-British Gothic fantasia as a group of badly disorganized German troops is shelled in a civilian cemetery. Graves are torn asunder, coffins are hurled in the air, old cadavers are flung out – and the narrator and his chums preserve themselves by crawling into the coffins and covering themselves with the stinking cerements. This will remind us less of *Hamlet* than of, say, *The Monk*" (196).

What is far more modern in this novel than anything found in Fussell's repertoire, however, is its cinematic telescoping of time – from its present-tense narration and its cinematic straight-cuts to its final, unaccountable shift of perspective from the first person to a camera eye that continues, as it were, to roll after the narrator's death (as if to show how memory were being displaced all along from a person to an instrument) – in effect producing a non-stop invasion of the present by moving images from the past. The past *qua* past has ceased to exist. One remarks something else as well in the narrator's scorn for books he has loved, as well as for the wider authority of the written word, insisting that he and his fellows have finally "learned to see" (13). The past no longer serves as a credible

category of temporality in war novels like these; the present is omnipresent in the new filmic epistemology produced by moving images on-screen.

The specular immediacy of events in *All Quiet* nonetheless gives
way to a sense that the narrator, trapped in an endless film-loop of
the continuing present (literally, in a "past-progressive-present"
tense), prefers death to the ongoing collapse of time and personality.
In 1929, one hostile German critic intimated as much in faulting
Remarque for "arrogating to himself the rôle of the omniscient recording angel of the Great War, the sole repository of the whole
truth about the armed conflict on the Western front" (Barker and
Last 42). "Recording angel" would not be such a bad conceit, were
there not already machines available in 1928 to do that sort of
thing. In fact, the recording of time in the modern world is governed largely by the implicit epistemology of film.

Matt K. Matsuda argues in *The Memory of the Modern* (1996)
that modernity, like the cinema, was a French invention, following
upon the disaster of the Franco-Prussian War and the collapse of the
Second Empire in 1870–71. The "breaking of time" for Matsuda is
"the deep logic" of a number of social and technical developments
in Paris thereafter, from the "ritual acts" of the Communards (34) to
"an accelerated history of the present, bought and sold around the
world" (59) in the frenetic activity of the Bourse. Above all, the
"cinematographe" of the Lumière brothers (1895), and the motion-
picture industry begun by Georges Méliès, resulted in what Matsuda
describes as "an 'accelerated memory,' a relentless telescoping of
time" (166). This new structure of memory is analyzed in detail in
chapters 5 and 6 of this volume; suffice it to say here that it depends
on a number of interlocking elements: the immediacy of the visual
image; the invasion of the present by the past; the simultaneity of
past and present; and the presentness of viewing – which I parse
quite literally as a new verb tense in the grammar of existence, con-
jugated in a "past-progressive-present" tense. "With its ability to
capture and collapse time," as Matsuda explains, "the cinema camera was an utterly modern marker for the accelerated memory of the
late nineteenth century, a machine which generated superbly real living records while simultaneously creating its own fantastically unsettling perceptual and temporal frameworks" (167).

In his very narrow focus on British combatant writings of the
Great War, Fussell is almost oblivious to other media, except for a

few scattered references to works such as John Dos Passos' *Three Soldiers* (1921), an American novel that Fussell regards, somewhat parochially, as "the most notable piece of Great War writing which makes extensive use of cinematic rather than traditional stage parallels," and where, in a clichéd assumption about film's cultural effect, the protagonist's "dreams 'of glory' fall naturally into the shape of the visual clichés of such cinematic costume melodramas as Griffith's *Birth of a Nation* (1915)" (221). Otherwise, Fussell insists on a "more kinetic sense of cinema attaching," in the main, to "later wars, wars characterized by a new geographical remoteness, mobility, rapidity, complex technology, and ever-increasing incredibility."

The farther afield one looks, however, the more signs there are of cinema's pervasive effect on our "modern memory" of the First World War. Lewis Milestone's film adaptation of *All Quiet on the Western Front* (1930) remains "one of the great classics of the cinema," in spite of its experimental position as "one of the early talkies" (Barker and Last 41). Its continuing resonance suggests that it likely depends on the same perceptual framework as Remarque's novel, and that part of its enduring place in the antiwar canon is attributable to its structuring of memory in terms of its filmic epistemology. *Generals Die in Bed* (1930), a Canadian novel mentioned before as part of the antiwar canon, is likewise narrated in the present tense, and uses some of Remarque's narrative techniques to dramatize the simultaneity of past and present. It remains to be seen if the restructuring of memory in film had as much to do with these novels entering the literary canon as did their anti-war sentiments. For now, it suffices to note that the "memory" of cinematic forms of seeing preceded the Great War by almost twenty years.

While both of these "foreign" works stand outside the British framework of Fussell's cultural history, a poem like Wilfred Owen's "Dulce et Decorum Est" also shares a filmic sense of the invasive power of the moving image. Owen's speaker's dramatic distaste for the classics likewise leaves Remarque's narrator sounding discursive by comparison. The visual immediacy of a soldier without a gasmask who "plunges at me, guttering, choking, drowning" ought to make Owen's poem "gothic," in Fussell's terms, were it not so filmic in its use of the present tense. For Owen also says, "If in some smothering dreams, you too could pace / Behind the wagon that we flung him in, / And watch the white eyes writhing in his face," and then, anticipating the "talkies" of a decade later, "If you could hear, at every jolt, the blood / Come gargling from the froth-corrupted lungs," surely you would not repeat "with such high zest ... the old lie" of classical culture. In its haunting, visual immediacy, in its tele-scoping of past and present, and in its decisive rejection of written, classical culture, "Dulce" is a cinematic *actualité* of the Great War.

In the longer view, too, "modern memory" should not have been wrapped in Cold War rhetoric of "adversary proceedings" – the hidden implication of Fussell's second chapter – any more than it should have been reduced to the ironic mode. Indeed, we have wit-nessed a wholesale rewriting of Great War literature throughout the Commonwealth in the three decades since Fussell's book appeared. Particularly in Canada, the influence of new media looms not only in the web-based *Memory Project* (described in chapter 10) or in History Channel broadcasts of *For King and Empire* (discussed in chapter 9), but in novels and plays where newer media – the real epistemological ground of these works – are the subject of "modern memory" as much as is the Great War itself. Evidently the percep-tual frameworks of these new media continue, without our atten-tion or knowledge, to alter the structure of memory and our relationship to the past as much as cinema first did at the beginning of the twentieth century. As late as 1977, for example, it is still pos-sible for a novel like Timothy Findley's *The Wars* to say something fresh and original about the Great War in terms of the way photog-raphy may be used (in an anti-war era) to distance us from history, or even to free a protagonist (who is really like "us") from his own time, in order to bring him riding down the light rays, in an implicit filmic movement, into the more congenial company of our own time. But before we can consider such works, we need to ask how, and in what ways, memory is "mediated."

2

Mediated Memory

Plato was the first *writer* to condemn writing as a lasting threat to memory: "If men learn this," his Socrates warned Phaedrus, "it will implant forgetfulness in their souls; they will cease to exercise memory because they rely on that which is written, calling things to remembrance no longer from within themselves, but by means of external marks. What you have discovered is a recipe not for memory, but for reminder" (Hamilton and Cairns 520). True memory, in this view, "is written in the soul of the learner" (521). To attempt to preserve memory on any material surface would be to relinquish the deep, indwelling memory of divine Ideas. For Plato, the medium was the message, and the message was purely and simply one of loss, of the corruption of "nature" by *techne,* by the machine.

Contrary to Socrates, however, Plato issued his verdict against writing in writing. This may be less contradictory than it seems, if only because Plato's own epistemology was grounded in writing, as Eric Havelock has shown (14, 200 ff). Doubtless Plato was also familiar with an older "art of memory" taught by the rhetors, which ignored "natural" writing "in the soul." Attributed to "Simonides of Ceos" (*c.* 556–468 BCE), this ancient art of memory "belongs to the pre-Socratic age" (Yates 27), and so stands apart from a doctrine of innate ideas or even a pre-scriptive fear of amnesia. As taught, the "art of memory" functioned by converting material objects into an alphabet of mental images that could be set in imagined (usually architectural) spaces. As Frances Yates explains, "Those who know the letters of the alphabet can write down what is dictated to them and read out what they have written" (6). The earliest surviving text to codify the rules of this ancient art was written in Latin, not Greek, suggesting that "the art of memory" must have been transmitted orally at first, if as a mental instance of writing. Even in ancient times, it appears, orality was always already a variant of literacy.

The anonymous Roman author of *Ad Herennium* (*c*. 86–82 BCE) taught his pupils that the *loci* or "places" of memory "are very much like wax tablets or papyrus, the images like the letters, the arrangement and disposition of the images like the script, and the delivery is like the reading" (Yates 7). One is hardly surprised by such an image in an age when every schoolboy learned to form his letters on reusable tablets of wax, and where even the poet wrote on papyrus scrolls. But what is fresh and surprising in Yates's history of memory is its brilliant premise: that memory itself can and should be periodized according to the prevailing media of each era. Put epigrammatically, "Memory obeys periods" (Matsuda 12).

In great detail, Yates traces the transformation of memory in the Middle Ages, as it moved out of the Roman temples and other edifices that had served as the *loci* of memory and into the Gothic cathedral, which offered new surfaces of remembrance. Here,

> The extraordinary thought now arises that if Thomas Aquinas memorised his own *Summa* through "corporeal similitudes" disposed on places following the order of its parts, the abstract *Summa* might be corporealised in memory into something like a Gothic cathedral full of images on its ordered places ...
>
> On the walls of the Chapter House of the Dominican convent of Santa Maria Novella in Florence, there is a fourteenth-century fresco glorifying the wisdom and virtue of Thomas Aquinas. (79)

What Yates sees in this grouping of figures around St. Thomas sitting on the throne is an image "not only [of] the learning of Thomas but also his method of remembering it" (80).

Imagining a Gothic cathedral as a "surface" for "inner writing" profoundly revises our understanding of literary structure in the Middle Ages. "That Dante's *Inferno* could be regarded as a kind of memory system for memorising Hell and its punishments with striking images on orders of places, will come as a great shock" (95). The point is not so much that Dante consciously structured his poem on a Gothic architecture of memory, but rather that such medieval habits of memory and forms of knowledge underlie the epistemology of *The Divine Comedy,* making the focus and structure of memory in the greatest poem of the Middle Ages a work written in "stone" quite as much as in words.

Renaissance memory would in turn be informed by such humanist edifices as the "memory theatre" of Giulio Camillo, in which images of the devout Middle Ages "are transformed again into magically powerful images" derived from Hermetic lore (157). An epistemological determinant appears as well in "the Shakespearean theatre" and its "marvelous synthesis of the immediate contact between players and audience of the classical theatre with a hint of the hierarchy of spiritual levels expressed in the old religious theatre" (363). Very likely, the "memory system" of the seventeenth-century English physician and occult philosopher Robert Fludd was "based on the Shakespeare Globe Theatre," making it "a last outpost of the art of memory itself, a signal that the ancient art of Simonides is about to be put aside as an anachronism in the seventeenth century advance"(368). Even here, Yates thinks that the art of memory may have contributed to "the growth of scientific method" (369). The most vivid feature of her groundbreaking history of memory is not its content, however, but its enabling premise: that memory is a mediated construct, its underlying structure shaped by the dominant mode of communication in any given culture. The structure of memory, in other words, is not a constant but a cultural response to changing media environments.

More recently, the German cultural theorist Andreas Huyssen has speculated in *Twilight Memories: Marking Time in a Culture of Amnesia* (1995) about how digital media are altering the forms of cultural memory. By situating his argument entirely in the digital age, however, he ignores cinema as a prior marker of modern epistemology; at the very least, there exists in film a compelling explanation for the truism he cites, "that to be radically modern means to sever all links to the past. Such was the credo of an un-self-critical modernity and many of its avant-gardist aesthetic manifestations earlier in this century" (250). As suggested earlier, the immediacy of the moving image and the presentness of cinematic experience appear to inform the deep structure of modernist presentism. Historically speaking, a process of devaluing the past and valorizing the present was well under way before the Great War even began; the process was merely accelerated by the hypocrisy of power and the death of idealism in that war.

Huyssen's argument regarding "the draining of time in the world of information and data banks" (9) is nonetheless relevant and urgent, if digital media have the power he ascribes to them to alter the structure of temporality in postmodern culture. As he sees it, the "accelerated pace" of "information networks that function entirely according to principles of synchronicity ... threatens to make categories like past and future, experience and expectation, memory and anticipation themselves obsolete." Thus, "[t]he more we live with new technologies of communication and information cyberspace, the more our sense of temporality will be affected." Inasmuch, Huyssen writes, as "the media are the hidden veil through which I am looking at the problem of cultural memory and the structures of temporality at the end of the twentieth century" (4–5), the threat of forgetting in digital writing may yet be balanced by the promise of another mode of remembering.

Still, Huyssen warns, "At a time when the notion of memory has migrated into the realm of silicon chips, computers, and cyborg fictions, critics routinely deplore the entropy of historical memory[,] defining amnesia as a dangerous cultural virus generated by the new media technologies" (249). A decade after Huyssen's analysis, humanists continue to bemoan the virus of technological amnesia in terms echoing the *Phaedrus,* but without any of the saving grace of Plato's paradoxical use of a world-altering medium in his own diagnosis. "Although perhaps it cannot be proved," John Paul Russo laments in *The Future Without a Past* (2005), "some hidden connection exists between the ahistoricism of the technological system and the utter lack of interest in memory as an educational value" (36). The threat to the traditional humanist, of course, is a general forgetting of the classic texts, not the loss of the Ideas belonging to Plato's inner writing. "Yielding to the tide," Russo fulminates, "colleagues shun the arts of memory as things of the past, vestigial organs. Yet as Gombrich points out, the original task of the humanities had been to preserve the memory of classical culture. Carved over the entrance to the Warburg Institute, London is MNEMOSYNE, Memory, the mother of the Muses" (47).

If this seems like déjà vu to the media historian, the prospect of cultural amnesia is nonetheless frighteningly real to the humanist. And yet there may be some compensation in what should otherwise be dismissed as a reaction formation: "The undisputed waning of history and historical consciousness, the lament about political, social, and cultural amnesia, and the various discourses, celebratory or apocalyptic, about *posthistoire*," Huyssen reminds the anxious humanist, "have been accompanied in the past decade and a half [i.e., since about 1980] by a memory boom of unprecedented proportions" (5). Although "cultural memory" differs in significant ways from history – at least from more professional forms of historical understanding – it does not end in amnesia. "Certainly, there is evidence for the view," Huyssen allows, "that capitalist culture with its continuing frenetic pace, its television politics of quick oblivion, and its dissolution of public space in ever more channels of instant entertainment is inherently amnesiac" (7). But if electronic amnesia is also causing a memory boom, then what is taking place is rather more like an exchange of one form of remembering for another. Of course, it still offers a salutary reminder that "we are living through a transformation of this modern structure of temporality itself" (8), a transformation familiar to Western culture from the advent of writing to the invention of the printing press to the appearance of cinema. To his credit, however, Huyssen is not content to valorize new structures of temporality any more than he is willing to privilege memory over history. Rather, he realizes that "[t]he difficulty of the current conjuncture is to think memory and amnesia together rather than simply to oppose them" (7). (In part, this is my project in my concluding chapters 9 and 10.)

What, then, is the proper way to "think memory"? One has first to understand its location, Huyssen claims; memory is located not in the past, but in the present:

> The temporal status of any act of memory is always the present and not, as some naïve epistemology might have it, the past itself, even though all memory in some ineradicable sense is dependent on some past event or experience. It is this tenuous fissure between past and present that constitutes memory, making it powerfully alive and distinct from the archive or any other mere system of storage and retrieval. (3)

The strength of this account is the way that a "tenuous fissure" in memory "between past and present" is reconcilable with recent findings of "neuro-physiology and neuro-biology," since memory by both accounts is "a cultural construction in the present rather than a storage and retrieval system" (Huyssen 261, n. 1).

Contrary, to what might seem "natural" in a digital age, individual memories are not stored on a biological hard drive, but are fresh "perceptions newly occurring in the present" (Eakin 19). As Gerald Edelman discovered in his groundbreaking theory of "neural Darwinism," the "brain's neural organization is constantly modified – both phylogenetically and ontogenetically – to adapt to the ever-changing demands of experience" (13). For this reason, personal memories are bound to change in the light of new experience. In neural terms, the past is only ever a construct of the ever-changing present.[4] If, at the level of the species, such a "capacity to formulate concepts" of the past confers "a distinct evolutionary 'value,' freeing 'the individual from the bondage of an immediate time frame or ongoing events occurring in real time'" (Edelman, cited by Eakin 14), it is surely of equal importance, at the level of human culture, to understand how our "culture constructs and lives its temporality" (Huyssen 2). How a culture's memory changes and why it does so are questions that are vital to the culture's survival.

A shift from "proper" history to the "memory boom" of new forms of media is clearly manifest in historical fiction and drama about Canadians in the Great War, as well as in programming on the History Channel – such as *For King and Empire,* Norm Christie's popular telehistorical supplement to his battlefield guide books – or, since 2003, on the website of *The Memory Project,* "the Dominion Institute's flagship educational programme, designed to connect veterans and students online and in classrooms across the country" (www.thememoryproject.com). All these forms, as Huyssen suggests in another context, are "a potentially healthy sign of contestation: a contestation of the informational hyperspace and an expression of the basic human need to live in extended structures of temporality, however they may be organized" (9). But in our ongoing cultural mutation from history to "memory," what are we forgetting in new ways of remembering? And how "do the technological media affect the structure of memory, the ways we perceive and live our temporality?" (252).

"Our sense of the past," as one apologist for historical film has recently argued, "is shaped and limited by the possibilities and practices of the medium in which that past is conveyed, be it the printed page, the spoken word, the painting, the photograph, or the moving image" (Rosenstone 59). Starting from the example of film, one finds a new grammatical tense structuring the way we perceive and live our temporality. On film, the past of written history becomes a hybrid of past and present progressive tenses, wherever and whenever the past enters the present tense of our viewing. The moving image "shot" in the past then has a power without precedent in prior history "to invade the present" (Matsuda 174). Henceforth, it functions as the visual equivalent of the verb in a hybrid past-progressive-present tense, marking a new temporality in the grammar of existence.

In part III, "The End of the Book and the Beginning of Cinema," I explore the temporal effects of this new cinematic epistemology on fictional memoirs and poetry written during and soon after the war. My argument assumes that the military crisis was confused with, and compounded by, a deep cultural crisis brought on by film. In other words, a film-induced alteration in the structure of perception invaded the book in the wake of the military invasion; older cultural defenses were now fully and finally breached. This alteration in the structure of perception appears, for example, in the present-tense narration and camera-eye techniques of Erich Maria Remarque's *All Quiet on the Western Front* (1928) and of Charles Yale Harrison's *Generals Die in Bed* (1930), discussed in chapter 5. In Remarque's novel, there is also a signature rejection of the classics, like Wilfred Owen's stinging rejection in "Dulce et Decorum Est" of the Horatian ode and its long-standing heritage in Western literature. In the case of Owen and Harrison, "fake" propaganda films such as *The Battle of the Somme* (1916) called for more authentic *actualités* in print, while the opening scenes of *All Quiet* likely have more to do with German propaganda films than with Remarque's own limited experience on the Western Front. At the very least, the poet and both novelists gravitate toward a filmic epistemology in order to discredit the ancient forms of written culture.

Chapter 6 explores Siegfried Sassoon's investment in filmic ways of seeing from his first postwar poetry collection, *Picture Show* (1919), through to his fictional *Memoirs of George Sherston* (1928–36), where "spectral images" often illustrate this cinematic invasion of the present by the past. The "double vision" of the soldier-poet is something more than the poet's rewriting of his own Achilles-like absence from the battle (which is how I first saw it); it is larger, too, than the Jekyll-and-Hyde complex that Pat Barker envisions in her rewriting of Sassoon's trilogy in her own *Regeneration* trilogy of novels (1991–95). Very likely it comes closest to the

experience of early filmgoers watching themselves on screen, as
happened to Messrs Janssen and Lagrange at an initial exhibition of
the Lumière brothers' invention at "the Congrès des Sociétés Fran-
çaises de Photographie in Lyon" in June 1895, where both these
men appeared as "collaborators in a fantasmagoria of impersonation in which the actors astonishingly appeared to be alive on the
screen, yet were seated nonetheless in the audience, watching themselves" (Matsuda 174). Matt K. Matsuda reminds us how odd this
experience must have been at the time: "To see oneself would be an
impossible exteriority, a doubling of bodies, of presences, a simultaneity of past and present in time and space" (174). And yet these
ontological doublings, together with other displacements in time,
would shape the memoirs of Siegfried Sassoon to an extent that his
books suddenly seem new and strange when read in terms of their
cinematic epistemology.

If much of this latter argument depends on the emergence of new
perceptual frameworks implicit in a filmic use of form, there is another argument about time to be made in later works. Timothy
Findley, for example, wrote his Great War novel at the height of
public opposition to the Vietnam War, as appears in a remark of
Marian Turner, a nurse who is asked to recall what she remembers
of Robert Ross, the war-resister and deserter from the Canadian
Field Artillery: "Robert Ross? Well – it was just so tragic. When
you think that nowadays so many people – young people especially
– might've known what he was all about" (10). Another eyewitness, Lady Juliet d'Orsey, recalls a "marvellous thing" that she
quotes verbatim from Sassoon's *Memoirs of an Infantry Officer*: "*I
still maintain that an ordinary human being has a right to be horri-
fied by a mangled body seen on an afternoon walk*" (114). But *The
Wars* (1977) is an historical novel, not a combatant's memoir of the
Great War, recreating events from archival documents. More signif-
icantly, the structure of memory in the novel is photographic, that is
to say, it is built out of verbal analogues of the photographic image
to distance the protagonist from his own era; indeed, the quest of
the archival narrator is to rescue this long-dead soldier of the Great
War from the "insanity" of his own era. Writing with "light" serves
to fix the image in the distant past, in order to deliver Robert Ross
out of his dark age into the "clearer light" of our own day. And it
succeeds insofar as the past-as-context remains frozen within the

static frame of the photo. Conversely, the narrative reconstruction frees Robert's image from a world of dead ideas to come riding, in cinematic fashion, down the light-rays into the more congenial social and political context of "our" day.

The new perceptual frameworks created by Joseph Nicéphore Niepce and his partner Louis Daguerre in the 1820s approximate those of the new discipline of academic history that would emerge in roughly the same years. The use of photography as an agent of distancing, difference, and decontextualization in *The Wars,* however, is only half of the story of how "light writing" has altered our sense of temporality. In the second half of part IV, "Photo/Play: Seeing Time and (Hearing) Relativity," I show how the epistemology of cinema – the setting back into motion of an arrested ray of light – is related to the epistemology of Einstein's special and general theories of relativity. In *The Lost Boys* (2001), a recent play by the Canadian actor and playwright R. H. Thomson, Einstein takes the stage with five brothers lost in the Great War as their respective photos appear on screens in projected beams of light, in brief film clips, and in the context of other visual and aural multimedia. In a remarkably apposite way, Thomson revisits the theme of the historian's quest in Findley's *The Wars* to locate the "lost boys" in the great curve of "spacetime," at about the same moment that Einstein announced his General Theory of Relativity. Lost in the war, the five boys are nonetheless recoverable by another form of memory: "a play of light" in which Einstein's theories come to life in a multimedia staging of projected photographs, film clips, and sound recordings, and are embodied in an actor who not only plays every role himself, but narrates his own quest for "the lost boys," culminating in "a dizzying prospect of curving space-time" (48). Through the "gravity" of the actor's performance, we feel how the past could be just "over there," and that we might "get there from here" if only we could travel down the light-rays. In other words, the play of light and sound are used to transport us beyond the weightlessness of light itself, and so beyond the past-progressive-present tense of film, into a future perfect tense where what was "lost" is now "found," only *there,* not *here.*

The relationship between time and space in *The Lost Boys* points to something else that was lost in the print revolution, perhaps as early as the seventeenth century:

Historians such as Reinhart Koselleck have shown how the specific tripartite structure of past-present-future, in which the future is asynchronous with the past, arose at the turn of the seventeenth to the eighteenth century. The way our culture thinks about time is far from natural even though we may experience it as such. In comparison with earlier Christian ages that cherished tradition and thought of the future primarily and rather statically, even spatially, as the time of the Last Judgment, modern societies have put ever more weight on thinking the secular future as dynamic and superior to the past. In such thinking the future has been radically temporalized, and the move from the past to the future has been linked to notions of progress and perfectibility in social and human affairs that characterize the age of modernity as a whole. (Huyssen 8)

Oddly, Thomson's final vision in *The Lost Boys* enacts a secular revival of this traditional Christian notion of a spatialized eternity, although his version of timeless time does not seem static. Rather, it is dynamic, as if in this re-mediated memory of the "lost boys" they could still be waiting for us in the future-perfect tense of "a dizzying prospect of curving space-time." By such means, a secularized space-time may surmount the horrors of a dark age, even as it reminds us that the past has an independent existence.

In part V, "Virtual Presences: History in the Electronic Age," I explore the new domains of History Television, *The Memory Project*, and interactive war museums in order to test Huyssen's theory that we are being carried beyond time in any meaningful sense, at least insofar as the accelerating speed of information technology supposedly produces a synchronic present where all times are simultaneously present, and time ceases to "pass" in any conventional sense. A measure of support for this view may be found in the work of Mary Ann Doane, an American theorist of television, who sees "a pervasive ideology of 'liveness'" enveloping broadcast television, even forty years after it was first taken over by videotape. Because "the recorded material it uses – including the material recorded on film" – is "instituted as actual in the production of the television image," then the "transformation of record into actuality or immediacy" is reduced to "a function of a generalized fantasy of 'live broadcasting'" (274). History on television then tends to be experienced as something occurring in the moment, even when it represents the past. Contrary to the tense of the photograph – the image of *"That-has-been"* identified by Roland Barthes (32) as a sign of both "the reality and the 'pastness' of the object photographed" – the verb tense of the television broadcast "would seem to be that of an insistent 'present-ness' – a *'This-is-going-on'* rather than a *'That-has-been,'* a celebration of the instantaneous" (Doane 269). In draining the past into this timeless present of viewing, television could even be contributing to what Doane calls "an absence of memory" in contemporary culture (274).

It strains credulity, however, to believe that viewers could mistake televisual history for the evening news or a live sporting event. Far more likely is the notion that history comes to life by virtue of the ontology of "live broadcasting." It is still a form of history, for all that it comes leaping off the page; it just isn't "book" history now, not if it realizes the unique properties of the medium. Even when it is distributed through a "live" broadcast, it still originates in film, notwithstanding its video format. In terms of "the special capabilities of the medium" that shape its approach to the filmic past, one notes "the closeup of the human face, the quick juxtaposition of disparate images, the power of music and sound effect," all of which are used "to heighten and intensify the feelings of the audience about the events depicted on the screen" (Rosenstone 56). Visual history on film or on television is then likely to differ in important ways from written history: "The word works differently from the image. The word can provide vast amounts of data in a small space. The word can generalize, talk of great abstractions like revolution, evolution, and progress, and make us believe that these things exist … Film, with its need for a specific image, cannot make general statements about revolution or progress. Instead, film must summarize, synthesize, generalize, symbolize – in images" (62). And television, which John Fiske tends to see as a medium that has much in common with oral culture (105–7), is more likely, anyway, to divert history into an ancient "channel."

The irreducible truth about visual history is that the properties of the medium – its basic means of mediating memory – "ensure alterations in the way we think of the past" (Rosenstone 59). But how, and in what particular ways, would television alter our sense of history? To listen to Ken Burns speak about the success of his popular documentary history, *The Civil War* (1990), is to hear a voice speaking as if from the ancient world: "I would like to suggest that television can become a new Homeric mode. What other form would allow such powerful emotions of the war to come forward, would allow you to follow the spear carriers as well as the gods?" (cited by Edgerton 306). The extraordinary thought arises, to adapt a phrase from *The Art of Memory,* that electronic media are returning us to a Homeric world rather than to the synchronic world that Huyssen sees.

Indeed, the astonished response of the conservative columnist George Will to *The Civil War* suggests that the American past has already found its true kinship in the ancient past: "Our *Iliad* has found its Homer ... [I]f better use has ever been made of television, I have not seen it" (cited by Edgerton 304). The public seems to agree with this estimate for two reasons: first, the compelling sweep of national history emerging from Burns's handling of period documents; and, second, his subdued, but genuine, celebration of the heroism of ordinary men and women on either side of the conflict in a period of great human tragedy. The popular success of *The Civil War* is all the more extraordinary, given the almost insuperable difficulty of making an historical film without one frame of archival footage. As Taylor Downing, a BBC documentary filmmaker, admits with great humility, "Ken Burns showed in his epic series *The Civil War* how marvelously creative it is possible to be with a supply of faded photographs, a cache of letters, and a few good songs" (297). But Burns also depended on a creative vision that said, "Once you've taken the poetry of words and added to it a poetry of imagery and a poetry of music and a poetry of sound, I think you begin to approximate the notion that the real war could actually get someplace, that you could bring it back alive" (cited by Edgerton 311).

Bringing it "back alive" ultimately depends on the power of "live" television to deliver the past-progressive-present tense of film to mass viewers simultaneously. And so a "new Homeric mode" may be strengthened on the one hand by the "direct address/appeal to the viewer" of television news (Doane 278), and on the other by distinctive properties of film that still emerge on television: "Film insists on history as the story of individuals ... singled out by the camera," Robert Rosenstone says (55). It also "offers us history as the story of a closed, completed, and simple past." In other words, film does not ask us to believe that things could ever work out differently. Moreover, if it is to make effective use of its emotive and individualizing properties, it cannot rely too much on either sober analysis or cautious skepticism, since it is "designed to strike by its evidence and through immediate contact, instead of convincing through reason and deduction" (Sorlin 26).

History as the story of individuals is what one finds in spades in the Canadian television series *For King and Empire* (2001), a six-part documentary filmed for History Television, the Saskatchewan Communications Network, the Knowledge Network, and the Access Network, based on host Norm Christie's self-published guidebooks to the major Canadian battlefields of 1915–18. Distributed by Breakthrough Entertainment, the series website (www.breakthroughfilms.com) speaks of Christie's portrayal of "the experiences and emotions of the Canadian soldiers, their remarkable endurance and their supreme sacrifices." One anonymous viewer has posted this online review:

> A walking tour of WWI graveyards sounds like it might make for tedious TV, but not in the hands of Norm Christie. Christie is an historian and has a deep appreciation for these gravesites, and what happened to the soldiers that lie within them. He's created a series that brings the stories of the Canadian soldiers alive in an extremely personal way. The series combines archive [*sic*] footage, narration, actor's voices, still images, soldiers [*sic*] letters and Christie's on-camera descriptions of the battles and soldiers' lives. (www.imdb.com/title/tt0308270/)

Each episode in the series observes familiar conventions of the historical film, beginning with an "establishing shot" of Christie at a Canadian cemetery, monument, or battlefield memorial, and voice-over narration by R. H. Thomson, before moving back and forth through time from archival film to photos to letters to newspaper clippings. But it also makes frequent use of the "following shot," which turns the "camera of now," the medium of television, into a "call" to the viewer to follow the "camera of then," on black-and-white film, even as he or she watches in the progressive-present of "live" TV.

Chapter 9, "Electronic Memory: 'A New Homeric Mode' on History Television," examines Christie's television series for these and other conventions of documentary history, in order to determine how visual history creates a new form of cultural memory. Overall, I am guided in my reading by Robert Rosenstone's arresting conclusion in "Looking at the Past in a Postliterate Age":

We must begin to think of history on film as closer to past forms
of history, as a way of dealing with the past that is more like oral
history, or history told by bards, or *griots* in Africa, or history
contained in classic epics. Perhaps film is a postliterate equivalent
of the preliterate way of dealing with the past, of those forms of
history in which scientific, documentary accuracy was not yet a
consideration, forms in which any notion of fact was of less
importance than the sound of a voice, the rhythm of a line,
the magic of words. (65)

Finally, in chapter 10, "Sound Bytes in the Archive and the Museum," I turn to the impact of digital media in two conservative institutions of memory that have been profoundly altered by digital
technologies. The online format of the Digital Archive in *The Memory Project,* for example, enables the user to sort soldiers by province of origin or branch of service, or even by "digital objects" (i.e.,
the type of memorabilia put online). More powerfully still, the
voice of an old soldier recalling life at the Front, or the voices of descendants reading letters and diaries to pass on oral stories of the
veteran's experience, allow digitized sound to play as large a part as
digitized photos, or Attestation papers, medals, badges, regimental
insignia, and other images in the repository. The interpretive focus
is kept on the soldier and his family, much as Homer's focus was
trained on Hector and Andromache, as well as on soldiers like Achilles,
Patroklos, and Agamemnon. But the belated creation of a digital archive in 2003 by the fledgling Dominion Institute of Canada has
meant that a majority of contributors are likely to be family members a generation or more removed from the combatant. Voluntary
inclusion in the Digital Archive is also likely to create a repository
that is not fully representative.

What emerges from *The Memory Project*, however, is a type of
oral memory, even when it takes the form of a family member reading a letter from the Front. In the recital of anecdotes from the
Western Front, memory is shaped by orality in two more ways: a
grandnephew transmits a story that has been handed down by family tradition; or a solitary veteran tells a story of hardships at the
front that is tailored (and self-edited) to be heard by schoolchildren.
Tinged by his awareness of the audience, the old soldier's reminiscence turns rose-tinted, even nostalgic, about friendship and thus

represses the real hardships and horrors of war. Throughout, the format of *The Memory Project* also encourages a type of volunteerism that parallels the ethos of a volunteer army, while its inclusive, democratic character links it to the district "histories" peculiar to centenary celebrations in many Canadian communities – "histories" usually composed of family reminiscence in the context of communal givens. At the same time, the Digital Archive allows for individualized pathways through the past of memory that are quite as evocative of the Homeric mind as the films of Ken Burns and Norm Christie, since the "'pathways' *(oimai)* of oral traditional epic" (Foley, "What's in a Sign?" 10) constitute that nexus of choices from a traditional repertoire that the oral poet has to make in performance.

To appreciate what is implied in this attribution of "Homeric" qualities to history on television and in the digital archive, I see no other way to begin the substantive argument than with the thorny question of oral memory in the *Iliad*. Begging the indulgence of readers who prefer to go immediately to the First World War, I remind them that all memories are mediated, and that memory itself is a medium. Our focus in a study like this has to be dual: How has the particular medium of memory shaped the character and structure of what is remembered? And how does "memory" reveal its own changing history as a series of mediated forms? The problem for a history of memory that has as its primary referent the Great War is that this war came at the end of the great age of print, perhaps decades before the emergence of electronic "orality," but several millennia after the end of ancient oral culture. To place a discussion of ancient culture at this point is to risk losing readers who want "modern," or even postmodern, "memory." And yet, since a history of "mediated memory" would be woefully incomplete without this history of "oral memory," I have opted to start with the classical period, and its dependence on the stabilizing force of tradition, to ground my history of memory.

In chapter 3, "Oral Memory and the Anger of Achilleus," I follow as far as possible the work of John Miles Foley and his many followers in the biennial proceedings of the Mnemosyne conference of oralists, since it offers fairly solid ground for my own view of the *Iliad* as a traditional poet's response to the "shock of the new" – at base, the warrior's angry doubt of oral memory and the oral poet as offering more than a reification of political power. In its largest extent, I think that the *Iliad* offers a forceful illustration of the emerging threat to traditional memory of script, still a nascent new medium, as well as of the oral poet's effort to outflank the warrior's doubt in a manner that preserves the integrity of this ancient medium of cultural memory. In tracing out the tensions within this conflicted medium, I seek to anticipate the ways in which cultural memory appears to be riven in our day by similar tensions implicit in differing forms of new media, with various consequences for our sense of temporality. Most of all, however, I want to show how the old form (oral memory) is not abolished by the new form (written memory), but makes it rather its implicit content in the longing of Achilleus for a more durable medium than that of oral memory. The astounding success of the Homeric poet is our first indication that media change does not have to entail a "law of obsolescence."

In the second chapter of part II, "Classical Memory: Orality and Literacy," I begin what I hope is a clear tack back toward "modern memory" with a fourth chapter on "Scripts of Empire: Remembering Virgil in *Barometer Rising*." Starting with a scene from Virgil's *Aeneid,* in which Jupiter unrolls the scroll of Fate in order to "read" the future of Roman empire and reassure the anxious mother of Aeneas,[5] I try to show how far the culture of writing informs the injunction of Anchises to his son in the Underworld, "*Romane memento*" (VI 851), and what such a "scripting" of empire really entails. At the same time, these two great Roman scenes of "memory" play directly into my reading of Hugh MacLennan's *Barometer Rising* (1941), a Great War novel that first appeared at the beginning of the Second World War. My reading challenges the canonical version of George Woodcock's "Odysseus ever returning" from the "Trojan" War, showing how MacLennan's novel has nothing to do with the Greek *Odyssey* and everything to do with a Roman *Aeneid,* particularly its scripting of empire. Although the prescriptive influence of Virgil carries the novel well out of the orbit of oral memory, the trajectory of written epic does have one crucial thing in common with *Iliad* – it depends on tradition to cushion its represented world from the "shock of the new," so helping to stabilize cultural memory in the face of the relentless dislocations of modernity. If the Halifax harbour explosion in December 1917 literally brought the Great War home to Canada, the Virgilian *pax Canadiana* of *Barometer Rising* at minimum freed the classically trained novelist to negotiate his country's distance between Britain and America, or, more generally, between the continuities of imperial tradition and the "shock" of modernity.

To this end, I turn to Homer's *Iliad* to develop a theoretical definition as well as a practical illustration of oral memory, both to begin my periodic history of memory and to contextualize the great changes still being wrought by new media in our understanding of the Great War and modern memory.

PART TWO

Classical Memory:
Orality and Literacy

3

Oral Memory and the Anger of Achilleus

The spectre of written communications makes a single appearance in Homeric song – in the sixth book of the *Iliad* – as Glaukos, an ally of the Trojans, presents himself to the Greek Diomedes as an heir of "Bellerophontes the blameless" (Lattimore, *Iliad* 6.155). In recalling a wicked plot against his ancestor, Glaukos tells of "murderous symbols" which King Proitos had "inscribed in a folding tablet, enough to destroy life, / and told him to show it to his wife's father, that he might perish" (6.168–70). In *Homer's Traditional Art* (1999), John Miles Foley has shrewdly observed that Homer "is identifying a technology he does not possess – writing and texts – as a species of the sign-language that he does possess – traditional, idiomatic representation" (3). The new technology, in Foley's view, is thereby assimilated to the old system of representation as one more element in a long-established "sign-language" of poetic tradition. The fable of "Bellerophontes' Tablet" is a fine example of Foley's nuanced approach to reading signs, or "*sêmata,*" as part of a larger language of poetic tradition with its richly connotative idioms. Indeed, the whole of *Homer's Traditional Art* proves our need of fluency in this specialized poetic register.

As a non-specialist, I take it on Foley's word that *writing* is just one more instance in Homeric art of verbal signs whose "secrets" would doubtless remain a mystery, were it not for "an audience or readership who knew the code, someone who could read the signs on their own terms and in their own context" (4). What Foley's elegant solution offers is a new way out of irresolvable debates about whether Homer composed orally, or dictated from memory, or wrote as he composed. Foley announces his own intention to "proceed under what I take to be the minimal defensible assumption – that the *Iliad* and *Odyssey* are *oral-connected* works of verbal art, that they employ the idiom of oral tradition and assume an audience fluent in that idiom" (xiv). It is a method that yields rich results.

And yet, as a media theorist, I hear another kind of "secret" in the fable of Bellerophontes' tablet – in the image of a singer looking ahead, as much as back to the old sign-system, in order to deal with these "murderous *sêmata*, / which he inscribed in a folding tablet, enough to destroy life" (Foley 2). Reading the fable as a brief allegory of the oral poet having to adjust to written communications, I ask a simple question (that has no simple answer): What difference does the written sign make to the story of the *Iliad*? Does it figure in any meaningful way in the anger of Achilleus, or in his thoughtful debates with the envoys in Book 9? Would it have any bearing on the image of a world turned upside down in his withdrawal from the fray of "the best of the Achaians" (1.412)? Or what about the flagrant reversal of custom in Priam's piteous suit to recover the body of his son Hektor? What if the "Homeric Question" were itself turned around to ask not how oral traditions differ from written memories but how the traditional poet might be seeking to outflank, or even to absorb, the threat of written signs that are indeed "enough to destroy life," or at least the living voice of a poet in the act of performance?

Tradition on the cusp of change is the other side of the story that I would set against Foley's handling of the fable of Bellerophontes' tablet. I want to know what may be learned from looking ahead, as much as back, at Homer's "traditional art." The old ways still appear most clearly in this liminal moment between two dominant modes of communication. We would first need, however, to rehearse old debates, and even some outmoded suppositions, about a supposed culture of "absolute non-literacy," the subject of Eric Havelock's *Preface to Plato* (1963), a book studiously avoided by Foley.

PREFACE TO HOMER

What are the conditions of cultural memory in a society that lacks "Bellerophontes' tablet"? What sort of information is preserved by oral traditions, and by what means is it reliably remembered? In Western history there is "what might be called a controlled experiment in absolute non-literacy" among archaic "Greek-speaking peoples" after the fall of Mycenae in the twelfth century BCE when "Linear B script perished" (Havelock 117). Although Homer "talks a great deal about Mycenae and is familiar with her history," is this "oral memory of Agamemnon and company" (116) historical in any meaningful sense? Would the oral tradition, in a nearly total absence of written records, recall and preserve something that remotely resembles our literate notion of "history"? Or are archaic Greek memories of the Trojan War "extrapolated from relatively few remains" (Kullmann 113)?

In his study of the oral technology of archaic Greek culture, Eric Havelock saw Homer as a "tribal encyclopedist" (66) whose *Iliad* is really "a kind of metrical text book" (87). In this "encyclopedic" reading, the tale of Achilleus' quarrel with Agamemnon is "designed as a kind of convenience" to serve "as a kind of literary portmanteau which is to contain a collection of assorted usages, conventions, prescriptions, and procedures" (66). The dispute among the Greek leaders most obviously derives from a violation of custom-law "governing the division of spoils" after the sack of a city. The rights of "Chryses, priest of Apollo" (*Il.* 1.11)[6] have in this case come into direct conflict with the political and military rights of the Greeks; the daughter of a priest is not a lawful war prize. Although "the distribution of these shares was governed by strict convention which accorded preferential choice to men of superior station" (Havelock 67), Agamemnon has been left with no choice but to observe religious custom. By convention, his "sole recourse would be to cancel the entire previous distribution and start again. The complications would be enormous, and indeed this solution was impossible. It is left to Achilleus to point out the fact, and incidentally to put on record the convention governing distribution" (67). The only way left for Agamemnon to save face, and thus to preserve the social hierarchy, is to claim for himself Achilleus' prize, "... the fair-cheeked Briseis, ... that you may learn well / how much greater I am than you, and another man may shrink back / from likening himself to me and contending against me" (*Il.* 1.184–7).

Agamemnon's preservation of the political hierarchy comes, of course, at the expense of military hierarchy, so calling into question both the legal and moral authority of the ruler. With forceful acuity, Achilleus challenges the decision, apparently in defence of the public right as much as of private interest: "King who feed on your people" (*Il.* 1.231), he begins, denouncing this abuse of authority (even the king's abuse against his own office) before dismissing all whom the king rules as "nonentities," since they dare not defend law, or custom, or common usage. But then, "[t]he sweep of his anger is interrupted," writes Havelock, "by an excursus on the staff as a symbol of authority; how you go into the woods and cut it, what it looks like, and who is entitled to hold it" (67):

> But I will tell you this and swear a great oath upon it:
> in the name of this sceptre, which never again will bear leaf nor
> branch, now that it has left behind the cut stump in the mountains,
> nor shall it ever blossom again, since the bronze blade stripped
> bark and leafage, and now at last the sons of the Achaians
> carry it in their hands in state when they administer
> the justice of Zeus. (*Il.* 1.231 ff)

Undoubtedly, Achilleus' "pronouncements conserve the legal precedents" (Havelock 68), for this excursus is a very effective means of "illustrating the public law, what we might call the governing apparatus of the Achaean society" (66). Doubtless, too, "the story is told in such a way that the rules themselves are continually recalled. The record is indirect but it is a record" (72).

For Havelock, there is always an ulterior motive in Homeric verse to memorialize "familiar and proper customs," as well as to endorse "acceptable and worthy habits and attitudes" (76). The problem with this view, however, is that it reduces the poet to a court reporter or legal recorder, lacking freedom to reshape, rethink, or transform his metrically transmitted materials. To John Miles Foley, this is the crux of the problem: "Although Homer's epics and countless other works are straightforwardly credited with having originated from an oral tradition, a composite poetics – an approach that takes account of both traditional character and what some have construed as 'literary' quality – has been elusive" ("What's in a Sign?" 6). Foley nonetheless has good reason to protest "that oral tradition never was the 'other' we accused it of being; it never was the primitive, preliminary technology of communication we thought it had to be" (1).

Havelock did make some allowance for the "literary" quality of Homeric song, however, admitting that the poet who simply recited formulaic precedents "would be dull if he performed those functions as would a literate poet composing for readers" (89–90). By way of illustration, he returns to Achilleus' excursus on the staff of authority to show how Homer has made it relevant to the motives of the speaker: "Yet it is also true that as the listener hears him describe this piece of a tree which will never burgeon again, for it has become something else, he would catch a note of relevance: the separation of the wood from its tree is irrevocable and so is to be the separation of Achilles from his own parent body the army. A piece of reporting turns into a dramatic device" (90).

If one sees the "separation of the wood from its tree" from another angle – that of the medium itself – the relevance of Achilleus' anger appears in yet another light. For the staff, insofar as it is a cultural and material record, encodes a set of social and legal customs that do distinguish it from the organic branch that would alter with the growing tree. What Achilleus appears to question more is the organic "living tradition" that could easily lose touch with its own material "history," with the very prescriptions it has adopted as a bulwark against change in the environment. At bottom, Achilleus seems to doubt the efficacy of the medium itself – both the oral tradition and the singer's art – to preserve the discrete artifact that is in some ways analogous to Bellerophontes' tablet.

The story of Achilleus' anger holds other clues to the question of whether the poet is bound by the formulaic constraints of oral memory, or whether the tradition is flexible enough to accommodate innovation. While I have enormous respect for Foley's scholarly attention to "*traditional referentiality* – the resonance between the singular moment and the traditional context" (*Homer's Art* xiv), as well as his "carefully measured yes" to the question of whether "we need a special poetics, an approach uniquely tailored to works that emerge from oral tradition" (xiii), I suspect that we also need an approach tailored to the exigencies of the medium. While I do not see how to avoid the conclusion that the "oral state of mind" is in some respects "Other" to the literate state of mind, I seriously doubt that writing was the first, or only, medium in history to be self-questioning. It may be useful then, to revisit Havelock's sweeping claim that "the spell of the tradition" of oral memory had to be broken by the method of Platonic dialogues, as if, "in asking a speaker to repeat himself and explain what he had meant," the "dream so to speak was disrupted" (199, 208, 209). Does Greek poetry not begin with this sort of question, which instantly disallows the "pleasurable complacency" that Havelock takes to be a given "in the poetic formula or the image" (209)? To understand how oral memory could still be preserved under conditions of self-questioning, we would first need to ask why "literates" would like to rule a self-reflexive orality right out of the court of inquiry.

THE ORAL TRADITION AS "OTHER"

For Havelock, it was Plato who made the oral poet and "the 'poetic' or 'Homeric' or 'oral' state of mind" an "arch-enemy," implicitly setting aside the historical conditions of oral communication and "entering the lists against centuries of habituation in rhythmic memorised experience" (47). Although Havelock wants to defend the "Homeric state of mind" on historical grounds ignored by Plato, the implicit logic of his defence is already signalled in his title. The Homeric poems can only be a necessary "preface to Plato," since Homer is "the representative of that kind of poetry which has to exist in a culture of oral communication, where if any 'useful' statement, historical, technical, or moral, is to survive, in more or less standardised form, this can be done only in the living memories of the members who make up the culture group" (91). A listening audience will be an indispensable part of cultural memory in a society without writing, since it is in their hearts and minds that the public record is ultimately kept. Metaphorically, if not literally, "[t]he memoranda of a culture of wholly oral communication are inscribed in the rhythms and formulas imprinted on the living memory" (107).

Poetry and the "oral state of mind" are thereby reduced to an automated technology, a type of pre-literate word-processing program that is quite as necessary to the preservation of the culture's total knowledge as it is to "the preservation of group identity" (100). Here, Havelock verges on technological determinism in regarding the epic "not as an act of creation but as an act of reminder and recall" (91). He frankly affirms the role of the poet as an "unconscious vehicle of repetition and record" (48), whose formulaic technology mandates a constant repetition of "*custom-laws* and *folk-ways*" (62). Implicitly, he adopts the perspective of the Platonic philosopher determined to overcome an "'oral' state of mind" as "the chief obstacle to scientific rationalism, to the use of analysis, to the classification of experience, to its rearrangement in sequence of cause and effect" (47). More explicitly, Havelock valorizes a type of poetry whose "patron muse is indeed *Mnemosune* in whom is symbolized not just the memory considered as a mental phenomenon but rather the total act of reminding, recalling, memorialising, and memorising, which is achieved in epic verse" (91). At this far end of a range of numerous oral "Others," the poet becomes a virtual captive of his medium, bound to recall what he has heard and to repeat whatever is needful to be known, in terms that will be hard to forget. The daughters of Memory, reduced to conservative agents of recall, are really "not the daughters of inspiration or invention, but basically of memorisation. Their central role is not to create but to preserve" (100).

More recently, in *Memory in Oral Traditions* (1995) David C. Rubin has explored this theme from the vantage point of cognitive psychology, conducting memory research on modern subjects in order to lay bare the mechanisms of recall in genres remote in time or place: epic, ballads, and counting-out rhymes. The processes described by Rubin "are not those of a single creative mind trying to be novel, but of many minds trying to be conservative" (10). On Darwinian grounds, Rubin justifies the conservatism of each genre as a survival mechanism, given evidence that "[s]ongs with highly constrained choices will be more stable than those with fewer constraints" (178–9). Still, "A premium must be put on solutions that are not repetitious. In addition, the constraints must be weak enough to allow variation. Nonetheless … creativity that leads to novel changes is a failure of memory" (179). Worse yet, true novelty is maladaptive, and likely doomed to extinction.

Among the productive constraints described by Rubin are theme, or "meaningful structure" (15), whereby both "the singer's and listener's tasks are made easier because they have a familiar structure in which to place the tale" (19); scripts, or "knowledge structures" (24), in which multiple details, or actions, or series of actions, such as a warrior arming for battle, can "fill the same slot or role in a script" (25); and "stereotyped *causal chains*" that serve "to preserve the temporal order of events in the theme and usually the actual order of the presentation of the events in the piece itself" (25). In general, Rubin claims, "Meaning constraints, such as scripts, causal chains, and story grammars, tend to preserve sequential information, and poetic constraints tend to preserve the exact wording" (63). Chief among poetic constraints are rhyme (in later, non-Homeric verse), alliteration, assonance, and meter, where "the intonation unit" (68) – a unit of four or five words that "corresponds to the contents of working memory" (69) – assists by "cuing and limiting the choice of both words and larger units to those with the correct rhythmic pattern" (85). With the help of "controlled experimental data," Rubin can then advance a theory of "recall in oral traditions as serial recall guided by multiple constraints" (176).

One predictable result of such a theory appears in a chapter on imagery, where the subheadings tell a story familiar to any formalist New Critic: "Imagery Aids Memory" (46); "Imagery Is for the Dynamic" (48); "Imagery Is for the Spatial, Not the Sequential" (49); "Imagery Is a Type of Organization" (52); "Imagery is Specific" (54). And yet what far exceeds the expectations of any mere formalist is this (translated) account of "a storyteller in the oral tradition of South Uist" who claims to remember the story he is telling as if it were a cinema running in his mind's eye: "I could see, if I were looking at the wall there, I could see just how they were – how they came in – the people – and how this thing was and that and the other ... Yes, it's easier to tell a story right through, from the beginning, because it's there in front of you to the end, all the way. All you have to do is to follow it" (59–60). The oral poet seems to be watching an inner film for which he alone has the soundtrack; at the same time, the precision and specificity of his visual recall is able to evoke comparable images in the minds of auditors.

One recent Homerist – who "examines from a cognitive perspective a typical if not a defining feature of the epics: the Homeric simile" (Minchin, "Similes" 25) – is evidently indebted to Rubin's memory studies, even when she stresses her dependence instead on the cognitive research of Allan Paivio. "According to [the latter's] theory," writes Elizabeth Minchin, "when we name a familiar object, two kinds of memory traces will be evoked simultaneously, a visual response (we see an image) and a verbal response (we register a word). The advantage of such dual coding ... is the probability that recall for the material in question is increased because the concept has been stored in two ways: 'there are two paths to an idea rather than one'" ("Similes" 28). But Homer's extended similes do not just constrain word choice or cue recall, as Rubin would have it; they also provide "a commentary on the scene which runs in the cinema of his mind's eye" (Minchin 44). Here, Minchin's cognitive approach can allow for much more creative freedom than the social scientist's conservative function of recall. Take, for example, the fall of the Trojan Asios at the hands of the Greek Idomeneus in *Iliad* 13 (a scene that introduces a formula used again at *Iliad* 16.482–4 to describe the fall of Sarpedon in battle with Patroklos):

> He fell, as when an oak goes down or a white poplar,
> or like a towering pine tree which in the mountains the carpenters
> have hewn down with their whetted axes to make a ship-timber.
> (*Il.* 13.389–91)

"What brings the description to life," writes Minchin, "is one particular item: these men are said to be ship-builders. But the ship-builders are not crucial to the comparison" (40).

Why extend the simile, then, from warrior through woodcutter to an irrelevant shipbuilder? Beyond the three reasons offered by Minchin – the fearsome image of a gigantic foe; a helpful explanation of what the men are doing in the woods; the terrible pathos of battle's destructive waste in contrast to more constructive action – there is another motive that defines and illuminates the hidden artistry of the oral "Other." The simile of a warrior cutting down his own "keel timber" implicates the audience in the longing of every Greek to hasten his "Return Song" through victory in battle. In cutting down the giant Asios, Idomeneus takes a long step toward the vessel of his homecoming. But the epic simile, on its second appearance, is now tinged with irony. In *Iliad* 16, the fate of the Greek warrior Patroklos is no longer in his own hands, since the "keel" that should hasten the homecoming of Idomeneus has been cracked by the anger of Patroklos' friend Achilleus. The art of the oral "Other" need not be lumbered, then, with inferior materials or be hampered by a technique of limiting constraints. Within the *enabling* constraints of his tradition, the Homeric poet enjoys a large measure of creative freedom. This would seem to be Foley's meaning when he observes, "We understand oral traditions best not when we worry over their superficial narrowness or limitations, but when we seek to discover their enhanced signification and rich coding – what lies behind their signs or *sêmata* ... In this respect they are usually more densely idiomatic and resonant than everyday registers; they work like language, only more so" ("What's in a Sign?" 11).

In *Homer's Traditional Art,* Foley redirects attention from a supposed art of oral composition to an audience's fluent reception of the oral tradition: "Whereas many have described the utility of ready-made diction and narrative machinery, restricting their attention to *compositional* values, I emphasize the inimitable usefulness of the signs as speech-acts, as signals that point toward emergent realities, as keys that unlock the word-hoard of traditional associations" (34). One accidental consequence of Milman Parry's epoch-making study (1928) of the practices of oral composition in South Slavic epic had been the way it hid the larger question: "We can see in retrospect that the composition-in-performance hypothesis was a necessary first step, awakening us to the possibility of 'another' kind of composition, audience, and verbal art" ("What's in a Sign?" 5).

And yet Eric Havelock had already recognized that "the element of improvisation is wholly secondary," even if he did offer a caveat that "the minstrel's personal invention is secondary to the culture and folkways which he reports and preserves" (93). In other words, techniques that "facilitate versification" (Sale 54) have ceased to be the main concern or focus of oralists. As Foley says with epigrammatic force, "[T]he crucial term in the phrase 'oral tradition' is not the former but the latter one" (13). Or, as he phrases it in one of his "six homemade proverbs," "Performance is the enabling event, tradition the enabling referent" (*Homer's Art* 5, 6). But to what does tradition refer, in fact?

ORAL TRADITION AND HISTORICAL MEMORY

When we turn from the question of *how* an oral poet remembers to the question of *what* is remembered, the minstrel soon reclaims his uncanny resemblance to Havelock's Platonic "Other." For, as Wolfgang Kullmann maintains, "The political geography of the Mycenaean age, such as we can reconstruct it from the Linear-B tablets, was quite different from that of the Catalogue of Ships" in the second book of the *Iliad* (101). The singer, or singers, did not even "know that all the palaces on the Greek mainland had been destroyed around 1200 BC, whereas Troy VII survived until about 1000 BC; only then did Troy become a ruin, to be resettled by Greeks" (102). In fact, the Homeric poet was demonstrably unaware that the Mycenaean world had already fallen some two centuries before the destruction of Troy.

Among other anachronisms, "the *Iliad* locates Agamemnon in Mycenae," although it "also shows awareness of the version that he resided in Sparta together with Menelaos and ruled over Messenia. Otherwise, Agamemnon's attempt to reconcile Achilleus by offering him seven Messenian cities (*Il.* 9.149 ff) would be unintelligible. He could do this only as a king of Sparta. This means that the poet anachronistically presupposes the result of the First Messenian War that led to the extinction of Messene" (105). With some justice, Kullmann concludes, "The image given by Homer contradicts everything that the Mycenaean archaeological finds reveal about the considerable extent of the territories in the Mycenaean age" (110).

Further anachronisms include the "loose coalition" from the Catalogue of Ships that "corresponds to the political situation that we can presuppose for the time of the poet of the *Iliad*" (110). The new pan-Hellenic feeling that appears among the "29 contingents of autonomous states that have only temporarily put themselves under the command of Agamemnon" had not begun to emerge until the eighth century in the organization, for example, of the Olympic games, celebrated for the first time in 776 BCE: "The degree of inter-Greek communication that is characteristic of the world described in the Homeric epics corresponds fairly exactly to the degree of communication necessary for the organization of common Greek festivals and games: this is actually attested to in inscriptions from the 7th century onward" (111). The world of the *Iliad* apparently has more to do with the culture of Greek-speaking peoples of the eighth and seventh centuries BCE than it has to do with any "history" from 400 or 500 years before. And yet the Homeric poet makes no reference whatsoever to the recent past, much less to a time of "origin" before the Mycenaean period. He keeps his focus solely on the culture of Mycenae.

Why, then, if "the historical core of the *Iliad* is very small" (Kullmann 112), is the poet so "fixated" (100) on a period about which he knows so little? Are "the ruins of the palaces" really an answer in search of a question, or are the "single pieces of old bronze weapons that were still extant" just so imaginatively compelling, that they require a "constructed history" to be conjured out of the oral tradition (113)? Havelock reminds us, for example, that in the Homeric poems "Mycenaean ancestors are not thought of strictly in historical perspective as they would be if history-making were a literate process. They are part of the present consciousness. The Ionic Greeks are still Mycenaeans, or re-enact the Mycenaean past" (121–2). But this re-enactment has little to do with what we regard as "historical consciousness." Nor is the "conservation of Mycenaean memories in Homer … a symptom of romantic nostalgia,"

Havelock concludes. "Rather it provided a setting in which to preserve the group identity of the Greek-speaking people. It was a matrix within which orally to contain and preserve their *nomoi*
[custom-laws] and *ēthē* [folk-ways]" (118–19). And what setting
had a larger geographical area for contemporary cultural unifica-
tion of the Greek-speaking peoples than the "memory of Troy"?

Havelock has grasped the principle that "the confusion between
past and present time guarantees that the past is slowly but continuously contaminated with the present as folkways slowly change. The
living memory preserves what is necessary for present life" (122).
More recent scholars, however, turn to anthropological research to
shake "all confidence in the idea that historical traditions could be
transmitted orally from Mycenaean times ... As early as 1968 Jack
Goody and Ian Watt drew attention to the interplay of remembering
and forgetting in oral cultures ... They claimed that in an oral society the tradition is always adjusted and assimilated to the conditions
of the present by eliminating everything that is no longer relevant"
(Kullmann 97–8).

Since "oral societies live very much in a present which keeps itself
in equilibrium or homeostasis by sloughing off memories which no
longer have present relevance" (Ong 46), the real question has to
be, How long can oral memory persist? In this regard, the sociolog-
ical researches of the French scholar Maurice Halbwachs (1950)
show that "the oral memory of man does not go back further than
about 80 years; it results from his own experiences and his social
communication, and has as its last component information handed
down by grandparents" (cited by Kullmann 97). "[H]istorical
memory," under conditions of oral transmission, thus "seems to be
confined to the normal memory of about 80 years" (99).

Although the "Trojan War retained its absolute chronological
place through its connection with the ruins of Mycenae and Troy"
(101), there is good reason to believe that "the historical memory
underlying the *Iliad* does not go back much further than 80 years"
(100). From the other end of the genealogical chain, it might be
more useful to ask how Achilleus would view this lack of "history"
under conditions of oral memory. The warrior at least gestures toward this sort of question in the first book, when he wonders what
will guarantee his "honour" after death, if it can be so easily re-
voked while he yet lives. Here, in fact, is how he grieves his case to
his divine parent, Thetis:

Since, my mother, you bore me to be a man with a short life,
therefore Zeus of the loud thunder on Olympos should grant me
honour at least. But now he has given me not even a little.
Now the son of Atreus, powerful Agamemnon,
has dishonoured me, since he has taken away my prize and keeps it.
(*Il* .1.352–6)

Far from petulance, the anger of Achilleus appears to be directed
against a cultural system that he regards as powerless to preserve
his good name. Thus the anger of Achilleus may be read as a sign of
his impatience with the oral tradition itself. Achilleus might have
some claim to being a proto-historic man wanting to be judged in
the "clearer" light of history.

THE WARRIOR AND THE POET

In the ninth book of the *Iliad,* as the embassy of Achaians approaches the "shelters and ships" of the Myrmidon leader, hoping
to win the peerless warrior's aid with an abject apology from
Agamemnon and an extraordinary offer of compensation,

> … they found Achilleus delighting his heart in a lyre, clear-sounding,
> splendid and carefully wrought, with a bridge of silver upon it,
> which he won out of the spoils when he ruined Eëtion's city.
> With this he was pleasuring his heart, and singing of men's fame,
> as Patroklos was sitting over against him, alone, in silence,
> watching Aiakides and the time he would leave off singing.
> (9.186–91)

Elizabeth Minchin has argued that this story of Achilleus' lyre draws
on a "knowledge structure" that she calls "a description-format"
("Describing" 56), thus integrating a part of Achilleus' personal history into the narrative through a material object that "reminds us of
the life he has led and the successes he has enjoyed" (59–60). No
doubt "it is a striking image of Achilleus, whom we remember from
his previous appearance in the narrative as the combative hero, ready
to stand up to his king." But it hardly suffices to say that "the lyre
suggests something about Achilleus' state of mind now that he is in
self-imposed exile from the active life. He is searching for a means to
fill in time. And, for all that, the lyre – paradoxically – is a reminder

of that life for which he yearns" (59). In truth, the image of the warrior, "delighting his heart in a lyre," says far less about Achilleus with his occupation gone than about the poet himself "singing of men's fame." For the warrior has taken a determined step toward another occupation – singing the heroic song he fears will be denied him and his fame.

The problem of the warrior-poet, of course, is that it is simply impossible for the oral singer to be two things at once: both a fighting machine, and a recording instrument. Achilleus admits as much when, rising "to his feet in amazement / holding the lyre as it was, leaving the place where he was sitting," he greets the envoys as follows: "'Welcome. You are my friends who have come, and greatly I need you, / who even to this my anger are dearest of all the Achaians'" (9.193 ff). It is a strange thing for the recusant to say, particularly if he is still "sulking" in his tent, this warrior in rustication who had sworn "a great oath" that "you will eat out the heart within you / in sorrow, that you did no honour to the best of the Achaians" (1.239, 243–4). Nor does the warmth of his greeting now have much to do with reconciling himself to the reviled Agamemnon. While receiving the embassy as friends, he also acknowledges his "need" of them, a need that is as much public as it is personal. For the song he was "singing of men's fame" as the delegation arrived has no words that are heard – neither by the envoys themselves, nor by any audience of subsequent poetic performances. By such means, a powerful point is made: the warrior cannot preserve the memory of his deeds without the help of oral tradition. He can sing his own praises all he wants, but when he is dead, the story of his fame can be preserved only by voices other than his own. There is no medium in which his history and his integrity may be preserved apart from the living memory of the culture. If the song he sings in Book 9 is not preserved in words, but only in its theme, then the reason is obvious: a singer will not survive himself.

By contrast, one thinks of the Latin poet Horace, fighting on the side of Brutus and Cassius at Philippi with every confidence in the scroll as his means of immortality. The ground of his conviction is simple: "non ego, pauperum / sanguis parentum, non ego, quem vocas, / dilecte Maecenas, obibo / nec Stygia cohibebor unda" (*Odes* II 20.5–8) ["Not I, the son of parents poor, not I, who hear your voice, beloved Maecenas, shall perish, or be confined by waters of the Styx"] (Bennett 165). The difference in the cultural situation of

Horace is most evident in the "double form" of his medium: "On no common or feeble pinion shall I soar in double form through the liquid air, a poet still" ["Non usitata nec tenui ferar / pinna biformis per liquidum aethera / vates"] (II, 20.1–3). The "pinna biformis" is literally the "double form" on which his fame depends – the double scroll, and those "twin wings" of speech and writing on which the poet hopes to ascend.

A suitable modern analogy appears in the career of the warrior-poet Siegfried Sassoon who, leaving the fray to question the Great War from Craiglockhart War Hospital, is able to mount a furious *Counter-Attack* (1918) by means of writing against the powers that be. A paperless Achilleus, on the other hand, lacks the option to write poems of protest; he is reported to be "singing of men's fame" in "winged words" never recalled in performance. Without this "double form," or "folding tablet," in which his voice will be heard, the warrior-poet can only admit, "Greatly I need you."

Odysseus now responds by reciting every formulaic line of Agamemnon's magnanimous offer of reparation, save for the deal-breaking requirement: "And let him yield place to me, inasmuch as I am the kinglier / and inasmuch as I can call myself born the elder" (9.160–1). So why does Achilleus still refuse the formula of the oral tradition? Not from stubborn pique or any other character flaw. He does so for just one reason:

> Fate is the same for the man who holds back, the same if he
>   fights hard.
> We are all held in a single honour, the brave with the weaklings.
> A man dies still if he has done nothing, as one who has
>   done much.
> Nothing is won for me, now that my heart has gone through
>   its afflictions
> in forever setting my life on the hazard of battle. (9.318–22)

How does one dispute this claim if "honour" (or integrity) is just as easily taken away as it is given in oral memory? Achilleus' hard lot is to learn this painful truth that oral "traditions are displaced when they are no longer relevant to present life" (Kullmann 98). Is it any wonder, then, that "all of them stayed stricken to silence / in amaze-ment at his words"? After all, "[h]e had spoken to them very strongly" (9.430–1).

At the same time, "Phoinix the aged horseman" recalls with kindly tact the relevant precedents and principles from tradition to restore his surrogate son to the *ēthē* of the Greek-speaking peoples. "The very immortals," he reminds Achilleus, must be open to "supplication" (9.497, 501), else how could they demand "sacrifices and offerings" (499) much less "libations" (500)? In "the old days," too, "[t]he heroes would take gifts; they would listen and be persuaded" (524, 526). But Achilleus has just seen through what stands revealed as an empty form: "Phoinix my father, aged, illustrious, such honour is a thing / I need not" (9.607–8), especially if it denies him his integrity. It is left to the blunt-spoken warrior Aias to berate his fellow warrior for having "made savage the proud-hearted spirit within his body" (629). The angry doppelgänger is at some pains to remind Achilleus of the binding force of custom, of a Greek man's duty to accept

> … from his brother's slayer
> the blood-price, or the price for a child who was killed, and
>   the guilty
> one, when he has largely repaid, stays still in the country,
> and the injured man's heart is curbed, and his pride, and his anger
> when he has taken the price. (9.632–6)

Given the didactic tone of this scene, Havelock concludes: "The ninth book of the *Iliad,* crucial for the movement of the tragic plot, is an epic essay in the education of Achilleus: his early training is described by Phoenix; his present instruction (which fails) is narrated by Homer as it is received at the hands of his peers. In the phrases and formulas of their exhortations we hear the preserved voice of the community affirming its manners and mores and imperatives" (120). But the lessons are not all on one side; nor, it seems, is the tragic failure to learn. Indeed, if the instruction in Book 9 "fails," it is not because of Achilleus' failure to speak with force and acuity about a cultural system that is fatally ill-equipped to keep faith with its fighting men. For if fame is exposed as a "winged word," then who would be willing to settle for "a short life" (1.352)?

RIGHTING THE WORLD TURNED UPSIDE DOWN

The warrior's loss of faith in the cultural system to preserve his story, his fame, and his integrity is not total and absolute, of course, else Achilleus would not have set any limits on his subaltern Patroklos going out to fight in terror-inducing armour borrowed from his formidable commander: "When you have driven them from the ships ... / you must not set your mind on fighting the Trojans, whose delight / is in battle, without me. So you will diminish my honour" (16.87 ff). Even now, his hope of being remembered continues to drive what Achilleus does. If he could write, he would be ready to sign his name in blood. But the oral tradition knows no signatures; the outsize image is the only mark of uniqueness it can entertain. As David C. Rubin explains, "Images in oral traditions are often exaggerated by normal standards. They are of epic proportions," largely because "exaggerated images will be remembered better than common images" (55). By holding out for so very long, Achilleus does guarantee that his name will be recalled as the exception to the rule. Thus his grief at the death of Patroklos is excessive, his revenge on Hektor as his friend's slayer too extreme, his heart of "iron" (24.521) at Priam's request for his son's body too obdurate. Achilleus makes himself a prototype for what Athenian drama would later regard as tragic excess, as the hubris of an individual who threatens the social order. Doubtless the challenge of Achilleus to the oral tradition is responsible for this image of an entire world turned upside down.

Such, at least, is the state of affairs the poet describes when old Priam pleads with Achilleus for the release of Hektor's body, that a father might have his son's corpse returned to him with a modicum of dignity, and that the people may yet honour their fallen champion: "I have gone through what no other mortal on earth has gone through; / I put my lips to the hands of the man who has killed my children" (24.505–6). "The world," notes Mary Sale, "as well as the formulaic words are upside down. But just as the poet made the formula partly by a strict, and partly by a strange interpretation of the rules, so Priam is obeying the old rules in a unique fashion, and we expect Achilles to obey them too" (74). Indeed, the aged king of Troy reminds us that, if the old rules do obtain, it is only in this particular way they have to be adjusted to new circumstances.

The oral poet thus shows how a profound challenge to the tradition may be absorbed only by a thoughtful response to the criticism, not by a silencing of the critic. For such reasons, the poet truly serves his own ends by making Achilleus a model leader at the funeral games he hosts in honour of his friend Patroklos. With an adroitness beyond what we see of the political leadership in the first book of the poem, Achilleus settles a series of disputes in the penultimate book. In what appears as the echo scene of Agamemnon's incompetent handling of a disputed war prize, Antilochus protests: "Achilleus, I shall be very angry with you if you accomplish / what you have said. You mean to take my prize away from me" (23.543–4). So Achilleus "answered him and addressed him in winged words: 'Antilochus, / if you would have me bring some other thing out of my dwelling / as special [sic] gift for Eumelos, then for your sake I will do it" (557–9). The leader's exemplary generosity prevails as well with Menelaos, who says, "Antilochus, / I myself, who was angry, now will give way before you, /... I will be ruled by your supplication. I will even give you/ the mare, though she is mine, so that these men too may be witnesses / that the heart is never arrogant nor stubborn within me" (23.601 ff).

Achilleus displays beyond all doubt a proper form of rule in honouring the aged Nestor with a prize, "since never again will you fight with your fists nor wrestle /... since now the hardship of old age is upon you" (23.621 ff). Setting the seal of tradition on this image of a truly magnanimous ruler, Nestor says, "I accept this from you gratefully, and my heart is happy / that you have remembered me and my kindness, that I am not forgotten / for the honour that should be my honour among the Achaians" (23.647–9). In such fashion, Achilleus is made a true ally of the poet in saving the same cultural system he had just exposed in all its contradictions.

In Achilleus' lack of pity for the supplicant Priam, however, we see how fully the challenge of the warrior to the medium of the poet may turn the world upside down, and leave it turned. For no good models exist in the oral tradition for a grieving father who has to find his way through "what no other mortal on earth has gone through." Except for one thing: the proud heart of Achilleus is suddenly broken by the father's pained humility:

So he spoke, and stirred in the other a passion of grieving
for his own father. He took the old man's hand and pushed him
gently away, and the two remembered, as Priam sat huddled
at the feet of Achilleus and wept close for manslaughtering Hektor
and Achilleus wept now for his own father, now again
for Patroklos. The sound of their mourning moved in the house
... (24.507–12)

The image of two traditional enemies sitting and remembering together their joint losses recalls us to the presence of the real enemy

– our common end in death. And so the moral and the social order alike do reassert themselves as the challenger gives way before the inescapable conditions of human existence. The image that lingers in the mind long after the tumult of Achilleus' anger dies away is of the impermanence of human life, not the transience of oral memory.

So it is that the anger of Achilleus allows the oral poet scope to rethink the whole *ēthē* of the oral tradition, as well as the means of his communication. And, this time, it is left to the "enemy" to sum up the traditional view, much as when the Trojan Sarpedon says to his friend Glaukos at the midpoint of the poem:

Man, supposing you and I, escaping this battle,
would be able to live on forever, ageless, immortal,
so neither would I myself go on fighting in the foremost
nor would I urge you into the fighting where men win glory.
But now, seeing that the spirits of death stand close about us
in their thousands, no man can turn aside nor escape them,
let us go on and win glory for ourselves, or yield it to others.
(12.322–8)

By the end of the poem, the anger of Achilleus has managed none-theless to force a telling revision of this ancient ethic. The last lines gesture toward the material signs of a way of life that is nearly over:

They piled up the grave-barrow and went away, and thereafter
assembled in a fair gathering and held a glorious
feast within the house of Priam, king under God's hand.
Such was their burial of Hektor, breaker of horses. (24.801–4)

What we are left with at the end of this deeply moving oral poem is something quite different from the philosopher's "encyclopedia," or "metrical textbook" of tradition, much less different from the cognitive psychologist's "word-processing program" of oral com-position. For what the oral poet has taught us, in the largest sense, is the capacity of his medium to absorb its own negation, to assimi-late the threat of "murderous symbols" of a new "folding tablet" of writing that is "enough to destroy life," and so to emerge more memorably than ever as an enduring vehicle of cultural memory, even when it has finally been gathered into tablet form.

4

Scripts of Empire: Remembering Virgil in *Barometer Rising*

Today's oralists speak of the oral and the written as a "false dichotomy," obscuring more than it reveals. "We know now," John Miles Foley says, "that cultures are not oral or literate; rather they employ a menu or spectrum of communicative strategies, some of them associated with texts, some with voices, and some with both" ("What's in a Sign?" 4, 3). This altered emphasis on communicative strategies, rather than on differing media properties of voice or text, has made orality a species of literacy, freeing critics to read the oral work in terms of "fundamental rules that govern its composition and reception" (14). To Egbert Bakker, for example, "Speaking and writing are different activities that call for different strategies in the presentation and comprehension of a discourse." To that end, "each medium, speech and writing, comes with its own set of associations, and even its own mentality. To bring out this aspect, we might speak of 'oral' as the *conception* that underlies a discourse, and oppose this quality not to 'written' but to 'literate" (30). One "important consequence of the conceptional understanding of 'oral' is ... that the orality of a discourse is perfectly compatible with writing" (31), as will be obvious from any first-person narration written in a vernacular style.

On the other hand, to grasp the potential impact of a discourse that is conceptually literate, one need look no farther than the figure of Jupiter as a *reader* in the first book of Virgil's *Aeneid*.[7] "Know, I have search'd the mystic rolls of Fate," the father of the Roman gods assures Aeneas's anxious mother Venus (in the epochal translation of John Dryden, made at the beginning of the first British empire and still a standard for The Harvard Classics as late as

1909): "Thy son (nor is th' appointed season far) / In Italy shall wage successful war, / Shall tame fierce nations in the bloody field, / And sov'reign laws impose, and cities build" (Dryden 84). "Unfolding secret fated things to come" in the more precise, yet somehow more evocative, modern translation of Robert Fitzgerald, Jupiter unrolls a papyrus scroll to reveal the future of Aeneas to a race of people fated to rule in his name: "For these I set no limits, world or time," the father of the gods concludes, "But make the gift of empire without end" (Fitzgerald 12–13). So a "fated" text comes to shape the future it contains as the "prescript" of empire. In other words, the text precedes what it creates, much as the blueprint antedates a building it conceptualizes.

Like the Roman god who is surely his metonym, the Roman poet stands in a new conceptual relation to time, not as the oral voice of an absolute tradition or unchangeable past, but as the architect of a time to come, of this new and better future that is supposed to emerge out of the poet's script. In historical fact, Virgil seems to have fashioned an image of historical possibility out of the myth of Aeneas to represent his own hopes under the rule of Augustus. For it was still quite possible at the time of writing

> to view Augustus, and consequently the future, in a much darker light – the uncontrolled domination of a man whose whole career was illegal, whose first act had been to raise an army and march on Rome, who had signed the lists which proscribed innocent citizens, committed unforgotten crimes in the civil wars and climbed to tyranny over the bodies of his enemies and the ruin of the constitution ... The epic would celebrate his achievement but, at the same time, it would attempt to influence it. Augustus would be shown an image of heroic splendour, moral elevation, true patriotism. Judicious praise – praise of the virtues of a ruler – could be a form of pressure on him to exhibit those very virtues. (Griffin 57)

At root, a literate prescription might then promote this change, and not simply preserve the history that it names. Aeneas need only learn to follow the script set down by the Fates, as Augustus need only learn to follow the script written for him by the poet.

Scripts are not unique to conceptually literate discourse, of course; they appear with remarkable frequency in oral traditions. Because oral discourse is made up of multiple "collections of concrete actions, scripts are well suited for their description. Longer sequences can be diagrammed in terms of grammar-like structures, though the rules for these structures need to vary from tradition to tradition" (Rubin 11). Recalling cybernetic scripts that have been "developed in an effort to provide knowledge structures that would allow computers to understand and make appropriate inferences about such trivial, everyday human activities as going to a restaurant or a dentist's office," David C. Rubin maintains that "members of a culture" also "have considerable knowledge about the kinds of routine activities that scripts describe, and they can use this knowledge to make inferences and set expectations" (24).

Supporting "schema theory" with cognitive experiments, Rubin concludes that "[a] major function of scripts in the real world of undergraduates and in oral traditions is to preserve the order of events" (26). Since "[t]he order-preserving aspect of scripts can also be observed in tasks that measure the time required to produce a response," they come as a godsend to the oral singer pressed by metrical constraints to make an instant response. Any omission or deviation from the standard order of events carries a larger significance than an unscripted event would bear, for the same reason that an interruption of the usual order draws on the knowledge of how things ought to be. For example, "The *Odyssey* is about the return of Odysseus after the Trojan War, and yet no sooner does the story begin than there is an interruption in the plot. Odysseus's son, Telemachus, goes on his first adventure, but does nothing to help Odysseus's return" (16). The interruption is more than memorable, however, since it also incorporates a script of the novice hero familiar to audiences. In fact, the "story of Telemachus fits the *Odyssey* because, in large part, it parallels and utilizes many of the same components as the story of Odysseus's return to Ithaki ... The example of the theme of the novice hero" thus "demonstrates how themes function to lighten the memory load on the singer and his audience" (18).

In a wide-ranging discussion of imagery as a cue to memory, Elizabeth Minchin identifies another form of "script" in Homeric song. When "the poet accesses imagery, he calls up also the relevant scripts from episodic memory, where his experience of event-sequences is recorded in minute detail" ("Similes" 38). If such scripts are usually brief – hardly more than "the contents of working memory" (Rubin 69) – they point all the same to a dimension of

"writing" in oral composition that often goes unnoticed. Oral memory follows scripts scored in the mind by daily events or procedures
that are read off the "page" of working memory. Such scripts differ
from those of long-term memory insofar as they participate in the in-
termittent structures of episodic memory. In other words, one image
prompts a memory that cues another image leading to another memory. These "'pathways' *(oimai)* of oral traditional epic are important
not chiefly in and of themselves but rather because of where they
lead" (Foley, "What's in a Sign?" 10). Where they lead is to another
memory cue, if also to a choice that is rarely single, having to do
with episodic structure. Under conditions of oral composition, large-
scale structures inhere in the genre to the extent that they belong to
"an organized set of rules or constraints that are set by the piece and
its tradition. In literary terms, this claim makes the structure of the
genre central to the production of the piece" (Rubin 7).

By contrast, a literate conception of a "script" allows for the invention of "tradition" that would make the past into a useable future. A failure to understand this literate conception is what led
W. H. Auden to misread Virgil in a poem entitled "Secondary Epic"
(a term too credulously borrowed from the classicist C. M. Bowra):

No, Virgil, no:
Not even the first of the Romans can learn
His Roman history in the future tense,
Not even to serve your political turn:
Hindsight as foresight makes no sense. (Auden 455)

Auden's mistake was to identify Virgil with "the first of the Romans" rather than with the father of the Roman gods. Virgil's
"hindsight as foresight" is indeed justifiable if he is writing "Roman history in the future tense," setting up a pattern of events that
extends not only throughout the centuries, but through several
widely separated passages in Books 1, 6, and 8 that simply do not
belong to the traditions of epic, but rather to the prescriptive, orga-
nizing functions of long-term memory – to that which requires a
written script that may be read periodically in order to look beyond
the fixed horizons of tradition.

What offends the modern poet, however, is evidently this static
conception of "scenes of a glorious Roman future transposed to the
decorative panels of the shield of Aeneas. What disturbed Auden

about the nature of the Vergilian shield has disturbed many readers of the *Aeneid*. As the modern poet protested, Roman history did not 'so abruptly, mysteriously stop'" (Gurval 209) in the wake of Antony's defeat at Actium in 31 BCE. Conversely, the figure of Augustus at the prophetic centre of Aeneas's shield was never the end, nor even the centre, of "eternal" Western history. What Auden truly failed to see, however, was that it was Virgil, not Augustus, who had created a "script" of Roman empire that was to endure for four more centuries in the political capitol of the West, for a millennium after that in Byzantium, and for the better part of two millenia in the spiritual capital of Christendom. Indeed, this "conceptually literate" script appears to underwrite the whole project of empire in later eras, in nineteenth-century British India, for example, or in the trenches of the Great War, or even in the streets of Baghdad today.

This static (or "inscribed") surface of Aeneas's shield in Book 8 doubtless "complements the prophecy of Jupiter to Venus (1.257–96) and the pageant of Roman heroes in the underworld (6.756–886)," both "in the content and tone of its message; it is the culmination of Vergil's efforts to link Caesar Augustus with the poem's hero, Troian Aeneas" (Gurval 211). What the vaulted arch of Roman script reaches toward, however, is something quite foreign to the oral conception of "[t]he tragedy of Achilles" that "subsumed the universal dilemma of mortal man" (210). For what is everywhere conveyed in Virgil's conceptually literate script is a promise, as well as the price, of Roman power. The shade of old father Anchises instructs his son in the Underworld:

> Tu regere imperio populos Romane memento
> Hae tibi erunt artes pacisque imponere morem,
> Parcere subjectis et debellare superbos. (*Aen.* 6.851 ff)

What the Roman is called upon to remember are his true arts – the reason he is destined "to rule earth's people by imposing the habit of peace, by sparing the humble and warring down the proud" (my translation).

In these pregnant lines, Jasper Griffin sees more than a little of "the human cost of empire. The career of conquest and dominion was not to be presented as enjoyable or as making the imperialist happy; the sacrifices so sternly demanded from Aeneas stand for the self-abnegation involved in turning away from the arts, from philosophy, and from ordinary life, to the exacting service of destiny" (17). For a Briton like Griffin, however, this is quite literally to read "memory" in hindsight, not, as Virgil conceived of it, as foresight. *Romane memento* – "Roman, remember" – is rather more than the injunction of a father to a son; it is the announcement of paternity of a discourse. For Virgil as its scriptor is mapping a singular path to peace through a maze of treacheries, civil wars, and barbarous acts identified throughout the epic with the "furor" of Achilles[8] and an old-style Greek hero. In style, as well as theme, Virgil scripts a very different past from the one his hero recalls in musing on scenes of fallen Troy that he sees on the wall of the Carthaginian temple of Juno in *Aeneid* 1, where his own nostalgia for that past verges on narcissism, and where the future suddenly threatens to be a fatal repetition of that past.

What Virgil seeks, however, in returning to the past in search of a better future proves to be as conservative as the Homeric effort to outflank the "shock of the new" in the challenge Achilleus presents to oral memory. For the situation in Rome in 29 BCE, when Virgil began his poem, was unprecedented. A republic founded on the myth of resistance to tyranny – the historical example of Lucius Junius Brutus sacrificing his sons for their support of a tyrant – had endured for five hundred years only to now fall into potential tyranny. And yet the Princeps presented the poet a way out of this dilemma: "Although he was such an innovator, or because he was, Augustus made a show of conservatism. He claimed to follow ancient precedents, revived or invented ancient rituals, disclaimed untraditional honours. That cast of mind naturally fitted well with the antiquarian aspects of the *Aeneid*" (Griffin 18). The truth of the poem, like the truth of politics in Rome, is that Virgil had to resort to a traditional myth of Rome and its founding – a myth entirely at odds, amidst the civil wars, with a far more relevant story of Romulus the fratricide – in order to give legitimacy to the benevolent tyrant.

Here, too, the prescriptive power of the literate conception could shape history in ways that were well out of the reach of an oral conception:

The symbolic framework of Vergil's *Aeneid* did not so much reflect a public image of Actium as it created or redefined the role of this victory in Augustan political culture. Vergil gave Augustus and his regime what Actium had previously lacked, not simply

poetic expression and epic grandeur (what any composer of hack-
neyed verses might provide), but political interpretation, meaning, and import. Viewed from the perspective of more than a
decade that witnessed an enduring, if at times fragile, political
success, the Augustan victory entered the Roman public consciousness as a critical moment of a collective history and national culture, what Auden disparaged as the poet's "grand
panorama" of history without end. (Gurval 246)

In the end, what Virgil achieved in his script of empire was to out-
last the empire itself.[9]

REMEMBERING VIRGIL

"*Forsan et haec olim meminisse iuvabit*. Only one who had experienced ultimate things could comprehend the greatness of that line"
(200), muses Neil Macrae (his own surname recalling that of the
"national" poet John McCrae), the protagonist of *Barometer Rising* (1941), a canonical novel about the Great War by the Canadian
Hugh MacLennan. The Latin line recalled by a soldier from the
Western Front is uttered by Aeneas (*Aeneid* 1.203) in the first public words he speaks in Virgil's poem: "Some day, perhaps," Aeneas
encourages his men still shaken by the furious tempest that has
claimed part of the Trojan fleet, "remembering even this / Will be a
pleasure" (Fitzgerald 10). Concealing his own despair at loss of
Troy and at the daunting task of founding a successor city, Aeneas
barely manages to conceal the death wish that had been his private
thought just hours before: "Triply lucky, all you men / To whom
death came before your fathers' eyes / Below the wall at Troy!"
(*Aeneid* 1.94–6; Fitzgerald 6). Given the circumstances of his utter-
ance, Neil Macrae's quotation from *Aeneid* is most felicitous. For
Neil, like the Trojan hero before him, must come to terms with the
destruction of his city in the Halifax Harbour explosion of 1917
that has struck it with all the force of a nuclear explosion.

Neil's recollection of Virgil at such a crucial moment casts him as
the Canadian Aeneas, seeking to script a future out of the wreckage
of the past. MacLennan, a classical grammar school teacher with a
Ph.D. in Latin literature from Princeton University, thus casts himself as a Canadian Virgil revising the established script of empire to
arrive at a redemptive version of the *pax Canadiana*. Like Virgil

before him, MacLennan chooses to confront "the shock of the new" – a devastatingly literal shock in this instance – by returning to tradition for an explanation of the present moment and for a vision of a better future. Like Aeneas, Neil is required to carry the burden of this vision, a deeply conservative pedagogy that is intended to transform the shockingly "new" into something more familiar. In the largest sense, MacLennan's decision to follow, and even to revise, the Virgilian script of empire is fully justifiable in 1940, his starting date of composition, since the outbreak of another World War is reminiscent of Rome's own situation in the renewed cycle of civil wars during the two decades before Virgil began to compose his epic.

What has stood in the way, however, of a legitimate Virgilian reading of a Latin-inspired novel of the Great War is the classic misreading of MacLennan as a minor Joyce who ransacked Homer to produce a Canadian *Ulysses*. In "A Nation's Odyssey" (1961), George Woodcock was the first to set MacLennan criticism on this path by claiming that "his development of the problems of individuals in an emerging nation" was achieved "by means of action built on a simple but powerful foundation of universal myth" (8). In a sense, Woodcock was merely seeking to justify an embarrassingly nationalist pedagogy in *Barometer Rising* through the simple expedient of universalizing it: "The myth is that of Odysseus translated into terms of modern living; the *Odyssey* itself was the product of a people in the process of becoming aware of itself, and, appropriately, the theme which MacLennan uses it to illuminate is the growth of a Canadian national consciousness."

National history is clearly retold in *Barometer Rising,* as it is in Joyce's *Ulysses,* from the ex-centric perspective of a colonized subject rather than from that of an imperial centre; and yet MacLennan's novel is neither liberal in its politics nor experimental in its form, unlike the modernist masterpiece. There are other difficulties, too, inhering in the choice of the Homeric script for MacLennan to follow. The first "difficulty," as Alec Lucas pointed out long ago, "arises from Ulysses' unsuitability as a symbol in this book as a whole, and generally throughout MacLennan's fiction, for Woodcock's thesis presents some problems when examined closely in the context of the novels" (Lucas 46). The most obvious problem is that absolutely nothing in the *Odyssey* corresponds to the Halifax Harbour explosion. If Ithaka is not destined for demolition in

Homer's epic, the "suitors" are not destined for punishment in MacLennan's novel. The plots of the two works are so incongruous that the new "Odysseus" does not even need to try the fidelity of his wife and son before reclaiming the "throne" he had left; rather, he must, like wandering Aeneas, envision a new social order for his wasted homeland. By contrast, the old order is what waits to be restored, not destroyed, in Homer; the future in the *Odyssey* is likely to be much the same as the past. Everything in the plot of this purportedly "universal myth" of Odysseus looks rather incongruous in *Barometer Rising*.

A second difficulty grows out of another inconsistency in Woodcock's thesis that takes him from an essentially comic myth in the *Odyssey* to a vision of Attic tragedy in *Barometer Rising* and the other novels. "MacLennan was a Classical scholar," Woodcock opines, "before he became a novelist, and a Calvinist before he became a Classicist, and the inexorable pattern of Greek tragedy still broods over his writing" (10). But no tragic hero broods over the end of *Barometer Rising* to evoke the pity and fear that one feels in the Oedipus or Orestes cycles. In its structure, as in its title, *Barometer Rising* operates quite openly in the comic mode, purging the old order and forming a new society in ways that do not permit us to skip from *Odyssey* to *Oedipus Rex*.

Of equal significance, perhaps, is the fictional mechanism by which MacLennan's comic plot is resolved. The modern "Odysseus" has no need to avenge himself because his potential "usurpers" are taken care of by accident (the force of the blast) rather than by design. This latter difficulty is at least acknowledged by Woodcock: "More serious because it seems to spring from a philosophic fatalism perennial in MacLennan's attitude, is the mechanical impetus that at times – and particularly during the explosion – takes the action wholly out of the hands of the characters" (10). But the solution offered by Woodcock only compounds the problem by failing to explain why Neil's ultimate success should be tinged with the aura of destiny.

A third, extrinsic difficulty appears in Woodcock's booklet *Hugh MacLennan* (1969). After outlining yet once more the Odyssean "analysis, which has generally been accepted by other critics," Woodcock is forced to confess, "I was astonished to receive a letter from him [MacLennan] in which he expressed his surprise at the parallel I had suggested, though he did not deny its validity" (52–3). "Until I read your essay," MacLennan wrote the critic, "it had never consciously occurred to me that I was following the Odyssey-myth in these books. The choice of the name Penelope in *Barometer Rising* may have been subconsciously prompted, but the passage at the end where it seemed most obvious that I was rubbing the symbol in was not much more than a device, and rather a corny one at that, used by an inexperienced author to conclude his book" (MacLennan, "Post-script" 86). MacLennan then tactfully suggests a simpler explanation for his "returning" heroes – the communal waiting of a seafaring people "for their fathers [and husbands] to return" (86) – while wisely refraining from taking a critic's role by remaining silent about the script on which his novel was modelled.

The Virgilian script has two evident advantages over a supposedly Homeric scripting of *Barometer Rising*: it accounts for the "fatalism" of MacLennan's work in terms more true to its artistry; and it puts MacLennan's didacticism in the more favourable light of a poetics designed to absorb and assimilate the "shock of the new." For, in "remembering Virgil," MacLennan was in fact doing what Pound had insisted the modern artist must do to give life to any script drawn from the past: "Make it new."

THE SHOCK OF THE NEW

The horrors of a war that had spared no one – civilians were just as likely to be vaporized in the blink of an eye as soldiers on this field of horror – were visited upon the city of Halifax, Nova Scotia, in a catastrophic blast on 6 December 1917 that killed and wounded thousands. While suspicion initially fell on German sabotage, the real fault was soon assigned to the usual suspects: negligence, incompetence, and chance:

> Shortly before nine o'clock a French ship, the MONT BLANC, was proceeding up the harbour at a rate of six knots, towards the Narrows. This was a cargo steamer of 2,250 tons, which had been loaded at Gravesend, New York, with high explosives and was coming to Halifax to proceed to her destination under convoy. Her cargo consisted chiefly of picric acid, of which she carried 2,300 tons, including moist and dry. Sixty-one tons of gun-cotton were stowed forward, and 225 tons of T.N.T. abaft the engineroom ... The MONT BLANC also carried a deckload of benzine in drums. (MacMechan 12)

Proceeding out of Bedford Basin, the Norwegian freighter IMO was laden with supplies for Belgian Relief. An "American tramp steamer ... desiring to anchor on the western side of the Basin turned to the left instead of to the right and forced the IMO" out of her lane, where a tug, towing two barges some four hundred feet in length, forced her farther left. The Norwegian ship was now on a collision course with the French ship still out of sight around a bend in the Narrows. "At the last moment, the MONT BLANC turned out of her course, directly across the bows of the IMO. Why she did so can perhaps never be known. One plausible theory is that the pilot's order at the critical moment was misunderstood, owing to the difference between the French and English words of command ... Almost at once the MONT BLANC was observed to be on fire" (13).

The *Mont Blanc*, "with 2,925 tons of explosives in barrels and kegs, packed in hermetically sealed holds inside a super-heated hull, was now the most powerful bomb the war and the world had ever produced" (MacDonald 61–2). Twenty-two minutes later, her blazing cargo "was converted in a split second into a hemisphere of intensely hot gas which sprang up into the air for possibly a cubic mile" (MacMechan 13). While the French ship was vaporized in the blast, a great

> fireball, which was invisible in the daylight, shot out over a one- to four-mile area surrounding the *Mont Blanc*. Richmond houses caught fire like so much kindling. In houses able to withstand the blast, windows stretched inward until the glass shattered around its weakest point, sending out a shower of arrow-shaped slivers that cut their way through curtains, wallpaper, and walls. The glass spared no one. Some people were beheaded where they stood. (MacDonald 63).

The blast left more than 2,000 people dead, over 6,000 wounded, and more than 9,000 homeless. Forty-one people were completely blinded, while another 249 were half-blinded (MacDonald 291). To modern eyes, photographs of the ruins of Richmond Hill, the Dockyard, and its environs bear an uncanny resemblance to Hiroshima and Nagasaki in August 1945, where the order of magnitude of each atomic blast was six times as great. The Great War had come home with a vengeance to citizens of a belligerent nation on a distant continent. Here, too, civilians were suddenly at risk with their fighting men.

In 1917, a ten-year-old Hugh MacLennan was leaving for school when his mother called him back to wash his knees "in the bathroom of his home on South Park Street" (Cameron 13). He was inside when a terrific blast rocked the house. His father, an army surgeon at Camp Hill Hospital, would treat many of the 1,200 victims admitted on that day. As an eye specialist, he was called upon to deal with a vast number of eye wounds and extractions that resulted; "buckets filled up with eyeballs beside the operating table" as Dr Sam "dealt with hundreds of eye and facial wounds" (13). Not surprisingly, "[t]he explosion, combined with the stories his father had brought back of the waste of life and the sheer brutality of the war overseas, made the sensitive boy a pacifist."

In 1947, this writer with pacifist inclinations would recall coming home in June 1940 to Halifax, "right after France surrendered" in the Second World War. In a moment of painful recognition, this peace-loving man was brought face to face with the stern realities of war:

> I looked out over the roofs of the city to the harbour ... By 1940, she had become the funnel through which the life-giving supplies of the western hemisphere were flowing ... That morning Halifax was the most vital city in North America, and she was completely unconscious of the fact. Almost, one might say she was unconscious of herself.
>
> At that instant the whole movement, drama, pathos, and unwitting loneliness of Halifax and of the country behind it surged through my mind. I decided, not knowing how it could be done, to put something of the essence of this city into a book. The result was my first published novel, *Barometer Rising*. (MacLennan, *Vogue* 136)

But it is the soldier invalided out of the battle, not the writer, who returns in *Barometer Rising* to find that the war has preceded him: "Neil's eyes ranged dizzily over the slope of the hill. It was a devastation more appalling than anything he had witnessed in France. The wooden houses had been punched inward and split apart, some of them had been hurled hundreds of feet; furniture, clothing, and human bodies were littered in swathes and patches among this debris" (161). He likens "blackened figures" climbing out of the rubble to "soldiers crawling out of shelters into the smoking, heaving

earth after a bombardment has passed." Making his way with difficulty to Barrington Street, "Neil noticed the inordinate number of
eye- and face-wounds caused by flying glass. Almost everyone he
saw was hurt and there were so many stretcher cases that an artillery brigade would not have had the transport necessary to evacuate
them" (164). As soon as transport could be found, "[h]e climbed
into the driver's seat and looked at his watch. It was nearly half-
past twelve: a little over three hours since the ship had blown up.
During that time Halifax had come to look like a city caught in the
fulcrum of a battle" (177). Later that night, in the midst of a winter
blizzard impeding his rescue efforts, Neil regards "the thin line of
men working methodically" as if they were "the vanguard of an attacking army stopped in its tracks and digging in under fire" (195).

Typical of his perspective from the home front, Neil's twelve-
year-old cousin Roddie Wain prefers to see the ruined city in terms
of military training and embarkation: "By early afternoon, individual citizens were establishing food-kitchens in churches and private
homes, and units of the Army Service Corps set up so many tents on
the Commons that the area looked like a military camp" (180).
Later, Roddie watches "[t]he stream of traffic on the roads about
the Citadel ... but now all adventure had gone out of the sight of it
and the people huddled together on the trucks and carts looked mis-
erable and hungry, and this was not a vision transported from
France or Serbia or some country that was never immune to such
things, but an actual occurrence in Halifax" (187). The reality of
the war brought home in such a brutal fashion may be difficult for a
New World child to fathom; but the returned soldier doesn't fare
much better.

Near the end of the novel, Neil muses, apropos of the war and local scenes of devastation all around him, that

> he and his countrymen had been a part of it. Why should Canada
> escape the results? There were thousands of dead Canadians and
> hundreds of thousands of living ones fighting over there now.
> Yes, but though a part of the war, they were innocent of the cause
> of it. They were explorers of an alien scene; they were adventur-
> ers, idealists, mercenaries, or merely followers of the herd. But no
> matter what the Canadians did over there, they were not living
> out the sociological results of their own lives when they crawled
> through the trenches of France. The war might be Canada's

catastrophe, but it was not her tragedy. Just as this explosion in
Halifax was catastrophic but not tragic. (200–01).

Remarkably, the veteran soldier defends his nation's innocence
against the evidence of his senses. Canada, he thinks, is not com-
plicit in the global conflict; to him, her people are no more than
hapless victims of a catastrophe, not moral agents in a global tragedy that has brought destruction to their city. The moral outlook of
the soldier is not far, in other words, from that of a child who says,
What have I done to deserve this punishment?

Of course, the veteran is in fact returning to prove his innocence of
the charges brought against him by his uncle and commanding officer, Roddie's father Colonel Wain. Geoffrey Wain has been reas-
signed to duty as a Transport officer on the home front in the wake
of his blundering attack in Flanders. There, he had managed to shift
responsibility for his poor planning and catastrophic judgment onto
his subaltern nephew, and would have secured his court martial were
it not for the accident of an artillery shell apparently blowing his
nephew to bits. Neil's return from the "dead" to vindicate his honour and recover his rightful place in the world is thus a story of the
revenant come to claim his lost innocence. While worse melodramas
have been structured on such a plot, this one is problematic because
of its arbitrary resolution. The ruthless Colonel Wain dies in the
Halifax explosion; justice is meted out by chance, if not by purblind
natural forces. Worse yet, Neil completely forgets, during his heroic
efforts to save blast victims, to secure the testimony of the one man
who could exonerate him – big Alec MacKenzie, the battlefield runner who had brought Colonel Wain's contradictory order to Neil as
the last surviving officer in the field.

In various ways, critics have seen this resolution as a crippling
weakness in the structure of the novel, even when they allow for its
descriptive strength: "The most vivid writing in the whole book is
that which concerns the explosion, but ironically this is in a sense
an artistic flaw, for it fixes attention on an event that, albeit spectacular, is not organically the climax of the novel" (New 302). "It is
frequently pointed out that the explosion in *Barometer Rising* operates as a kind of *deus ex machina* which dispenses an arbitrary,
though poetic justice. It interferes with the action, and prevents the
confrontation that the early development of the book would seem
to demand" (Arnason 70). "This discordant element pervades the

novel from beginning to end; one is made uncomfortable by the idea that the explosion is being used merely as a gigantic purge to cleanse Halifax (Canada) of her old 'insecurity'" (Cockburn 44). The problem is both formal and ethical: the form supplies no logical reason for the triumph of innocence; and so the moral vision of the novelist seems hollow at best. Neil's question is merely rhetorical – "Why should Canada escape the results?" – since he immediately rejects it, clinging like a child to his (and his nation's) sense of invincible innocence.

As early as 1961, Woodcock had isolated many of these faults in MacLennan's artistry. He recognized, for example, how "one of the most striking characteristics of *Barometer Rising* and MacLennan's four later novels is their relative conservatism. They are unashamedly didactic; they rely heavily on environmental atmosphere and local colour; their characterization is over-simplified and moralistic in tone; their language is descriptive rather than evocative; and their action tends to be shaped externally by a Hardyesque use of circumstance and coincidence" ("A Nation's Odyssey" 7–8). But Woodcock's solution – a "universal myth" that occludes more than it reveals of the novel MacLennan actually wrote – fails to explain the author's "didacticism" about a nation at war to secure a greater peace. To understand that, one needs to understand Virgil's "script" of empire.

THE ODYSSSEAN *AENEID*

"Forsan et haec olim meminisse iuvabit," Aeneas had said at the outset of Virgil's epic. "One day, perhaps, remembering even this will be a pleasure." Yet how can he truly believe it? How many heartaches and horrors must a man endure without beginning to think that forgetting is a better path to pleasure? "Virgil's essential insight, out of which seemingly the whole *Aeneid* grew, was the perception that this hero would have to struggle not only against external *furor* and passion but against the same elements within himself and that he could become the Roman-Augustan ideal only by rising above his original nature to a wholly new and quasi-divine kind of heroism" (Otis 219). For the true enemy of the Virgilian hero is himself – that primal nature that must be overcome. Thus,

the distinction between Aeneas and any genuinely Homeric hero is quite fundamental. His ethos is utterly different from that of

Achilles, Hector or Odysseus. Aeneas' goal and object in life is not merely in the near but in the remote future, in Augustan Rome itself. Thus all the intelligible goals of Homeric epic or Greek tragedy, indeed of all Greek literature, are not available to him. His fate is to sacrifice every present enjoyment or satisfaction to an end he cannot hope to witness himself ... He is thus the great exhibit of *pietas* or of the willing service of destiny. This is emphatically not a Homeric but a Stoic and, above all, a Roman-Augustan attitude. Augustus, himself, was the avowed founder of the future. (Otis 222)

This formation of a new kind of hero required Virgil to literally recall, even as he subverted, Homeric narrative. "An epic poem in twelve books challenged Homer, but it also made towards him an immediate gesture of submission. For each of the two Homeric epics had twenty-four books and Virgil's total of twelve must have been meant to suggest a certain modesty – the *Aeneid* is only half of the *Iliad* or the *Odyssey*. Yet at the same time the *Aeneid* aspires to comprehend both Homeric epics: Odyssean wanderings in the first half, Iliadic battles in the second" (Griffin 14). Even at that, Virgil's reprise of the wanderings of Odysseus in the first half can never move toward the homecoming, but only away from a nostalgic attachment to the past in order to found a just *imperium*. The survivor of Troy will only ever redeem her loss by "a radical repudiation of his Trojan home" (Otis 232). "So it is part of the cruelty of Aeneas' destiny that he must sacrifice everything to the god-given task of founding Rome and yet that he will not be allowed to do it. He must take it all on trust up to the end" (Griffin 63).

For most of the first six books, Aeneas is unable to master his nostalgia, sinking into an ecstasy of self-pity at first sight of Juno's temple in Carthage, where images of the fall of Troy adorn every wall: "What spot on earth ... what region of the earth, Achätes, / Is not full of the story of our sorrow?" he laments. "Even so far away ... they weep here / For how the world goes" (1.459 ff; Fitzgerald 20). Yet self-pity is the one luxury that the founder of Rome can least afford. Again and again, he is forced to master his nostalgia for anything that could be called home. Even then, his re-formation still requires him to forsake his Carthaginian lover Dido, and to bury his father in a strange land – even to "die" himself in a perilous descent into the Underworld – "The way downward is easy from Avernus," says the Sibyl. "But to retrace your steps to heaven's air, / There is the trouble, there is the toil" (6.126 ff; Fitzgerald 164) – a descent from which he will be stoically reborn as the hero of the future. "The sixth book of the *Aeneid* is the turning point, the death and resurrection piece, that converts the defeat, passion, and uncertainty of Books 1–5 into the victorious and un-shaken valour of Books 8–12" (Otis 218).

In the Underworld, Aeneas is at last reunited with the shade of his dead father, who shows him "What famous children in your line will come, / Souls of the future, living in our name" (6.758 ff; Fitzgerald 186). One of these ("Hic vir, hic est") "is the man, this one, / Of whom so often you have heard the promise, / Caesar Augustus, son of the deified, / Who shall bring once again an Age of Gold" (6.791 ff; Fitzgerald 187). But was ever the Age of Gold harder to achieve in myth or legend? "It was fundamental to Virgil's plan ... that the founding of Rome should be seen as labori-ous and also morally painful, since the Italians are to be part of Rome and the struggle has much of the horror of civil war" (Griffin 91). What Aeneas must always remember, his father Anchises as-sures him, is his definitive difference from the Homeric hero:

> Roman, remember by your strength to rule
> Earth's peoples – for your arts are to be these:
> To pacify, to impose the rule of law,
> To spare the conquered, battle down the proud.
> (6.851 ff; Fitzgerald 190)

"This is a proud claim," Jasper Griffin remarks, "but also a fearful renunciation. In the middle of the greatest work of Latin literature Virgil feels obliged to ascribe to Rome not the sciences and the arts but only the hard and impersonal 'arts' of conquest and rule. That, too, is part of the price of empire" (87).

If human hardships and dangers are not enough, there is also the fury of a god against which the Roman must contend. "In her divine pride," Juno hints at a ruthless power at the root of exis-tence, a hatred so extreme that even the narrator is forced to ask, "Can anger / Black as this prey on the minds of heaven?" (1.11; Fitzgerald 3). Juno may be a terrifying emblem of "savage and bar-baric violence," of everything "that opposes *pietas* and *humanitas*" (Otis 330, 323); but she is far more than an image of the "brutal self-seeking" (382) of older civilizations. To Virgil, she is a divine embodiment of an implacable "Counter-Fate" (Otis 223) which is opposed to Fate itself – *fatum,* that which is spoken by Jupiter as Heaven's will – a perverse negation in the order of things. Even Juno's husband cannot control her, although Jupiter assures the council of the gods in Book Ten that "the Fates / Will find their way" (10.113; Fitzgerald 297). If the "function of Juno and her hostility is to delay the founding of Lavinium and to cause suffering to Aeneas," it is still the case that "the reader is encouraged to speculate on the justice of heaven and the hardness of a divine will which does indeed demand of the Romans a standard higher, in some ways, than it chooses to accept for itself" (Griffin, 75, 96).

In *Barometer Rising,* it is Neil who shares this destiny of Aeneas to transform himself into the servant of the future. Despairing at first, he sees only how "[o]ne chance must lead to another with no binding link but a peculiar tenacity which made him determined to preserve himself for a future which gave no promise of being superior to the past. It was his future, and that was all he could say of it. At the moment it was all he had" (7). No augurs, no prophecies, no divine messengers appear in our time to inform the hero of his destiny. He knows only that an implacable foe is determined to destroy him. At his reunion with his lover Penny, he protests: "Oh God – it's impossible! Here you are – living in your father's house, everything the same, nothing different! He'd still have me shot if he knew I was alive where he could get his hands on me" (109). Geoffrey Wain's hatred, his daughter knows, does not come just from his need to make Neil a military scapegoat. It began long ago with his sister's marriage to a man he considered their inferior: "Father hated him. I think he hated him from the time he was born" (35). In fact, Neil is opposed at every step by this man who hates the thought of his existence.

Geoffrey Wain is an unlikely substitute for the Roman goddess Juno, but he does function as a blocking figure in the novel to resist change and oppose the founding of a new social order. Colonel Wain, a descendant of "a privateer in the war of 1812," is a conservative in the worst sense of the word, whose "fortune had remained stationary" (19), given that his sole concern has been to maintain his social caste and privilege. "There was something in the man not even his most intimate associates had ever been able to calculate, a discrepancy between the sense of ruthless and indifferent power he radiated and the mediocre record of his achievement" (26). In a realist novel, Wain would be a self-hating colonial, a type to which he appears to subscribe on several occasions: "I've wasted a whole lifetime in this hole of a town. Everything in this damn country is second-rate. It always is, in a colony" (101). And yet Wain has his eye on bigger things, if in a way quite distinct from his author, whose own eye is fixed on the Virgilian script.

What Geoffrey-Juno wants, and why he would gladly destroy Neil-Aeneas to get it, emerges in a conversation with Angus Murray, once a surgeon in his battalion: "After this war the entire world will be bankrupt," he assures the doctor. "It has already become a military society for purposes of the war. Do you think it will slip back into the old mould again? After this war, anyone outside the army or navy will be a nobody" (101). While Angus Murray sees through Wain's transparent offer of his daughter as a bribe to assist him in checking the progress of Neil Macrae, he cannot hide his contempt for Wain's political machinations. "As he turned to leave he muttered, 'At least your notion of a military dictatorship in this country is a lot of balls'" (104).

The Roman Juno could well be "a lot of balls," too, were it not for Geoffrey Wain's sense of playing a role in a cosmic drama (although he cannot see the "script"):

> "Remember that we must avoid a court-martial. The only way that can be done is for him to leave the country at once. *Try* to persuade him that no matter what sense of grievance he may feel he hasn't a chance if he remains here. *Try–*"
>
> "Grievance?" Murray interrupted sharply. "What do you mean by that?"
>
> "Nothing definite. I suppose he feels the world is against him, that's all. He ought to. The world *is* against him." (99)

Indeed, the *world,* in the person of Geoffrey Wain, is against Neil in much the same way that Juno, as the embodiment of Counter-Fate, is against Aeneas.

This is not to say that *Barometer Rising* is a slavish allegory. The danger of "remembering Virgil" anachronistically is largely neutralized through a simple expedient of giving Wain a second role as Turnus. The Rutulian hothead had led Italian forces against Aeneas to abort his truce with Latinus, King of Latium, in a vain hope of stopping the marriage of the Trojan to the Latin princess Lavinia. A human agent of Juno's divine anger, Turnus is Virgil's version of an Achilles figure, roused to a fury by Allecto, the Fury whom Juno summons from "the world below" (7.312; Fitzgerald 206). So it is that Angus Murray comes to see how "underneath the urbane exterior the older man was seething with anger and wounded pride, with humiliation at the steps necessary to advance his career, with outrage over the need of disclosing so much of his private affairs to a stranger" (104). Even so, the former commander of a battalion "comforted himself with the reflection that by the time the war ended, familiar conventions would be broken down entirely, and a new age would be at hand of power and vulgarity without limitation, in which the prizes would not be won by the qualified but by the cunning and the unscrupulous" (126). In this second role, Wain does make a satisfactory Turnus, hostile to the values of civility, self-mastery, and the common good that will come to define the character of the true Roman hero.

Angus Murray might have a better claim to be Turnus, pressing his suit for the hand of "Lavinia," were it not for the grace with which he gives way when Penny reveals her love for Neil. At any rate, Angus has a better claim to play Father Anchises, both in name and deed, since it is he who will protect his "son" by getting the testimony of Big Alec to exonerate Neil from military charges. More importantly, it is Angus-Anchises who assumes a Virgilian function as "the agent of Jupiter and the very embodiment of the new *pietas* of Rome and the future ... the great symbol of *conscience* (*pietas* personified) that broods over the whole Odyssean *Aeneid*" (Otis 250). Much as Anchises enlightens Aeneas in the Underworld about the future history of Rome and the duties of the Roman hero, so Angus gives Neil a vision of the nation's future and the hero's destiny.

At first, of course, Angus-Anchises fails to see beyond the horizons of an eternally unchanging "Troy": "The creeping noises of this old town never ceased; for as long as there were wars and she remained the terminus of the longest railway in the world, her back to the continent and her face to the Old Country, she would lie here in all weathers unchangeably the same, and her bells would ring in the darkness" (32). Angus knows that an "inability to alter the nature with which he had been born, had made him a fatalist against all his wishes. And Halifax, more than most towns, seemed governed by a fate she neither made nor understood, for it was her birthright to serve the English in time of war and to sleep neglected when there was peace" (33). But after the old "hierarchy ... had been blown wide apart" (191) in the blast, Angus gains a very different vision of the future:

> We're the ones who make Canada what she is today, Murray thought, neither one thing nor the other, neither a colony nor an independent nation, neither English nor American. And yet, clearly, the future is obvious, for England and America can't continue to live without each other much longer. Canada must therefore remain as she is, noncommittal until the day she becomes the keystone to hold the world together. (208)

Murray is conscious that there is no place for him in this future, "caught" as he is "somewhere between the two extremes, intellectually gripped by the new and emotionally held by the old, too restless to remain at peace on the land and too contemptuous of bourgeois values to feel at ease in any city" (208). Like Anchises, he is fated to disappear before the new order he anticipates can be established.

Of course, the ultimate function of the Anchises-figure is to envision a future that Neil-Aeneas would want to serve: "Canada," as Neil comes to see it, "was still hesitant, was still ham-strung by men with the mentality of Geoffrey Wain. But if there were enough Canadians like himself, half-American and half-English, then the day was inevitable when the halves would join and his country would become the central arch which united the new order" (218). Although this vision does follow the script that put Augustan Rome at the centre of Aeneas' shield, making the battle of Actium the keystone to Roman "*imperium sine fine*" (*Aeneid* 1.279), there is one telling difference in the way that this vision is realized in each work. Virgil had the incalculable advantage of an actual cult of the Sibyl that was very much alive and active at Cumae, only a short distance from his home on the Neapolitan shore. And so he could count on public belief in the gods, of "Actian Apollo [who] / Began to pull his bow" (8.704; Fitzgerald 255) in the decisive victory of Augustus over Antony and Cleopatra, over all the "barbaric wealth" (8.684) of the East, and those "monster forms / Of gods of every race, ... the dog-god / Anubis barking" (8.698; Fitzgerald 254) in futile opposition to the king of Heaven.

The only equivalent of Heaven's will in a "realist" novel such as *Barometer Rising* is the three-kiloton blast that reduces modern "Troy" to rubble. The new Aeneas is not fated to found a new *imperium,* but only to be a bridge between Britain (the *Empire*) and America (the Roman *Republic*). Somewhere between imperial and democratic rule, the "new order" will apparently be "half-American and half-English," and yet be neither; in fact, it will simply be "the central arch" that unites the two. Aside from the vague identity, or indeterminate *political* form, of this "arch," MacLennan faces another problem that Virgil had managed to solve by narrative structure: Neil-as-Aeneas has descended into the Underworld and returned before his story even begins. And so we are back to the problem that has bedeviled criticism of the novel from the beginning, if with a new difficulty. MacLennan uses the Halifax explosion in a symbolic way as the judgment of Jupiter, or an expression of the will of Heaven, although he lacks Virgil's greatest symbolic asset: the death of the hero at the midpoint of the story (his descent into the Underworld), and his rebirth as a new type of "hero who has subjected his own desires to a social purpose, who wins because he has put courage and toil – duty – above success" (Otis 381). Put in this way, how might the Halifax explosion form a *narrative* arch that, instead of splitting the two parts, would join the first to the second half of the story?

THE ILIADIC *AENEID*

"The Neil of the first part of the novel and the Neil of the second part are each in his own way convincing," one of MacLennan's defenders has noted. "Neil number one is indecisive and paranoid, and his actions confirm this. Neil number two is smugly selfish and competent, as is shown by his handling of things after the explosion. The difficulty is that it takes an unusually powerful ability to suspend disbelief to be convinced that the two are one, and that is a chief flaw in the book" (Arnason 71). Seen in its Virgilian context, however, the novel is true to its script. The hero of the *Aeneid* is necessarily conceived as two characters: one who must be filled with all the *furor* of an old-style *Iliadic* hero, before he succumbs to the lachrymose nostalgia of Odysseus on Calypso's island; and another figure who, "at the crisis of his career," finds himself reborn by virtue of "the acquisition of an historical perspective which

includes Augustus and the Augustan *pax Romana.* Only so can he
bring the civilized future to bear upon the primitive or Homeric
present in which he, as *dramatis persona,* is supposed to stand. In
this sense we can partially describe the *Aeneid* as the creation of
Roman civilization out of Homeric barbarism" (Otis 384–5). As
even Brooks Otis will concede, however:

> The interest of the hero's bitter, personal struggle for self-mastery
> is, for at least many moderns, far greater than that of the tangible
> narrative of a battle whose outcome is certain. Nor does Virgil
> seem to make it easy for us: he now presents Aeneas as a quite
> static figure, unchanging and foursquare in his *pietas* ... Nor does
> Virgil share with Homer any particular zest for battles or the inci-
> dents of battle: he does not in fact hide his aversion to war or his
> strong preference for peace; all his own tastes and values seem to
> contradict and discount his martial subject. (313)

Given the sequence of events, "Aeneas Number One" can't take
us with him into the Underworld in MacLennan's novel to witness
his rebirth or see his will steeled against trials to come. Neil as the
old-style Aeneas is angry, rash, and self-pitying; even Penny fears
that this "Neil had not changed as much as she had feared; he was
still impetuous, still explosive and oblivious to what other people
might be thinking" (113). To his credit, however, MacLennan's portrait of Neil after the blast is more interesting than that of Virgil's reborn Aeneas. Part of the compelling power of these scenes is the way
in which the soldier suffering from "shellshock" moves through a
landscape that reminds him of the battlefields of France. "Neil Macrae could see nothing but a blazing light behind his own eyes and
could hear nothing but the thunder of explosions in his head ... The
blazing whiteness at the heart of the explosion, the whirling nose of
the approaching shell, my own number inscribed in German on its
nose *nummer sieben hundert tausend acht hundert* – "(159). And
yet, after his initial shock, "suddenly he felt all right. It was as
though the prospect of shock had torn at his nerves all these months
and now he found his nerves better than he hoped" (161). MacLennan does allow the revenant to "die" a second time in the blast, if
only to emerge with a new sense of duty to help the wounded and
dying in any way he can. When "[a] doctor came running up the
drive with an instrument-bag in his hand, glanced at him and said,

'Hello, Neil,' and hurried on," he does not flinch, though he may have "blinked. It was only then that he realized that he no longer cared who recognized him. Even though he was still subject to court-martial, his personal danger had ceased to matter" (166).

So it goes, as Neil responds time and again to this unprecedented disaster without any thought for himself:

> "You don't look like a shellshocked man to me," Murray suddenly said.
> Neil glanced sideways in surprise. "Why do you say that?"
> "I thought you'd been shellshocked in France."
> "I was. But I feel fine now." They were nearing the bottom of the hill and the truck was swaying drunkenly. "Watch for the ditch. Here we go!" (170)

Nor will he give up when, "[a]fter the panic and excitement of yesterday their work had descended to a killing routine of digging in the frozen earth, heaving away fallen beams, and clearing foundations. The longer they worked, the fewer bodies they found; but because they always found one here and another there, the work had to continue. Most of the bodies brought in within the last six hours had been dead a long while, and all were frozen stiff. The men had not slept the night before and had taken little food" (197). And yet the volunteers obey his commands exactly as the men in the trenches had once done. The disgraced soldier is redeemed by his actions; his every act is now one of mercy and pity, not one of aggression. Only at the end of two days on his feet (199) does Neil arrive at his saving moment of Virgilian recognition: "Some day, perhaps, remembering even this will be a pleasure." Shortly thereafter, "a plank broke loose and the man's face was revealed; Neil stood staring as the beam of the torch fell on the frozen, familiar features of Geoffey Wain" (202).

One of the problems Virgil had faced in making Aeneas the hero of civility, rather than of "brutal self-seeking," was how to depict his war against Latium and future fellow citizens as something more than civil war. More than a hundred years before Virgil, "the Elder Cato had said in his *History of Rome* that Aeneas and his Trojans came to Latium ... According to Cato, the Trojans were plundering the countryside, when the local people gave battle under their king, Latinus, who was killed" (Griffin 60). Worse still, this

outcome now recalled two decades of civil wars in the deadly ri-
valry of Caesar and Pompey, and then of Octavian (Augustus) and
Antony. If Virgil were to save Aeneas as the prototype of an "innocent" Augustus, he would have to make Aeneas the injured party in
his war with Latium, just as he would have to make Octavian the
injured party in his conflict with the "foreign" despot Antony. And
so Virgil chose to portray King Latinus as an ineffectual ruler who
unwillingly breaks the truce because he fails to control the Latin
hotheads who support Turnus in his furious self-seeking. Unlike the
latter, Aeneas "does not manifest any eagerness for fighting, except
when dominated by a special emotion such as his affection for Pallas.
Unlike them, he regrets and sorrows over the war. He alone thinks
throughout of the peace to be gained ... He alone avoids the sin of
hybris and feels the sadness of success" (Otis 315).

Similarly, it is very much to MacLennan's purpose to make his
Canadian Aeneas an innocent who regrets, although he cannot prevent, the disaster that befalls the city. By the simple expedient of
making the Halifax explosion an expression of Fate, MacLennan
clears Neil from the taint of fratricide or civil war. Colonel Wain as
Turnus must suffer the judgment of Heaven, while Geoffrey Wain as
Juno must be thwarted by a script that entirely neutralizes Counter-
Fate. But, to do this, the nation must first be cleared of fratricidal
guilt in its war in Europe. That is why Neil "knew beyond any
doubt that the war was not all-powerful. It was not going to do to
Canada what it had done to Europe. When it ended, there would be
madness in the Old World. Men would be unable to look at each
other without contempt and despair. How many in Europe would
have the will-power to live naturally under such an intolerable burden of guilt as theirs would be?" (200). The Canadian Aeneas has
to remember, like Virgil's hero before him, that fratricide will only
undermine the foundations of the nation.

If there is something truly Virgilian about Neil's final vision, it
would not beg belief to see him "whispering sweet nothings to
Penny," while "his mind is elsewhere, 'identifying ... with the still-
hidden forces'" (Cockburn 43). Only recall the vast distance we
have already come from the *Aeneid,* where Lavinia, the destined
bride of Aeneas, is not allowed to speak, and is not at all a match
for her future husband, contrary to Penelope in Homer's *Odyssey.*
In fact, MacLennan makes us privy to Penelope's thoughts on the
last page of the novel, giving us access to the heart of a woman in

love who has no illusions about her lover's limitations: "Neil knew next to nothing of his own country. He had never been able to see how it was virtually owned by people like her father, the old men who were content to let it continue second-rate indefinitely, looting its wealth while they talked about its infinite opportunities. And meanwhile the ones like Neil, the generous ones who had believed the myth that this was a young man's country, were being killed like fools thousands of miles away in a foreign world" (217). Penny makes herself the equal of Neil in a way that Lavinia can never be in the Augustan world of the *Aeneid*. And so she remains as true to her Homeric original as Neil is to his Virgilian one. Here, and only here, does MacLennan come close to being Greek in his classicism. All the rest is decidedly Latin, as Neil concludes in his vision of Canada at the centre of his own "shield of Aeneas": "For better or worse he was entering the future, he was identifying himself with the still hidden forces which were doomed to shape humanity as certainly as the tiny states of Europe had shaped the past" (218). These "still hidden forces" bear more than a passing resemblance to the discursive forces that were to shape Rome's destiny in the age of Augustus. Not the least of these was Virgil's poem, which, when it was published after his death in 19 BCE, carried public opinion before it in the great debate raging in poetry and in the wider culture in the decade after 31 BCE.

ACTIUM AND AFTER

Outside of Classics departments in recent decades, there has been something like a conspiracy to make us *forget* Virgil. "The painful experience of two world wars," as Robert Gurval writes, "had made the twentieth-century poet especially distrustful of the fraudulent and boastful claims of extreme nationalism, imperial power, and manifest destiny" (Gurval 238). So Auden protests more harshly yet at the end of his "Secondary Epic": "No, Virgil, no: / Behind your verse so masterfully made / We hear the weeping of a Muse betrayed" (Auden 456). This very modern suspicion of Virgilian epic depends on a faulty perception of the role of poetry in the early days of Empire, where, it is often assumed, "the Augustan poets felt compelled by the political regime to incorporate recognition and praise" (Gurval 6) of Octavian's victory at Actium. Indeed, "[t]he remark by one scholar that 'the poet discharges his

obligation to commemorate the conclusion of the civil war' by the
inclusion of Actium on the shield of Aeneas characterizes the modern approach to the passage" (Gurval 12). The accretion of poetic
riches around the literary patron Maecenas has been unfairly dissolved in an acid bath of cynical modern assumptions that Virgil,
Horace, and Sextus Propertius were glorified political hacks justify-
ing the overthrow of the Roman Republic.

It is nonetheless the burden of Gurval's *Actium and Augustus*
(1995) to show how these assumptions are fundamentally mis-
guided, given that Augustus himself would downplay his victory in
what was really a civil war. In his triple triumph of 29 BCE, he
would focus public attention instead on the fall of Alexandria and
on Cleopatra's suicide (33). Gurval traces in meticulous detail the
fears and anxieties, the doubts and suppressed hostilities of the Augustan poets in a number of works referring to Actium in the decade before Virgil's death and the subsequent publication of the
Aeneid. Particularly in his discussion of Horace's *Epode* 9 and several elegies by Propertius (2.1; 2.15; 2.16; 2.34; and 3.11), Gurval
fulfills his stated intention "to perceive more clearly the Augustan
image of Actium, a mixed portrait of victory and defeat, joyful celebration and bitter sorrows, a public ideology, slow, if not reluctant
to emerge, and a wondrous and inspiring myth shaped more by the
verses of individual poets, elated, angry, and at times indifferent,
than by the concerted actions and directives of an imperious and
vainglorious ruler" (17).

What emerges from a literary and cultural history of this decade
(29–19 BCE) is a clearer picture of the decisive "contribution of
Vergil's *Aeneid* to the glorification of Actium" (213). For the reception of this one great rival to Homer put an end to the "battle of the
books" over whether Rome had been saved or destroyed by the actions of one man. "To the contemporary reader of the *Aeneid*, the
victory can be seen not only as a spontaneous occasion of celebration but as the fulfillment of dreams, the final cessation of hostilities, and the embarkation of a new age" (246). At the same time,
"[t]he Vergilian shield is a much more complex and critical reflection on Rome, past and present, than any absolute expression of national pride or unrestrained eulogy of Augustan might and
authority" (215). At the centre of the shield is "Augustus Caesar
leading into battle / Italians, with both senators and people, /
Household gods and great gods" in his rout of "the power of the

East, of Egypt, / Even of distant Bactra of the steppes. / And in his wake the Egyptian consort came / So shamefully" (8.678 ff; Fitzgerald 254).

So it is that civil war is finally transformed into a defeat of the "barbaric" East, even when the border of the shield is ringed by "encircling images of warfare, treachery, and civil conflict" (Gurval 230), including the recalcitrant fratricide Romulus, the raped Sabine women, "Porsenna ordering Rome / To take the exiled Tarquin back," the Gauls' assault on "the Tarpeian Rock," and the rebel General "Catiline, on a precarious cliff / Hanging and trembling at the Furies' glare" (8.668 ff; Fitzgerald 253). Virgil never lets us forget the long history of internecine conflict that underlies the walls of Rome, or to shrink from the implication that Actium was part of that conflict. The difference is that Augustus alone is capable of giving a "divine" purpose to Rome, by enabling it to "bring the whole world under law's dominion" (4.231; Fitzgerald 103).

It is wholly in keeping with this script that a Latinist like Hugh MacLennan – still a teacher of Latin literature and history at Lower Canada College in Montréal – wrote his first script about Augustus the year before he began to write *Barometer Rising*. In 1939, "he tried his hand at a short radio drama, *Augustus*"(Cameron 125), which was never produced. As Elspeth Cameron summarizes the theme of this drama, "Octavius defeats the decadent 'fascist' Marc Anthony, partly through the political compromises which involve the death of Cicero." Doubtless, "the play's subject is fascinating. Through classical history MacLennan examined the world of 1939 … In *Augustus* he revealed that for him organization and freedom are the two essentials of political life" (125–6). As Augustus says in the play, "I intend to marry freedom to organization" (125). And yet, "if either is missing, he suggested, war is more than likely" (126). Here is the true import of remembering Virgil in the next work MacLennan would write about internecine warfare in Europe. Neil-Aeneas is less significant as a prototype for a future Canadian Augustus than he is as a cultural script for remembering Virgil in a manner that would put the protagonist – and the reader – at liberty to realize "what being a Canadian meant."

Paradoxically, what "being a Canadian" seems to have meant to MacLennan in 1941 was freedom from further European wars (the battle of Passchendaele following hard upon the Trojan war and the battles of Latium and Actium). For, as Neil realizes, "[t]he life he had led in Europe and England these past two years had been worse than an emptiness. It was as though he had been able to feel the old continent tearing out its own entrails as the ancient civilizations had done before it. There was no help there" (79). There is no help anywhere, it seems, save in this Virgilian script of a *pax Canadiana*.[10]

PART THREE

The End of the Book and the Beginning of Cinema

5

Cinematic Memory in Owen,
Remarque, and Harrison

"When at the end of the spring term of 1932," Hugh MacLennan's
biographer writes, "he went down from Oxford, having taken a
third class in Literae Humaniores, the occasion was hardly auspi-
cious. Twenty-five years old, with his Oxford BA in Classics, he
could not have known that the Depression would deepen and that
the field he had worked so hard to master was quickly fading from
significance in North American education" (Cameron 62). This unprecedented change in the culture of American universities was accelerated by several factors foreign to Oxford. The rate of
technological change, of urbanization and industrialization, and of
corporate and bureaucratic centralization after the American Civil
War had served to make public utility the guiding principle of public education. A subsequent rise of "the sciences and social sciences
not only physically crowded out the classics; they also recruited
new sources of intellectual authority that challenged the traditional
claims of classics" (Winterer 103). New sciences, with their quanti-
tative methods and epistemologies, swiftly undermined the verbal
epistemology of the ancients.

Even staunch defenders of the Classics helped both directly and
indirectly to undercut the "relevance of antiquity to 'modern' civilization" (107), particularly in the new Humanities (as opposed to
the old Divinity). By 1884, Charles Eliot, president of Harvard (and
future grandfather of T. S. Eliot), saw how "'Modern education'
demanded that 'new sciences' like history and political science join
the group of ancient studies considered essential to a liberal education. 'Are our young men being educated for the work of the twentieth century or of the seventeenth?' he asked" (106). Historicism,

in addition, required an altered conception of time, replacing older notions of temporal cyclicality with a progressive view of "linear, directional change over time" (133). Implicitly, "Such reasoning invoked the present rather than the past as a source of authority" (108). This new, uniquely modern relation to temporality has been lucidly defined by Matei Calinescu as "an awareness of time as an historical movement that is linear and irresistible, directed toward the future" (cited by Matsuda 11). Within this altered paradigm of temporality, "[t]he lessons of antiquity now lost their didactic clarity. No longer could the classical past instruct Americans to escape from time; no longer could it offer itself as a mirror of the present" (Winterer 133).

Similarly, "reform movements in French secondary education favoring scientific and technical instruction" after 1871 vilified "classical education as elitist and ill-suited to a complex, modern society, blaming it for the humiliation of France by Germany" in the Franco-Prussian War (Matsuda 75). "A government body, the Ribot Commission, was established to consider reforms and pursued hearings and depositions from 1899 to 1902, inciting long debates between Ancients and Moderns." In Britain, where education had been modelled for four hundred years on the Renaissance grammar school, reform continued to lag. "In the lengthy public debates," however, "which followed the passage of the 1902 Education Act, the public-school classical curriculum became a major target for progressive and radical critics" (Stray 4). W. H. D. Rouse, Headmaster of Perse Grammar School, Cambridge, and "a fierce advocate of the retention of Compulsory Greek," organized a "Greek Defence Committee" (31) for the retention of entrance requirements at the ancient universities (matriculation in both Latin and Greek), as well as for a standard Arts curriculum (the Cambridge "Tripos," where "History" still meant ancient history). Not until the setbacks and reverses on the battlefields of 1915–16 did a majority of Britons begin to question the utility of a Latin grammar school education:

The debates on education stimulated by the activities of the Neglect of Science Committee in 1916 led to the appointment of a series of official committees (on science 1916; modern languages 1916; English 1919; and Classics 1919). The pro-science campaign was led, among others, by the biologist [E. R.] Lankester and by H. G. Wells. Their manifesto, which appeared in *The Times* on February 2nd 1916, pointed to the inadequacy of British industrial production in meeting the demand for war material, and identified the continued domination of the public-school curriculum by the humanities, especially Classics, as a major culprit. (Stray 49)

Thus, by the time Hugh MacLennan went up to Oxford in the 1920s, the Ancients had become largely irrelevant to modern civilization. Indeed, the eighteenth-century Battle of the Books was won by the Moderns in the mud of Flanders.

In retrospect, the logical outcome of this battle ought to have been legible on facing pages of the Loeb Classical Library at its founding in 1911. W. H. D. Rouse, co-editor with T. E. Page of the Loeb series, had to acknowledge "the existence of a readership interested in, but not wholly competent to read, classical literature" (Stray 1). And so the Loeb Library, with its Greek and Latin texts printed on the left-hand page and its English translations filling the facing page, sent out the Classics in modern dress, where the English text had the last word in evolutionary adaptation to this new, modern environment of efficiency and utility. By making the Classics accessible to vernacular speakers, Rouse actually helped to hasten the process of social change, opening the groves of ancient learning to lesser folk outside the leisured class. Henceforth, the ancients would have to become moderns instead of the moderns becoming ancients.

AN ANTI-HORATIAN ODE

In his posthumous edition (1920) of war poems, collected by his fellow officer Siegfried Sassoon, Wilfred Owen made the decisive break in modern British literature with Classical culture. While some of Owen's titles such as "Arms and the Boy" may continue to orient a reader through familiar echoes of Virgil, the tone is clearly parodic. For the sonorous music of the opening line of *Aeneid*, "Arma virumque cano," has been reduced to the bitter truth that modern wars are fought by children lacking the man's knowledge of "arms," whether they be the arms of love or death. "Let the boy try along this bayonet-blade / How cold steel is, and keen with hunger of blood," the speaker urges in "Arms and the Boy." Then he may

judge for himself what was always occluded in Virgil's stately Latin
music, "Of arms and the man I sing."

> Lend him to stroke these blind, blunt bullet-heads
> Which long to nuzzle in the hearts of lads,
> Or give him cartridges of fine zinc teeth,
> Sharp with the sharpness of grief and death. (Owen 58)

While the careful reader of *Aeneid* may note a similar conjunction
of love and death in Virgil's efforts to evoke "the pity of War" – a
phrase used by Owen in his fragmentary "Preface" (40) – it is nonetheless obvious that Owen's pity will not extend to poets or to poli-
ticians who dignify the sacrifice of children with the name of manly
valour (*virtus)*.

Indeed, the ode from which Owen took that most sonorous of sentences – "dulce et decorum est" (III 2.13) – builds to Horace's quintessentially Roman ideal of "Virtus, repulsae nescia sordidae" (III
2.17) ("True worth, that never knows ignoble defeat" (Bennett 175).
"True worth," Horace sings, "opening Heaven wide for those de-
serving not to die, essays its course by a path denied to others"
(Bennett 177); ["Virtus, recludens immeritis mori / caelum, negata
temptat iter via"] (III 2.21–2). Owen's poem – ending in its stinging
denunciation of "The old Lie: Dulce et decorum est / Pro patria
mori" – makes brilliant use of the guttural harshness of Anglo-Saxon
speech to contradict the fluid polysyllables of Horace's line and to expose the actualities of modern war: "'Here is a gas poem, done yesterday,' [Owen wrote his mother from Craiglockhart]. 'The famous
Latin tag means of course *It is sweet and meet to die for one's country. Sweet! And decorous!*'" (Hibberd 276). If the ignobility of fighting wars with poison gas gives the lie to the noble sentiment of the
Roman poet, it is the "foreign" word that masks the "old lie" of culture. In the modern world, what do dead languages produce except
more death? The blunt "truth" of native speech insists on being
heard instead, essentially souring the assonance of Horace's fluid *e*'s
and *o*'s, his chiming *d*'s and *c*'s, his lulling *m*'s and *p*'s:

> If you could hear, at every jolt, the blood
> Come gargling from the froth-corrupted lungs,
> Bitter as the cud
> Of vile, incurable sores on innocent tongues,—
> My friend, you would not tell with such high zest

To children ardent for some desperate glory,
The old Lie: Dulce et decorum est
Pro patria mori. (Owen 66)

The final rhyme (glory / mori) puts paid to any debt owed the Classics, given that terminal association of the word glory (L. *gloria)* with death *(mori)*. Old men, desperate to preserve their power, have merely used the foreign word to buy off children with "the old Lie" – that empty promise of glory – *Sweet and fitting it is to die for one's country.*

On one level, it is doubtful that an Oxbridge product could write such a blatantly anti-Horatian ode. Sassoon would have been the one to do so had he not left Cambridge after two years' immersion in Classics: "[T]he History Tripos did not appeal to him, so he left without taking a degree – nine years before Owen recognized it as one of his 'most terrible regrets' that he never had the chance of going to Oxford" (Stallworthy 205). Owen failed to get a "first" when he went up to London on 9 September 1911 to write the university entrance exam, and so failed to win the scholarship he needed (61–2). His subsequent failure to gain "a scholarship to University College, Reading" (92) would leave him even more open to the type of cultural forces that had been at work in America since 1865, or in the educational reform movement in France after the debacle of 1871.

Other forces were at play, of course, in the making of a neo-romantic like Wilfred Owen into a truly modern poet – forces that loom out of "Dulce et Decorum Est" to show how and why the authority of the classical word was so swiftly eroded. One such force appears in the cinematic memory of Owen's anti-Horatian speaker. Indeed, his projection of a mini-"newsreel" from the battlefield encapsulates the whole process "of a newly visual culture eroding the standards of a literate one" (Matsuda 177). For the cinema camera had bestowed on modern life "a machine which generated superbly real living records while simultaneously creating its own fantastically unsettling perceptual and temporal frameworks" (167). More to the point, this unsettling agent of modernity had been at work for two decades before Owen found himself at the Western Front. Indeed, "[t]wentieth-century historians seem to forget that the film was a perfectly common information vector well before the First World War" (Sorlin 31). What remains to be seen is how film was revolutionizing perception in the decades leading up to the Great War.

CINEMA AND MODERN MEMORY

"In 1894, Louis Lumière began experimenting with Edison's Kine-toscope and Kinetograph; making the improvements necessary for projecting filmstrips, which were lacking in Edison's machines, he in-vented the *cinématographe*" (Barsam 20). Weighing just one percent of Edison's cumbersome contraption and operating with a hand-crank, not with electricity, Lumière's device "was actually three ma-chines in one – camera, developer, and projector" – allowing scenes to be shot anywhere that light permitted. "The first motion pictures ... were 'actualities,' short films of actual people, conditions, or facts, constituting ... 'unmanipulated activity of more or less general inter-est'" (17). (In this word *actualités* Barsam has missed the connota-tion of *actuellement* [*now, at the present time*], implying immediacy, or the simultaneity of the event with its viewing.)

The next year, on 22 March 1895, Louis and his brother Auguste "were invited to show their first film, *La sortie des ouvriers de l'usine Lumière (Workers Leaving the Lumière Factory),* at the meeting of a scientific group, the Societé d'encouragement à l'In-dustrie Nationale, an event that is considered by many as the world's first successful projection of a moving picture" (21). Later that spring, on 10 June 1895, "they showed an expanded program of eight films to the meeting of the Sociétés Photographiques de France at Neuville-Saint-Vaast near Lyons. There, they added to the excitement provoked by their invention by making films of the dele-gates arriving at the congress hall and projecting them two days later" (21). After the passage of two days, amazed delegates found themselves back at the beginning of the congress, watching the past come crowding into their present moment. Although "[t]hese first films were no more than 30 seconds long, shot by a stationary cam-era from a fixed point, ... each encompassed a new world of move-ment. Almost one hundred years later, viewers still find the inescapable shock of the new in these first films" (22).

Early accounts of these screenings hint at a momentous shift in our human relation to time, to memory, and to language. After "the first public performance for a paying audience on December 28, 1895, in the Salon Indien, a room in the basement of the Grand Café on the Boulevard de Capucines in Paris" (21), the journalist was almost lyrical. "As tramways, cars, and passersby made their way across the screen, movement itself was truth. *Le Radical* of

December 30, 1895, reported these first moving images as 'astonishing'; rolling waves and seaside bathers 'excited enthusiasm' and were commented to [sic] describe 'a marvelous realism'" (Matsuda 167). Indeed, the same reporter for *Le Radical* grasped at once how the word was undercut by the power of the moving image to collapse both past and present into the past-progressive-present tense of cinema: "Already, words are collected and reproduced; now life is collected and reproduced. We can, for example, see our dear ones again long after they would be lost to us" (cited by Matsuda 172). The past on film, it seemed, was qualitatively different, maybe different in *kind,* from any past represented in language, much as the past of the daguerreotype, at the other end of the temporal spectrum, would also differ in kind from the fixities of print. For the photograph only "fixed a particular past moment. The cinematic image seemed rather to reproduce actuality, to invade the present" (174).

It was this strangely invasive power of cinema that effectively overturned familiar notions of temporality. For the new "machine did more than preserve the past; the authenticity of the moving image was so authoritative, so *real,* that filmed subjects seemed to exist not as records of a point in time, but in the present projection" (166–7). The result was "a relentless telescoping of time in which the boundaries between past and present appear to dissolve, and all [filmed] time and space are rendered apparently simultaneous in the present" (166). For a past *actualité* appeared *actuellement* (at present, here and now), to invade the present, making the pastness of the past seem "unnatural." In a sense, the *cinématographe* was creating a new verbal tense in the grammar of existence, collapsing familiar distinctions between the progressive tenses of past and present.

Modern memory was further shaped by cinema in terms of "the directness of image and compression of time which the camera itself created, an immediacy which annihilated temporal order, distance, and reflection" (170–1). A French airplane disaster captured on film in December 1910 illustrates the nature of these effects: "Before the events were scarcely comprehended by those at the scene, they were witnessed by a distant public viewing 'the last word' in *actualités.* Image preceded understanding; the experience of tragedy and the memory of an event was the shared viewing of the projection itself, all the more striking and apparently real for its immediacy" (171). In the rush to screen the latest *actualité,* "the camera allowed the past – or what used to be the past – to be almost instantly displaced into the present." And so the immediacy of the moving image had precisely the opposite effect of the still photograph: the hidden dimension of *actuellement* (at the present time) of the *actualité* worked to bridge the gulf between then and now, collapsing temporal sequence into a cinematic past-progressive tense.

The collapse of time in the immediacy of the image was likewise repeated in the presentness of viewing. "Sensibilities of temporal depth and sequence which gave reality to the past were dominated by the spectacular immediacy of the image. Striking images would become the viewer's memory of events, shaping recollections to the measure of filmed and projected scenes" (167). Even the distant past, let alone recent events on film, became mobile; even memory came to be structured by the site of viewing. ("Where were you when that plane came crashing down?" "I was in the dark, watching with you.")

Within three years of the first screening of cinematic *actualités,* the outbreak of the Spanish-American War gave the public a chance to witness the assault on "San Juan Hill in Cuba by Theodore Roosevelt and the Rough Riders" in July 1898 (Barsam 31). In fact, the "charge up San Juan Hill" was unique to print; the *actualité* showed a guerilla-style attack of creeping riflemen through wooded terrain. While filmic "truth" thus gave the lie to print, it failed to satisfy the public's hunger for drama. In consequence, "British and American films made in the Spanish-American War and the Boer War" began to take divergent routes: "[S]ome filmmakers traveled to the battle to record the action while others stayed at home and staged war scenes for their cameras" (Barsam 31–2). In order to hide their differing order of truth from *actualités,* "many of the faked films were carefully produced to seem authentic; Thomas Edison, who 'shot all his Boer War series in the Orange Mountains of New Jersey, was particularly adept in this respect' " (32).

The demand for "authenticity" was weakened, however, by two crucial factors. In the first place, the Lumières became victims of their own success; they had "emphasized movement for its own sake, but the public grew weary of the novelty as it became increasingly aware of the medium's theatrical potentialities" (29). Secondly, theatrical impresarios like Georges Méliès soon grasped the potential of the *cinématographe* to tell stories that looked like *actualités.* "At the end of

1897, although the Lumières had successfully exhibited and exploited more than 750 *cinématographe* films around the world," they abandoned the new medium to the storytellers, and "withdrew from film production, discontinued the exhibition tours, and concentrated on manufacturing and marketing the *cinématographe* and films already in their catalog" (24). At the same time, their film catalogue for 1900, "*Catalogue Général des Vues Positives,*" is revealing of the depth and extent of the craze for *actualités* that their invention had created, since it lists "1299 titles by the Lumières and others, almost all of which became world famous."

And yet, "[e]ven as the nonfiction film became less and less a part of film programs, World War I created a new audience interest in both nonfiction and narrative films about war" (30). Recognizing the value of public desire to see the war as it was being waged, "a nearly secret propaganda effort" of the British government, "[t]he War Propaganda Bureau, was established in Wellington House, its headquarters, where it operated from 1914 to 1916" (33). The War Office reached an agreement with the British film industry to supply all the transport and budget, and the industry to "supply the necessary equipment and expertise" (34) in order to slake the thirst for war films on the home front.

On the Western Front, in "theatre," there was an astonishing appetite for cinema, though of a type distinct from that on the home front. As Kevin Brownlow reports, "One American observer saw motion pictures run in an old dugout that held fifty men. 'Those ragged, dirty fellows, caked with mud and covered with vermin, did not want to look at the pictures that well-intentioned folks thought they would be interested in, but were eagerly enthusiastic over scenes of city streets of Paris, London, New York. You see, they had got in a state of mind where none of them believed they would ever see a city street again, and a city street with well dressed crowds walking about' " (45). The cinema became "a regular feature of life at the front from August 1915. Initiated by wealthy citizens of France to entertain French troops, they were converted from any building within easy access of the front lines that was still upright. When a show was announced, it was a foregone conclusion that it would be packed. By mid-1916, there were twenty cinemas within the British sector" (43). Even more telling are the military euphemisms of the battlefield as a "picture-show" that, taken together, serve to define and to refigure the soldiers' endless "fascination with pictures ... Trenches were called 'Picture house tea rooms' by British troops, who referred to machine guns as 'cinema cameras,' and instead of being ordered to open fire, they were told to 'turn the crank.' An offensive was a show, and ... '[t]he pictures' was a euphemism for the operating theater" (46).

By contrast, audiences on the home front were eager to watch British war films by the dozen, although four in particular have been credited with conveying "'an entirely new understanding of the complexity of modern warfare, and a picture of mud, cheerfulness and death in the trenches...': *The Battle of the Somme* (1916), *St. Quentin* (1916), *The Battle of Ançre* (1917), and *Advance of the Tanks* (1917)" (Barsam 34).[11] The first of these four was filmed in the last days of June and on the first of July, 1916, by Lt Geoffrey Malins, "an official War Office 'kinematographer'" (Horrall 208). "[O]ne of two cameramen who filmed the first day of the Battle of the Somme" (the other was John McDowell), Malins "always claimed that he had filmed men going over the top in the first wave and being cut down. He wrote as much in his cockily self-regarding memoir, *How I Filmed the War*. Lieutenant Malins, dynamic and egotistical, a showman to his fingertips, was the driving force behind the film as it appeared" (Hudson, online 1). Historians do not dispute that "Malins filmed the starting gun for battle on the Somme – the explosion of a tremendous mine laid under German positions at Hawthorne Redoubt" (2). What they doubt is Malins' claim that "he then 'swung the camera round' to capture the visual climax of the film – scenes of British soldiers going over the top." For, "[a]s Roger Smither, keeper of the Film and Photograph Archives at the Imperial War Museum, points out, the trench is unwired, far too shallow and open to sniper fire. The troops appear not to be carrying all the notoriously heavy equipment that weighed down soldiers on July 1, and the camera angle is such that the cameraman would be exposed to enemy fire." But matching-shot techniques do authenticate other scenes.

For example, "immediately after the allegedly staged scene comes the recently discovered footage of real combat, some of the most telling and heart-rending scenes on that first day on the Somme." As Christopher Hudson notes in his *Sunday Times* feature article of 8 October 2006 on the occasion of the re-release of the film in a digitally mastered version, "*The Battle of the Somme* thus becomes the first film in screen history to have footage of men being killed in combat" (online 2), and the deaths that it records make up one of the most painful moments in Newfoundland history. "From his precarious position in the now-abandoned trenches, overlooking the ground ahead, Malins' camera records the fateful advance of the 1st Newfoundland Regiment down a slight incline in the middle distance... In the remastered film we see the tiny figures, rifle bayonets on shoulders, advance down the ridge, then crumple and fall, while the others march on to their deaths" (3).

For all the recent controversy over faked scenes of "going over the top" and of "sequences that were later inserted into *The Battle of the Somme*, including mortars being fired and shells bursting at a trench mortar school" (2) behind the Front during the rain delay of a late June downpour, viewers of the time were drawn like moths to the flame. "Reports of the battle had primed audiences' interest, and this, along with the unrelenting advertisements, made *Battle of the Somme* [sic] the greatest craze in British cinema history" (Horrall 209). By 1916, "There were some 4,500 cinemas in Britain, and a population of [43 million]. *The Battle of the Somme* opened in 34 cinemas in London alone. People queued all day to book tickets; thousands were turned away from the doors" at the film's release on 21 August 1916 (Hudson, online 1). Many of these viewers were within earshot of the big guns (the *actualité* more *actuellement* than ever) as the battle continued to rage just across the Channel. "The film broke box-office records," which have never been matched, "wherever it was shown" (Hudson). "As many as one million Londoners saw the film ... Twenty million more people throughout the country saw the film in its first six weeks" (Horrall 208). "It was eventually shown in eighteen Allied countries," and was even "screened for British soldiers at rest areas in France, to provide new recruits with some idea of what they were about to face" (Gilbert 149–50).

Clearly, the War Office's publicity campaign, including "endorsements from Lloyd-George and the King" (Horall 208), helped to make *The Battle of the Somme* the first mass media event in history. Nor should one discount word-of-mouth publicity, given the "unprecedented reactions from audiences who believed it to be the first 'true' representation of how their friends and relatives were fighting in France" (209). "Frances Stevenson, Lloyd George's secretary and mistress who had lost her brother Paul in the fighting," speaks with a lack of emotional reserve that, being quite untypical of her social milieu, speaks volumes about the event: "It reminded me of what [her brother] Paul's last hours were. I have often tried to imagine to myself what he went through, but now I know, and I shall never forget. It was like going through a tragedy. I felt something of what the Greeks must have felt when they went in their crowds to witness those grand old plays – to be purged in their minds through pity and terror" (Hudson, online 1).

Even more remarkable, perhaps, is what this response of a well-educated woman suggests about social class and film: "At the start of the war, according to a war-cabinet report in 1917, the cinema 'was almost universally regarded as an instrument for the entertainment of the masses'" (Hudson, online 2). If the masses got their impressions from flickering images, the educated classes acted and thought on the basis of print. And so authorities felt it necessary to ban print journalists from the Front lines after "an impudent *Times* correspondent had visited a forward observation post without Haig's permission" in May 1915, drawing enemy artillery fire on the post. "Paradoxically, the rules would be relaxed for newsreel cameramen. The authorities, brought up long before the age of moving pictures, didn't take them seriously, unlike newspapers, which were read in the London clubs" (Hudson, online 2). But Frances Stevenson's response suggests that such class distinctions could no longer be based on the mode of communication.

Nor did the epistemology of cinema preclude the memory of Greek tragedy or Aristotelian catharsis in this educated woman's moving encounter with the terrible "*actualité*" taking place on the Somme. But the social actuality was more likely to be shaped by the temporal immediacy of the *actualité*. For the home front was henceforth assaulted continually by moving images that crossed the Channel from France, and "what was then still a novelty" quickly "became an established phenomenon in British society" (Barsam 35). In a sense, the collapse of temporal boundaries in the newsreels of battle now worked to erode old boundaries of class, at least to the extent that no educated Briton could look again at modern war as a continuation of Homer, and no undereducated Briton could look again at the past as a foreign country. *The Battle of the Somme* had made the underclass genuine contemporaries of the upper class.

OWEN'S AMBIVALENT RESPONSE
TO CINEMATOGRAPHY

Why, then, did Wilfred Owen famously write in one of his letters to his mother while on rest out of the line at Beaumont-Hamel in January 1917, where the Newfoundland Regiment had been wiped out six months before: "Those 'Somme Pictures' are the laughing stock of the army – like the trenches on Exhibition in Kensington" (*Letters* 429)? His biographer, Jon Stallworthy ventures the interpretation that "like many another soldier who at the time made little of his own suffering in the trenches, Owen resented 'the illusory War Films' currently showing in England such a bowdlerized version of the truth" (170). While there is support for this view in Owen's, let alone other soldiers', writings, one ought first to remark how his early ambivalence to cinema might bear on this much-quoted remark.

The first mention of cinema in Owen's collected correspondence appears in a letter, written at age seventeen, from the home of relatives in Torquay to his mother in Shrewsbury. In this letter, postmarked 5 August 1910, he tells of a visit to Plymouth where he "saw principal sights, e.g., Mayflower Stone, Guildhall, Hoe, etc." But, when an afternoon visit to the Dockyard was spoiled by a downpour, "we had to content ourselves with 'Buffalo Hunting in Indo-China' in Animated Pictures, (1s. seats)" (*Letters* 60–1). The tone is one of wry amusement and keen awareness of the incongruity of the content. And yet a later remark that same year is almost breathless about the medium. From Alpenrose on a visit to his cousin Leslie, he writes to his mother on 29 December 1910: "In the afternoon Leslie took me in to Reading to see West's wonderful Pictures (animated.)" [*sic*] (66). The editors note that "West's Picture Palace, at 33 West Street, Reading, was one of the earliest cinemas in the town. There were regular advertisements in Reading for 'West's Pictures – travel, sport, drama, comedy, new spectacle, tragedy, and farce, 3d, 6d, and 1/-" (note 1). The placement of the adjective "wonderful" between "West's" and "Pictures" hints that it was the medium itself – "animated" – rather than the several types of picture shown, that was "wonderful." Two days later, a verse letter to his youngest brother Colin (1 January 1911) is more revealing of his attitude to the content: "That afternoon we also saw the 'Pictures' / The French boys always charm me, but the mixtures / Of

Blood and Thunder Stories sometimes shock me" (67). Wilfred is evidently capable of alarm, in addition to the irony, indifference, and wonder with which he views the *cinématographe*.

Two years later, he offers a rather more sophisticated critique of the medium in a letter written to his mother from Dunsden Vicarage on 22 September 1912:

> On Sat. Afternoon, I saw *Queen Bess* by Sarah Bernhardt in Cinematograph, (with Leslie, Uncle, & Vera.) All very well; but it is positively painful to me not to hear speech; worse than the case of a deaf man at a proper Shakespeare play; for all the finer play of mouth, eye, fingers, and so on, is utterly imperceptible, and so are the slower motions of the limbs spoiled, and their majesty lost, in the convulsed, rattling-hustle of the Cinema. Certainly, the old impression of driving through an electric hailstorm on a Chinese-cracker is not now so easily got, as of old; but still, I cannot enthuse over the things as Leslie does. His infatuation would speedily vanish if he knew "the real thing." (162)

On one level, this critique resembles that of Maxim Gorky, the Russian novelist, who famously complained in his 1896 review of the first Lumière program in Russia "that he was disturbed and depressed by the depiction of a gray and irrelevant world: 'Last night I was in the Kingdom of Shadows. If you only knew how strange it is to be there. It is a world without sound, without colour" (Barsam 24).

Not surprisingly, Gorky does anticipate the frequent complaint of British soldiers who saw *The Battle of the Somme* in rest areas. "As it was a silent film, the soldiers' main complaint was its failure to capture the sound of the battle" (Gilbert 150). This is also the basis of Owen's complaint about *Queen Bess,* where Sarah Bernhardt is rendered speechless. But there is another side to Gorky's complaint about watching "not life but its shadow; it is not motion but its soundless spectre" (cited by Barsam 24). So, too, for Wilfred Owen, the greatest stage actress of the era becomes the ghost of herself on film; the medium leaves her not just speechless, but expressionless in muscle and limb.

Early in the second decade of motion pictures, convention still dictated that shots be taken from "stage distance," i.e., "twelve feet away from the camera, in compositions that showed part of the floor or ground in front of their feet and the top third of the frame above their heads" (Bowser 94). Today, we more properly understand the power of the close-up to express the poetry of each muscle in the human face. But, in *Queen Bess,* the great Sarah Bernhardt still could not let the camera do what it does best in close-up shots. And so Owen sounds rather like a deaf man on the verge of losing his sight. Part of his distaste for the "Somme Pictures" would appear to spring from the same source: the lack of sound, and the lack of expressiveness in "tiny figures, rifle bayonets on shoulders, advanc[ing] down the ridge, then crumpl[ing] and fall[ing], while the others march on to their deaths" (Hudson, online 2). Of more obvious importance, however, is Owen's bitter experience of "the real thing," and his revulsion from the slightest indication of fakery.

On the other hand, Wilfred writes to his mother from the company of fellow officers in training at Fleetwood (near Blackpool) on 23 November 1916, contrasting the "dead letter" of print to the "animation" of the film image: "I haven't seen 'L'Amour' [a poem by his cousin Leslie Gunston] in print. I don't like Print, now that I see what a dead letter it is to all these living men about me." A few lines later, he notes, almost as an afterthought, "I have quite a veneration for Charlie Chaplin by the way" (*Letters* 416).

The aesthetic distance covered in these same years of film history (1910–16) now feels like light years. In 1956, Roman Jakobson famously remarked, "Ever since the productions of D. W. Griffith, the art of the cinema, with its highly developed capacity for changing the angle, perspective and focus of 'shots,' has broken with the tradition of the theatre and ranged an unprecedented variety of synechdochic 'close-ups' and metonymic 'set-ups' in general. In such pictures as those of Charlie Chaplin, these devices in turn were superseded by a novel, metaphoric 'montage' with its 'lap dissolves' – the filmic similes" (Jakobson and Halle 92). Given Wilfred Owen's fondness for Keats and for what Jakobson calls "the metaphoric pole" of human expression, one is not surprised to find the poet writing to his mother from Craiglockhart Hospital in Edinburgh on 22 August 1917, "The most momentous news I have for you is my meeting with Sassoon … German is getting on. Saw Ch. Chaplin again" (*Letters* 487–8). One cannot discount the fact that "the hospital cinema" (Stallworthy 201) at Craiglockhart is mentioned in the same breath as Owen's fateful meeting with the war poet he idolized, or that he might have seen, a short time before he wrote his "gas poem" (499) in October, 1917, a way to improve on *The Battle of the Somme* by making a "filmic" *actualité* that would show "the real thing."

Before we turn to the signs of this cinematic epistemology in "Dulce et Decorum Est," however, we need to look again at that letter of 19 January 1917 in which Owen is so dismissive of "Somme Pictures," since the remark has rarely been read in light of its historical context, or even as the dramatic record of his first encounter with a gas shell:

> Last night indeed I had to 'go up' with a party. We got lost in the snow. I went on ahead to scout – foolishly and alone – and when, half a mile away from the party, got overtaken by

> GAS

> It was only tear-gas from a shell, and I got safely back (to the party) in my helmet, with nothing worse than a severe fright! And a few tears, some natural, some unnatural. (428–9)

The isolation of the word "GAS" – white space divorced from human expression – is an eloquent reminder of his position in No Man's Land, far from his fellows and the relative safety of box-respirators. The isolation of the word GAS on the page – recalling the spatial isolation of the figure at the centre of his poem – serves as a visual memory of his terror of isolation, with nothing but wordless space filling with gas: "In all my dreams, before my helpless sight, / He plunges at me, guttering, choking, drowning." Whether or not this moment in the letter is the "source" of the image in "Dulce," it functions as the filmic analogue of an image from the past – erupting into and invading the present as a "cinematic memory." Both "GAS" and the "drowning" man depend on the invasion of that past image into our present of reading, evoking this recurring nightmare where the immediacy of the visual image and the presentness of viewing both serve to translate the fixities of print into a cinematic *actualité*.

"DULCE ET DECORUM EST" AS *ACTUALITÉ*

While Owen's double sonnet is carefully structured as a cinematic newsreel, climaxing in a rhetorical unmasking of the "foreign" word as "The old Lie," its structural power comes from a recurring image of a respirator-less man who, the speaker recalls,

> was yelling out and stumbling
> And floundering like a man in fire or lime. –
> Dim through the misty panes and thick green light,
> As under a green sea, I saw him drowning. (66)

And then the figure returns, at the very centre of the poem, in two lines that stand out quite starkly from what Stallworthy calls the "*exemplum,*" or the octave and sestet of the opening, which is then "followed by a *moralitas* of passionate indignation" (228) in the last twelve lines of the double sonnet following those two lines set off as nightmare.

Both the specular immediacy of this haunting image and its recurring power to invade the present suggest that we need to look again at Owen's language to see how it mimics the effects of cinema from the opening lines. Read in this light, the poem opens in a long shot that follows a column of soldiers – "Bent double, like old beggars under sacks, / Knock-kneed, coughing like hags," as they "cursed through sludge, / Till on the haunting flares we turned our backs, / And towards our distant rest began to trudge." After this establishing shot, the "camera" begins to move closer: "Men marched asleep. Many had lost their boots / But limped on," as the "camera" quickly closes to an extreme close-up of feet that are "blood-shod," before panning over to show how "All went lame, all blind." The cinematic focus at this point remains on the group, not on any one person.

A careless reader could be lulled by the past tense of the verbs into a sense of being at a safe distance in time and space from a scene where men are "Drunk with fatigue; deaf even to the hoots / Of gas-shells dropping softly behind." Of course, "sleep," like "fatigue" or deafness, will not be as deadly to readers who fail to stay awake, to be alert to danger from behind. Yet, when danger does strike in the ninth line – the sonnet's traditional volta – the warning voice is not even set off in heard speech, within quotation marks, but rather in words that appear to be mouthed, as if read like lips in a silent film:

> Gas! GAS! Quick, boys! – An ecstasy of fumbling,
> Fitting the clumsy helmets just in time.

A sudden switch in tense from the past to the present-progressive tense in two participles ("fumbling," "fitting") alerts the reader to the clear and present danger, until "the clumsy helmets [are fixed] just in time." Then, just as the speaker breathes a sigh of relief (into his clumsy respirator), his attention is drawn to one still "yelling out" and "stumbling / And floundering" in a terrifying extension of the present-progressive participle, the "progress" of which must lead, unless the viewer is willing to give up his own respirator, to a horrible spectacle of agonizing death – "As under a green sea, I saw him drowning."

While the sestet of the first sonnet still holds out a prospect of temporal distancing from death – at least in the past tense of "saw him drowning" – the second "sonnet" begins, or rather returns, with a vengeance to the cinematic immediacy of this image from the past, which appears, again and again, to invade the present:

> In all my dreams before my helpless sight
> He plunges at me, guttering, choking, drowning.

The visual separation of these two lines from the rest of the poem ensures that the present sight cannot be shaken off; the speaker is "helpless" to save the man, unless he should offer to hand over his own gas mask and die in the other's place. Still, the dying man "plunges at me," asserting his *actualité*, his visual immediacy; there is no saving distance possible now, no retreat into the past tense. Instead, the speaker stares directly into the face of death, while shrinking from the damning implication, "Better him than me."

Of course, readers are not let off the hook, either. The way we are implicated in the scene makes us combatants, too, since the speaker's words, like the cinematic image, continue to invade our present, dissolving the usual boundaries between past and present, making other times and places simultaneous with our place of viewing. In this changed environment of the simulated moving image, the horror now moves inside the reader:

> If in some smothering dreams, you too could pace
> Behind the wagon that we flung him in,
> And watch the white eyes writhing in his face [...]

The point, of course, is that, in making his language move with the immediacy of the cinematic image, Owen makes his readers see (and relive) his memories. And so we cannot help but "watch the white eyes writhing in his face," or "hear, at every jolt, the blood / Come gargling from the froth-corrupted lungs." We are involved from the outset of the poem in the "truth of cinematic seeing" (Matsuda 170), and will hardly shake off its effects with any more ease than the speaker shrugs off his haunted memories.

One of the underlying reasons, then, why the Great War has not yet ended – not even after the better part of a century – is that it is the very first war to be viewed on film. And where the memories of combatant-poets begin to take the form of verbal films, they begin to invade our present, to become our memories, too, by means of the invasive power of the "cinematic" image.[12] The result, however, is mixed: while Owen's mimesis of cinema strikes a blow against "The old Lie" of classical culture, denying its relevance for modern memory, the all-consuming nature of that memory has not allowed us to escape thralldom to his particular past. For the past (on film) is still too much with us, speaking with all the force of "specular immediacy" to our present age.

ALL QUIET IN THE PRESENT TENSE

Erich Maria Remarque's novel *All Quiet on the Western Front* (*Im Westen nichts Neues*) (1928) follows a similar cinematic logic, challenging the authority of the word by means of language, even as it converts that language into a verbal form of "motion pictures." In such writing, traditional values of distance, detachment and reflection give way to a new epistemology of visual culture with its values of immediacy, temporal simultaneity, and "accelerated memory" (Matsuda 166). But the novelist's cinematic techniques are far more extensive than those of the poet, helping to lay the ground for a popular success that culminated in Universal Picture's film adaptation by Lewis Milestone, a film that "was one of the early talkies" and also "one of the great classics of the cinema" (Barker and Last 41).

All Quiet first shares with "Dulce" a blatant distrust of the authority of the written word. Thematically, its narrative builds to an explosion of moral outrage at "The old Lie": "It must be all lies and of no account,"[13] the narrator Paul Bäumer remarks acidly, "when the culture of a thousand years could not prevent this stream of blood being poured out, these torture-chambers in their hundreds of thousands. A hospital alone shows what war is" (263). If Bäumer refrains from making the Latin word a perpetrator of the "old lie," it is likely because of a difference in his education. For some time, the authority of the Classics was attenuated by a German romanticism that took its authority from native Idealist philosophy. The thought of Fichte, Schelling, and Hegel – those late-eighteenth- and early-nineteenth-century successors to Kant – but most of all, Hegel's "idea that each age possesses a particular spirit to which all artistic work must inevitably conform" (Gelernter 200), had helped to make discontinuity the norm, ending the ancient faith in cultural continuity encouraged by and through the classical grammar school.

For example, when Remarque's narrator comes home on leave, he sits in his old bedroom staring at a shelf full of books: "Many of them are secondhand, all the classics for example, one volume in blue cloth boards cost one mark twenty pfennig. I bought them complete because it was thoroughgoing, I did not trust the editors of selections to choose all the best. So I purchased only 'collected works' " (170). His ensuing confession that "I preferred the other books, the moderns, which were of course much dearer," marks him as a child of his culture. Longing to recover the "quiet rapture" (171) he had known in books, he says: "Images float through my mind, but they do not grip me, they are mere shadows and memories" (172). The insubstantiality of the word is what now strikes him: "Words, Words, Words – they do not reach me" (173). Profoundly alienated from family and neighbours who do not share the horrors he has seen, he is also alienated from any past found in books. "A terrible feeling of foreignness suddenly rises up in me ... Slowly I place the books back in the shelves. Nevermore. Quietly, I go out of the room" (172–3). Yet this is but a late, not final, step he takes away from a world shaped by print.

As early as his first chapter, Bäumer has offered several reasons for what he sees as the declining authority of the word:

We often made fun of [our elders] and played jokes on them, but in our hearts we trusted them. The idea of authority, which they represented, was associated in our minds with a greater insight and a more humane wisdom. But the first death we saw shattered this belief. We had to recognize that our generation was more to be trusted than theirs. They surpassed us only in phrases and in cleverness. The first bombardment showed us our mistake, and under it the world as they had taught it to us broke in pieces. (12–13)

This discovery that the "authority" of books is not much more than empty rhetoric turns on a trope of vision that evokes the "privileged relationship of memory to vision in the late nineteenth century" (Matsuda 168). As Bäumer recalls: "While they continued to write and talk, we saw the wounded and dying. While they taught that duty to one's country is the greatest thing, we already knew that death-throes are stronger" (13). At the same time, he says, "We loved our country as much as they; we went courageously into every action; but also we distinguished the false from true, we had suddenly learned to see. And we saw that there was nothing of their world left."

Here is the crux: *We had suddenly learned to see.* For what Paul Bäumer and his generation do see gives the lie to "the whole gamut of culture from Plato to Goethe. With our young, awakened eyes we saw that the classical conception of the Fatherland held by our teachers resolved itself here into a renunciation of personality such as one would not ask of the meanest servants" (22). *Patria* and *pietas,* Fatherland and the renunciation of personality, are nothing more than political alibis to justify the sufferings of a Virgilian hero for the sake of empire. As political ideas, both have been corrupted at the source. And yet, "the whole gamut of culture from Plato to Goethe," from the greatest of the Greeks to the greatest of the Germans, is dismissed as mere words, without reality.

Are we then to read *All Quiet on the Western Front* as a postmodern novel turned back on itself, in which language undermines its own claims to representation? Likely not, given the narrator's claim to having "distinguished the false from true" by "suddenly learn[ing] to see." It could be this naive confidence that inspired one parodist,[14] not long after the novel's German publication, to pillory Remarque for "arrogating to himself the rôle of the omniscient recording angel of the Great War, the sole repository of the whole truth about the armed conflict on the Western front" (Barker and Last 42). In *Vor Troja nichts Neues* (*All Quiet before the Walls of Troy*), he appears as an egotist for whom "the whole Trojan war seems to be taking place simply so that he can write a book about it … 'Thus it is that I am writing a war diary. It will contain a great deal about me and just a very little about the war.' The rest of the world is in a state of utter confusion; the soldiers alone have retained their clear-sightedness and integrity" (41).

What the parodist fails to see, however, is that Paul Bäumer is not writing a diary or a memoir or anything else in the narrative. "It is strange to think," he muses at the outset of the second chapter, "that at home in the drawer of my writing table there lies the beginning of a play called 'Saul' and a bundle of poems. Many an evening I have worked over them – we all did something of the kind – but that has become so unreal to me I cannot comprehend it any more. Our early life is cut off from the moment we came here" (Remarque 19). What do we read, then, if he does not write? An interior monologue, perhaps, told "principally in the historic present" (Barker and Last 46)? If it is an interior monologue, it suffers nevertheless from a disastrous rupture in form. The subject dies, and yet the story, carried until now in the first person, continues for another page in the third-person voice of an unnamed narrator. After three hundred pages of following Bäumer's thoughts through to his last word, the idea of now hearing the voice of an author-god is hard to credit: "The life that has borne me through these years is still in my hands and my eyes. Whether I have subdued it, I know not. But so long as it is there it will seek its own way out, heedless of the will that is within me" (295). Such are Bäumer's last words.

But now a god-like, third-person voice takes up the narrative on the last page, if only for the space of an obituary: "He fell in October 1918, on a day that was so quiet and still on the whole front, that the army report confined itself to the single sentence: All quiet on the Western Front" (296). Who speaks these words, if there is no precedent in the story for this egregious violation of narrative perspective? Or how does the narrative account for the metamorphosis of an interior voice into an external eye? No fictional editor enters the stage at the end to identify a (non-existent) manuscript; no Daniel Defoe precedes the narrative to edit the diary of a Robinson Crusoe, or to tone down the confessions of a Moll Flanders. It is either the artless device of an incompetent author, or else it is a symptomatic break with the conventions of narrative in the first person.

In fact, even in the present tense of narration, there had been signs of a break with novelistic conventions in order to evoke an unusual temporality. The opening sentence had set us in the here-and-now: "We are at rest five miles behind the front" (1). While a succeeding compound sentence recalls the recent past – "Yesterday we were relieved" – the second main clause returns to an ongoing present:[15] "and now our bellies are full of beef and haricot beans." The scene is as immediate as it is visual: "The cook with his carroty head is begging us to eat; he beckons with his ladle to every one that passes" (1). It is as if we are watching events through the camera-eye of a narrator whose every glance determines our field of vision. So we are present a few pages later at mail call: "To-day is wonderfully good. The mail has come, and almost every man has a few letters and papers. We stroll over to the meadow behind the billets. Kropp has the round lid of a margarine tub under his arm" (7). Recalling this experience behind the line, the narrator projects it without analysis or reflection; instead, we see what he sees, as if he were a cyborg with camera implants for eyes in a futuristic novel by William Gibson.

In *Representing War* (1993), Evelyn Cobley remarks that, in war narratives like this one, "the narrator's function is analogous to that of a camera, he is confident that he can reproduce accurately whatever he chooses to 'frame'" (11). The "camera" that she envisions, however, takes snapshots; it is far better suited to past-tense images than it is to motion pictures. Back in the continuous present of the narrator's field of vision in the line, one does not meet still images: "We see men living with their skulls blown open; we see soldiers run with their two feet cut off, they stagger on their splintered stumps into the next shell-hole" (134). *We see*, while the camera goes on running, "men without mouths, without jaws, without faces; we find one man who has held the artery of his arm in his teeth for two hours in order not to bleed to death." In view of hundreds of such passages, the "memory" of the narrator seems to have been "displaced from persons to instruments. Acting as a 'witness,' the new machine [of a camera-narrator] would be, in effect, the dispassionate eye of history, a scribe whose power was rooted in the recording of time through seeing" (Matsuda 168). But time is continuously visible only if the narrator records and relays events as they happen, if he functions anachronistically as a television camera sending a "live" flow of images in high definition.[16]

Flashbacks, on the other hand, show how even the past tense can offer a form of cinematic vision in *All Quiet,* where the shift to the past in the "domestic" idyll of the first chapter is made in filmic terms. Here, for example, is the narrator's memory of basic training, presented without comment as a cinematic straight-cut: "I wish he was here," Müller says bitterly of Kantorek, their hated drill-sergeant. Then, across a visual break in the page, there appears an image of the man himself: "Kantorek had been our schoolmaster, a stern little man in a grey-tail coat, with a face like a shrew mouse"

(10). Again, in the third chapter, when "the conversation turns to drill[, ... a] picture comes before me. Burning midday in the barrack-yard. The heat hangs over the square" (41). Another straight-cut in chapter six conforms to, and confirms, the type: "It is chilly. I am on sentry and stare into the darkness ... The parachute-lights soar upwards – and I see a picture, a summer evening, I am in the cathedral cloister and look at the tall rose trees that bloom in the middle of the little cloister garden where the monks lie buried" (119).

The point is not just that the narrator sees "a picture" whenever he thinks of other times; rather, the "accelerated memory" of the moving image produces, as it does on film, "a relentless telescoping of time" (Matsuda 166). In these filmic scenes of "memory," the past is every bit as immediate to Bäumer as the things he sees in his cinematic present. The collapse of time into a continuous present would seem to lead, in terms borrowed from the emerging field of the sociology of memory, to a "loss of trust of the future," since the future has by this time been thoroughly displaced by the "instantaneous time" (Urry 52) of cinematic culture.[17]

Only in rare folds between the present and future are we able to glimpse the logic of this presentness of things in *All Quiet*. Memories of home and basic training, with their accompanying reflections on "learn[ing] to see," invariably break off in straight-cuts back to the present: "Before going over to see Kemmerich we pack up his things; he will need them on the way back" (13). Yet what appeared to begin as idyll now ends at the dressing station with Bäumer and his friends acknowledging that Kemmerich won't be going home alive: "The skeleton is working itself through. The eyes are already sunken in. In a couple of hours it will be over" (28). The immediate future only ever leads to death in Paul Bäumer's line of sight, as it does most graphically in this scene:

> The shelling has ceased, I turn towards the crater beckoning to the others. They take off their masks. We lift up the wounded man, one taking his splintered arm. And so we stumble off hastily.
>   The graveyard is a mass of wreckage. Coffins and corpses lie strewn about. They have been killed once again; but each of them that was flung up saved one of us. (70–1)

If the narrator survives the barrage, it is only because the dead "have been killed once again." But how will he keep "next time" at bay when even the "instantaneous time" (Urry 52) of the continuous present cannot save the dead from dying again and again?

The High Command makes no bones about forcing the soldiers to look into the immediate future, there to read the likely end of their story. As chapter six begins:

> There are rumours of an offensive. We go up to the front two days earlier than usual. On the way we pass a shelled schoolhouse. Stacked up against its longer side is a high double wall of yellow, unpolished, brand-new coffins. They still smell of resin, and pine, and the forest. There are at least a hundred.
>
> "That's a good preparation for the offensive," says Müller astonished.
>
> "They're for us," growls Detering. (99)

So the narrative logic of a continuous present, or "instantaneous time," looks inescapable: "We sit as if in our graves waiting only to be closed in. Suddenly it howls and flashes terrifically, the dug-out cracks in all its joints under a direct hit" (110). Bäumer sees how, "If we were in one of those light dug-outs that they have been building lately instead of this deeper one, none of us would be alive." His only consolation is: *Not yet.*

But death and the future do not always strike from afar. Take the scene in the shell-hole where a French soldier lies dying with a dagger-wound Bäumer has given him: "But every gasp lays my heart bare," the narrator confesses. This "camerade" for whom he feels such pity, but from whom he cannot free himself under the sweep of machine-gun fire, is the image of his own near future, the embodiment of his death. He now thinks, "This dying man has time with him, he has an invisible dagger with which he stabs me. Time and my thoughts" (221). The near future inevitably and invariably leads to death. So better to remain in "instantaneous time" and not think about time past or time future.

The problem, of course, is that living in the instant offers no better prospects for life than the near future or the distant past. Reflecting on what Albert means in saying, "The war has ruined us for everything," Bäumer comes to see their true predicament:

> He is right. We are not youth any longer. We don't want to take the world by storm. We are fleeing. We fly from ourselves. From

our life. We were eighteen and had begun to love life and the world; and we had to shoot it to pieces. The first bomb, the first explosion, burst in our hearts. We are cut off from activity, from striving, from progress. We believe in such things no longer, we believe in the war. (87)

The saving grace of the continuous present is turning into the bane of their existence, draining away all hope of a future. This "draining of time" and general collapse of temporality that Andreas Huyssen situates "in the world of information and data banks" (9) has evidently been present all along in the structures of cinematic temporality. Thus Bäumer finds that he is locked into the "spectacular immediacy" of a "cinematic" existence that continues to function like an endless film-loop. "Cut off" from past and future, he is then trapped in the eternal present of an unending war. Indeed, the war itself has become synonymous with the filmic present. Past and future are already obsolete in this unrelenting destruction of time and distance, of detachment and reflection.

And so we come at the end of the novel to the death of this narrator who has shown us the war through the lens of a subjective camera. What we find on the last page is the camera left running, as if one of Bäumer's comrades were merely picking it up to turn it back on its fallen operator. The precedent for this type of narrative handover was established in a scene where Müller "handed over his pocket-book to me, and bequeathed me his boots – the same that he once inherited from Kemmerich. I wear them, for they fit me quite well. After me Tjaden will get them, I have promised them to him" (279). Now another buddy is designated to take up the camera and keep it running after Bäumer's death. But, as the camera turns back on its former operator, we see that "[h]e had fallen forward and lay on the earth as though sleeping. Turning him over one saw that he could not have suffered long; his face had an expression of calm, as though almost glad the end had come" (296). Such is the predicament of this "cinematic memory" of war, where even death is preferable to the hell of a never-ending present.

ACCELERATING MEMORY AND MORE LIES

The moderns are firmly in the field, the ancients nowhere in sight, in *Generals Die in Bed* (1930), the one canonical Great War novel to be written by a Canadian combatant. Charles Yale Harrison

(1898–1954) – a native Philadelphian who went to work for the *Montreal Star* at the age of sixteen before joining the Royal Montreal Regiment – lacked the necessary formal training (claiming to have left school in Grade Four) to feel the least bit ambivalent about the authority of the ancients. To the contrary, the newspaper was for him the real purveyor of printed lies and false ideals. "Strangely," his nameless narrator remarks, "we never refer to the Germans as our enemy. In the week-old newspaper which comes up from the base we read of the enemy and the Hun, but this is newspaper talk and we place no stock in it. Instead we call him Heinie and Fritz" (44). In the present-tense experience of these Canadian soldiers, "We have learned who our enemies are – the lice, some of our officers and Death" (43).

The same can be said of press reports of troop morale: "*Camaraderie – esprit de corps* – good fellowship – these are words for journalists to use, not for us. Here in the line they do not exist" (91). To the contrary, the narrator says, "We know what soldiering means. It means saving your own skin and getting a bellyful as often as possible ... that and nothing else." What "soldiering" means in linguistic terms is the ability to translate false names into "true" names, to replace the lies of military-speak with real-speak:

> We have long since learned that the word *rest* is another military term meaning something altogether different ... We are taken from the trenches and march for endless hours to billets. The first day out we really rest. Then begins an interminable routine of fatigues. We march, drill, shine buttons, do guard duty, serve as batmen for the officers, practice grenade-throwing, machine gunnery, and at night we are taken by lorry behind the lines to do wiring and trench-digging. This is called out on rest. (36)

The same principle applies to *artillery duel:* "We cower behind the sandbags, trembling, white-faced, tight-lipped. Our own guns reply. ... The infantrymen on both sides suffer, are killed, wounded. This is called an artillery duel." This assault on the spoken and printed word is premised on the same distinction that Owen and Remarque make between reading or hearing what the culture teaches, and seeing for oneself the truth of things.

In technique, Harrison also follows *All Quiet* in his use of the cinematic present tense and the immediacy of the visual image to open a gulf between print memories and screen memories. At one point,

Harrison's narrator even refers to film to describe what soldiers must endure in a bombardment: "The force of the detonations cause [*sic*] the light of the candle to become a steady, rapid flicker. We look like men seen in an ancient, unsteady motion picture" (97) (see p.295). That a technology only twenty years old is now termed "ancient" speaks volumes about the narrator's investment in "instantaneous time," where even the cultural regression of a world at war is preferable to "ancient" time (i.e., any time before the modern era with the advent of film, not to mention "talkies" or CinemaScope).

From its opening line to its final sentence – "I am carried up the gangplank" – *Generals* is narrated in this relentlessly continuous present where the past has virtually ceased to exist. "It is after midnight on pay-day" (3), the narrator begins his story in an army barracks in Montréal. "Outside in the streets we hear the sounds of celebration. Fireworks are being exploded in our honour" (8). As the battalion marches to the train, "We are heroes, and the women are hysterical now that we are leaving" (9). In the railway car, "We wait, for hours, it seems ... The boys lie like sacks of potatoes in the red plush-covered seats. Some of us are green under the gills. White-faced, we reel to the toilets. The floor is slimy and wet" (11). A straight-cut to the next chapter, "In The Trenches," serves as a new establishing shot. Now, "[w]e leave the piles of rubble that was once a little Flemish peasant town and wind our way, in Indian file, up through the muddy communication trench" (15). Here, the narrator sits down on a firing-step and tries "to imagine what Montreal looks like. The images are murky. All that is unreality. The trench, Cleary, Fry, the moon overhead – this is real" (20). Out of sight, out of mind; the past is visible only as a distant memory before vanishing for the remainder of the novel. "Instantaneous time" appears at once to replace any other mode of temporality:

> Over in the German lines I hear quick, sharp reports. Then the red-tailed comets of the *minenwerfer* sail high in the air, making parabolas of red light as they come towards us. They look pretty, like the fireworks when we left Montreal ...
> In that instant there is a terrific roar directly behind us.
> The night whistles and flashes red.
> The trench rocks and sways.
> Mud and earth leap into the air, come down upon us in heaps.
> (23)

The past is obliterated in the instant as time collapses in on itself. Now, there is no time but the present tense of experience; the narrator refuses to take refuge in the distance of either past time or distant space. Instead, what readers see is akin to what filmgoers see: "projected images of a past more immediate than their own present" (Matsuda 166).

The actors themselves affirm that they no longer exist outside the present moment: "We do not know what day it is. We have lost count. It makes no difference whether it is Sunday or Monday. It is merely another day – a day on which one may die" (27). There are just two verb tenses left in a soldier's experience, even when he is out of the line: the immediate present and the near future. "It is strangely quiet. Only in the distance do we hear the rumbling of massed artillery fire." And yet: "We never escape this ominous thunder. It is the link which binds us to our future. Out on rest, miles behind the lines, we hear it. It is a reminder to us that the line is still there; that we must return" (71). If the near future approaches in the sound of the guns, it is an ever-present reminder of the narrator's loss of faith in any meaningful future.

Even in the momentary freedom of a swim in the Somme, this futureless future is pressing against the present instant: "In the distance the rumble of the guns is faint but persistent like the subdued throbbing of violins in a symphony. I am still here, it says ... I am the link that binds you to your future" (86). The nearness of the link is graphically displayed at the end of the scene in which cavorting boys confront the body of a French soldier that has been "carried to us from the front by the sparkling, sunlit water of the Somme" (88). *Et in Arcadia, ego,* the classicist murmurs on viewing this convergence of past and present as if through a camera lens. But only neoclassicists are likely to recall Nicolas Poussin's painting of *Les bergers d'Arcadie;* otherwise, the camera eye will not recall it for you. And yet there is far more here than Cobley sees in reducing the scene to documentary realism, where, "[w]ith naturalistic precision ... Harrison elects to focus on external features, refusing to elaborate on his own more personal reactions" (*Representing* 77). For the River Somme is characterized as a messenger from the near future with a grim announcement to make: "He is different, this Frenchman, from the hundreds of corpses we have seen in the line. We thought we were safe. We thought we could forget the horrors of the line for a brief few weeks – and here this swollen reminder drifts from the battlefield" (88) to shrink the men's temporal horizons even further.

Time is further compressed through establishing shots in each chapter that confine the reader to a continuous present. After his leave in London, the narrator returns, in "Over the Top," to find himself, "[b]ack at the front. I find the battalion a few miles behind the reserve lines" (177). After a visual break between paragraphs, there is another location shot: "In the front line. It is midnight. We are to go over at five" (182). Soon, "[w]e clamber up the ladder and out on to the field. All along the line men are advancing with their rifles on guard. We walk slowly. The curtain of fire moves on, methodically. Out of the smoke behind us tanks crawl like huge beetles spitting fire. They pass us. From one of the holes a hand waves to us. On and on!" (185). So *on and on* it goes, with nothing to hope for beyond the present moment: "To-morrow we may be dead. The world is shot to pieces. Nothing matters. There are no ten commandments. Let 'er go!" (138).

What choice do these men have but to live for the moment in a "relentless telescoping of time" (Matsuda 166)? If not television broadcast news, the narrative does approach early cine-journalism, where events are "reported not even as they [have] been witnessed, but as they [are] *being* witnessed" (Matsuda 171). Distance is no longer possible in this type of media environment. Harrison's *you-are-there* technique virtually excludes the possibility of temporal depth, much as had the same-day screening of film. "The element of time which had depended upon distance in reporting information was being destroyed ... Speed and immediacy were all; the camera allowed the past – or what used to be the past – to be almost instantly displaced into the present" (Matsuda 171).

This loss of distance nonetheless produces what is likely the most gripping scene in *Generals,* a scene that cites the better-known one in *All Quiet,* where Paul Bäumer's regret at stabbing a French soldier when he tumbles into the same shell-hole turns into a plea for forgiveness. But Bäumer's report of this intimate drama differs in two respects from Harrison's scene: Bäumer imagines the past life of the French bookbinder from documents he finds on the body, before entering into his imagined dialogue to make things right with the dying man's family. Because the dying French soldier is beyond speech, however, the scene in *All Quiet* is played entirely as a monologue.

Harrison's narrator, in contrast, looks straight into the eyes of the German soldier he bayonets as the other "reaches for his revolver":

> I lunge forward, aiming at his stomach. It is a lightning, instinctive movement.
> The thrust jerks my body. Something heavy collides with the point of my weapon.
> I become insane ...
> I have a man at the end of my bayonet, I say to myself.
> His shrieks become louder and louder ...
> I move to seize the butt of my rifle. Once more we are face to face. He grabs the barrel with a childish movement which seems to say: You may not take it, it is mine. I push his hands away ...
> Suddenly I remember what I must do.
> I turn around and pull my breech-lock back. The click sounds sharp and clear.
> He stops his screaming. He looks at me, silently now.
> He knows what I am going to do. (110–14)

The short, stabbing sentences allow for no reprieve; the narrator is condemned to live in a recurring nightmare, where a dying man's shrieks do not die away. Only the dying victim is able to escape the scene; the narrator is condemned to suffer as long as this scene replays itself in his mind.

A second notable difference from Paul Bäumer's situation emerges in the next scene where Harrison's narrator is forced to witness the pain of a surviving brother, when one of his German prisoners stumbles across the body of the man he has just killed:

> He looks up at me with the eyes of a dog and says:
> "*Mein Bruder – eine minute – mein Bruder.*"
> The red flares grow brighter in the sky over my shoulder.
> The other prisoner looks at me with sad eyes and repeats: "*Ja, ja, das ist sein Bruder.*" 16–17)

The narrator had tried to march the prisoners past the body, "quickly[,] as though I do not know him" (116). Now, however, in view of a family member's pain, "I want to tell these boys what I think, but the gulf of language separates us" (120). His human

respect for the dead man's brother – giving him a minute alone with
the body – allows the latter to pat his hand in gratitude. "'*Du bist ein
gutter Soldat*,' he says, his eyes filling with tears. I pat his shoulder"
(120). The irony is lodged in the sequence of events, not in the narrator's subsequent reflection, for this guilty killer praised for his tender-
heartedness is instantly mortified, though he is unable to say so. Even
then, the brother is not really mistaken: "You are a good soldier," he
says. And we know, from the immediacy of what we have just witnessed, that the "killer's" heart is indeed in the right place.

If "reflection" is impossible in the immediacy of present-tense
narration, there are still ways for other, later perspectives to be
grafted onto the sequence of immediate events. Take this early scene
where the narrator suffers his first shell concussion:

> A shell lands with a monster shriek in the next bay. The con-
> cussion rolls me over on my back. I see the stars shining serenely
> above us. Another lands in the same place. Suddenly the stars re-
> volve. I land on my shoulder. I have been tossed into the air.
> I begin to pray.
> "God—God—please ..."
> I remember that I do not believe in God. (26)

Evidently, the sequence of events has been structured to create irony
in the present tense. In particular, "I remember" becomes the voice of
a later time intruding on the "present" moment, producing a structural "reflection" on what is dramatized as immediate experience.
The scene is designed, in other words, to catch one unawares, to
bowl the reader over in the narrator's present moment of experience.
It is no more than a verbal trick by which two distinct verbs of reflection are rendered in the present tense: "I *remember* that I *do not believe*." The voice of the future may then be projected onto the voice of
the past in a sharp compression of time that literally aims at liberation from the past, at a present-tense modernity freed from history.

What Matsuda calls the "accelerated memory" (166) of cinematic narration is nonetheless destined to recoil upon itself. Such is
the case in the final chapter, whether the narrator (or his author)
notices it or not. "It is the first week in August," 1918 (243), when
the Canadian Corps is marched down to Amiens to begin the battle
that will result in the decisive Allied breakthrough on the Western
Front. "Our faces are as red as the poppies of which the war poets

are writing back home" (244), the narrator says with mordant irony, given the nature of this scene in which the troops are preparing to fight:

> An aide hands the brigadier-general a paper and he reads to us:
> "... and after the *Llandovery Castle* was torpedoed, not a helping hand was offered to our wounded comrades ... no instance of barbarism in the world's history can equal the sinking of this hospital ship ... think of it, more than three hundred wounded Canadians struggling in the choppy waters of the English Channel ... the lifeboats ... sprayed by machine-gun fire as the nurses appealed in vain to the laughing men on the U-boat ..." (245)

The narrator's own use of ellipses in these lines points to the brigadier's editing, to what is pointedly left out, even as it produces in the reader a sense of *in medias res*.[18]

The military consequences are of course predictable: one "good" war crime deserves another. Equally predictable, however, is the cinematic playback of the next scene, in which such archaic behaviour is rendered in terms of an archaic technology, almost like that of a previous scene recalled as "an ancient, unsteady motion picture" (97):

> The figures run with funny jerky steps towards us, holding their hands high above their heads.
> We open rifle fire as we advance. The silhouettes begin to topple over. It is just like target practice ...
> There are hundreds of them. They are unarmed. They open their mouths wide as though they are shouting something of great importance. The rifle fire drowns out their words. Doubtless they are asking for mercy. We do not heed. We are avenging the sinking of the hospital ship. We continue to fire ...
> "*Bitte—bitte* (please—please)."
> Their voices are shrill. They are mostly youngsters.
> They throw themselves into the crater of a shell-hole. They cower there. Some of our men walk to the lip of the hole and shoot into the huddled mass of Germans. Clasped hands are held up from out of the funnel-shaped grave. The hands shake eloquently asking for pity. There is none. Our men shoot into the crater. In a few seconds only a squirming mass is left. As I pass the hole I see the lips of a few moving. I turn away. (254–6)

Yet it is still impossible to turn away, as even the truncated length of this quotation attests – although the sharp compression of time in this scene also makes it impossible to cut. It is a filmed scene that is by now horrifyingly familiar, replaying for us this "squirming mass" from the Nazi death camps to Rwanda to Srebrenica to Darfur.

After ninety years, however, what is most horrifying is the realization that this past is still our present. In fact, "they" do not have a monopoly on mass murder, not if "we" initiated it. Because the scene is so immediately traumatic, it leaves the narrator scant room for reflection, since it goes on and on, playing in his head even as he is carried aboard a hospital ship. Only now, cinematic "truth" is framed by a second lie quite as culpable as "the old Lie" of classical poetry: "'The *Llandovery Castle*?' [The orderly] laughs contemptuously. 'That was bloody murder, brother. Our officers oughta be shot for that. She was carryin' supplies and war material – it's a god-damned shame, that's what I say'" (268–9). It is this bitter "irony" that is "carried up the gangplank" with the narrator, now condemned to an endless replay of his cinematic memories:

> The *Llandovery Castle* – carrying supplies – war material –
> I see the general reading us the report of the sinking just before
> the battle of Amiens – I see the bright sun shimmering on his
> brass – I hear his cold, dispassionate voice – "couldn't swim,
> poor chaps – wanton act – must not go unavenged …"
> I remember the funny jerky steps of the prisoners as they came
> running towards us with their hands held high above their heads
> – I see the clasped hands lifted over the lip of the shell-hole as we
> fired into it – clasped hands silently asking for pity … (269)

The unique power of cinema to displace the past into the present has indeed turned into "the funny jerky steps of the prisoners" through which "The old Lie" of patriotism begins to mutate into the continuing trauma of cinematic seeing.

And yet there is a second, concealed "lie" at the end of this book that should not be ignored or forgotten. "The *Llandovery Castle*, a British merchant vessel serving as a Canadian hospital ship," writes the official military historian of the Canadian Expeditionary Force, "had been torpedoed on 27 June 1918, while returning to England from Halifax. Of a Canadian crew and medical staff totalling 258 all ranks, only 24 survived. Among those who perished were the fourteen Canadian Nursing Sisters aboard" (Nicholson 398 n.). As one recent historian writes, "There were 94 Canadian Army Medical Corps personnel on board, including 14 Canadian Nursing Sisters. In the ensuing exodus from the sinking H.S. Llandovery Castle, all Canadian Medical staff made their escape to the lifeboats. In an act of barbarity, the U-Boat Captain ordered the survivors machine-gunned. The 14 Canadian Nursing Sisters perished as their lifeboat vanished into the sucking vortex of the sinking ship. Eighty-eight of the 94 Canadians drowned" (Christie 1).

Nothing can or should excuse the wanton murder of German soldiers surrendering at the Battle of Amiens. And yet the historical context (or temporal depth of events) still has to be remembered in judging events.[*] For it was not one lone general and his troops who howled for revenge: "The newspapers and the propaganda machine played up the atrocity so by August 1918, the Amiens operation was code-named 'Llandovery Castle'" (Christie 1). Such reflection afforded by the distancing of print thus allows for other temporal perspectives to be added to the "truth" of "cinematic seeing." "The old Lie," in other words, is not to be found just on the lips of old men, or even in the pages of poets speaking "To children ardent for some desperate glory." It lurks in our peculiarly modern bias toward visual immediacy that too thoughtlessly privileges the present moment without true regard for the past.

[*] See Tim Cook, *Shock Troops: Canadians Fighting the Great War 1917–18, Vol 2* (Toronto: Penguin, 2008), for more nuanced accounts of the "treachery" of German troops who chose either to fight on, ignoring their own white flag, or else to ambush Canadians leaving cover to take them prisoner. The next white flag to be waved by Germans would indeed be ignored by the Royal Montreal Regiment who spared no one "when the garrison stepped out with raised hands–they were annihilated almost to a man" (426).
DW: 27 January 2011

6

"Spectral Images": The Double Vision of Siegfried Sassoon

In May, 1919, Siegfried Sassoon received "the proofs of *Picture Show,* his privately produced collection of which 200 copies were printed by the Cambridge University Press under the supervision of Theo Bartholomew" (Egremont 236). "By 24 July," the collection "had sold a disappointing thirty copies in four weeks" (237), despite the fact that one-quarter of its thirty-four poems concern the war, and that the collection ends with one of today's most-anthologized war poems, "Everyone Sang." An explanation of sorts may be found in the title poem, "Picture-Show," where "The brave despair of men flings onward, ever the same / As in those doom-lit years that wait them, and have been ... [*sic*] / And life is just the picture dancing on a screen" (www.bartleby.com/137/). As Max Egremont shrewdly notes of "the dreamy 'Falling Asleep,'" the penultimate poem in the collection, "time dissolves into nostalgia almost before it has been lived" (273). The same thing is quite as true of the ten-line "Picture-Show," where "life" is reduced to "just the picture dancing on a screen." Time "dissolves," in other words, into languorous melancholy where the viewer is hopelessly excluded from the world of the moving image.

Such a reading nonetheless distorts the haunting sense of the opening lines, where the immediacy of the visual image invades the present with a force that now collapses time, leaving the speaker spellbound in his presentness of viewing: "AND still they come and go: and this is all I know – / That from the gloom I watch an endless picture-show, / Where wild or listless faces flicker on their way." The problem is two-fold: the structure of the poem alienates the reader from this visual immediacy, reducing the "wild or listless faces" that the speaker sees "dancing on a screen," to mere "flick-ering," distant images; and the speaker's nostalgic tone cuts him off from active involvement in the scene.

Another reason for critical neglect of "Picture-Show" is that it begs belief to say that Siegfried Sassoon's memories of war are structured cinematically. For the former subaltern of the Welch Fusiliers appears, in genre after genre, as one of the leading print *writers* of the conflict. Even before the Armistice, 2nd-Lt Sassoon had published two books of poetry – *The Old Huntsman* (1917) and *Counter-Attack* (1918), and he would spend the better part of the next two decades adapting his diaries into the fictionalized *Memoirs of George Sherston,* a trilogy of war novels comprising *Memoirs of a Fox-Hunting Man* (1928), *Memoirs of an Infantry Officer* (1930), and *Sherston's Progress* (1936). To this trilogy he would later add an "authorized" autobiography, *Siegfried's Journey 1916–1920,* which also appeared in print at the end of World War II. Most of this writing seems obsessively focused on getting his ex-perience down in *book* form, "'Going over the ground again,'" as Paul Fussell says in another context, in a recurring "act of memory conceived as an act of military reconnaissance" (260).

Sassoon's recourse to the stabilizing power of print has also been viewed, with justice, as his therapeutic response to trauma. To Mi-chael Thorpe, it is the raison d'être of his war writings: "We have seen in these two volumes of memoirs, not only a mind trying to achieve 'some sort of mastery over the experience,' but also a mind striving to know and govern itself" (105). On this account, writing and, more generally, the book as a cultural form, have a crucial role to play in self-formation, as the nineteenth-century bookman him-self suggests in *Infantry Officer,* where an untested George Sherston writes, "It was no use regretting the little room at Flixécourt where I had been able to sit alone every night, reading a good book and calling my soul my own" (21). Here, the book is figured implicitly as an analogue of the self-bounded individual, a self-governing soul.

In terms of his medium, Sassoon's writing also raises print-de-fined questions about the intrinsic differences between a traditional combatant, like Achilles, depending on the oral poet to keep his memory alive, and the literate soldier telling his own story in the en-during medium of print.[19] In his diary entry for 17 December 1915, for example, Sassoon clearly views the *writing* of poetry as his best bid for immortality: "Reading the new volume of Eddie Marsh's

[*Georgian*] poets, nothing new to me in it. Wish the Kaiser would let me go back to my work at writing poems. Slow and sure is my way, I'm sure, and the good work was bound to come along sooner or later. And now, if I get done in, I leave only a sheaf of minor verse, mostly derived from memory" (26). Several months later, he will take a wider view of heroic action as a necessary precondition of poetic fame (if in the Pateresque language of his times)[20] in his diary entry of 31 March 1916: "Great thing is to get as many sensations as possible. No good being out here unless one takes the full amount of risks, and I want to get a good name in the Battalion, for the sake of poetry and poets, whom I represent" (51). The poet needs to speak and to act with authority if he is to become the keeper of his own memory, the sole guardian of his fame.

Late in the war, however, Sassoon begins to see a fatal opposition between the warrior and the writer, as in this diary entry of 15 June 1918:

> I am beginning to realize the difficulties of combining the functions of soldier and poet. When I was out here as a platoon-commander I spent half my time in day-dreams. I avoided responsibilities. But since I've been with this battalion responsibility has been pushed on to me, and I've taken soldiering very seriously. A conscientious and efficient company-commander has rather a harassing time, especially during prolonged periods of training. For several weeks I hardly thought of anything but the Company. Now that their training is coming to an end I've been easing off a bit; have allowed myself to enjoy books. The result is that I immediately lose my grip on soldiering, and begin to find everything intolerable except my interest in the humanity of the men. One cannot be a good soldier and a good poet at the same time. (270–1)

Indeed, this rift between the soldier and poet had been looming for a year, ever since Sassoon had torn the ribbon of the Military Cross off his tunic after writing to his regimental commander on 6 July 1917 to protest, as he put it in his *Declaration*, "against the political errors and insincerities for which the fighting men are being sacrificed" (*Diaries* 174).[21] Temporarily invalided out of the Battle of Arras in April, he would choose for the rest of that year to take the part of a modern-day Achilles, not out of any sense of having been dishonoured, but out of a professed sympathy for his fellow soldiers (the illusion of public sacrifice likely sparing him the consciousness of heroic egotism). Convinced that he (and his fellows) had been deceived by the High Command in the conduct of "this War, upon which I entered as a war of defence and liberation," and which had "now become a war of aggression and conquest" (173), he refused in the most public way possible to return to the battlefield.

More than twenty copies of "A Soldier's Declaration" were sent to public notables, including writers and philosophers, like-minded editors and journalists, friends, and sympathetic Lords and Members of Parliament.[22] On the evening of 30 July, H. B. Lees-Smith, the Labour MP for Northampton, read out the full "Declaration" in the House of Commons, thereby entering it into the printed record of Hansard's *Parliamentary Debates*. The next day, under the headline "An Officer and Nerve Shock," the *Times* of London reported the story, quoting the full text of the decorated war hero's "Declaration."[23] The story enjoyed wide circulation in the press outside of London. "The *Bradford Pioneer* had already jumped the gun, publishing the statement in full on 27 July" (Wilson 384). The full text was subsequently published in the *The Manchester Guardian*, excerpts and commentary being printed in nine more regional newspapers. Indeed, "A Soldier's Declaration" would continue to circulate in newsprint, fiction, memoirs and diaries, which poured from Sassoon's pen for another thirty years. Far from suggesting a mode of cinematic memory, the memoirs of the soldier-poet Siegfried Sassoon seem to be an epitome of the book, a moral declaration by a modern-day Achilles sitting out the battle to ensure his own fame in the fixities of print.

Even so, another clear pattern runs through Sassoon's writings, sharply qualifying this portrait of the bookman – a modern pattern of questioning the value of heroic poetry and the hidebound culture of antiquity. On 3 June 1916, he writes in the *Diaries:* "I was thinking this evening (as I sat out in the garden with the sun low behind the roofs and a chilly wind shaking the big aspens) that if there really are such things as ghosts, and I'm not prepared to gainsay the fact – or illusion – if there are ghosts, then they will be all over this battle-front forever. I think the ghosts at Troy are all too tired to show themselves – they are too literary – and Odysseus has sailed into the sunset never to return" (71).

This reduction of Achilles and Odysseus to literary ghosts, to mere forms without substance, constitutes a rejection as decisive in its own way as Owen's later rejection of "the old lie" of Horatian patriotism. Long before he was to meet Owen, also suffering from "shell-shock" at Craiglockhart Hospital in the summer of 1917, Sassoon felt that the traditions of heroic poetry were worn out. Too many "ghosts" of men he knew now cast the old stories in a new light; the "truth" of books looked pale as ghosts in the dawn.

Fourteen years later, Sassoon was to question more directly the truth of print in *Memoirs of an Infantry Officer:* "What use," he thought after hearing yet another account of a botched operation from a friend visiting him on sick leave, "were printed words against a war like this? Durley represented the only reality which I could visualize with any conviction. People who told the truth were likely to be imprisoned, and lies were at a premium" (253). Something similar appears in his antipathy to wartime journalism: "I wondered why it was necessary for the Western Front to be 'attractively advertised' by such intolerable twaddle. What *was* this camouflage War which was manufactured by the press to aid the imaginations of people who had never seen the real thing?" (262).

Given such a fatal hemorrhaging of faith in war journalism, the only saving grace must be to let people who had "seen the real thing" write their own stories, i.e., to make combatant narratives a norm in representing it. Writing his own "normative" story a dozen years later, however, Sassoon is uneasily aware of the fallibility of even some regimental historians who had served at the Front:

> Someone (it must have been Dunning) had sent me some details of the show[24] they'd been in on April 23d. The attack had been at the place where I'd left them. A little ground had been gained and lost, and then the Germans had retreated a few hundred yards. Four officers had been killed and nine wounded. About forty other ranks killed, including several of the best N.C.O.s. It had been an episode typical of uncountable others, some of which now fill their few pages in Regimental Histories. Such stories look straightforward enough in print, twelve years later; but their reality remains hidden; even in the minds of old soldiers the harsh horror mellows and recedes. (253)

If regimental histories (written after the fact) cannot be trusted to tell the truth, what about eyewitness accounts written in the smoke and heat of battle? Memoirs, based on diaries written at the time, could, for all their subjectivity and restriction of perspective, be more "true" than retrospective histories written by those who were there.

And yet the problem of writing memoirs, as we see from the second page onwards in *Infantry Officer*, is that memory and diary tend to disagree: "There were several of us on board (each Battalion in our Brigade was sending two officers) and we must have stopped at the next village to pick up a few more. But memory tries to misinform me that Flook and I were alone on that omnibus" (10). And so he moves from such fallible recollection to more precise quotation from his daily record: "I remember him talking about the hard times he'd had in Canada, and how he used to get a meal for twelve cents. In the meantime I made a few notes in my diary" (29). What is written in the medium of a daily diary is better able, it is supposed, to preserve the "truth" of immediate experience, and so must take precedence over the soldier's own memories:

> "*Tuesday evening, 8.30. At Becordel cross-roads.* On a working party. A small bushy tree against a pale yellow sky; slate roofs gleaming in the half light. A noise of carts coming along with rations. Occasional bang of our guns close to the village ...
> "*Wednesday, 6.15. p.m. On Crawley Ridge.* Ormand up here in the Redoubt with a few men. I relieve him while he goes down to get his dinner. Very still evening; sun rather hazy. Looking across to Fricourt; trench mortars bursting in the cemetery; dull white smoke slowly floats away over grey-green grass with buttercups and saffron weeds. Fricourt; a huddle of reddish roofs; skeleton village; church tower, almost demolished, a white patch against green of Fricourt wood (full of German batteries) ..." (30)

Yet even this passage – a close adaptation of Sassoon's diary entries for 22–23 May 1916 – is used to dramatize a basic difficulty in the posture of the observer in the novel: the diarist is excluded from any role as actor. As Sassoon had lamented in his diary for 5 February 1916, "The mare brought me home straight as a die across the four miles of plough and mud – gloom all around and stars, stars, overhead, and hanging low above the hills – the rockets going up behind, along the line – brief lights soon burnt out – the stars wheeling changeless and untroubled, life and deathless beauty, always the same contrast. So I still see the war as a looker-on" (38). The diarist, it seems, is necessarily cut off from the soldier's pursuits; at the very least, he cannot be at once both a poet and a soldier.

Only in *Siegfried's Journey 1916–1920* (1945) does Sassoon find a way to explain how these contradictory roles of observer and

actor can be joined in one person. It dawns on him, from a reitera-
tion of a scene of personal trauma recorded in his diary and then repeated in *Infantry Officer*, that his personal trauma is symptomatic
of a wider trauma resulting from new structures of perception. Here
is how he generalizes from his personal experience of trauma in a
recognition scene penned some thirty years later:

> No longer feeling any impulse to write bitterly, I imagined myself
> describing it in a comprehensive way, seeing it like a painter and
> imbuing my poetry with Whitmanesque humanity and amplitude
> ... Or it seemed that I was looking down on a confusion of
> swarming figures in some battle-ravaged region – an idea derived,
> perhaps, from the scenic directions in Hardy's *Dynasts*. These
> spectral images, seen from the borderland of sleep, brought me a
> delusive sense of power to put them into words. There was a
> haunting appeal, too, in the sad anonymous faces which emerged
> on that dream cinematograph, faces pale and passionless, as
> though from a sculptured frieze. Thus might the dead have re-
> turned in apparition, silently censuring the cause for which they
> had given their lives. (70)

If "spectral images" and "that dream cinematograph" announce
his investment in cinematic modes of remembering, Sassoon also
gestures more largely than he had done in "Picture-Show" to this
mode of remembering. For Sherston the diarist functions as the
camera eye, recording "raw" footage, while the shaping mind of
the poet is evident in the series of "edits" by which memory will
later be restructured in the novels. In these twin technologies of recording and projection, the autobiographer develops a conscious
figure of what he has managed intuitively to do all along. For it is in
his "dream cinematograph" that these two moments of primary
and secondary viewing are made one thing, joining the soldier to
the poet in what now appears as a filmic mode of remembering.

"THAT DREAM CINEMATOGRAPH"

To begin exploring the cinematic epistemology at the base of
Sassoon's fiction, one has only to compare his immediate impressions in the war diaries with his revisions of them in the novels,

particularly in scenes where later perspectives are added. For example, on 23 April 1917, the wounded officer lies in a hospital bed, recording his impressions of a daytime world veiled in a fog of words, as compared to his nighttime world graphically invaded by terrifying images, now that he has returned to London:

> In the ward they talk of little else but the war:
> 'counter-attacked from the redoubt'
> 'permanent rank of captain'
> 'didn't draw any allowances for six weeks'
> 'failed to get through their own wire' and so on. [...]
> All day I have to talk to people about the war, and answer the questions of friends, getting excited and over-strained and saying things I never meant to. And when the lights are out, and the ward is half shadow and half glowing firelight, and the white beds are quiet with drowsy figures, huddled out-stretched, then the horrors come creeping across the floor: the floor is littered with parcels of dead flesh and bones, faces glaring at the ceiling, faces turned to the floor, hands clutching neck or belly; a livid grinning face with bristly moustache peers at me over the edge of my bed, the hands clutching my sheets. Yet I found no bloodstains there this morning. (161)

The scene is especially disturbing in its vivid particularity, hinting at a mind unhinged by "horrors" that "come creeping across the floor." The diarist may try to ward them off by likening them to "dummy figures made to deceive snipers: one feels that there is no stuffing inside them"; and yet they are so real that he is constrained to check his sheets for "bloodstains." Because he is safe and they are fatally damaged, their very "blood" accuses him "like ink spilt on blotting paper" (162). Reduced once more to the role of quintessential onlooker, he now feels condemned to write in the blood of his accusers. Nor will he spare himself by claiming to suffer from nightmares; he ends the paragraph wishing that he "could sleep." The "horrors," he leaves us to think, are indeed real ghosts.

Should we then infer that he is close to mental breakdown, as some of his closest friends are wont to do in Pat Barker's novel *Regeneration* (1991), her creative retelling, from a variety of historical documents, of this fascinating story of Sassoon's treatment for

"shell-shock"? Doubtless, the protagonist does find that his friend
Robert Graves has inferred as much, since the fictional Sassoon
feels obliged to defend his sanity:

> 'You can't put people in lunatic asylums just like that. You
> have to have *reasons.*'
> 'They've got reasons.'
> 'Yes, the Declaration. Well, that doesn't prove me insane.'
> 'And the hallucinations? *The corpses in Piccadilly?*'
> A long silence. 'I had rather hoped my letters to you were
> private.' (7)

In his private diary, however, the historical Sassoon had already cast
reason aside in his account of the hallucinations. The "horrors"
keep him awake, they do not trouble his sleep.

In his adaptation of the diary into fiction, Sassoon tries nonetheless
to render this scene of "corpses in Piccadilly" acceptable to reason.
So Sherston begins: "More than once I wasn't sure whether I was
awake or asleep; the ward was half shadow and half sinking firelight,
and the beds were quiet with huddled sleepers. Shapes of mutilated
soldiers came crawling across the floor; the floor seemed to be littered with fragments of mangled flesh" (248). The scene builds
through now-familiar details of "the horrors" to conclude with the
same image of an "English private" fumbling "in his tunic for a letter." Then, "as he reached forward to give it to me his head lolled
sideways and he collapsed; there was a hole in his jaw and the blood
spread across his white face like ink spilt on blotting paper ... Vio-
lently awake, I saw the ward without its phantoms." These ellipses
erupt in the text as if to mark the boundary between nightmarish
sleep and waking sanity, in this public restatement of a privately recorded vision. Order, reason, and civility are restored not only in the
act of waking, but in one further, anticlimactic, sentence of homely
description: "The sleepers were snoring and a nurse in grey and scar-
let was coming silently along to make up the fire" (248). Sherston
thus "blots out" the more disturbing implications of this scene with
borrowed "blotting paper." The technology of writing comes to serve
as a defence against the invasive power of the cinematic image.

It will take another fifteen years for Sassoon, in *Siegfried's Journey,* to view his memories in terms of "that dream cinematograph."
Here, the "horrors" are no longer rationalized as a bad dream, but

are directly aligned with film's power "to reproduce actuality, to invade the present" (Matsuda 174). In a way that had largely escaped his conscious notice before now, Sassoon is able see the war "in a comprehensive way," because he now views himself simultaneously as a soldier-camera and a poet-projector. In the field, he is a "camera" recording "spectral images" of the battle (presumably the images in his diary), but in his memoir, he is a "projector" casting moving images on a screen where the past invades the present. The private "ghosts" of a haunted imagination are thus transposed into the public spectacle of the "ghost in the machine," since the fundamental effect of cinema is to make us see ghosts – or "spectral images" – at will.

As Matsuda suggests in his title, "Spectacles: Machineries of Magic," film is a crucial determinant of modernity by virtue of its "relentless telescoping of time in which the boundaries between past and present appear to dissolve" (166). One recalls how these boundaries are dissolved in Wilfred Owen's "Dulce et Decorum Est" by a nightmare image that comes to haunt the present with its vivid actuality: "In all my dreams before my helpless sight / He plunges at me, guttering, choking, drowning" (66). But, as we have seen, Owen's "nightmare" image also depends – even more than Sassoon's – on several cinematic techniques such as the long shot, the panning shot, and the extreme close-up, all juxtaposed in an artful montage. Sassoon has merely to invoke the "spectral" character of the image to let us see its true relevance to "that dream cinematograph" whose images can be "real" and "ghostly" in the same instant. And we grasp at last why the "double vision" of the war-haunted poet is neither morbid nor insane, but is more likely a basis for "modern memory," where the present is regularly invaded by the past and where the immediacy of the "specular image" makes distance difficult to achieve. Indeed, the larger story of Sassoon's personal journey concerns his largely instinctive struggle with several kinds of temporal displacements, as well as with these new and unsettling perceptual frameworks created by cinematic technology.

TEMPORAL DISPLACEMENTS

The ghost-in-the-machine had immediately enabled film to generate "superbly real living records while simultaneously creating its own fantastically unsettling perceptual and temporal frameworks"

(Matsuda 167). When *The Memoirs of George Sherston* are set in this light, the structure of memory in parts of the trilogy becomes less incomprehensible to print-formed minds. Paul Fussell, for one, has judged *Sherston's Progress* to be "the least artistic among the three volumes" of Sassoon's "memoirs," since "there are signs of impatience and fatigue. One such sign is the frequent and sometimes embarrassingly self-conscious auctorial intrusions which shatter the verisimilitude, like this chapter opening: 'Sitting myself down at the table to resume this laborious task after twenty-four hours' rest, I told myself that I was "really feeling fairly fresh again"'" (100). What Fussell laments as a loss of verisimilitude looks different, however, in light of film's temporal paradigm, where the viewer is overtaken by "the directness of image and compression of time which the camera itself created, an immediacy which annihilated temporal order, distance, and reflection" (Matsuda 170). Within this new perceptual framework, reason is easily overwhelmed by playback – or by the invasive power of the image – much as the narrator finds himself overwhelmed by the apparitions threatening his reason. Initially, the narrator can do little but erect defences against the immediacy of the invasive image. In other words, the constant replay of his "camera-eye" memories sharply interferes with the shaping vision of the poet; the soldier's instant "playback" even threatens to eclipse the narrator's reflection.

"Another index of fatigue," in Fussell's print-formed estimate, "is Sassoon's leaving seventy-three pages in something close to their original form as diary, without troubling to transmute them into something closer to fiction" (100). What this critique ignores is the filmic immediacy of events recalled from the diary; quite literally, the diary annihilates the historical order by importing the present tense of the event, here and now, into the novel's past-tense narration. One of the usual comforts of first-person narrative is its assurance that the teller has lived to tell the tale; the crisis or danger or misunderstanding has already been surmounted in a retrospective telling, or is otherwise disarmed by distance in time. A brother officer's story in *Infantry Officer* is paradigmatic: "It had been his first experience of shell-fire. Narrating his numerous escapes from hostile explosives, he continually invoked the name of the founder of his religion; now that it was all over he enjoyed the retrospective excitement, roaring with laughter while he told us how he and his men had flung themselves on their faces in the mud. Rees never minded making himself look ridiculous, and I began to feel that he was capable of taking care of himself"

(211). In effect, a relieved chronicler gains control of the threatening event by speaking from a later time; he has lived to tell the tale. And yet Sassoon, who often mixes diary entries with past-tense narration in earlier volumes of *The Memoirs of George Sherston,* now seems compelled to relive the very moments that had threatened to destroy him. So the past comes back to invade the present of reading in the present-tense form of the diary, thereby interrupting the past-perfect tense by which the narrator would otherwise gain distance on events. (What this assumption most obviously ignores is the distance already achieved in the author's naming of the diarist as George Sherston rather than Siegfried Sassoon. But more of this ontological doubling later.)

Just as revealing in terms of perceptual frameworks is Fussell's assumption that Sassoon's diary intrudes on Sherston's past-tense narration only in the final volume of the trilogy. One need but recall the longing for immediacy in that earlier diary scene quoted from *Infantry Officer* to recognize the consolations of presentness. To extend the extract: "Sky full of lark songs. Sometimes you can count thirty slowly and hear no sound of a shot; then the muffled pop of a rifle or a slamming 5.9 or one of our 18 pounders. Then a burst of machine-gun fire. Westward the yellow sky with a web of filmy cloud half across the sun; the ridges with blurred outlines of trees. An aeroplane droning overhead" (30–1). A verbal analogue of an "establishing shot," or even the pictorial and auditory details of the images, are not what makes them filmic; rather, it is the collapse of temporal boundaries in that long interval between the narrator's "I remember" (29) and the diarist's immediate image of "an aeroplane droning overhead" (31). Such a dramatic collapse of temporal boundaries makes sense only in terms of film's epistemic bias.

Take another scene from *Infantry Officer,* where George remembers (in the past tense) watching the opening of the Somme offensive on the first of July, "[f]rom the support-trench, which Barton called 'our opera box'" (74). Only now, he does more than cast himself as a compulsive watcher recording images that pass before his eyes like "the horrors" later crawling across his floor; he explicitly renounces any claim to later perspectives in time, resorting instead to a "small shiny black note-book" that "contains my pencilled particulars," since "nothing will be gained by embroidering them with afterthoughts. I cannot turn my field-glasses on to the past." In a single, decisive gesture, he exempts his narrator from further obligation to distance himself from events, or to arrive at a new understanding based on his later position in time. To the contrary, he seems perfectly willing to let his past self speak for his present self.

By reproducing a long excerpt from his diary at this point in his past-tense account, the narrator of *Infantry Officer* also succumbs to his longing for "presentness," or immediacy, most notably where it is expressed in the untransmuted present tense of the past – or what I call the "past-progressive-present tense" – of raw film footage:

7.45. The barrage is now working to the right of Fricourt and beyond. I can see the 21st Division advancing about three-quarters of a mile away on the left and a few Germans coming to meet them, apparently surrendering ...

9.30. Came back to dug-out and had a shave. 21st Division still going across the open, apparently without casualties. The sunlight flashes on bayonets as the tiny figures move quietly forward and disappear beyond mounds of trench debris. A few runners come back and ammunition parties go across ...

9.50. Fricourt half-hidden by clouds of drifting smoke, blue, pinkish and grey. Shrapnel bursting in small bluish-white puffs with tiny flashes... I can see seven of our balloons, on the right. On the left our men still filing across in twenties and thirties. Another huge explosion in Fricourt and a cloud of brown-pink smoke. Some bursts are yellowish.

10.5. I can see the Manchesters down in New Trench, getting ready to go over. Figures filing down the trench. Two of them have gone out to look at our wire gaps! Have just eaten my last orange ... I am staring at a sunlit picture of Hell, and still the breeze shakes the yellow weeds, and the poppies glow under Crawley Ridge where some shells fell a few minutes ago. (74–6) (ellipses mine)

Many of the more picturesque elements in this "sunlit picture of Hell" support Sassoon's later claim in *Siegfried's Journey* that he had become intent on describing the war "in a comprehensive way, seeing it like a painter" (70). And yet the presentness of his diary account does not suggest distance and reflection, or even expansion toward some sort of "transcendent" perspective. Rather, the reverse is true: that he greatly constricts the moment by conflating past and present in a fundamental reordering of represented time.

Other passages in *Infantry Officer*, however, show the mind of a poet (or novelist) at work in editing the soldier/diarist's raw "footage." Cinema, of course, is an art form that is born on the cutting room floor, demanding decisions on images that are inevitably mediated for all their seeming immediacy. A remarkable example of such editing emerges from a scene, first recorded in his diary of 21 July 1916, where Sassoon is waiting for elements of the battalion to return to rest-billets from a week of fighting in the Somme Offensive: "The road where I sat was a moonlit picture (I sat among some oats and watched the procession of the Seventh Division). Guns and limbers, men sitting stiffly on tired horses – transport – cookers – they rolled and jolted past in the moonshine. Then, like flitting ghosts, last began to come the foot-weary infantry – stumbling – limping – straggling back after eight days in hell – more or less" (97).

In the novel, the scene has a similar beginning: "An hour before dawn the road was still an empty picture of moonlight ... Then the procession of the returning troops began. The camp-fires were burning low when the grinding jolting column lumbered back. The field guns came first, with nodding men sitting stiffly on weary horses, followed by waggons [*sic*] and limbers and field-kitchens" (116). But at this point one finds a marked elision: "After this rumble of wheels came the infantry, shambling, limping, straggling and out of step. If anyone spoke it was only a muttered word, and the mounted officers rode as if asleep" (116). What had appeared with such immediacy in the *Diaries* – the infantry passing "like flitting ghosts" – is delayed by a gradual recognition of a significance still latent in the scene: "Thus, with an almost spectral appearance, the lurching brown figures flitted past with slung rifles and heads bent forward under basin-helmets" (117). An "almost spectral appearance" of war-weary soldiers may well recall other men in ancient epics returning from the banks of the Stygian shore, many of them more dead than alive. But it is the living men in *Infantry Officer* who take on the appearance of the "spectral images" first described in the *Diaries* as "the horrors" that had "come creeping across the floor" (161). The novelist's distance in time from "the horrors" finally enables him to conflate his private "ghosts" with the more public image of "spectral" survivors, thereby comprehending the unnerving spectacle of the death-in-life that he meets at "the crossroads" (*Infantry* 115).

It is the filmmaker's temporal vision that is also projected onto the screen of memory in three sentences added to the original account from the diary: "Soon they had dispersed and settled down on the hillside, and were asleep in the daylight which made everything seem ordinary. None the less I had seen something that night which over-awed me. It was all in the day's work – an exhausted Division return-ing from the Somme Offensive – but for me it was as though I had watched an army of ghosts" (117). What the novelist reserves for a climax to this scene works like a tiny film clip, where "an army of ghosts" appears to be both dead (the "spectral" image captured in a sequence of still frames) and alive at the same time (the moving image resurrected in a beam of projected light). "It was as though I had seen the War as it might be envisioned," he concludes in one haunting, fi-nal sentence, "by the mind of some epic poet a hundred years hence." What he appears to foresee is how the future will henceforth be in-vaded by the past (or is it the present?) through the power of the "spectral image." The "filmmaker" has done more than to escape the catastrophe; he has made himself ubiquitous in time.

A second vision from the future offers a different sort of "spec-tral" image in *Infantry Officer,* in a scene where Sherston waits in the Hindenburg Tunnel to lead his bombing party in support of an-other regiment at the Battle of Arras. (The vision is missing from the diary's account of the attack on 16 April 1917.) When the signal to move finally reaches him after an interminable wait of two hours, George is startled by what he sees: "As I got up from the ta-ble on which we'd been leaning our elbows, a blurred version of my face looked at me from the foggy mirror with an effect of clairvoy-ance. Hoping that this was an omen of survival, I went along to the rendezvous-shaft and satisfied myself that the bombing Parties were sitting on the stairs in a bone-chilling draught, with my two subor-dinate officers in attendance" (230). What he spies is literally noth-ing more than a mirror image of himself; but what he sees figuratively is an assurance of his survival in the form of a clairvoy-ant double who stands outside this time of danger, another version of himself existing in doubled time and doubled space where he is bound to appear again. In other words, what the novelist adds to his diary account of the scene is an image of this later perspective in time, where the self who survives the battle looks back on a "spec-tre" of himself, itself the perfect analogue of a moving image. If the teller has survived to tell the tale, his double has also survived the moment of danger, appearing now to be as "real" on the "screen" of the teller's memory as the latter is in the camera-eye of the soldier. The two times are thus telescoped into a single instant.

ONTOLOGICAL DOUBLINGS

Paul Fussell identifies "a habit of simpleminded binary vision" (100) in *The Memoirs of George Sherston* that "is elaborately structured to enact the ironic redemption of a shallow fox-hunting man by terrible events" (102). To support his thesis "that there seems to be one dominating form of modern understanding, that it is essentially ironic; and that it originates largely in the application of mind and memory to the events of the Great War" (35), Fussell derives this binary habit of mind from "the binary deadlock" of the war (77). But to impose a series of oppositions on the external world – a series rooted in the reductive absurdity of "'us' and 'them' " (79) – is far more likely to occlude a more significant habit of double vision in Sassoon's writing that leads to a very different binary of selves doubled in space and time, thereby producing something akin to the ontological confusions of the first viewers of film.

There are some obvious ontological confusions in the mirror scene in *Infantry Officer*, as Sherston finds himself staring back at himself from both sides of the glass. In that fleeting instant, is the soldier still the observer, or is he the one being observed? Similar confusions abounded at the unveiling of the Lumière brothers' projection system in Lyon in June, 1895. The newspaper *Le Progrès* reported that a certain M. Janssen and a M. Lagrange were both present in the room where their moving images appeared to the assembled viewers. Disconcertingly, their "gestures were reproduced with such accuracy that one could have supposed behind the screen the complicity of two characters playing a fantasmagoric story, and yet there they were in the room" (cited by Matsuda 174). But how could they be present simultaneously in the time of the moving image and in the time of collective viewing? How could they be present in two places at once? Indeed, the very presence of Messrs Janssen and Lagrange to their own moving images raised deeply unsettling questions. Who was observing whom? Could these spectral doubles be watching them as intently as they were watching their own moving images?

Neither *Le Progrès* nor *Memoirs of an Infantry Officer* was to make the dizzying leap of Lewis Carroll's Alice through the looking glass. Sherston, for example, does not think that he has ceased to occupy ordinary space in the mirror scene, only that he has come to occupy other spaces (and times) simultaneously. So, too, in *Sherston's Progress,* George is suddenly conscious of hearing himself speak "as though I were a third person in the room – saying, rather hurriedly and not at all in the grand manner, 'I was getting things into focus a bit while you were away and I see now that the only thing for me to do is to get back to the front as quick as I can'" (60). At this moment, he does not yet see himself retrospectively as a different person, acquiescing in the sensible advice of his psychologist Dr. W. H. R. Rivers to explore his moral contradictions. To the contrary, he sees himself in the instant as both the observer and as the one observed. In some respects, he continues to struggle with his old "difficulties of combining the functions of soldier and poet," which is to say the opposing roles of an actor and a watcher, as well as those opposing functions that had troubled him in the *Diaries* as early as 1918 (270). And so Sherston's "progress," which is announced in 1936, has finally to be measured in terms of the means his author uses to reconcile him to his "double vision."

At the beginning of part II, "Liverpool and Limerick," George still measures "progress" by the device of temporal doubling, through which he is able in a conventional way to look back (and down) at several selves who have passed this way before:

It is not impossible that on my way back to Clitherland I compared my contemporary self with previous Sherstons who had reported themselves for duty there.

First the newly-gazetted young officer, who had yet to utter his first word of command – anxious only to become passably efficient for service at the front. (How young I had been then – not much more than two and a half years ago!) Next came the survivor of nine months in France, (the trenches had taught *him* a thing or two anyhow) less diffident, and inclined, in a confused way, to ask the reason why everyone was doing and dying under such soul-destroying conditions. Thirdly arrived that somewhat incredible mutineer who had made up his mind that if a single human being could help to stop the war by making a fuss, he was that veritable man.

There they were, those three Sherstons; and here was I – the inheritor of their dim renown. (93–4)

This is fairly conventional as a recognition scene, structured as it is by the rule of an observed and observing self, first employed at the end of the fourth century in Augustine's *Confessions*.[25] The observing self (or, rather, the one who writes) becomes the successor to the one who acts (or is observed), and so stands as both an "inheritor" and a judge of the former's "dim renown."

Given the traditional character of this narrative self-division, a modern reader might not be prepared at all for what is truly modern in Sherston's next confession: "A ruminator really needs two lives; one for experiencing and another for thinking it over. Knowing that I *need* two lives and am only allowed one, I do my best to *lead* two lives" (104). Flouting the Christian tradition of conversion, or the supersedence of a "fallen" self by a "redeemed" self, Sherston quite abruptly (and alarmingly) insists on maintaining their simultaneous existence.

Pat Barker has dramatized this trope of a "double life" in *The Eye in the Door* (1993), the second novel in her *Regeneration* trilogy about Sassoon and his era, in terms of a Jekyll-and-Hyde complex that she regards as a normal, rather than pathological, instance of personal identity. In a variety of ways, her fictional character Billy Prior comes to the same conclusion as her "real-life" characters, Sassoon and Dr. Rivers, about leading two lives at once. Here, the conflict between the soldier and the poet, the actual conflict endured by the historical Sassoon, is generalized as a psychological law, brilliantly analyzed by Barker's Rivers:

> Siegfried had always coped with the war by being two people: the anti-war poet and pacifist; the bloodthirsty, efficient company commander. The dissociation couldn't be called pathological, since experience gained in one state was available to the other. Not just *available*: it was the serving officer's experience that furnished the raw material, the ammunition, if you liked, for the poems. More importantly, and perhaps more ambiguously, that experience of bloodshed supplied the moral authority for the pacifist's protest: a *soldier's* declaration. No wonder Pinto's innocent question had precipitated something of a crisis. (233)

Rivers' analysis of Sassoon's condition now enables the psychologist to reach a universalizing conclusion about his own experience, given fairly similar oppositions in his life between his past identity as an anthropologist in the Solomon Islands and his present identity as a neurologist at Cambridge University. "It had not been merely a matter of living two different lives," he thinks,

> divided between the dons of Cambridge and the missionaries and head-hunters of Melanesia, but of being a different person in the two places. It was his Melanesian self he preferred, but his attempts to integrate that self into his way of life in England had produced nothing but frustration and misery. Perhaps, contrary to what was usually supposed, duality was the stable state; the attempt at integration, dangerous. Certainly Siegfried had found it so. (235)

If it is impossible to overcome psychic duality in *The Eye in the Door,* it is likely because Pat Barker imagines Sassoon as being unable to live his differing selves simultaneously.

It is nonetheless possible to read *Sherston's Progress* as a textbook case of how to lead two lives at once. The poet who wrote most of *Counter-Attack* in Craiglockhart Hospital as a protest against the war did return to the Western Front in the summer of 1918, just in time to raid another German trench (though apparently without aggressive intent), before turning back toward his own front line where a sentry furrowed his scalp with a bullet, sending him back to a London hospital. "I wanted to do something definite," the man of action says, "and perhaps get free of the whole thing" (259). Here, the reflective man adds that, "I should admire that vanished self of mine more if he had avoided taking needless risks. I blame him for doing his utmost to prevent my being here to write about him. But on the other hand I am grateful to him for giving me something to write about" (259–60). Even at this late date, the reflective man likes to think of himself as two distinct beings whose actions are separated by a tract of years.

But then he catches sight of "a sort of intermediate version of myself, who afterwards developed into what I am now; I see him talking volubly to Velmore and Howitt on the way back to company H.Q., and saying good-bye with a bandaged head and assuring them that he'd be back in a week or two" (270). And so this "intermediate" self literally comes to mediate between his "vanished" self and "what I am now," much as all three novels mediate among the diaries and the formal autobiography, *Siegfried's Journey.* In the formal doubling of a man variously identified as George Sherston and Siegfried Sassoon, we follow the process by which such temporal and ontological doublings of the self converge on an "intermediate version of myself," literally a self located in the space *between* differing media and among all these doubled texts.

In terms of the cinematic epistemology that authorizes this all-embracing "double vision" of Siegfried Sassoon, it seems that the only possible way to lead two lives at once is to be, as it were, on-screen and off-screen simultaneously. In terms of the medium in which the writer works, however, his ontological double is literally generated by his inclusion of two kinds of texts that stand side by side: the text of the "thinking" man and the text of the "experiencing" man, in which both voices come to occupy the same space: "And two days later he is still talking rather wildly, but he is talking to himself now, and scribbling it down with a pencil as he lies in a bed at No. 8 Red Cross Hospital, Boulogne. It is evidence of what I have just written, so I will reproduce it" (270).

In each of these ongoing acts of "reproduction" – both in the sense of making and of preserving simultaneous images of the soldier and the poet, Sassoon the "ruminator" intervenes to set his double vision in a perpetual present, "talking to himself now," but also talking to us who exist both in the future and in his past, watching a whole "army of ghosts" go by in living, moving images that hauntingly compel us to believe we have in fact "seen the War as it might be envisioned by the mind of some epic poet a hundred years hence" (*Infantry* 117).

PART FOUR

Photo / Play:
Seeing Time and (Hearing) Relativity

7

Photographic Memory:
"A Force of Interruption" in *The Wars*

That memory is structured photographically in Timothy Findley's *The Wars* (1977) is a critical commonplace. But, despite a wealth of commentary on the novel's photographic technique, we have yet to understand the real significance of its shift from the present-tense immediacy of combatant narratives like *All Quiet on the Western Front,* or the blending of diaries and retrospective narration in *The Memoirs of George Sherston,* to the photograph as "a force of interruption." Part of this critical neglect originates in Timothy Findley's own comments on photography as a generative force in the writing: "I began to get flashes of something, and what it was, was a sentence I put down. 'Robert Ross arrived at Boulogne and got off the ship and walked across the encampment toward the train.' Then the image continued with the number of tents: the picture – it's like a developing picture in the pan, that comes more and more into focus, and more and more into view" (Aitken 80). In another interview given to his partner William Whitehead for the *Findley* special issue of *Canadian Literature* in 1981, the novelist focused more on the visual structure of his novel and rather less on its composition: "*The Wars* unfolds as a series of pictures. Pictures and interviews." Of course, he added, the problem was "to find the right pictures and find the right characters to interview" (Findley, "Alice" 16).

In the interview with Johan Aitken, Findley also offered an extratextual image of the novel – ignored for the most part in the criticism – that makes the literary text a virtual mutation of a visual medium. This image is all the more telling because it emplots the story as a long avenue of time down which Robert Ross comes riding on a horse past "billboards [set] on an angle on either side of this avenue. Flashing on these billboards are the selected photographs, the images that I wanted to imprint of moments from that war, moments from Robert's life, moments from history" (84). The literary text has yet to be integrated with this informing image in ways that reveal the larger significance of photography as a force of interruption, which is to say a force of mutation, in the novel.

In the photograph, as in its verbal equivalent, a new phenomenology of time begins to emerge, a phenomenology in which the cyclical experience of daily or yearly time, or the linear sense of time as historical continuity, gives way to an atomized sense of time whereby distance, difference, death, delay, danger, and discontinuity become the rule. In a crucial way, Findley's protagonist, Robert Ross, is distanced from his own contemporaries by an archival narrator and differentiated from his historical moment by a photographic technique that would sever all continuity between his era and ours, freeing him to come riding down the light rays, in cinematic fashion, into our age. As a book of interruptions, *The Wars* dramatizes a photographic structure of delay that then leads to a belated recognition of the image's latency, its danger, and its discontinuity. But, as a formal expression of writing with light, the novel also embodies this medium that first enabled us to "see" history. *The Wars* asks to be read, in other words, as a text about historicism, about the hidden connections between history and photography, so reminding us why history as a modern discipline should attend the advent of photography.[26]

CAMERA OBSCURA

Treating the photographic technique of *The Wars* in thematic terms, critics tend to obscure the philosophical implications of this medium in the novel. John Hulcoop, for example, writes in the Findley special issue of *Canadian Literature* how "Findley's fascination with stories told in the form of pictures (as in picture-books and films) is obvious. Much of his own story-telling has been done in the medium of television, and a great part of the TV script consists quite literally of visuals" (Hulcoop 39). While Hulcoop's subtitle urges the necessity of "Paying Attention to Timothy Findley's Fictions" (22), his essay stops short of identifying photography as the silent protagonist of the novel. Conversely, Eva-Marie Kröller makes photography an antagonist in *The Wars* in an essay published in the same year,

arguing that it revolved "around a series of experiences each implying a *camera obscura*" (70). She isolates a series of confining rooms
(*camerae*) in the novel, all of which connote "the threatening posses-
sion of dark boxes," sharply limiting Robert's perception. Suffering
from the inherent violence of "Western frames of thought" which
destroy, as much as they confirm, "man's central position" (69) in
the world, the protagonist is thus set at odds with this apparatus of a
sovereign Cartesian cogito that enforces its dominance over both the
human and non-human world. But to claim that "Robert is a long-
distance runner either evading still frames or exploding them once
he is trapped in them" (71) is finally to argue that the narrator is his
enemy, and to say that Robert is a victim, not the heroic destroyer, of
this supposed photographic technology of suppression.

Sensing that it "is the photographic style which accounts for much
of the powerful impact of *The Wars*," Lorraine M. York (1988) focuses more properly on "Findley's growing awareness" of the "suspended quality of certain moments in our existence" that, in this
novel, "accompanies an increasing value for the past and for human
memory" (76, 77). Rejecting Kröller's notion of the "threatening enclosure" of the *camera obscura*, York argues that the archival narrator and soldier join in a "conception of the photograph as the
preserver of all that is precious and alive" (84). Much as Robert tries
to save the lives of animals amidst the brutalities of war, the archival
narrator makes a narrative "attempt to capture the essence of Robert
Ross's life" (84). Were this the whole of the story – that photography, like memories preserved in narrative, are life-sustaining – the
ambivalence about photography that Kröller rightly sees in the protagonist would not be so disturbing. The novel will not allow us to
forget that the photograph, in its pre-digital history, has to take the
form of a ghostly negative before it is made into a positive print.

Evelyn Cobley does not neglect the ambiguous status of photography in *The Wars*, allowing that its documents are all "mediated by a
researcher-narrator who interposes himself between the reader and
the already technically reproduced reality they denote. This double
mediation signals an acknowledgement of fiction-making which the
earlier war narratives sought to ward off through documentary
guarantees" ("Postmodernist" 108). In this way, Findley escapes the
usual trap of combatant narratives that document the horrors of
war, only to reproduce "the ideological assumptions of modernity"
in its lamentable failure "to deliver the promise of universal human

emancipation" (99). As Cobley sees it, "duplication" and "duplicity" are the ground of the photograph, which, in Derridean fashion, dooms it to "*différance*" instead of "sameness." Given its status as a supplement marked by the absence of the subject, the photograph reveals why "Findley should have chosen the theme of death to illustrate this process of sense-making as a process of substitutions" (112). For "neither verbal nor visual images can recuperate what is lost; they can only interminably speak their nostalgia for the traces of the past." Oddly, Cobley ends by reinscribing "an ethic of nostalgia for origins, an ethic of archaic and natural innocence, of a purity of presence and self-presence in speech" (Derrida 264), so undermining her own deconstructive project.

The first essay to remark the interruptive force of the photograph in *The Wars* is still unsurpassed. Laurie Ricou's "Obscured by Violence" (1979), too rarely cited, shows how "the narrator is repeatedly and uneasily trying to establish his distance from Robert Ross" by means of narrative interruptions. "Breaks and pauses, involuntary repetition, and occasional complete stoppage of words," as he inventories Findley's style, "are characteristic of the stammering, interrupted syntax and structure of the novel" (133). Therefore, "[t]he brevity of sections, paragraphs, and sentences catch the fragmentary, but also suggest that the narrator cuts himself off: there is so much that 'could not be told' " (135). While the narrator may rely on photographs as "the art form of the Great War, the chief means of remembering that war, as film might be the art form of the Second World War, or videotape of the Vietnam war" (132), Ricou stops short of recognizing them as Findley's means of detaching Robert from his own time; rather, it is the narrator's story that "opens stammering" (129), in much the same way that Robert does himself, as doubt "stammers in his brain" (*Wars* 6). Should the narrator's story end only if and when he accepts Ross as a mirror of himself, then distance becomes more a dramatic condition in need of resolution than a property of photography itself. If one were to see, rather, how the narrator's position echoes that of Robert jogging with a coyote on the prairie – "Distance was safety. Space was asylum" (32) – then the quest of the protagonist would be better aligned with the narrator's quest. In words borrowed from the narrator himself, "There was nothing to be won but distance" (25) by such a photographic technique.

A FORCE OF INTERRUPTION

In his illuminating monograph on Walter Benjamin's "persistent recourse to the language of photography in his discussions of history"
(xix), Eduardo Cadava argues that Benjamin's concept of the "thesis" is "[l]ike the gaze of the camera that momentarily fixes history
in an image ... A photograph in prose, the thesis names a force of
arrest" (xx). Because Benjamin holds that "historical thinking in-
volves 'not only the movements of thoughts, but their arrest as
well,'" Cadava concludes that, "For Benjamin, there can be no history without the Medusa effect – without the capacity to arrest or
immobilize historical movement, to isolate the detail of an event
from the continuum of history" (59). In his "Theses on the Concept
of History," for example, "Benjamin traces the effects of what he
calls 'the caesura in the movement of thought'" (xx). What Benjamin
sees in the instant of a shutter-click is a "Medusa's gaze [that] stalls
history in the sphere of speculation. It short-circuits, and thereby
suspends, the temporal continuity between a past and a present."
Indeed, it is this "break from the present" that "enables the reread-
ing and rewriting of history" (59). What Benjamin isolates in his
"Theses" is "the caesura of the historical event, the separation and
discontinuity from which history emerges" (xx).

Such a "caesura in the movement of thought" is evident in the repeated starts and stops of the opening chapters of *The Wars*. An image of a horse, a dog and a man in the "Prologue" forms a virtual
snapshot of immobility before it gives way after six staccato paragraphs to motion: "They rode down the track towards the road to
Magdalene Wood." But no sooner is the horse in motion than it
halts, whinnies, and is answered "from inside" an abandoned railway car. Four sentences later, "Robert was riding" again, this time
"behind a hundred and thirty horses with the dog trotting beside
him ... This was when the moon rose – red" (2). Here is where the
prologue breaks off and the first chapter – a single paragraph –
begins: "All of this happened a long time ago" (3). Such a shift from
historical subject to historian is not as complete as it might seem,
however, in this move from the past progressive into the past perfect
tense. First-person witnesses to events remain in the narrative – if
not combatants, at least those "who played a part in it." But these
witnesses won't say what they have seen: "Ask what happened,

they say: 'I don't know.' Mention Robert Ross – they look away. 'He's dead,' they tell you. This is not news. 'Tell me about the horses, you ask. Sometimes, they weep at this. Other times they say: 'that bastard!' " "In the end" – a brief chapter is further foreshortened – "the only facts you have are public. Out of these you make what you can" (3).

"You" make what you can out of what every historian has to work with – primary sources. "You begin at the archives with photographs" (3), but only a glimpse is given of the bundles of letters Robert sent home from the Front – "All these letters neatly folded and tied" (73) after being "numbered and catalogued and memorized" (153) by his long-suffering mother. Two brief excerpts (51, 71) of this word-hoard are all that enter the record, amounting to barely a page in a novel of 218 pages. Closing the book on an epistolary narrative that could have recounted events in the first person, Findley thus eschews a major convention of Great War combatant narratives. (He was born too late himself – 1930 – to have served in the First World War, and not soon enough to have served in the Second.) From the outset, his soldier is thus distanced from us in time and narrative perspective.

A more formal "interruption" will emerge in an archival scene of looking in the next chapter, composed as a photographic layout: "Spread over table tops, a whole age lies in fragments underneath the lamps" (3). Composed of a single paragraph, this tiny second chapter manages to cram seventeen sentences into fourteen lines. By its end, we know that the story is going to be made out of fragments and displayed, as it were, in an "album" of fragmented instants: "As the past moves under your fingertips, part of it crumbles. Other parts, you know you'll never find. This is what you have" (4).

From a theoretical, rather than formal, point of view, what we have is a stoppage in the flow of time; the "force of arrest" in the photographic technique literally disrupts the organic continuity of older notions of temporality, whether these be governed by an idea of historical cycles – the Eternal Return, the Great Year, etc. – or by a Heraclitean model of "time as a flow, or river" (Bal 7). Although the photographic image is "cut from that flow, a frozen moment, or suspension" of it (7), it marks "[a] return without return," an "eternal return" that "tells us that the photographed, once photographed, can never return to itself – it can only appear in its withdrawal in the form of an image or reproduction" (Cadava 42).

Isolating the moment from its context, the photograph breaks the cycle, for "what is repeated is a process of becoming, a movement of differentiation and dispersion – and what is differentiated and dispersed is time itself" (31).

Conversely, since "the photographic event interrupts the present" as a continuous flow, it "interrupts history and opens up another possibility of history, one that spaces time and temporalizes space. A force of arrest, the image translates an aspect of time into something like a certain *space,* and does so without stopping time, or without preventing time from being time" (61). "Looking both backward and forward," Cadava writes, "this figure marks a division within the present. Within the almost-no-time of the camera's click, we can say that something *happens.* For Benjamin, however, for something to happen does not mean that something occurs within the continuum of time, nor does it imply that something becomes present. Rather, the photographic event interrupts the present; it occurs *between* the present and itself, between the movement of time and itself" (61).

By separating the moment from itself, the photographic event actually atomizes time, making it possible to "see" time as a conglomerate of particles. The result is a phenomenology that differs from older conceptions of time as "eternal return" or as linear flow. And since the photographic event marks a division within the present, it "names a process that, seizing and tearing an image from its context, works to immobilize the flow of history" (xx). More precisely, "in the interruption of its movement," the photographic event "tears the image to be read from its context. This tearing or breaking force is not an accidental predicate of reading; it belongs to its very structure. Only when reading undoes the context of an image is a text developed, like a photographic negative, toward its full historical significance" (65).

The verbal snapshot of "1915" that opens the overwrought third chapter of *The Wars* is but one example of this tearing or breaking force in the medium of photography. "The year itself," which "looks sepia and soiled," turns remote, as if "muddied like its pictures" (4). "Part of what you see you recognize," but the images of recruitment parades still bristle with interrupted motion: "Everyone is focused, now, shading their eyes against the sun. Everyone is watching with an outstretched arm – silenced at the edge of wharves and time" (5). It is this silence, as much as the sepia colour of the images themselves, that works to distance us from a scene we contemplate, but in which we do not participate. As readers, we are now firmly detached from the objects of our gaze.

At least until "*Robert Ross comes riding straight towards the camera ... There is mud on his cheeks and forehead and his uniform is burning – long, bright tails of flame are streaming out behind him. He leaps through memory without a sound*" (5). A sudden eruption of italics prepares us to see this latter image as existing in another dimension – one that has already been interiorized, or moved into "memory" – if it exists at all on paper (shutter speeds in 1915 making it unlikely that an image of Robert's equestrian leap would come into focus anywhere but in memory or imagination). In fact, the narrator tells us, "*You lay the fiery image back in your mind and let it rest. You know it will obtrude again and again until you find its meaning – here*" (6). "Here" is most likely the page itself, if not "here" in the domain of memory. Although a moving image thus arises to challenge a static photograph, the narrator prefers for now to "let it rest." Another dynamic of narrative may then emerge out of this tension between distance and proximity, between the externalized image and one that has already been interiorized.

PROXIMITY AND DISTANCE

A dynamic "oscillation between space and time, between distance and proximity," Cadava suggests, "touches on the very nature of photographic and filmic media, whose structure consists in the simultaneous reduction and maximization of distance" (xxv). While the photograph appears "to reduce ... the distance between people and events, or people and places," this effect "only enables it to install a greater distance. If it brings people and events or places together at all, it is only in order to keep them apart" (xxiv). This is surely the case in *The Wars* where images of *Thomas Ross and Family* are brought together in 1915 with images of crowds on the home front. On the one hand, the family "stand beside a new Ford Truck" in a picture printed "in the *Toronto Mail and Empire*" (6), trumpeting the family's donation of an ambulance to a Field Surgery Hospital that will bear their name. If the Ross family is brought close to the public as a model of sacrifice in the cause of "King and Empire," they also remain distant, their private life veiled by several levels of absence, most notably that of Rowena, their eldest child, who "is not shown. She is never in photographs that are apt to be seen by the public" (6). Although a "*hydrocephalic*" (7) child might "taint" the family's public image, "Robert has her picture on his bureau" (6) in a private expression of fraternal love. His preservation of his sister's portrait in the sanctum of his bedroom thus links him to the narrator who has already preserved his image in this act of interiorization.

In parallel fashion, the narrator acts in the preceding paragraph to distance Robert from a public absolutely besotted by marching troops and martial music: "A Band is assembled on the Band Shell – red coats and white gloves. They serenade the crowd with 'Soldiers of the Queen.' You turn them over – wondering if they'll spill – and you read on the back in the faintest ink in a feminine hand: '*Robert*.' But where? You look again and all you see is the crowd. And the Band is still playing – quite undisturbed – and far from spilled" (6). The narrator's act of turning a photograph over, wondering if its contents will spill, is both close to, and distant from an image of toy soldiers spilled out of a box by a child ignorant of war's reality. In this case, however, it is not the soldiers but an image of Robert himself that "tumbles" out of the frame: "Then you see him: Robert Ross. Standing on the sidelines with pocketed hands – feet apart and narrowed eyes … He doubts the validity in all this martialling of men but the doubt is inarticulate" (6). By such means, Robert is brought closer to us, but is also distanced from us by his marginal position in a distant epoch. In effect, he comes to occupy a role already constructed for the reader: he is also a watcher detached from the object of his gaze.

In other ways, as well, the narrator seeks to isolate Robert from his own historical moment, as if to "rescue" him from a time and place uncongenial to them both. To do so, he enlists contemporary eyewitnesses who are able to speak for the silent images of history he finds in photographs, but who also replicate the operations of photography in tearing the image from its context. Marian Turner, for example, the war nurse who once tended to the burned body of Robert Ross in a field hospital after his desertion, recalls in words the narrator has recorded and preserved on magnetic tape, "that nowadays so many people – young people especially – might've known what he was all about" (10). Her assessment of the war is far from the common opinion of the era in which Robert Ross was court-martialled: "Looking back, I hardly believe what happened.

That the people in that park are there because we all went mad"
(10). At the end of the novel, Marian Turner will once again come
to the aid of the narrator in his "photographic" project of tearing
Robert from his immediate social context and arresting the flow of
time: "I'm a nurse. I've never offered death to anyone. I've prayed
for it often enough. But I've never made the offer. But that night –
surrounded by all that dark – and all those men in pain – and the
trains kept bringing us more and more and more – and the war was
never, never, never going to end – that night, I thought: *I am
ashamed to be alive.* I am ashamed of *life.* And I wanted to offer
some way out of life – I wanted grace for Robert Ross" (215). Although the memories of a Marian Turner bring us closer to the
burned soldier, they also illustrate the significance of a temporal
maxim she takes from Robert: "Not yet" (216).

Further examples of this tension between proximity and distance
appear in the testimony of another eyewitness who, as a twelve-
year-old girl, had fallen in love with the mutinous Canadian soldier.
An elderly Lady Juliet d'Orsey assures the narrator: "You can not
know these things. You live when you live. No one else can ever live
your life and no one else will ever know what you know. Then was
then. Unique" (114). But the intent of her words, like Marian
Turner's "nowadays" – presumably the Vietnam War era in which
the novel was published – is meant to establish Robert as a "hero"
(10) of the future who looks back on the era of the Great War from
the distance of a later age. Both women occupy a position similar to
the narrator who, speaking from this later age himself, constructs
an image of a soldier whose conformity with his era is kept at a distance, but whose contemporary pacifism is portrayed in extreme
close-up.

DIFFERENCE

Where the logic of photographic "arrest" will lead for Benjamin is
to a separation of the thing photographed from itself. In effect,
there is "a withdrawal that is fundamental to the temporal structure of the photograph." Indeed, "[t]here can be no photograph
without the withdrawal of what is photographed" (Cadava 10).
If what is photographed is infinitely reproducible, then what is
reproduced is no longer singular; it "is itself already a reproduction
– and as such, separated from itself" (xxvi). This photographic

separation of the object from itself is also a determining feature of the medium for Siegfried Kracauer, a contemporary of Benjamin whose thinking on photography had an influence on his thought. For Kracauer, "the significance of photography lies not with its ability to reproduce a given object but rather with its ability to tear it away from itself. What makes photography photography is not its capacity to present what it photographs, but its character as a force of interruption" (Cadava xxviii). What the photographic image comes to interrupt is the *being in time* of the object, its radical separation from its own future.

That this is the goal of the historical album chapter in *The Wars* emerges in a later sequence of captioned images, from "*Meg – a Patriotic Pony*" to "*Peggy Ross with Clinton Brown from Harvard!!!* Nothing in Clinton Brown from Harvard's appearance warrants three exclamation points" (7–8). That Robert is supposed to be out of step with his own era is demonstrated long before his enlistment, when he refuses to fight another man, "Because he *loves* me" (13), Heather Lawson says, trying to provoke a jealous response. On what authority this scene is recounted, however, is not made clear.

Nor is it clear by what authority the literal sense of Robert's letters can be denied. The pacifist, or the type, at least, of a more doubtful, questioning warrior is not at all manifest in Robert's letter of embarkation from St. John harbour: "I've written these last few words by lantern light. Green for starboard looking towards the sea. I hope you all can read this – because I can't. So – adios! as the bandits say. Robert Ross. Your son" (51). The swagger of his concluding formula hardly fits the image of his later actions. Nor does the postscript he writes in a second letter sound like the gun-shy officer who supposedly struggles to shoot a horse with a broken leg: "P.S. Do you think you could send the automatic soon? I want it very much. Battery Sergeant-Major says if you could get a Webley .455 Mark I they're the best there is. They're wonderful to fire, and they kill at fifty yards" (71).

Irony – or a hypocritical difference between the outer and inner man – fails to explain, since the private letter really inverts his tenderhearted actions in the hold of the ship. By reducing his cache of letters to two brief fragments, and by framing his literal words with verbal analogues of photographs, the narrator thus manages to tear this image of an eager enlistee away from himself. The photographic image and the man are made to differ conspicuously from one another. But only when the narrator's reading of events undoes the context of the historical image is his text capable of development, like a photographic negative, towards its "full" historical significance.

THE PHOTOGRAPHY OF TIME

Roland Barthes – likely the most influential theorist of photography after Benjamin – writes in *Camera Lucida* (1981) that, in an age before photography, people were resistant "to believing in the past, in History, except in the form of myth." However, "[t]he Photograph, for the first time, puts an end to this resistance; henceforth the past is as certain as the present, what we see on paper is as certain as what we touch. It is the advent of the Photograph – and not, as has been said, of the cinema – which divides the history of the world" (Barthes 87–8). The fact that history and photography both had their birth in the nineteenth century is no coincidence. Benedict Anderson recalls how "the establishment of the first academic chairs in History" took place in 1810 (Berlin) and 1812 (La Sorbonne); but it was not until "the second quarter of the nineteenth century" that "History had become formally constituted as a 'discipline,' with its own elaborate array of professional journals" (194). It was also in this second quarter of the nineteenth century (1827) that Joseph Nicéphore Niepce produced the first "photograph," a blurred image that he called a "heliograph" and that required eight hours of exposure to a silver plate. After his death in 1833, his partner Louis Daguerre helped to revolutionize this cumbersome process of capturing light emanations. "Daguerre's photographs were iodized silver plates exposed in the camera obscura, which had to be turned this way and that until, in the proper light, a pale gray image could be discerned" (Benjamin, "Little History" 508). For obvious reasons, "[t]he procedure itself caused the subject to focus his life in the moment rather than hurrying on past it; during the considerable period of the exposure, the subject (as it were) grew into the picture, in the sharpest contrast with appearances in a snapshot" (514). Talbot Fox's invention of the calotype in 1841 finally reduced the twenty-minute exposure of the daguerreotype (Benjamin 528, n. 1) to something like shutter speed. Thereafter, "advances in optics made instruments available that wholly overcame darkness and recorded appearances as faithfully as any mirror" (517).

If photography influenced the birth of history as a discipline, it did so because it authorized a new view of time. Both Benjamin and Barthes claim that historicism was necessarily founded on the new epistemology of photography,[27] a medium which was obviously "false on the level of perception, [but was] true on the level of time: a temporal hallucination, so to speak, a modest, *shared* hallucination" (Barthes 115). Or, "[i]n the wording of Siegfried Kracauer, 'historicism is concerned with the photography of time' " (Cadava xviii). In Barthes's terms, the viewer of the photograph gains a position outside of time, unlike the viewer of cinema who remains immersed in its flow. "I don't have time," Barthes complains, to think about the images in movies; "in front of the screen, I am not free to shut my eyes; otherwise, opening them again, I would not discover the same image; I am constrained to a continuous voracity; a host of other qualities, but not *pensiveness;* whence the interest, for me, of the photogram" (55). It is only the force of arrest in the photographic image, and its separation from the subject, that enables a viewer to see what is preserved in the image.

More largely still, Barthes expresses a preference for the static image on the basis of its ontology: "I decided I liked Photography *in opposition* to the Cinema, from which I nonetheless failed to separate it. This question grew insistent. I was overcome by an 'ontological' desire: I wanted to learn at all costs what Photography was 'in itself'" (3). What he discovers is that, "[l]ike the real world, the filmic world is sustained by the presumption that, as Husserl says, 'the experience will constantly continue to flow by in the same constitutive style'; but the Photograph breaks the 'constitutive style' (this is its astonishment); it is *without future* (this is its pathos, its melancholy); in it, no protensity, whereas the cinema is protensive, hence in no way melancholic" (89–90).

If cinema speaks in the present progressive tense of images that move in our time, the photograph speaks in "the aorist" tense or absolute past of the arrested image, unlike memory, "whose grammatical expression would be the perfect tense" (91). Unlike the past perfect of a completed action, the aorist tense of the photograph suspends the image in a past forever closed to the future. "This brings the Photograph (certain photographs) close to the Haiku. For the notation of a haiku, too, is undevelopable: everything is given, without provoking the desire for or even the possibility of a rhetorical expansion. In both cases we might (we must) speak of an *intense immobility*" (49). This is the ultimate significance for Barthes of the aorist tense of the photograph: "By giving me the absolute past of the pose (aorist), the photograph tells me death in the future" (96).

DEATH

Such is the significance for Findley's narrator of his penultimate image of Robert Ross which he reports in the *Epilogue:* "Robert is seated on a keg of water. This is at Lethbridge, in the spring of 1915" (217). In his hand Robert seems to "be holding something alive or made of glass. But the object – once you have made it out – is nothing of the sort. It is white and slightly larger than his fist. Magnification reveals it is the skull of some small beast – either a rabbit or a badger. Robert's middle index fingers are crooked through its eyes. You put this picture aside because it seems important" (218). Its importance consists in an "Alas poor Yorick" moment of recognition – a true *memento mori* – that telegraphs Robert's "brotherhood" with the animals, even anticipating his fiery death with the horses. Indeed, in this image of intense immobility, everything is already given; Robert's image is without future except for the death that awaits him. The past is thus absolute, as if the picture were incapable of further development.

Death similarly shadows Benjamin's "little history" of photography, from his commentary on the technology's early requirements to his discussion of the "loss of the aura" in the process of mechanical reproduction. Those portraits, for example, that he reproduces of the pioneering British photographer, David Octavius Hill, "were made in the Edinburgh Greyfriars cemetery" ("Little History" 512), a setting that "could never have been so effective if it had not been chosen on technical grounds. The low light-sensitivity of the early plates made prolonged exposure outdoors a necessity. This in turn made it desirable to take the subject to some out-of-the-way spot where there was no obstacle to quiet concentration" (514). Even when photography moved indoors, its association with death could not be dispelled: "The peeling away of the object's shell, the destruction of the aura, is the signature of a perception whose sense for the sameness of things has grown to the point where even the singular, the unique, is divested of its uniqueness – by means of its reproduction" (519). For that "strange weave of space and time" that Benjamin defined as the aura of the photographic subject, "the unique appearance or semblance of distance, no matter how close it may be" (518), was elided by the fact of its mechanical reproduction. "Seeking to eternalize its objects in the time and space of an image," Cadava enlarges on this premonition of the image's morbidity, "the photographic present returns eternally to the event of its death – a death that comes with the death of understanding. That the photograph is always touched by death means that it offers us a glimpse of a history to which we no longer belong" (Cadava xxviii).

That we no longer belong to a nineteenth-century cult of romantic heroism is writ large in the words a silent icon of Robert Ross is made to speak in his formal portrait:

Oh – I can tell you, sort of, what it might be like to die. *The Death of General Wolfe.* Someone will hold my hand and I won't suffer pain because I've suffered that already and survived. In paintings – and in photographs – there's never any blood. At most, the hero sighs his way to death while linen handkerchiefs are held against his wounds. His wounds are poems. *I'll faint away in glory hearing music and my name. Someone will close my eyes and I'll be wrapped around in flags while drums and trumpets-bagpipes march me home through snow ...* (48–9)

This risible image of the dead hero – a military volunteer who gets his "romantic" notions "from silent images" – reduces him to a ventriloquist's dummy for an imperial history whose icon is General James Wolfe. In the famous image of his *Death* (1771) created by Benjamin West, a colonial painter from Philadelphia, the subject is composed in the visual language of a *Pietà*, where the dying martyr is surrounded by a dozen disciples and is borne up by loving hands that need not stanch his wounds. The promise of this image, it seems, is death without dying, another analogue of the photograph's immortality.

As Cadava explains, "In photographing someone, we know that the photograph will survive him – it begins, even during his life, to circulate without him, figuring and anticipating his death each time it is looked at. The photograph is a farewell. It belongs to the afterlife of the photographed" (13). Nothing more clearly demonstrates this commodification of the soldier-subject in *The Wars* than the words of his photographic afterlife:

> Afterwards, my mother will escort her friends across the rugs and parquet floors to see this photograph of me and everyone will weep and walk on tip-toe. Medals – (there are none just yet, as you can see) – will sit beside this frame in little boxes made of leather lined with satin. I will have the Military Cross. *He died for King and Country* – fighting the war to end all wars.
>   5 × 9 and framed in silver. (49)

In the starkest of terms, the photo-ventriloquist shows how the soldier's image has begun "to circulate without him, figuring and anticipating his death" from the moment it is fixed on photographic paper. And so the logic of the larger narrative, its photographic emplotment, as it were, is that Robert should be required to step out of the picture, to shed his uniform, much as the narrator has already shed Robert's "uniform" image.

DELAY

To Benjamin, the isolation of a photographic image in an instant of time, outside a network of relations that would define it otherwise, opens up an "optical unconscious" ("Little History," 512). As he says, "it is another nature which speaks to the camera rather than to the eye: 'other' above all in the sense that a space informed by human consciousness gives way to a space informed by the unconscious" (510). What the eye sees is of a different order of being than what the camera records; indeed, "we have no idea at all what happens during the fraction of a second when a person actually takes a step. Photography, with its devices of slow motion and enlargement, reveals the secret. It is through photography that we first discover the existence of this optical unconscious, just as we discover the instinctual unconscious through psychoanalysis" (510, 512). In this way, Benjamin makes photography a tool for reading history that is analogous to psychoanalysis as a tool for reading personal histories: "In linking the experience of shock to the structure of delay built into the photographic event, Benjamin evokes Freud's own discussions of the latency of experience, discussions that are themselves often organized in terms of the language of photography"

(Cadava 102). For Benjamin, "[i]t is what is not experienced in an event that paradoxically accounts for the belated and posthumous shock of historical experience" (Cadava 104). For, in this "structure of delay" – a defining element of photography for Benjamin – the latency that is peculiar to individual psychic experience is also realized as being intrinsic to historical experience.

Once we recognize this structure of delay in the photographic technique of *The Wars,* we see what was always latent in the image of *"Robert Raymond Ross – Second Lieutenant,* c.f.a. ... *posed in mind and body"* (48) in full-dress uniform. As Roland Barthes remarks of this pose before the lens, "I constitute myself in the process of 'posing,' I instantaneously make another body for myself, I transform myself in advance into an image" (10). Something else is manifested in the military pose, however, since the image is prefabricated, or socially determined, by martial expectations of heroism. And so the subject of this type of photograph is given over to a loss of self, not only in the technical process of being "objectified, 'thingified,' imaged" (Cadava 8) by an instrument of mechanical reproduction, but also in the general social process of conforming to type: "*Dead men are serious* – that's what this photograph is striving to say. Survival is precluded. Death is romantic – got from silent images. I lived – was young – and died. But not real death, of course, because I'm standing here alive with all these lights that shine so brightly in my eyes" (*Wars* 48). Robert's photographic pose not only signals his withdrawal as a soldier about to embark, or even as an image withdrawing from himself, but as an image cut off from all but a photographic development.

DANGER

If there is a threat of violence in the technological reproduction of the image – as Benjamin maintained in "The Work of Art in an Age of Mechanical Reproduction" (1936), the essay in which he first described the loss of the "aura" or an art work's unique appearance in time and space (*Illuminations* 222–5) – there is also a more hopeful form of violence inherent in photography-as-history. "'To articulate the past historically,' Benjamin writes, 'does not mean to recognize it "as it really was." It means to seize a memory as it flashes up at a moment of danger.' History therefore begins where memory is endangered, during the flash that marks its emergence and disappearance"

(Cadava 63). In distinct opposition to the German war-novelist and fascist theorist Ernst Jünger, Benjamin transforms the notion of "a 'second' consciousness" – or the cold indifference to pain that is supposedly the result of a photographic subject's "ever more marked ability to see oneself as an object" (Cadava 52) – into an idea of the photograph as a "blast" that "'shatters the continuum of history' and in so doing reveals the history hidden in any given work. It discloses the breaks, within history, from which history emerges" (60). The "flash" of the moment in which memory is in danger is a moment for Benjamin in which the movement of history can be arrested, in which history can be thought.

There are many such moments of danger in *The Wars* where a "flash" of memory interrupts the flow of events, making it possible for history to emerge from the break. "There is," for example, "no good picture of this except the one you can make in your mind," as the narrator says in the first sentence of the opening chapter of Part Two. "The road is lost at either end in rain. Robert's perception of it is limited by fog and smoke" (75). The abruptness of the statement dislocates us in time and space; we only gradually come to see what Robert comes to see with horror – that he has led his men onto a crumbling dike where they barely escape drowning. But the role of the reader, like the role of the narrator in this scene, is to "make" in the *camera obscura* of the mind a picture that will interrupt the action, if not penetrate the enveloping fog. The narrator is even confident enough, in the midst of the suspended moment, to survey the topography through which Robert's supply convoy has travelled: "At the centre of the world is Ypres and all around the centre lie the flats of Flanders" (75). The "moment of danger" is now extended, but also arrested, in a series of four swift chapters, at the end of which Robert will extricate his convoy from the bottomless morass of Flemish mud.

A similar photographic technique structures the whole of Part Three, in which a crazed superior, Captain Leather, sends a mortar party under Robert's command to take a position in a deep shell crater where they nearly drown again. But they survive a chlorine gas attack because Robert recalls, in a flash of memory from his school days, how urine contains enough ammonia to neutralize chlorine gas, converting it to salt. This mental "flash" in a moment of danger becomes a formal feature of Part Three, in which the action is clocked in a series of sub-headings that first interrupt events at "*4 a.m.*" as "the mines went up" and "there was a sort of glottal stop – halfway to nowhere" (121). Soon, the "glottal stop" becomes an *f*-stop of a camera "flash," first at *4.25 a.m.* (126), and then again at *5.30 a.m.* (127); *6.10 a.m.* (128); *7 a.m.* (130); *7.30 a.m.* (130); *8.15 a.m.* (131); *8.50 a.m.* (136); *9.30 a.m.* (140); *10.30 a.m.* (141); *12.15 p.m.* (141); and *1 p.m.* (141).

As Laurie Ricou remarked of this formal device, "the parallel between Robert Ross's stammering thought processes and the narrator's difficulty with his story makes spasmodic fear an unmistakeable aspect of the narrator's character" (134). But the technique is likely less personal than historiographical in its motivation; in other words, the narrator's facsimile of a photographic style is what enables him to write "history" at all. Another narrator in *The Wars* does have a personal motive, however, for stopping the action in prose snapshots – the twelve-year-old diarist Juliet d'Orsey, who feels tortured by a scene she had witnessed between her sister Barbara and Robert, with whom she is helplessly in love: "I was standing on the third step from the bottom and I think I must already have come to a stop because what happened next is sort of like a photograph in my mind and I see myself in the picture. Robert Ross came out of Captain Taffler's room and the door, as it opened, gave a kind of click like a shutter of a camera" (171–2). Recording in her diary a sharp sense of self-division, the child splits herself into an object who loves without hope and a subject who fears her own belatedness. Later, she will suffer from, but also look back on, such self-division in a scene of adult sexuality: "This was a picture that didn't make sense. Two people *hurting* one another. That's what I thought. I knew in a cool, clear way at the back of my mind that this was 'making love' – but the shape of it confused me. The shape and the violence" (178). As things stand, the child writes, "I feel a dreadful loss. I know things now I didn't want to know." What she finally sees, however, as she "looks" at herself in the picture, is the very child she has ceased to be. The "historian" finds her *self* in the "blast" of a "photograph."

A POSTHUMOUS SHOCK

Although film has likely done more than still photography to produce shock in its "techniques of rapid cutting, multiple camera angles, [and] instantaneous shifts in time and place," Benjamin was to argue in "On Some Motifs in Baudelaire," "the 'snapping' of the photographer has had the greatest consequences. A touch of the finger now sufficed to fix an event for an unlimited period of time. The camera gave the moment a posthumous shock, as it were" (*Illuminations* 176–7). In Freudian terms, "the danger of the event renews its demand and opens another path for itself, emerging, symptomatically, as an image of what has happened – as a return of what was to have departed – without our acquiescence or understanding" (Cadava 103).

It is in these terms that the concluding pages of *The Wars* ask to be read. For the novel proper concludes with "a photograph of Robert and Juliet taken about a year before his death" (217). The man who had risked life and honour to save a herd of horses from senseless slaughter in the Canadian Field Artillery has been condemned by a military court, his sentence commuted to convalescent treatment in Lady Juliet's home because "there was virtually no hope that he would ever walk or see or be capable of judgement again" (216). In this last photograph, "[h]e wears a close-fitting cap rather like a toque – pulled down over his ears. He has no eyebrows – his nose is disfigured and bent and his face is a mass of scar tissue. Juliet is looking up at him – speaking – and Robert is looking directly at the camera. He is holding Juliet's hand. And he is smiling" (217). The photograph would be unremarkable were it not for the tender witness it bears to Lady Juliet's love. Latterly, it reveals how Robert has been put in the same position as Rowena when, out of love, he made himself his wheelchair-ridden sister's sole caregiver. Robert's fate, we recognize in an instant of "posthumous shock," is contained in the photograph of his sister. Here at last, we see how a "structure of delay" that informs the photograph has structured the narrative all along: Robert has always been "one" with Rowena.

In the *"Epilogue,"* another "posthumous shock" comes from one final photograph of Robert with his sister. For it speaks of "the return of the departed" (Cadava 11) whose image from before the war restores us to the beginning of the narrative. In this temporal hallucination, nothing (and everything) has happened. But it is the addition of Robert's written word to his silent image that now speaks volumes: "*Robert and Rowena with Meg:* Rowena seated astride the pony – Robert holding her in place. On the back is written: 'Look! you can see our breath!' And you can" (218). The sight of their breath, and Robert's confirmation of that sight, comes to "animate" us (Barthes 20) in much the same way that Marian Turner and Lady Juliet have animated Robert's memory. That is to say, it is our fate, as readers who "remember" Robert, to inspire his image with our own breath. This is the true latency of history – that it remains to be lived over again.

In what may be his boldest stroke, Findley invents an essayist, Nicholas Fagan, to explain our sense of closeness, and also of distance, from this temporal hallucination that appears in the medium of photography: "This is what he wrote: '*the spaces between the perceiver and the thing perceived can ... be closed with a shout of recognition. One form of a shout is a shot. Nothing so completely verifies our perception of a thing as our killing of it*'" (218, ellipses in original). One sees at last why the whole of the novel has sought to dramatize this ongoing oscillation between distance and proximity. For the narrator "verifies" his perceptions of the war, first by "killing" off the old-style warrior, and then by closing the distance with a "shout of recognition" at Robert who is made the "hero" of a new age.

In the end, one can see why those photographs Findley imagined as "flashing" on "billboards" down a long avenue of time did not move; they were irrevocably fixed in their own time. But the "hero" who comes riding down the light rays is not confined to his own historical moment: he could never be "contained entirely in a caught circle, back only in his own time" (Aitken 84), not if he could still be torn from his historical context to ride in cinematic fashion down a corridor of time into our future. And so the hero comes to join us in the present instant of a new *actualité* even as his photographic past is kept in check by these images of a history that would not, finally, become us.

A Play of Light: Dramatizing Relativity in R. H. Thomson's *The Lost Boys*

If it were possible to make a photographic negative of a novel, R. H. Thomson's *The Lost Boys* (2001) might well be read as a "negative" image of Timothy Findley's *The Wars*. A stage play rather than a narrative, Thomson's drama tells the story of a family of five boys (nary a deserter in this lot) who went overseas with the Canadian Expeditionary Force in 1914–18. Diving into a trunk-full of 700 letters sent by his great-uncles from the Western Front, Thomson reverses Findley's refusal to quote from the epistolary hoard of his soldier. More to the point, Thomson's subtitle "Letters From The Sons in Two Acts, 1914–1923," signals his intent to *perform,* rather than to quote, the words of these dead men. Even his use of "photographic memory" follows this line of reversal; where Findley offers verbal descriptions of photos to generate his story, Thomson projects actual photographs onto the back wall of his set. Because these photos are projections, they have an added dramatic effect of converting images back into light, as if returning them to their source. Above all else in his systematic reversal of the novelist's method, Thomson's narrator remains ever-present and visible in the midst of his story. Where Findley's "you"-narrator is never seen or named in his story, the "Man" who narrates *The Lost Boys* is omnipresent on stage. For it is Thomson, one of Canada's finest actors, cast in the role of his five uncles, who also plays himself as a middle-aged man in search of a story that had enveloped his childhood, since "there were some mighty goings on in that house though I never realized it then" (8). Thomson the actor is doubly present in body and in memory, "playing himself in *The Lost Boys*" in a one-hander that John Coulborn says "may rank as one of Thomson's finest performances" (online review).

Other reviewers have not been as kind in their estimates. Joel Greenberg impugns the performance as "long-winded and, in the last twenty minutes, too self-absorbed to allow the audience in" (online review). Jon Kaplan's judgment is harsher yet: "A trunkful [sic] of letters from the first world war [sic] is a potential dramatic gold mine in *The Lost Boys*. Writer R. H. Thomson unearths some of the precious material, but R. H. Thomson the performer squanders more of it" (online review). Most disappointingly, Christopher Hoile, the principal reviewer for *Stage Door*, writes, "A play that has seemed extraordinarily self-indulgent finally slips into the confessional and becomes embarrassing" (online review). For Hoile, "The overriding difficulty is that the letters are not inherently interesting and even less dramatic." As he phrases the problem, "Thomson had had the idea for 20 years that he should make something of one of his family's treasures – [these] letters"; he "initially thought of making them into a television documentary and indeed that's what he should have done. The letters could have acted as a Canadian family's voice in the Great War."

As the next chapter will show, however, Thomson had already acted in a six-part documentary for History Television, *For King and Empire*. So the question is rather why Thomson, with so much formal experience of history on television, should take a play to be the only form adequate to his material? What is there in his presence on stage that does what can't be done on film or television? Why, above all, when he admits his obsession with a film clip of his Uncle George's regiment, to a point that the performance nearly comes to a halt, does he refuse to work in a cinematic or televisual medium? As he says, "I found some actual film footage of George's regiment, 1917 the P.P.C.L.I. And I thought I saw him. There, the second in the line, there. Run it again. There, the one with the moustache. Run it again. There. No, no. Stop. Stop it. Stop it! I'm sorry. I'm obsessive" (56). Obsession is an answer of sorts, but a better answer may be found in the way that light plays a key role in the play, particularly in relation to Einstein's theory of relativity. Since Einstein himself appears in a projected beam of light on stage, and since his theory of relativity will ultimately be central to the theme of the play – the meaning of time in relation to memory – it ought to repay our efforts to rethink cinema, this time as a medium with hidden connections to relativity.

Admittedly, critics have not viewed kindly this attempt to put Einstein's thought on the stage. Kevin Connolly views it in terms of other clichés he finds in the writing: "Who of us does not remember the 'back by Christmas' estimates, the gas and rats stories, or even the tale of German and English soldiers sharing songs during a spontaneous Christmas ceasefire? Worse is Thomson's penchant for invoking big themes (Albert Einstein somehow figures into things) and his self-dramatizing discussion of his own motivations" (online review). In a more sophisticated way, Christopher Hoile also reduces Einstein's stage appearance to a thematic cliché: "Thomson's attempts to give his private ruminations greater resonance by contrasting the 'evolution' of Einstein's theories of the universe with the 'devolution' of the generals' approach to the war are too forced to seem like more than inept stabs at profundity." Here, in the failure of a critic who is not lacking in subtlety, one who even raises the central question – Why the stage and not a television documentary – we should infer our need of media theory. Why, indeed, has the narrator dramatized his refusal to tell his story on film or in a televisual text? Why should he risk stopping the show, unless to tell us that neither film nor television is capable of what he means to attempt: to give us the *experience* of relativity, to make us feel it in our very bones. If *The Lost Boys* turns its back on film and television in order to tell its time- and memory-haunted story, it can only be that an actor's body moving and speaking in the midst of these multimedia projections is required to realize the ongoing search for "lost time." Thomson's play, that is to say, appears to be a mediatized, postmodern version of a quintessentially modernist narrative, *À la recherche du temps perdu.*[28]

STAR-LIGHT, FILM-BRIGHT

On his second, triumphant tour of America in 1931, Albert Einstein was to sit beside Charlie Chaplin in the back of an open convertible as they rode down Hollywood Boulevard. Amid roars of approval from the crowd, Chaplin is supposed to have said to Einstein, "You see, they are cheering me because everybody understands me, they are cheering you, because nobody understands you" (cited by Lanczos 8). More than he realized, however, Chaplin's medium *had* prepared the public at the very least to sense the theory of relativity, at least to an extent that film had allowed them to *see* time on a flat motion-picture screen as being unified with space (if no more than the space of plane geometry). What a viewer sees in the two-dimensional space-time of the screen is nothing more than the motion of still photographs, each measuring $\frac{5}{8}$ by $1\frac{1}{8}$ inches, although when these "stills" are run before a beam of light focused through a lens, a visible dimension of time is projected onto space. Stop the motion (as Thomson's narrator does), and time as an integral dimension of space disappears. Time on screen is thus inseparable from the *motion in space* of light-borne images.

For his part, Albert Einstein modestly acknowledges in his "Autobiographical Notes" to the 1951 edition of *The Library of Living Philosophers* that the notion of time as a "fourth dimension" did not originate with him. What was unique to his theory was simply the idea of an *inextricable* link between time and space, the notion that time would not exist without, or apart from, space:

> Classical mechanics, too, is based on the four-dimensional continuum of space and time. But in the four-dimensional continuum of classical physics the subspaces with constant time value have an absolute reality, independent of the choice of the reference system. Because of this [fact], the four-dimensional continuum falls naturally into a three-dimensional and a one-dimensional (time), so that the four-dimensional point of view does not force itself upon one as *necessary*. (Schilpp 57, 59)

Einstein's rejection of an absolute value for time and his confirmation of the absolute speed of light[29] allowed him to conclude apropos of his special theory of relativity (1905): "There is no such thing as simultaneity of distant events; consequently there is also no such thing as immediate action at a distance in the sense of Newtonian mechanics" (Schilpp 61).

Writing in the same volume, the philosopher Hans Reichenbach illustrates the "relativity of simultaneity" as follows: "For instance, if a telephone connection with the planet Mars were established, and we would have to wait a quarter of an hour for the answer to our questions, the relativity of simultaneity would become as trivial a matter as the time difference between the standard times of different time zones is today" (Schilpp 308). These days, of course, the relativity of simultaneity is reduced to a truism by the legions of scientists one sees on television communicating with the Mars Rovers. At the same time, there is no longer any doubt "that time is not completely separate from and independent of space, but is combined with it to form an object called space-time" (Hawking 23). Contrary to classical mechanics, time does not have an independent being apart from three-dimensional space.

At the end of the nineteenth century, the new medium of cinema was already beginning to undermine the commonsense conviction that time was constant and unalterable. A decade before Einstein produced his famous paper "On the Electrodynamics of Moving Bodies" (1905), *Scribner's Magazine* (6 December 1895) had published a story entitled "The Kinetoscope of Time," concerning Thomas Edison's new (1894) peep-show box. The author, one Brander Matthews, professed to be astonished not only by "the marvelous vividness with which the actions had been repeated before my eyes, like life itself in form and in color and in motion, but also at the startling fact that some of the things I had been shown were true and some were false. Some of them had happened actually to real men and women of flesh and blood, while others were but bits of the vain imagining of those who tell tales as an art and as a means of livelihood" (cited by Pratt 11). The Kinetoscope's power to represent Achilles chasing Hector around the walls of Troy, or Don Quixote tilting at windmills, side by side with Custer's Last Stand, was understandably disturbing. But a far deeper fear was manifest in the narrator's next question to the peep-show exhibitor: "'You are not Time himself?' I asked in amaze" (12). While the exhibitor assures him to the contrary, the narrator's intuition is likely closer to the truth. The "movie screen" might well be the fourth dimension or, at least, the new medium might have the power, in its use of light, to annul the absolute value of time.

Motion pictures had had no appreciable influence, of course, on the thinking of Albert Einstein in 1905. "Influence" appears rather to have run in the opposite direction, from the physicist's separate and independent challenge to the temporal order toward a film-crazed public. As Philipp Frank recalls:

> In the fall of 1912 I first realized that Einstein's theory of the "relativity of time" was about to become a world sensation ...
> Einstein had succeeded in proving that under certain conditions time itself could contract or expand, that it could sometimes pass more rapidly and at other times more slowly.

This idea changed our entire conception of the relation of man to the universe. Men came and went, generations passed, but the flow of time remained unchanged. Since Einstein this is all ended. The flow of time itself can be changed. (Frank 61)

And yet even Frank concedes that, "to say that time *flows* is a figure of speech that is only partly appropriate to the description of the physical phenomena. To speak of 'more rapid flow' is to take a simple metaphor seriously" (63). At the same time, the metaphoric flow of time was to be thoroughly naturalized by the end of the first decade of the nickelodeon film craze (1905–16), by virtue of this new type of "flow" of light-borne images into the space-time of motion picture screens.

Terminology provides a more oblique, but likely more revealing, sign of the new epistemology that emerged in this decade (1895–1905) when Einstein first thought about light in ways that were to revolutionize our thinking about space and time. Unlike his "famous contemporaries [who] were then all concentrating on dynamics," Einstein chose rather to focus on *kinematics* – "the theory of the purely geometrical movements of bodies without any consideration of forces" (Fölsing 178). His rejection of the "ether theory" of light – that light requires a medium in which to move – enabled Einstein to redefine the properties of light apart from the forces of dynamics. It is this decisive "departure from Newtonian kinematics" that "links time with the spatial coordinates; it is the physical basis of the four-dimensional presentation of relativity theory, with time as the fourth 'dimension'" (Fölsing 189).[30] "Kinematics" was that particular branch of mechanics ideally suited to Einstein's speculations "on the properties of light," which he had begun "as early as the age of sixteen" (Frank 56) – as early, in other words, as 1895.

While the name "kinematograph" (1896, *OED*) – given by the Messieurs Lumière to their Lyonnaise invention of the first motion-picture camera with projector – was informed by a classical concept of Newtonian kinematics, the new device set figures of light in motion without subjecting them to gravity or other forces. In other ways as well, the *cinématographe* anticipated some of the epistemological effects of Einstein's theory of relativity. For film-light from "another time" now made it possible to *see* the "relativity of simultaneity," and to feel, if not to understand, what Einstein meant by his claim that, "two events that are simultaneous when observed from some particular coordinate system can no longer be considered simultaneous when observed from a system that is moving relative to that system. There are as many 'times' as there are inertial systems" (Fölsing 186). Literally, as well as figuratively, the Lumière brothers' *cinématographe* had introduced a second inertial (uniformly moving) system relative to viewers, which, by the nature of its light projection, was independent of their (terrestrial) inertial system.

As Stephen Hawking observes about the relativity of time, "[W]e do not know what is happening at the moment farther away in the universe: the light that we see from distant galaxies left them millions of years ago ... Thus, when we look at the universe, we are seeing it as it was in the past" (28). Similarly, in his study of the ontology of film, Stanley Cavell reminds us that what we are looking at in movies is quite literally the past written in light: "I am present not at something happening, which I must confirm, but at something that has happened, which I absorb (like a memory)" (26). In this sense, "[p]hotography maintains the presentness of the world by accepting our absence from it. The reality in a photograph is present to me while I am not present to it; and a world I know, and see, but to which I am nevertheless not present (through no fault of my subjectivity), is a world past" (23). For that reason, Cavell writes: "It is an incontestable fact that in a motion picture no live human being is up there. But a human *something* is, and something unlike anything else we know. We can stick to our plain description of that human something as 'in our presence while we are not in his' (present *at* him, because looking at him, but not present *to* him" (26–7). In this light, the brand name Lumière, with which the words "cinema" and "cinematography" are historically linked, like Einsteinean *kinematics,* need to be re-thought as epistemological markers of a whole era in which space and time were being reconfigured in two distinct forms of discourse – relativistic physics and motion pictures.

RELATIVITY AND MULTIMEDIA

In *The Lost Boys,* R. H. Thomson brings Albert Einstein to the stage in two significant ways. As an image projected in a beam of light onto a scrimmed screen, "*ALBERT... takes his place on the stool back to back*" with an actor who "*slowly spins in place from one to the other*" (30). The actor, identified only as "MAN" in this drama composed almost equally of narration and performance, describes a world being led in 1915 by Generals wanting to fight their "way back to the 18th century," if not back "to the 16th century," or even back to "the 1st century if the men will let us" (30). But this mention of the Generals is largely a device on which to pivot back toward something still unplumbed in Einstein's theory of time, at least in its significance to the drama: "And I ask myself," the narrator muses,

> how does such devolution that engulfed my "uncles" exist so precisely in time and space with such an evolution of vision and profundity? Because less than one hundred hours after my uncle George, seated by the brazier, finished this letter, ... this other young man, Albert, stood up in Berlin and spoke with genius about the bedrock of our being. Albert Einstein, [*sic*] leapt one hundred years ahead to describe a world which even today we are slow to comprehend. (30–1)

What we have been more "slow to comprehend" is a peculiar latency in cinematic images of human beings written in light – the very thing that almost stops the show as the narrator obsesses over a film-image of his uncle George. For what we see, ontologically speaking, when we regard a film image, is the relativity of time. "Albert" is present to us (and to the actor on stage) in projected light, but we are not present to "him." From this first appearance in light, Einstein thus serves to dramatize the relativity of simultaneity.

Thomson's work is hardly a conventional drama, however, since it refuses to dramatize a present conflict or even to represent more than our present reception of the past. What it chooses to represent instead is *time* as the fourth dimension on the three-dimensional space of the stage (a tall order, likely one of the reasons why critics have such uneven views of the play). To this extent, it *must* differ from film in which actors are present in forms of light, and where time is united with just two dimensions of space.

Insofar as it strains toward the condition of film-light, however, the play is really powered by its use of multimedia, particularly in the way each medium works to unite the present tense of the narrator with the past tense of the lost boys. Impersonating each of them in turn – along with himself as a boy – the Man seeks to recover their "lost time." His search is not reducible to a Proustian sacrament of memory, however, since lost time is not recovered involuntarily or spontaneously in anything like a *madeleine* dipped in tea. In fact, one cannot reverse the flow of time in this play; the gap is only ever crossed in one direction, on various bridging media, from *then* to *now* (and not, as happens in Proust's novel, in immediate transport from *now* to *then*). Thomson's choice of the stage means that "lost time" is not to be recovered, as it is for Proust, in the theatre of the mind. It has, rather, to be visibly realized in the public space of the theatre. And so it must be conjured – or made visible, i.e., mediated – by other means.

To make us see *time,* to make the temporal order literally *visible,* the actor resorts to a broad range of multimedia in a space that "*is a series of scrimmed screens on which appear the faces and war landscape of the play*" (3). Here, the photographic images of faces, landscapes, and letters take shape on a stage that even Christopher Hoile admits is a remarkable piece of stagecraft that advances the drama (just not far enough):

> The production's most notable aspect is its design. Astrid Janson has covered the otherwise bare stage with dirt and added a trench whence Thomson produces hidden props. Behind are three gauzy panels in front of a screen. Janson thus recreates the structure of the painting "La Rêve," owned [by] Mrs. Stratford, depicting soldiers asleep on the earth, their dreams appearing above the clouds in the background. To create this background lighting and visual designer Martin Conboy has done an extraordinary job of combining a wide range of lighting effects with projections, sometimes altered to create the illusion of motion, of facsimiles of letters, telegrams and other documents and portraits of the Stratford family along with archival photos from World War I on and off the battlefield. This and Duncan Morgan's vivid soundscape are ultimately more involving than any of Thomson's text. (online review)

Conversely, although the staging is "very imaginative," in Greenberg's view, "it keeps pushing us away from any emotional connection with the actor or his subject. Leaping into and out of the downstage trench loses its novelty early on, and the extensive use of projected images only occasionally rises above the level of research."

More revealingly, Greenberg concludes, "The playing space wants to be too many things and the staging wants to dazzle us with its virtuosity" (online review). To this critic, multimedia are really more of a distraction than a means to redefine the "playing space."

In a March 2002 review in *Lancette: Journal of the Arts*,[31] one reviewer stands apart in defining the temporal significance of a set which creates "a simple, yet complex image on stage. There is a trench, that symbol of wwi, there is sand and various objects that to this day still can be found in the fields of Belgium. They all help Thomson to tell his uncles' stories, but also that of hundreds of thousands more who fought on both sides of those trenches. Photos are projected onto the back wall of the stage to identify the five men. We see images of explosions, with full sound. They tell of the awful noises with which the men in the trenches had to live. And through it weaves a haunting melody" (Kohlhaas). And yet Kohlhaas stops just short, in her recognition of those "hundreds of thousands more who fought on both sides of those trenches," of showing how we come to witness the mystery of time turning into space-time in four dimensions on this stage.

One of the true strengths of the production, as Hoile sees it, is its use of recorded sound to bring the experience of trench warfare to life. Various aural media recall the sound of another era, including a period gramophone, tape-recordings of voices "speaking" the soldiers' letters or singing their wartime songs, of shells and other "detonators" bursting about the stage, of gas bells ringing, of motor ambulance and transport sounding their horns, and of strains of silent film music accompanying Albert Einstein's projection in light. In this vivid soundscape, we can see why the film-image of George marching in the ranks of the Princess Patricia's Canadian Light Infantry would be insufficient to realize the mystery of time and memory, much less to recover "lost time."[32] Although it figures a certain "lightness" of being, film will never be able to re-present the gravity of the situation in which these "boys" are lost.

The actor's self-confessed "obsession" with a film clip of George marching with the Princess Pats is thus a mirror image of the play's obsession with multimedia and their differing ways of communicating the past to an audience – what might be called their relativizing frames of reference. Once we *listen* to these aural media, we should begin to hear them as "characters" engaged in dramatic dialogue with the narrator. For this is a play that still conforms to the dramatic

norms of a form that has its origins in oral culture. In such terms, we
need to ask how each medium in this array of multimedia contributes
to the dramatic development of the play? Or, to return to the Proustian metaphor of an actor's search for "lost time," we need to ask
more precisely, What is the relationship in this play between one-
directional media forms of light and multi-directional, aural modes
of remembering?

DIALOGICAL MEDIA AND MEMORY

The dramatic motive for the actor's stage vigil is his painful memory of his youthful failure to have kept a vigil of remembrance:

> I was 16 and I was in Belgium. It was the usual European tour for
> teenagers... My vigil was in the actual battle chapel, a chapel
> created by the soldiers in the attic of a house in Belgium just be-
> hind the front line ... But the reality of the First War was dim.
> I mumbled my words, knelt for my vigil, gave back the sword
> and then stumbled back outside to the Belgian darkness. Standing
> there in the light of the stars I didn't get it, and of all the teenagers
> there, I should have been the one who did. Two of my great un-
> cles were buried there. A number of my family had been killed by
> that war. Did I have any idea of the story surrounding me? (3–4)

The actor's failure is all the more painful as he recalls what he
ought to have remembered from the family archive: "The letters
were a bit of a deal in my family... [They] had been typed out and
distributed. At 16 I'd read a few. There were hundreds of them. The
adults kept saying how important they were. I never got very far"
(4). If the written word has failed to take him very far, it is likely because of its endless repetitions (or what Hoile calls "unpromising
material"): "Could you send a couple of pairs of socks?" "Could
you send moth balls?" "The Belgian mud is something fierce." "I
could do with another pair of socks" (4). To the boy, the written
word is truly a dead medium that fails to *speak* to him. In its most
basic dramatic situation, *The Lost Boy* thus concerns the actor's
longing to *hear* those voices speaking to him from the mists of time.

   In his childhood, there was one visual image that did speak
vaguely to him, a battlefield painting that "hung in the hall on the
way to my grandmother's dining room ... It was about dreams and
the dawn. It was called 'Le Reve' [sic]" (6). As he begins to reflect

on it, "I remember this picture for as far back as I can remember – six years old, three" (6). And yet the sight of warriors marching in triumph in the air above the heads of actual soldiers sleeping on the ground remains "far away ... It's as if the dream soldiers were going to march off into the stars. And [then,] as I got older, a teenager maybe, it got clearer. It was about battle and death, and glory and victory" (8). What the teenager sees in Édouard Détaille's painting (1888; now in the Musée d'Orsay) hardly differs, however, from the painter's nostalgia for Napoleonic glory, or a late nineteenth-century, revanchist desire for a restored French Empire. What the boy does see, however, is the fixed distance between lofty ambition and lowly circumstance, that unbridgeable gulf between time past and time present. At first, the past seems hopelessly "far away."

Projected as an illuminated image, however, the frame of the painting disappears, and *"The actor walks into the picture"* (8). The landscape of "The Dream of Soldiers" now "enters" him, at least as much as he enters it. Therefore, he says, "I know it is about eternity, an eternity which is very close. I know now the dream soldiers marching in the clouds are dead, which is why their cries always came from somewhere far away. I know now that this picture hung in the house of a woman who had lost four brothers because of the war" (8). As the usual distance between past and present is crossed one way on a beam of light, that old distinction made by G. E. Lessing on "The Limits of Painting and Poetry" – the first art being limited to space, the second being limited to time – suddenly dissolves. For this metamorphosis of paint into light has just transformed a static painting into a temporal gateway to a unified dimension of space-time.

It is now that the actor is suddenly able to hear the *voice* of his uncle Art speaking a letter that we hear as a tape-recording: "The trenches here are only about 39 yds. apart. Only the other night a German soldier called over in good English, 'Will you surrender?' One of our fellows replied 'No, we won't, you fiddle faced ****.' It was an experience to hear that tommy swear. If it wasn't for the funny things I think we would all go crazy" (12). The actor then introduces "three German artillery sounds that we might become acquainted with, 'The Whiz-bang,' 'The Coal Box' so named because of the black smoke given off on detonation, and the 'Jack Johnson': *Sounds are provided. Actor disappears in trench on the explosion. When all is clear, he reappears with a windup gramophone. From this point on all letters are performed"* (12).

From this point, the actor's "obsession" with hearing, as well as seeing, all those things heard and seen by his uncles will lead him, however belatedly, to occupy their space, if not their time: "I went back to Belgium. When I read this letter I had to find the place where Art was hit. I had to walk in his footsteps" (19). In Art's words: "The Allemand copped me at last. A damned silly way to get plugged too. I was hit while in an ambulance" (18). Finding the very space where Art was hit, the narrator says, "I stand in the wet darkness. I actually stand here ... with Art. The rain. The mud. The night. I feel as if I am watching history with my skin" (20, ellipses in original).

Watching history with his "skin," the actor is now empowered to hear (and so act out) the Attestation papers of Art's brother, Joe, done to the accompaniment of silent film music: "*A Charles Chaplin romance is heard ... The Chaplin romance is JOE's theme*" (20, 22). There is something touchingly innocent about Joe's first letter from England that makes him seem Chaplinesque: "There is only one complaint and that is that our Cavalry unit is not at the front ... Can anyone imagine 50,000 in a Cavalry charge? It just makes my hair curl to think of it ... I do wish they would drop us in France or Belgium. I am crazy to get there" (22). In his next letter, it is Joe, rather than the narrator, who now converts the *"Punch cartoon acknowledging the Canadian fighting at Ypres"* into patriotic rhetoric: "Just didn't our Johnnie Canucks show them how to fight. They made the greatest stand that any army has ever made in the history of the world" (24). In his naïveté, there is also something troubling – quite un-Chaplinesque – about his innocence.

It is the narrator who is able, between his performance of these two letters, to draw upon a much longer history: "Poison gas was first used by the Greeks in the Wars of the Peloponnese around 410 BC. The Germans improved the chemistry and reintroduced it April 22nd 1915 around five in the afternoon." But the narrator's point is not jingoistic in the manner of his uncle: "The gas was 'improved' by Professor Fritz Haber in Berlin. Fritz Haber was a 'good colleague' of Albert Einstein" (23). So it is that Einstein appears as the antithesis of the Prussian patriot Fritz Haber who also worked at the Kaiser Wilhelm Institute in Berlin: "Albert saw the madness. He understood devolution. He spoke of relativity and astonished those who heard him by describing the very shape of existence" (31–2).

"But back in the mud," it is a third brother, George of the Princess Pats, who "waits for the next leap backward" (31). To our sense of sound and sight, George adds his own sense of smell. Through him, we *smell* the horrors of trench warfare: "George's world became an open latrine for men and horses. Rather than risk the open pits back of the lines, many men would rather shit in their helmets and throw it into 'No Mans Land'... It was said that you smelt the frontlines before you ever saw them. It was said that on a hot day the sounds of the fly's [*sic*] wings as they fed, could drown out the noise of approaching shells" (31). It is such visceral evidence of "devolution" that brings the first Act to its conclusion, as we crouch under an artillery bombardment in the trench with "*the actor sitting rodent-like in a gas mask under the fading projection*" (39), before the scene fades to "*Black.*" The total absence of light at this point is suddenly experienced as a metaphysical condition, as a loss of that "evolution of vision" whereby Einstein sought to pull "the world in [an] opposite direction" from his "poison gas" colleague, Fritz Haber.

What "*the distant sounds of the artillery from France*" (36) have come to drown out, however, is a vital counter-movement of the first Act, culminating in the arrival of the boys' mother in England in January 1917, where she hopes to see all five of her sons: "*MOTHER's letter is recorded, the first woman's voice in the evening. Her projection appears. The actor listens, gradually lying down in the light from the crack in the door*" (34).

While "Mother" will recount her meeting with each of her five sons, it is still a mediated encounter, presented as a light-projected image and as a voice-over of a *discarnate* being. Mother is no more present to the audience than are her sons. The only bodily presence on stage is the actor, who, unable to step through this portal into another time, must lie down, as we do, figuratively at least, "in the light from the crack in the door." And so "*[t]he rest of MOTHER's letter becomes difficult to distinguish because it is only one of many voices of the bombardment*" (38). What we notice, even so, in the midst of the growing concussion, is that a genuine door to the past has been left ajar, if only a little, and that voices can still be heard through the gathering darkness.

The second Act complicates our hope of passing through the "crack in the door," particularly when the actor begins to see that the past is not an open book, that its records are not exactly transparent. Now the historical archive itself is implicated in relativity theory, insofar as it enforces a principle of distinct referential frames for each "time." For George is unable to tell his mother the whole truth as he writes that he "is in hospital for his feet." The actor's research has dredged up "Army Form B.213," informing us that George was hospitalized on 6 May 1917 for gonorrhea, before he was transferred two days later to another hospital for treatment of syphilis. *"The actor now begins to realize how much is hidden from him in the letters"* (44). He is forced, in other words, to rethink his own faith in written documents as a reliable source for the recovery of "lost time": "The first level of deception in these letters is the triviality, the off-handedness. There was so much they could not write about ... The next level of deception is the nature of the deaths. But of course, why would anyone tell a mother how horrible some of the deaths were? 'He was killed instantly' was a well-worn phrase. Then there is the simplest kind of deception. In his hospital bed with syphilis George again writes his mother" (44–5).

To deal with the next dissembling letter, the actor reverts from narration to performance: "I went up for my final medical board and I was so hard of hearing that the doctor said I'd better take a few more weeks and have my ears attended to, so here I still am" (45). But the medium of the written word no longer suffices to represent the "truth" of history. The actor's appeal to the character to explain himself is doomed to failure: "Help me George. You were on leave in London a month before, was she English? ... [T]here's nothing in the letters George, nothing. It's a world unspoken" (46): *"Actor has reached a dead end. He passes the letter to* GEORGE. GEORGE *glances at it and crumples it up in silence, pitching it back into the trench. The actor searches the earth."* The written word will not redeem this absence at the source, not when the historical subject insists it should be lost. Much as his act of impersonation had failed to complete the "quest for lost time," so the actor's reading of letters becomes a "dead end." Except for one thing.

He suddenly picks up a high-explosives "detonator head from the war. I bought it in Belgium for about $4.00." The presence of a dramatic prop from the Western Front makes him wonder what else might be hidden from him on the battlefield: "[W]hen I walked in the fields it looked peaceful to my immediate eye. Peace and order were what I saw but they were just a small part of the story. The larger part of the story was that everything beneath my feet was moving. Through seasons of rain and heaving frosts, bits of rifle, detonators, barbed wire, helmets, artillery shells are slowly being pushed to the surface ... The larger story is that the earth is not at peace. The earth is reworking its memory of the war."

The possibility that the earth itself has repressed memories of the war, and that the actor's role – rather like a Freudian analyst – is to bring such memories to light, marks a dramatic turning point in the actor's quest for lost time. For now he begins to see "the larger story" in the "Iron Harvest" beneath his feet, as well as in "the dance of the dead soldiers" whose skeletons are slowly working their way up to the surface: "Up to 40 of these forgotten soldiers appear each year ... and the other thousands return to their dance. That is the larger story. That story was never told me by my senses" (47).

From this point, the actor's physical performance approaches dance in movements that Alidë Kohlhaas calls "graceful, precise, often balletic." Christopher Hoile also singles out this aspect of performance as one of the great strengths of Thomson's acting: "Where he is most effective is in mime as when he enacts the 'dance' of skeletons as they are pushed to the earth's surface." But Thomson's quandary is to put everything together in his quest for lost time – physical movement, visual image, taste, smell, hearing. And so it is to narration that he turns at last to get at the deeper problem revealed to him through relativity theory, the fact that "our senses are veiled," and are thus dependent on technological mediation to see what is not seen by human eyes or heard by human ears:

I wasn't designed to see the dancing soldiers in the earth or the stars in the daylight sky. I certainly wasn't designed to see dark matter and black holes out there. I wasn't even designed to experience the earth as round. Really, left to my immediate senses, there is nothing to tell me that the earth is round. The earth is flat ladies and gentlemen. Sorry but every bit of evidence that I see first hand, says it's flat as a table. Don't mention pictures and don't mention technology, they are not first-hand. My senses as designed told me only of a flat world. (47)

Comparing himself to Galileo's Pope in 1610, the narrator insists that, "it takes more than eyes to see ... It takes a suspension of what we believe makes sense" (47). And so he narrates another return to the story of Einstein, to the epoch-making physicist who "in 1915 read the larger story of relativity ... a dizzying prospect of curving space-time. And when will any of us be ready to 'know' that great,

great story relativity ... perplexing and mystifying ... the story conceived at the birth of the universe, the supreme contract between
matter and energy, a story that says there can never be an absolute
to physical existence" (48). Ultimately, the actor's quest for lost
time will depend on his ability to narrate "relativity." But, to do
that, he will have to dramatize Einstein's theory in a way that
would "unveil" our senses, or let us see (on stage, no less) beyond
the "first-hand" evidence to a more oblique, and perhaps "dizzying
prospect of curving space-time."

DRAMATIZING RELATIVITY

At first, the narrator appears to falter in his attempt to uncover "the
larger story." For he simply returns to performing letters by George
who is "fighting the battle of Passchendaele. Is that all you can ·
say?" the actor reacts in evident frustration to one such letter. This
time, however, it is not a sin of omission, but the irony of George's
imminent death by "drowning in mud at night" (49), that will
alienate the actor from the time and space of the Passchendaele
mud. "I'm about all that's left," George writes, "in the way of officers in this Company so you can imagine we have a pretty tough
time" (50). Even as the actor speaks these words, however: *"Ghost-
ing in is the projection of the Night Letter informing* GEORGE's
*mother of his death ... The actor now stands with his death notice
projected on him ... Silence. Night Letter is now heard in recording"*
(50, 52). What one feels in this scene is something akin to Einstein's
incorporation of gravity into the general theory of relativity (1915).
Much as Einstein came to see "that a strong gravitational force
causes light rays to bend," or that a "massive object like the sun
bends the nearby geodesics" because "the attraction of gravity"
causes "spacetime [to be] curved in toward the source" (Kosso 87–
8), so the narrator finally understands that the deaths of George
and Joe must act as massive attractions on him. "Did I have any
idea," he had once asked, "of the story surrounding me?" (4). Only
now does he finally gain a sense of the greater "surround" of the
story as an aspect of "curving space-time" (48).

The true "bent" of the actor – the way his situation is continually
modified by the "gravitational" pull of the "dance of the dead" – is
revealed at last in a projection onto his body of George's "death notice." The weight of mud now threatens to suck the actor down along

with his great uncle. At first, he laments this new-found knowledge that "[h]e was not killed instantly as the army had said. He died in pain. His body was never found. His grave became lost in the mud of Passchendaele" (63). But the gravitational pull of the mud also serves to explain an apparent digression in the play, where the narrator acts out his compulsion to touch the very spot where his father died in a car wreck: "I press my hands to the earth. What am I going to feel, my Father's body? There pressed deep was a part of his glasses, the left half, dirt smearing the lens" (57). Here is the actor's first return to "ground," unable to rest at this point in bodiless forms of light.

The death of the actor's father further lets us feel the absence of the boys' mother, who disappears too soon in the second Act to bear the climactic weight that was given to her "voice" at the end of the first Act. This time, her voice is heard speaking to her youngest son, Rick, attempting in her letter to allay his grief at the death of his brother George. Thereafter, her role is taken up by two dramatic substitutes; the first is a surrogate "French" mother, Madame Mialaret, writing to share in the mother's grief over George's death. Speaking her letter in French in voice-over, while *"The actor translates, the two voices intermingling"* (60), Madame Mialaret forces the audience to recognize its own part in the play, where receiving news from afar constitutes the only real action, thus making the audience a recipient of her letter, too. The play, in other words, has not been conceived, nor is it performed as a monodrama; we are put into the same position as the actor, on whom communications from a distant time and place have a lasting effect.

A letter from the mother's niece "MARGARET Osbourne," further dramatizes the significance of this temporal mediation. At first, it seems that Margaret's letter to the boys' mother, which *"is recorded and spoken as if in natural dialogue"* (53), simply tells of her last meeting with George, who took her to the movies not long before his fateful return to the mud of Passchendaele. *"[A]bsorbed in MARGARET's letter,"* the actor says: "I feel that if I read this letter closely enough, I might hear the last few breaths. Passing my fingers through those breaths I might touch George" (54). He cannot, of course, do any such thing. And yet the very terms of his desire show how the play has always dealt with the uni-directionality of time.[33] For it is finally the actor as recipient who is left to give these letters breath and weight, much as the audience becomes a recipient of each "message." Relativity, in other words, is not an escape from gravity.

Indeed, Einstein's general theory of relativity had predicted that the gravity of "Massive objects cause[s] a curvature of the spacetime, and massive objects respond to a curvature of the spacetime" (Kosso 88). "The presence of a massive object like the sun does not define the properties of spacetime," as this commentator explains; rather, "it modifies them" (Kosso 89). In analogous fashion, the grave of Joe comes to exert a massive pull on the narrator. He declares: "I must follow the body. I leave the woods by the only lane to the west to Dommartin. It must be the way. It is growing dark. I can sense my hand on the cart. Step by step I'm with Joe. It's evening by the time I return ... to the cemetery" (69). Like a "ball falling to the floor or the moon staying in orbit," the actor has responded to the gravitational pull of memory by following the straightest path he can find to the past. And yet this path is symbolically curved, as it were, because spacetime "is curved in toward the source" (Kosso 88). The "greater story" that "surrounds" the narrator has required this form of a parabolic return from the beginning.

The path of the parabola adds a further level of explanatory power to the actor's "obsessive" return to his film footage of *"halting images of the men of the P.P.C.L.I. marching. The actor points out his fantasy, asking for the footage to be played again and again"* (56). After his brief narrative "digression" about his father's death, and his need to place "my feet in his footsteps, to know him, to be there, to be here. That's all I can do. Witness," the *"Actor returns to the reanimated footage of the marching soldiers. It finally stops and is replaced by the projected letter announcing JOE's death"* (57).

So it is that the graves of the "lost boys" approximate the effects of gravity in a universe where time and space and matter are necessarily unified. Or, as Stephen Hawking puts it, "Before 1915, space and time were thought of as a fixed area in which events took place, but which was not affected by what happened in it ... The situation, however, is quite different in the general theory of relativity. Space and time are now dynamic quantities: when a body moves, or a force acts, it affects the curvature of space and time – and in turn the structure of space-time affects the way in which bodies move and forces act. Space and time not only affect but also are affected by everything that happens in the universe" (Hawking 33). What the actor suggests, in another way, is that the stasis of print needs to be accommodated to this model of a dynamic universe where every body is in motion relative to every other body in the universe. For such reasons, Hoile is utterly beside the point in concluding, "For all its surface motion the play is static." Rather, it is the gravitational force of the past itself that appears to curve space-time in these grave scenes, so shaping the narrator's parabolic movement toward the last moments of the lost boys.

This is why film as a form is inadequate to the content of the play, why the story of their several deaths must be staged. For, on the silver screen, there is no gravity or spatial depth. Without the sun, "[s]pace-time … would be 'flat'" (Kosso 89). But in the three-dimensional space of the stage, the narrator's time comes round again quite near to the time of the lost boys; the "real" effects of gravity are still in play in a four-dimensional space-time. Contrary to the special theory of relativity (and its analogue in film), in which gravity plays no part, the general theory of relativity makes it clear that "now space, time *and* matter [are] united into a single entity" (Lanczos 46). Dramatizing relativity in this play, then, is what takes us beyond the weightlessness and matterlessness of film-light. For the plot of the play carries us back, in a grand parabola, to the moment of its beginning, to the Actor standing under the stars, asking: "Have I come as far as I can? Is my vigil finally over? … Having come this far I now know how little of the world I see" (69).

What Thomson the performer, as well as Thomson the writer, asks us to see in the end is the human significance of relativity. He allows how "Albert had warned me; 'Nature's only showing us the tail of the lion'":

> *The actor lies back on the grave.*
> I want the great story. I want to see the body of the lion. But the light of the billions above me is part illusion. They have all moved or gone out. Even my sun and my planets are not where I see them. And while the earth and mud cling to my shoes and will claim my body as well, they have no absolute hold over me, since the earth is not absolute but the condensed energy of the light in which I live. (70)

Like vanished stars, the "light" of the lost boys is only reaching us now. If they were film "stars," they might be present to us, but we would not be present to them. And yet we *are* present to the actor on stage; it is through this performance of his vigil that we are finally able to approach the time of the lost boys.

The actor's final dance thus takes place in a universe of constant motion, where nothing is fixed or constant, but where nothing is lost, either. For the light from those stars that have already gone out keeps on arriving from the farthest reaches of space-time. In a universe measured by intergalactic distances, the relativity of simultaneity does approach to infinity. And, being in motion ourselves, we can only see time past and time present in relative terms.

As the stage directions now indicate, *"The music of the final dance appears,"* and the narrator sums up our journey through space-time: "What is absolute is the motion, lives come and lives gone. The motion is all that is left me ... the turn and dance of my uncles and the stars that are no longer there yet exist just the same" (70). All that remains, in this absolute sense, is the motion of the dance – of the stars, of the skeletons under the earth, of the actor above ground. And yet the dance itself *re-members* its protagonists, both human and non-human, as we come round again, in the great curve of space-time, to an "eternity which is very close" (8) to the play's beginning:

> I have come as far as I can. I've done as much as I can. All that's left for me now is to be here.
>
> The actor dances. He is eventually lost from sight.
> *Blackout.* (70)

Here, the absence of light is much less threatening, however, than it was at the end of the first Act. For we are finally able to see how light moves on, yet continues to exist elsewhere, long after every audience has left the scene.

PART FIVE

Virtual Presences:
History in the Electronic Age

Electronic Memory: "A New Homeric Mode" on History Television

Ironically, the stage embodiment of relativity in *The Lost Boys,* the writer-actor R. H. Thomson is no more than a disembodied voice of history in *For King and Empire,* a six-part series about "Canada's Soldiers in the Great War" produced by Ira Levy and Peter Williamson for History Television. As narrator, Thomson never appears on screen, but his magisterial voice-over can be heard for about one-third of the running time of each episode. Five of the series' six instalments open with establishing shots of present-day France or Belgium, in the northern regions where Canadians fought and died all those years ago. For example, a golden field of grain bends in a light breeze before the distant, reddish spires of Ypres in the series opener, "Baptism of Fire: The Canadians at Ypres – 1915." The site is St-Julien in northwest Belgium, where in April 1915 untested Canadian volunteers faced a chlorine gas attack in their first battle of the war. In the second episode, "Slaughter and Sacrifice: The Canadians at the Somme – 1916," the sun-winking current of that sleepy little river belies more bloody work to come in the Allied offensive of July–November 1916.

The third episode, "Storming the Ridge: The Canadians at Vimy – 1917," begins with a "tracking" shot of trees and lawns scarred by old shell craters as Thomson's voice-over leads us to the site of a victory where the French had failed in 1915, and the British had failed again in 1916: "The Canadian National Memorial Park on Vimy Ridge in the heart of France. People say there are 60,000 trees in this park, one for every Canadian killed in the Great War."[34] The shot dissolves after 22 seconds to a flutter of Canadian and French flags flying side by side as the narrator intones: "The park is a gift of the people of France to the people of Canada." Seven more shots over 46 seconds display the Vimy Monument from various angles, both in its parts and in its larger setting, before the voice-over continues: "But even as the grass grows over shell holes, mine craters, and trenches, *the land remembers*. Land given in gratitude for a victory no one thought possible, the capture of Vimy Ridge" (my emphasis). At this point, the shot of vibrant green craters fades to black and white, as if it were only natural that "the land" should "remember" its grassless, graceless state in a slow dissolve to a black-and-white image of a file of troops silhouetted atop the distant ridge. The memory of the *land,* it seems, is what conjures up the Canadian attack on Vimy Ridge before our eyes. The whole enterprise of *making* history is thus *naturalized,* not in direct acknowledgement of "the televisual recovery-demonstration-articulation" of a story structured as *"yesterday-today"* (Heath and Skirrow 18), but in the more equivocal mode of a medium that is all about time, especially the sale of an audience's viewing time to advertisers (Fiske 100).

The shifter, or device for getting us from *now* to *then,* in this series is usually the colour-fade to black-and-white, a visual marker used effectively in every episode to signal movement from one time zone (the present scene) to another (most often action in the distant past). At the same time, the source of any given shot, whether it be derived from a video camera in the "immediate" present or from a film camera in the "mediated" past, is also colour-coded. This simple technique of time-shifting is complicated, however, by a second form of temporal bridging that brings us to the heart of the difference between history on film and history on television. For the opening sequence in every episode is a call to the viewer to follow the series host, Norm Christie, on a tour of First World War cemeteries and monuments, beginning at home and continuing overseas. The specific camera work used to interpellate[35] the viewer in this way is the following shot.

In the first shot of the opening sequence in each episode, the camera tilts down from an empty blue sky to two dark figures cast in bronze. "This is the war memorial in Stratford, Ontario," a voice says off-camera, "so it's typical of all the war memorials across Canada, in every village, every town, and every city."[36] DISSOLVE to a following shot of a man moving toward the Stratford war memorial filling the background of the frame. A superimposed subtitle

identifies the man as "Norm Christie / Author & Historian" – as he
and the following camera summon the viewer – "and these memorials are gateways to the First World War." Three shots in quick succession dissolve from a close-up (CU) of a·brass Honour Roll
bearing the names of the dead to an extreme close-up (ECU) of a
sword, tracking up the jagged blade to the face of a hatless, shirtless
bronze "hero," before ending in a close shot (CU) of the middle column of names.

Meanwhile, the host chides, "most Canadians have forgotten the
First World War, and they don't realize that it was the greatest,
most traumatic episode in our history. Four hundred thousand Canadians went overseas between 1914 and 1918." At this point, the
shot dissolves to a mid-shot (MS) of Christie looking over his shoulder and speaking to someone nearby, though still off-camera. Both
statues now stand in the background of a long shot (LS, full height),
as Christie concludes, "Sixty thousand died for King and Empire."
No more than forty-two seconds have passed in this opening sequence, but it is sufficient to introduce each episode, commanding
our attention and calling us to follow one who has been there and
who offers to convey us, too, in the blink of an eye, to places distant
in time and space. The mode of address is really the polar opposite
of that disembodied voice of history about to follow in the establishing shot of each episode. Inevitably, these differing modes of address produce an ongoing tension between the "presentness" of the
host in his dual capacity as presenter and travel guide, and the invisible narrator, whose voice-over functions to recall a distant era.
While these two times and modes of address constitute a distinctive
feature of history on television, they also mark the crucial function
of sound in binding past and present together. Unlike the disembodied, even impersonal, role of a book historian, the television historian is a vocal "presence," summoning you to join "him" on this
excursion into the past.

At the end of the opening sequence, the screen fades to black for
an instant before the title sequence begins with a 4-second drum-
roll, and then a skirl of pipes in an up-tempo rendition of "The Maple Leaf Forever" as pipers march past in black-and-white archival
footage of an Embarkation Parade (thus dramatizing the "call" to
follow). This music is heard throughout fifty seconds of the title
segment of rapid edits of twelve shots, ranging from an artillerymen
ducking an explosion to infantrymen going over the top, and from

the Embarkation Parade to a Funeral Parade with coffins being carried on a line of stalwart shoulders. Out of several shots of mass
troop movement there now appear four individual soldiers, one after the other in matte shots, looking like still photos until each man
breaks into a grin, dispelling any fear that we may be watching
"lifeless" history. In a sequence of 1- to 4-second shots, the whole
course of the war is projected, culminating in a victory image of
troops waving wildly from the back of a transport, just before the
map of the Canadian sector appears and the camera tilts down a
line of place names, following the red line of the Western Front
from Flanders in the north to Amiens in the south. One final dissolve returns us to the full shot of troops waving from the back of a
truck, before a blasted wasteland appears on screen over which the
general series title is imposed – a seemingly still photo that suddenly
explodes in an artillery blast beyond the stumps of shattered trees.
This title shot is then followed immediately by the establishing shot
of that particular episode, and by the elegiac voice of the narrator,
R. H. Thomson.

This type of segmentation in the "call" and "title" sequences is far
more typical of television than of cinema. As John Fiske remarks of
this made-for-TV technique, "Title sequences frequently exploit this
segmentation by editing together shots from the forthcoming or past
programs in a rapid, highly enigmatic way." The technique is a staple of music videos as well, where logical causality is of negligible
import. "Even drama series and serials, where the narrative requires
the principles of logic and cause and effect, may be segmented into
short scenes with logical links omitted. The switching between one
narrative strand and another in multi-narrative programs such as
soap operas is frequently rapid and unmotivated" (Fiske 103). It is a
technique that supports Raymond Williams's claim that "the central
television experience" is "the fact of flow" (95).

And yet, within this visual stream, the segmentation of images in
For King and Empire still must produce a visual code, or system,
for reading such "flow." In the "call" sequence, for example, it is
those two brass figures that set the archival segment in its "heroic"
frame, reassuring us that the story will turn out well, and that these
flickering images in black-and-white have more than a passing
significance. Indeed, our guide calls us to inspect a local landmark –
the name of Stratford conjuring up both the history plays of Shakespeare and the dramatist's enduring fame. As soon as we answer the

"call" (by staying with the channel) to see the Stratford War Memorial as our host sees it – "a gateway to the First World War" – we are swiftly transported to another time and place.

And so we begin our discipleship in flickering recollection of a story told in tones of pride. For this, as the title shot reminds us, is our story as a *nation*, "the *Canadians* at Vimy – 1917," or "the *Canadians* at Passchendaele – 1917," as the subtitle of the fourth episode declares, or "*Canadians* in the Last 100 Days – 1918," as announced in the subtitle of episode 5. On each of these battlefields, "the land remembers" our valour. Of course, it is television that is the true agent of "national unity-within-diversity" (Fiske 55) – a virtual subtext of the medium *qua* medium – but, for all that, still a story of "*Canadian* Soldiers in the Great War," a national narrative of the country's coming of age. In the final episode, "Shadows of the Great War," this view will finally be overtly endorsed by the host amid the 11,000 graves of soldiers in Tyne Cot Cemetery[37] near Passchendaele: "The men who came here in 1914–1915 were British. The men who attacked and captured Vimy Ridge were Canadians. And that transition took place in the hearts and souls of the men who were the Canadian Corps. It was their ability, their pride, in being members of the Canadian Corps, that really created this whole concept of Canadian nationalism" (VI 44.39–45.07).[38]

CAMERA OF NOW AND THEN

In his reflections on "the ontology of film," Stanley Cavell notes a widespread "loss of conviction in the film's capacity to carry the world's presence," in consequence of which "the camera must now, in candor, acknowledge not its being present in the world but its being outside its world" (131, 130). Although the philosopher doesn't mention the impact of television, "this loss of connection" – amounting to a troubling awareness of film's lack of "presentness" – likely derives from the sense of belatedness that live television has imposed on cinema. The claim of television to be "there" with its camera, wherever "news" is being made, tends to marginalize any film camera that can take days or weeks to get its images "out there." That we see events as they occur on "live" television is a result of electronic scanning of the image, followed by its electronic transmission and reconstitution through a scanning beam in distant receivers where the image is rebuilt. Unlike the camera of "then" – film based on thousands of still photos that produce the illusion of motion – the camera of "now" transforms the notion of "live" from simultaneity in the same space to "live" in the same time, if in a displaced "space." As Jane Feuer remarks more sceptically, "Even the simplest meaning of 'live' – that the time of the event corresponds to the transmission and viewing times – reverberates with suggestions of 'being there' ... 'bringing it to you as it really is'" (14).

More disconcertingly, television "happens" in the immediacy and privacy of our homes, catching our attention intermittently in the domestic "flow" of noise, news, and on-screen drama. "Television, then, because of the property of flow, seems 'real' in another sense; unlike cinema, it is an entirely ordinary experience, and this makes it seem natural in a way going to the movies no longer does" (Feuer 15). The "camera of then" is henceforth relegated to cinema theatres and other public spaces. What once looked like the "presentness" of cinema is now exposed as an illusion, a filmic "superimposition ... of reality and of the past," which Roland Barthes claims is "the very essence, the *noeme* of Photography," nowhere more so than in its belonging to the temporal order of "*That-has-been*" (76–7). Whether or not we know that motion pictures are static images passing through a beam of light, we sense that what we are watching is no longer contemporary with us. "The temporal dimension of television, on the other hand, would seem to be that of an insistent 'present-ness,'" Mary Ann Doane says, "a '*This-is-going-on*' rather than a '*That-has-been*,' a celebration of the instantaneous" (269). Henceforth, as "[f]ilm presents itself as a record of what has happened, television presents itself as a relay of what is happening" (Fiske 22).

Television, of course, ceased long ago to be a live medium, increasingly so in an era of magnetic tape and then of digital harddrives, though it continues to present "live" daily broadcasts of news shows, sporting events and other public entertainments that are filled with taped reports, "instant" replays, and digital effects, all of which are "best described as a collage of film, video and 'live,'" all interwoven into a complex and altered time scheme" (Feuer 15). And yet, as television "becomes less and less a 'live' medium in the sense of an equivalence between time of event and time of transmission, the medium in its own practices seems to insist more and more upon an ideology of the live, the immediate, the direct, the spontaneous, the real" (14).

The pretense that "[l]ive television is *not* recorded," that "live television is *alive*," or even that "television is living, real, not dead" (Feuer 14), is maintained through a variety of institutional practices, from programming and public service announcements to production practices. For example, the videotaping of *The Tonight Show*, or *The Daily Show*, like the taping of quiz shows, still takes place before live audiences. In fact, "Quiz and game shows," and so-called "reality TV" shows like *Survivor*, "go to great lengths to disguise the fact that they are prerecorded, and the winners are known, in order to give the viewers the pleasures of engaging with the uncertainty, of predicting and then experiencing its resolution" (Fiske 97). Unlike location-shot dramas and cop shows, sitcoms require feedback (usually laughter) from studio audiences to put the viewer at the scene of what "is going on," rather than at the site of what "has been." Television as an institution must therefore seek to disguise or even repress the fact of its own pastness.

For such reasons, history on television should be a contradiction in terms. How can a medium given over to an ideology of "nowness," and structured in its delivery as "flow" – this term of Raymond Williams since glossed to mean "that television is a continuous succession of images which follows no laws of logic or cause and effect" (Fiske 99), apart from its own endless "flow of consumable reports and products" (R. Williams 105) – how can this medium of the *present tense* devote itself with any credibility to the *past tense*? Would not the "camera of now" and the "camera of then" present, even as they re-present, incompatible modes of vision? Would not history "in the present tense" differ, or even mutate, from history presented, as in the photographic object, in the past tense? And what, in the wider cultural sense, does an "'electronification' of memory" (Urry 63) imply for social memory, for *how* an electronic society remembers the past?

THE DOCUMENTARY LOOK

"[T]elevision," as Mary Ann Doane sees it, "tends to blur the differences between what seem to be absolutely incompatible temporal modes, between the flow and continuity of information and the punctual discontinuity of catastrophe" (270) – although the televisual "catastrophe" in the instance of the Great War is already situated decades in the past. Therefore, the ultimate "catastrophe" in

history programming must be located at the present site of a
viewer's forgetting – a cultural lapse that has produced a general
sense of "punctual discontinuity" in the temporal order. How is it
possible, then, for History Television to put the considerable
strength of this medium – the "nowness" of its continuous flow – at
the disposal of historical memory when its evident "enslavement to
the instant and hence forgettability" (Doane 270) – are at the same
time its Achilles heel?

By means of what John Caughie calls "the documentary look,"
television at least mitigates, if not escapes, the tyranny of what he
calls "the dramatic look" of the medium: "By the 'documentary
look' I mean the system of looks which constructs the social space of
the fiction, a social space which is more than simply a background,
but which, in a sense, constitutes what the documentary drama
wishes to be about, the 'document' which is to be dramatised"
(342). Due to the "nowness" of television, the "then-ness" of history can thus appear as "nowness." But drama, far more than documentary, has to hide its own fictionality. So various conventions of
"the dramatic look," such as the "eye-line match" and "field/
reverse-field" of dramatic interlocutors presented in a "two-shot,"
are meant to persuade us that we see the scene from both points of
view, as if our camera-generated ubiquity in space had also made us
omniscient. To escape the charge of "fiction," then, the historical
documentary cannot afford to put unhistorical images on screen.
Historical persons can appear only in their own image, whether in
photographs – the only "faces" available, for example, to Ken Burns
in his documentary of the American Civil War (1990) – or through
archival footage (a predictable amount of First World War film surviving in grainy black-and-white). The "document" to be "dramatized" must be composed of actual words of real people represented
by their "true" image. And those images of real persons must be integrated into a segmented "flow" which, though not presuming to
give unmediated access to the past, still offers more than the "look"
of the times; ultimately, they must communicate a sense that these
images are the true source of the "document" we are viewing.

Documentaries are by definition retrospective, from the heavily
scripted text of the historical narrator, to letters (most notably those
in *For King and Empire* of Agar Adamson, the commander of the
Princess Patricia's Canadian Light Infantry), to memoirs (notably
those of sharpshooter Will Bird and Chaplain Frederick Scott), to

the spontaneous, though still retrospective, comments of host Norm Christie. Although the documentary is less susceptible than drama to hiding its status as mediated text,[39] its mandate is nonetheless to *dramatize* the "document." To that end, there is some scope for unplanned, or unpremeditated, shots in a documentary. For example, Christie is diverted in nearly every episode by something he espies in a plowed battlefield, or in the woods, or at the side of a road. Suddenly, he will turn aside, or crouch down, to pick up an unexploded Mills bomb, as at the end of the first episode: "Here's a little bit of a find. It looks like – uh – an iron potato, but it's a British Mills bomb" (44.35). Or else he holds up an iron spike that once held a revetment together, if not a footbridge across a trench. Or he will be driving by a pasture fence made of metal posts once used to string barbed wire in No Man's Land, and will stop his van to point out the differences between the German and British implements.

Nothing better displays this "rhetoric of the 'unplanned' or 'unpremeditated' shot" than "the camera surprised by the action" (Fiske 29). And nothing confirms the "nowness" of our presence more than an unexpected shot of the host in *For King and Empire* demonstrating that "This-is-going-on" before our very eyes. "It just doesn't stop, does it, with the things that you find here," director Harvey Crossland says to Christie at one point in episode 2 on the Somme (21.25), as the host reaches down to hold up what he has found in a field of standing wheat: "This is a piece of driving band from off a shell." Of course, it doesn't stop; it must not, since the "surprise" of the host is integral to our sense of the continuing presence of the Great War on screen, even if it should take more threatening forms (such as unexploded 90 kg shells, or 21 cm shells that are "armed" and sensitive to the touch of a hand). The viewer is then positioned in a parallel state of surprise at what he or she has long forgotten, or, more likely, has never known.

By "the dramatic look," Caughie also means a larger "system of looks and glances which is familiar from fictional film, and which works to produce the consistency and movement of the narrative, placing the spectator in relation to it" (342). Although history is less open to this "dramatic look," there is another system of looks and glances at work in *For King and Empire,* appearing on two distinct planes of the camera work and style of editing. One recalls how the host looked back over his shoulder in the opening sequence to speak to someone off-camera (later, it will be director Harvey

Crossland, who walks into the shot with him on the Somme in episode 2, and who will do so again in episode 6 at the Vimy Monument). Here is one meaning of "the documentary look," where the
host virtually acknowledges our presence by looking near the camera, though still preserving the illusion of the camera's "objectivity"
by speaking to someone nearby who doesn't see quite what we do.
To Fiske, this "metadiscourse of camera work and editing is superior to that possessed by" (28) an off-camera listener, because we
see what he or she is unable to see – the host explaining to a well-
intentioned spectator what he already ought to know. Apparently,
we don't even need this lecture aimed at our surrogate: "The omni-
science given us by this dominant discourse of the camera" derives
instead from "our position as an invisible eavesdropper-voyeur who
can hear, see, and understand all" (28) without being put in the position of a pupil subjected to the master's authority. There is no con-
descension in the work of the camera, at least not to this viewer.

At other points, the camera literally precedes us, as in the fifth episode where we follow its uncertain progress through a maze of tunnels under the city of Arras. It is one of the sites where the
Canadian Corps was billeted at the end of August 1918, before
moving against the formidable defenses of the Drocourt–Quéant
Line to the east of the city in a decisive battle of the war. The carved
walls and chalky floor are bathed in a yellow glow as we overhear
the "voice" of Frederick George Scott – an army chaplain in the
First Division from Quebec City whose memoir *The Great War As I
Saw It* has been cited throughout the series – describing a "flight of
steps" which "led down to stone chambers below these and then
down a long sloping passage to a broken wall which barred the entrance into the mysterious caves beneath the city" (Scott 290). Because the light is yellow, we suspect that we are following the
"camera of Now" that was taking shots a moment ago of Christie
on market day in modern Arras. There is no attempt to make us
think we are watching non-existent archival footage of troops quar-
tered under the city in 1918. At the same time, because we follow
the progress of Scott's depiction of "the mysterious caves beneath
the city" (17:28), a substitution of sorts may be effected in the
enunciation. For the moment, it *is* Canon Scott, and not Norm
Christie, leading us on this tour that began with a shot of Christie
descending the slippery stairs of the *souterrain*. The work of the
camera thus manages, with the help of sound dubbing, to take us

down the well of memory. So we are back, by means of the "now-ness" of television, in the time zone of August 1918 with Canon Scott and the Canadian Corps.

Two similar sequences in episode 3 carry us more ambiguously between the two times. The first shot is archival footage of men in a tunnel, the voice-over matching text to image in the actor's reading from Will Bird's memoir *And We Go On* (1930): "[They lowered Tommy and me] down, by a ladder that was quite vertical, to a chalk tunnel" (26). A straight cut brings new archival footage of soldiers passing planks hand to hand, with Will Bird's text in voice-over: "[W]hen we got down there all sound stilled and it was warm. We had to shed our great coats and equipment at once." And then the black-and-white picture dissolves to a dim, yellow light as a camera trained at foot-level moves ahead of us in the chalk tunnel, rising to peer some twenty metres ahead. Meanwhile, the "voice" of Will Bird carries over the shot: "[We went crouching] on all fours, along a tunnel in solid chalk just four feet high and hardly three feet wide ... The chalk face was sprayed with vinegar. Then one man cut it with a knife as it softened and passed back large chunks to his helper ... At any moment, it was possible the removal of a newly cut chunk might reveal a German dugout filled with men! For weeks afterwards, my whole body would tense when I thought of that night" (26–7;15.34–16.11). FADE to black, and the lights rise on Norm Christie speaking to us over his shoulder as a following shot takes us through the Grange Subway under Vimy Ridge. The point is not that we have been tricked, but that the camera has been "there" long before us with Bird, and well before the arrival of the host. Christie is now catching up with us; we are not catching up with him.

Much later in the Vimy episode, after the host and narrator have laid out the tactics and their execution in the battle of 9–12 April 1917, Christie stands on the pedestal of the monument, looking past the statue of "Canada bereft" (Hucker 282) mourning her fallen sons as he gestures to the landscape beyond: "This is the view that they had ... [of] this beautiful, lush green territory. The Canadians were the ones that were in control. But they had one more attack to make, to secure the entire Ridge, and that was going to be at the Pimple. It would take place two days later." The shot dissolves to a black-and-white image of Christie moving ahead of us into the landscape. We watch his back moving away as the shot dissolves to black-and-white footage of shells exploding in the distance, the camera closing to a huge black plume, and then sudden darkness. It is this image of a subject who has been speaking to us over his shoulder walking into the past that truly authorizes this inverse "invasion" of television; contrary to the silent film image that has typically invaded the present, the vocal television image takes us with him in the opposite direction, "swimming" upstream of time, as it were.

Over this sequence there now sounds the "voice" of another soldier, Cpl Victor Wheeler, describing the novelty of following a creeping barrage (a tactic first employed successfully by the British at Vimy, and a prototype of the television tactic by which we now invade the past): "We went forward with chronometer accuracy, virtually touching the steel edge of the beautiful creeping barrage, always a few feet ahead of us. The whipping, cutting sound of hard, steel fury was music to our ears. The sight of the German parapets, dugouts, and machine gun emplacements exploding skyward" – as the screen fades to black – "was a pleasure." And the lights come up on archival footage of a soldier (CU) throwing a Mills bomb, then others in the shot rising to hurl grenades as well. "More like enraged avengers," Wheeler's voice-over continues, "than well-disciplined Canadian volunteer soldiers, we Mills-bombed, shot dead, grappled, and rifle-butted the enemy. And, within an hour" – the black-and-white footage dissolves to a colour shot of sunrise over distant trees – "we had succeeded in capturing The Pimple" (40.31–41.22). The visual novelty of this sequence has to do with Christie advancing as if into black-and-white footage of 1917, stepping through a curtain into this other time that has been awaiting his arrival, waiting all this time for us, as it were, to arrive on the scene as all hell breaks loose. It is in this sense, more than any other, that the camera produces its "documentary look" that also makes us part of its larger system of looks and glances.

FLOW AND REGULARITY

One of the more daunting things about attempting a full shot analysis of a single episode of televisual history – just forty-five minutes – is to find ways to stop the visual "flow" in words that may provide an "analysis of a heterogeneity, the range of codes and systems at work in television over and across its matters of expression (speech, music, sound effects, writing, moving pictures" (Heath and Skirrow

10). I necessarily narrow my focus to the Vimy episode of *For King and Empire,* the only one for which I have made a complete shot analysis. Even at that, there isn't space for an exhaustive analysis of a single episode composed of 359 shots – 171 of them from archival footage, 56 from black-and-white photos, 14 of colour maps, and 3 colour shots of war paintings, in addition to 115 shots taken with a video camera on location (44 with the host on camera) – as well as hundreds of bars of music, the sound of detonating shells and clattering machine guns, and thousands of words of script, both by series screenwriter Gilbert Reid and by combatants themselves in their letters and memoirs. How is this wealth of varied information also shaped by editor Paul Kilback into a coherent "document"? Of what does such heterogeneity speak, in fact? Do images and words tell the same story? If so, how? Where is structure to be found in the seemingly endless flow of images?

"[P]lanned flow," as Raymond Williams famously wrote, is "perhaps the defining characteristic of [television] broadcasting, simultaneously as a technology and as a cultural form" (86), although this is a dated notion now being questioned by theorists and practitioners alike. John Fiske points to Williams's "lack of sympathy with the nature of television and the reading relations it sets up with its audiences," arguing to the contrary that "[f]low, with its connotations of a languid river, is perhaps an unfortunate metaphor: the movement of the television text is discontinuous, interrupted, and segmented" (100, 105). And Stephen Heath, a maker of documentaries along with Gillian Skirrow, aims as well to neutralize the whole emphasis on "flow." To the contrary, Heath and Skirrow say that "The 'central fact of television experience' is much less flow than *flow and regularity*" (15).

A shot analysis of "Storming the Ridge" confirms a casual impression that several types of regularity occur in the editing, regularities that are meant to give us our bearings in the midst of "flow." One of these regularities in the flow of sound and image is voice distribution: the host gets roughly 18 minutes to the narrator's 15, while the letters and memoirs of combatants take up 13 minutes. (The "rule" has been established in the first episode, where the ratio is host:17; narrator:15; combatants:13. "Air" time given to the soldiers is thus a constant in the series, about 30 percent of each 45-minute episode. In the fifth episode, however, the host gets a bit less time than the narrator [15/16], and in the last episode, the ratio is actually reversed [15/17]). These, then, are the regular recurring proportions out of which the verbal document is made: 30 percent for the soldiers, with the host and narrator alternating between 37 percent and 33 percent of the time.

Similar regularities appear in the visual document, in terms of running times for images matched to voice. Location shots (with or without the host) take up some 13 minutes in episode 3, while Christie is heard speaking for another 8 minutes about various sites and objects in our field of view. Obviously, the narrator as a disembodied voice of history does not appear on camera, but his voice is often matched to images from archival footage or maps, or, at times, as in the opening sequence of cratered landscape, to the location shot itself. If the host has 18 minutes on (or just off) camera, there are some 20 minutes of images of combatant experience, inasmuch as photos of the speakers take up 6 minutes, with another 14 minutes given to archival shots of troops in action or in recreation. Add to these visual documents some 2 minutes and 15 seconds of colour maps and 36 seconds of paintings by war artists, and one has a rough idea of the true heterogeneity of this "flow," as well as the regularities of its appearance.

On the one hand, episode 3 is all about "flow," from the first tracking shot of Vimy's craters to subsequent shots of troops moving through its "moonscape," to a map shot of the region north of Arras. This whole segment flows in such a way as to set us down on the adjacent ridges of Notre Dame de Lorette and Vimy, as well as to situate us in the nearby villages of Mont St. Eloi and Neuville St. Vaast (2.35–3.14). The next set-up includes images of helmeted German troops moving toward us through a trench, and a column of Canadians coming up a road, "marching from the battlefield of the Somme," the narrator reports, "where they had suffered 25,000 casualties" (3.14–3.46). This information is followed by a straight cut to a shell explosion, followed by a blast, with the camera closing to a tight shot of a billowing cloud of dirt and gas. Another straight cut leads to a black-and-white photo of bodies laid in rows on a slight downward slope as a musical chord builds tensely to the narrator's announcement that the Canadians, exhausted from "a bloodbath" at the Somme, "are ordered to Vimy" (3.47–3.58).

At this point, a shot of corpses dissolves to a black-and-white portrait photo of Donald Fraser, "a cool, tough Scot from Alberta," before dissolving to a colour shot of the slag heaps of Lens north of

Vimy Ridge. In a broad Scots accent, an actor quotes a letter from Fraser: "We are treading the road again on the way to a new front. Slag heaps become a prominent feature of the landscape." The video camera obligingly pans right in a telephoto shot of slag heaps in the distance, rising like Egyptian pyramids out of the verdant landscape (3.58–4.15). In a curious way, the image of slag heaps appears to precede Fraser's description of them, as if the visual image were conjuring up his words. Commenting on this device, Heath and Skirrow stress the importance of giving priority to the image, even when it is merely there to fill the screen for words scripted before it and in need of a visual match: "Certainly … the commentary over in this section was written and read. Such anteriority, effectively sustained, would break the television present … [I]mages are proposed as the actuality of the commentary, the latter following them – it hardly matters what images as long as they always appear as the *cause*" (20). On this reading, it is the *present* of television that actually authorizes the colour-fade to black-and-white in the middle of that colour shot of slag heaps (4.19). It is also this shot that "causes" Fraser's next remark, "The countryside embracing Notre-Dame de Lorette is somewhat pretty" (4.15–4.21). Fraser's letter concludes with another brief comment, "Next to Vimy, the Lorette promontory has been the scene of such frequent and bloody combats that the French call it La Butte de la Mort, the Ridge of Death" (4.32–4.39). And the scene changes to a shot (in both senses) of the barrel of a German gun recoiling. The anteriority of the landscape shot – the functional marker of television's "now-ness" – thus works to set us down in the scene as if we were viewing the nightly news (on a black-and-white television set).

The voice-over of the narrator follows, as if commenting on footage of old news: "In 1915, the French had driven the Germans from Notre-Dame de Lorette, but they failed to take Vimy Ridge. After months of savage fighting, French missing, wounded, and dead numbered 150,000." At this point, the black-and-white footage of soldiers in a very long shot (VLS) advancing over a plain dissolves to a colour shot (5.03) of crosses marking the graves of thousands of French soldiers, and Norm Christie enters the shot, moving toward the camera trained on the apex of the converging rows of crosses: "We're at La Targette French Military Cemetery near Vimy Ridge," he says, speaking *here* and *now,* from the television *present;* then, for another 42 seconds, he speaks of the "fallen of 1915" and the reasons for the French "disaster."[40] In the middle of one ECU of a white cross with its brass nameplate of a dead French soldier, Christie begins to reveal his subtext: "The French built very big cemeteries." DISSOLVE to an overhead shot (OH), and we see dozens of rows of crosses stretching up and over a hill. The point hardly needs to be spoken: "massive cemeteries, and you – you feel the massive loss [DISSOLVE to Christie moving down a row and looking back, talking to someone just off camera], but at the same time you don't feel the individual loss. The British Commonwealth cemeteries are smaller and more individual" (5.49–6.16).

By this time, what Heath and Skirrow call "the *protocol* of the programme" (19) has been fully established. We anticipate, before it occurs, another dissolve to black-and-white footage of grave diggers at work in a field, as the narrator recalls how, "[i]n the winter of 1916, the dead of the year before are still unburied at Vimy Ridge [note the present tense] as Agar Adamson, the 53-year-old commander of the Princess Patricia's Canadian Light Infantry, soon discovers when he enters the trench." Adamson's identifying photo emerges from the dissolve and holds on screen for 7 seconds as the camera closes to an ECU (brow to chin) of his face – if the image doesn't move, the television camera must do so. "Dear Mabel," Adamson writes to his wife at home in Hamilton, describing the dead still scattered about, not to mention whole companies of Germans in a cave who "refused to come out," shooting "the French officer who went down. The French then put smoke bombs down the shaft [DISSOLVE to photo of dead bodies lying in a cave] and suffocated them all, 280 of them. They are still there [STRAIGHT CUT to a CU of a tangle of corpses], huddled together as they died. It is a dreadful and unsavoury sight with thousands of rats." STRAIGHT CUT to archival footage of troops digging with picks and hammers as Agar concludes, "I'm having the shaft closed and sealed up with cement. Well, that's it for today, old girl. Ever thine, Agar" (6.21–7.17). In less than a minute, the full horrors of a year of failed attacks on Vimy sweep into view in the verbal and visual text. But more than this spare performance will still be required to "dramatise the document."

As the narrator tallies the 140,000 dead on the German side, a black-and-white shot of a field of crosses turns to colour, and the camera pans across row after row, before dissolving to a following shot of Christie again walking down a row: "We're at Neuville St. Vaast German Military Cemetery near Vimy Ridge. It's the largest German cemetery in the area, and it contains about 45,000 burials." As the shot dissolves to a field of black crosses with shade trees in the background, Christie adds, "German cemeteries of this nature put four men to a cross. The ones that are headstones and not crosses [DISSOLVE to a following shot of Christie moving to a headstone and kneeling, the camera closing to a tight shot] are Jewish German soldiers. This is – uh – I don't know if I can pronounce it. Isidor Machol. He was killed in November 1916 [STRAIGHT CUT to an ECU of Machol's name below a Star of David; the image is held for 4 more seconds]."

The next dissolve leads to another following shot of Christie talking over his shoulder as he moves down the rows, describing how "German cemeteries have a different atmosphere, one of foreboding, and sadness, and pain." The shot then dissolves into a ground-level shot of black crosses with leafless trees in the background, before the camera pans over the rows. And Christie concludes, "It's a different ... a different ... atmosphere than a British cemetery, which is like an Edwardian garden" (8.20). And we begin to sense that this is one of the dramatic regularities of the program – the imagining of differing ways in which each society remembers its dead, while clearly privileging the intimacy of personal remembrance in English-speaking culture. More than this, we begin to suspect that the "nowness" of television is what has motivated this brief "timeout" in the action, for the "real" story is less about the past than about the television *present* mediating that past, and its availability to anyone willing to go over the same ground, to heed the "call" of the following shot.

The whole series, in fact, is punctuated by such regular visits to cemeteries. The first episode, "Baptism of Fire," is barely 5 minutes old when we get a location shot of Christie in a graveyard: "This is Voormezeele Enclosure Number Three Cemetery, and it's here at Voormezeele that the first Canadians came into the Line in the First World War. It started here in these peaceful fields. This is the grave of the first Canadian killed in the First World War. He was killed near here on the 8th of January 1915.[41] Lance-Cpl H. G. Bellinger, Princess Patricia's Canadian Light Infantry, 8th January 1915. Aged 39" (1 6.10–6.52). Three minutes later, Christie speaks again from a similar location: "This is Langemarck German Cemetery, the largest German cemetery around Ypres, and we're really here to illustrate the point of the failure of the Germans to capture Ypres in 1914." What emerges over 2 minutes 40 seconds of changing shots of the cemetery, however, is the discourse of cultural difference: "Each one of these blocks [close-up of a dark bronze block carved with tiny names swims on-screen] lists the names of approximately 500 German soldiers who were killed around Ypres and are buried in this mass grave" (1 10.09). There is no mention of the postwar German economy ravaged by runaway inflation, or of French reluctance to cede land to the invader, as it had done in gratitude to the Allies. Rather, we get a CU of Christie straining to pick out a single name, as if to redeem the anonymity of the 44,000 bodies in Langemarck Cemetery, 25,000 of which had to be dumped in a mass grave, given the limited space: "One of them here is a – uh – Franz Haber[42] who was killed in the battle in October 1914, who was one of those thousands that were shot down coming across the Salient." In such fashion, the discourse of the Name becomes a structural regularity in the series (see below).

For now, it is enough to observe three major forms of regularity in each episode:

1 A regular relay from voice to voice (usually in repeating sequence from narrator to assembled eyewitnesses – the testimony of Donald Fraser, Agar Adamson, and Canon Scott running through each episode, supplemented by such newcomers as Victor Wheeler [episode 2] and Will Bird [episode 3] – and so onward to Christie himself in the cemeteries, or else at the Crater Line, or later at the front door of the Château Camblain l'Abbé, where General Julian Byng and Lt-General Arthur Currie made their meticulous preparations for the assault on Vimy);

2 A regular relay of images from then and now, in fairly predictable sequences, as, for example, dissolving from a still photo of snipers seated in a trench, the camera closing to a full shot of one of them cradling a rifle, to another photo of an empty trench, except that now the picture begins to move while colour bleeds into a shot of feet moving in advance of the camera;

3 A building of each segment toward a dramatic climax that has to occur at least five times in the hour, for the break to commercial. (This latter regularity also marks the structure of commercial television, taking from 5 to 8 minutes to build each segment to a climax. Writer Gilbert Reid and editor Paul Kilback thus make good use of a five-act structure in every episode, with breaks left for commercials – the whole show taking 46.32 of running time, including title and credit sequences).

STRUCTURING THE "DRAMATIC DOCUMENT"

The first Act of "Storming the Ridge" builds through 10 minutes and 5 seconds to a climax, with the camera panning in archival footage over a Church Parade, while Canon Scott recalls: "At midnight, the buglers sounded the Last Post, and the Band struck up the hymn, 'O God, Our Help in Ages Past.' A mighty chorus of voices joined in the well-known strains." Bugles can be heard throughout this long, 28-second shot as the camera pans past the chaplain's flowing white robes to the ranks of men in soft hats standing at ease, and helmeted MPs standing to one side. "It was an inspiring sight," Scott recalls, "and we all felt that we were beginning a year that was to decide the destiny of the Empire" (11.11–11.39). The screen fades to black before a new segment (made up of several 30-second commercials) begins to decide the destinies of advertisers.

After the commercial break, the narrator begins again, reminding us where we are and what we are doing here: "When they arrive [in the present, it seems] at the Front, the Canadians have not recovered from the bloodbath of France. Their British Commander Julian Byng knows he has only a few months to transform his exhausted Canadians into a single, dynamic fighting force" (11.50–12.05). From here, the second Act builds through a winter of preparations to the eve of battle. Again, the testimony of Canon Scott is used to carry this segment to a climax: "What did the next twenty-four hours hold [archival footage of a big gun firing from beside a stone wall launches the verbal text towards an anxious resolution] in store for us? Was it to be [the shot cuts away to archival footage, a three-shot of artillerymen firing an eighteen-pounder from inside a low building] a true Easter for the world, a resurrection to a new and better life?" Another straight cut takes us to a shell exploding in the distance, and then a further series of explosions as the camera pans over the smoke and confusion of battle. "If death awaited us, what nobler passage could there be to eternity? Such a death in such a cause" (24.36–25.00), the Anglican chaplain says, rather in the vein of Jonathan Vance's title in his brilliant social history of Canadian commemoration, *Death So Noble* (1997).

The regularities of the third Act, used to dramatize the Canadian Corps's assault on Vimy Ridge in the first day of the battle, are largely those of rhythm, the high volume and rapidity of images achieved through rapid cutting to give us a sense of the battle for which little film exists. In 10 minutes of shots, 3 minutes are made up of only forty-three archival moving shots, a fairly moderate pace. But eighteen of these shots will come in the thick of the action: four take but a second each, four more appear for 2 seconds, four more are on screen for 3 seconds, and the rest run from 4 to 8 seconds. The most rapid shots are of a row of field guns firing from a wood, a large gun firing from a carriage on tractor wheels, another huge gun firing from a railway flatbed, and an eighteen-pounder firing from a thicket. The verbal text accompanying the visual text is little more than a part of speech in these shots: "The tempest of death" accompanies 2 seconds of big guns firing away from the camera; the noun phrase is followed by three shots running from the verb "swept" to the preposition "through" to the prepositional object "the air" (26.47–26.52). Much of the third Act sweeps by in such fashion, assaulting the senses of the viewer, until it climaxes in 4 successive shots: a map of Vimy with coloured arrows moving in the direction of each of the four attacking Divisions; a black-and-white photo of troops outdistancing the fallen, with the camera closing to a full shot of one corpse; then a photo of body parts beside a stretcher, with the camera pulling back from the shocking sight; and a final photo of corpses strewn about a wide hollow, with the camera panning slowly over the bodies. On the third-last shot, the narrator remarks in the present tense, "A German officer looks down on the dying of the Fourth Division." Then a German voice (presumably of "Ernst Jünger") speaks over the last two shots: "In the entanglements of the German line where the corpses lie in khaki heaps, the Canadian attack against us peters out in blood" (34.57–35.24). The climax is thus a searing reminder that "heroism" comes at a price.

The pacing is slower in the fourth Act, especially when the cost of taking Hill 145 and pushing the Germans off "The Pimple" is tallied in headstones at a nearby cemetery. To reach this spot, we must cross through a series of photographs (the photos and one painting suggesting a scarcity of moving images of the events of the assault on 12 April), the camera closing steadily on a figure of a blown-out tank, or a photo of troops running forward, the camera then drawing back to show the breadth of the attack. There are photos of corpses laid headfirst to the camera, and of distant troops disappearing over a ridge. A colour dissolve now leads to an unexpected painting of a blasted landscape tinted blue and splashed with red, with the camera closing to a full shot of a lone infantryman at its bleak centre (36.53–37.01). Out of a black-and-white "photo" of a Cross of Remembrance appears a sudden colour shot of the cemetery, with our host leading us through Givenchy-en-Gohelle Cemetery, "one of the nicest, and most remote, historically anyway, cemeteries on the Western Front. You can hear the cars speeding by on their way to Paris. And no one has any time for this sacrifice here." In another following shot, the camera turns a corner to find Christie kneeling by a headstone to read the inscription: "W. T. Hooper, 78th Battalion (which was the Winnipeg Grenadiers), 9 April 1917, Aged 38. 'Tell England that we Died for Her / And Here We Rest Content" (38.42). And we discover that another subtext of the series has just been unearthed.

The fourth Act will take another 3 minutes to reach its conclusion, however, with the host now tramping through a field of brown hay to write a coda to an action we have "seen" with our own eyes: "The Pimple was a position that ran from that wood, which is called Givenchy Wood, across that big mound. From these points, about two thousand men from Western Canada charged across No Man's Land in a blinding snowstorm and drove out the Germans from The Pimple. They fought in Bois de Givenchy, and in Givenchy Village, and by the end of the night, the battle of Vimy Ridge was over" (41.22–41.55). The identification of the Fourth Division as "men from Western Canada" completes the project of achieving unity-through-diversity; viewers from all parts of the country are now sutured into this text of the "birth of the nation."

If the fifth Act begins with a series of shots of Germans shuffling into prison camps, the balance of the segment returns to where Act One began, in Vimy Park, at the Memorial in the present-tense of the host who has called us to witness the hardships and the horrors, as well as the triumphs and joys, of those four days in April 1917, when the Canadian Corps, with men from every corner of the nation, came together for the first time to fight as a unified (and uniquely successful) force. In more following shots of Norm Christie walking up a path to the twin pylons of the Vimy Monument, or mounting the steps below allegories carved in stone, we hear how this memorial "commemorates the sacrifice of Canadians, over 600,000 who served in the War, and specifically those who died. The inscription here reads: 'To the valour of their countrymen, and in memory of their 60,000 dead, this monument is raised by the people of Canada" (44.17–44.49). And our host now points to

"This statue" which "is the soul of the Monument," while the shot dissolves to a mid-shot (MS) of Christie staring into the distance, with a long shot (LS) of the statue filling the back of the shot. "This is the Spirit of Canada weeping for her fallen sons. It's the center-piece of the whole – the heart of the Monument, really. It's a beauti-ful statue by Walter Allward of Toronto." DISSOLVE to the head and shoulders of the statue as the camera closes in soft focus, before sharpening to a very clear focus on the grieving face. "This Monu-ment," Christie affirms, "is just the most moving tribute to Cana-dian sacrifice." As the shot dissolves to a mid-shot of him with "the Spirit of Canada" at full-length to his left, he says, "As a Canadian, I'm instilled with pride when I come here. This is just the–uh – most magnificent monument I've ever seen." As the shot dissolves, the camera moves right and draws back to bring both pylons into final view, framing the Spirit of Canada at their centre. "In every detail. And the fact that it's Canadian just moves me incredibly" (45.43–46.33). Now the credits roll to the sound of pipes playing "The Maple Leaf Forever," as we digest the whole series of regularities that have flowed to this conclusion.

FILMED AND WRITTEN HISTORY

There is one regularity that is not a property of the televisual text at all, but is yet integral to its coherence: network scheduling. The Vimy episode, as well as two or three more of the Canadians at Ypres, at Passchendaele, or at the Somme (though rarely in the vic-tory of "The Last Hundred Days") are shown each year in broad-casts leading up to Remembrance Day. Part of their coherence derives from larger social practices of commemoration, from the way that our culture tends to make sense of our past. At less ritual-istic moments, perhaps, episodes of *For King and Empire* are shown on TV Ontario or the Saskatchewan Communications Network, these public networks having shared with History Television the cost of production. The Great War has not ended yet in our televi-sion present where "[m]emory-keeping is a function increasingly as-signed to the electronic media" (Samuel 25). But, given the "nowness" of television, what sort of "history" are we looking at? And how does it compare with written history?

From the perspective of the written document, including opera-tional reports of battalion commanders, Gary Sheffield makes a strong case that what we find in the story of Vimy is a folk memory with deep roots in British, as well as in Canadian, popular culture because of "the nationality of the troops selected to capture it; the proximity of Vimy to England; and the building of a visitor- (especially pupil-) friendly memorial, complete with artificially preserved trenches" (27). His reassessment, based on the scholarly deployment of documents, is very much at odds with the televisual history of "Storming the Ridge." In "Looking at the Past in a Postliterate Age," Robert A. Rosenstone reminds us, all the same, how "[f]ilm neither replaces written history nor supplements it. Film stands adjacent to written history, as it does to other forms of dealing with the past such as memory and the oral tradition" (65). While his topic has little to do with history on television, Sheffield's reappraisal of the folk memory of Vimy does fit within this pattern of differences between visual and written history. "Film," as Rosenstone argues, for example, "insists on history as the story of individuals, either men or women (but usually men) who are already renowned, or men and women who are made to seem important because they have been singled out by the camera" (55).

At least in part, the story of men of renown is typical of the kind of history one does find in *For King and Empire*, where the narrative is based on the words of war memoirists.[43] *The Great War as I Saw It* (2nd. ed. 1934) is surely the authorizing document for Canon Scott to appear as lead witness in episode 1 (and who then appears in episode 2 as the grieving father risking his life on the Somme to give his son's body a proper burial in No Man's Land). Scott is both the voice of conventional heroism and the prop of Empire in the third episode, while his testimony will recur at regular intervals in episode 4 at Passchendaele. In episode 5, he is finally wounded out of the battle in the decisive attack on the Drocourt–Quéant Line, but he leaves the field in the most stirring fashion possible: "Our journey lay over the area where we had just made the great advance. Through the open door of the ambulance as we sped onward, I could see the brown, colourless stretch of countryside fade in the twilight and vanish into complete darkness. And I knew that the great adventure of my life, among the most glorious men that the world had ever produced, had come to an end" (31.56). And one begins to hear the echoes of a new Homeric discourse on nobility and fame.

One of the most gripping memoirs on either side of the war is Will Bird's *And We Go On* (1930; republished in 1968 and after as

Ghosts Have Warm Hands). Bird, as one would expect, appears with increasing frequency in later episodes, following his arrival in theatre at Vimy Ridge. Bird's voice is the true "Homer," if there is one, of the Great War, raising vital questions about valour and immortality in an industrial age. But other voices, like those of Donald Fraser, Agar Adamson, Victor Wheeler, and John Harold Becker (who arrives in theatre in episode 4), are likewise crucial. Although these "ordinary" people are less renowned, the series would be diminished without their stories.

At the same time, an admirer of Will Bird's *And We Go On* is shocked to read his version of trench initiation after watching it in "Storming the Ridge." In the video, we see a series of archival images, ranging from Germans coming up a trench, to a German climbing a trench ladder, to more Germans in an overhead (OH) shot moving down a trench with a body sagging in a stretcher. The images on film are matched to the "voice" of Will Bird in a short passage from *And We Go On*: "The distance was not more than 100 yards and I had crosshair sights. It was not a good shot, but I had really killed a Hun, my first. A second German, wearing his full pack, appeared in the same place. I shot him as soon as he appeared. [sound of a rifle shot] He had his hair close-cropped and binoculars in his hand. I shot him [sound of another shot], and as he went down, the binoculars were flung in a high loop over his head" (14.39–15.10). The story of Bird's initiation ends at this point, as the shot dissolves to archival footage of Canadians coming up the trench. And the narrator conducts us underground to the story of tunneling through chalk, to which Bird brings further first-hand testimony.

An entirely different impression of the scene is given in the book, however, where there is far more space to complete the story. Bird writes:

> I shot him and as he went down the binoculars were flung in a high loop over his head.
> The fellow with him was aiming a rifle in our general direction. Pearce gripped my shoulder. He had been watching with the glasses outside the plate. "Shoot!" he rasped. "You won't get a chance like this all day."
> I drew back and handed him the rifle. A queer sensation had spread over me like nausea. "Go ahead yourself," I said. "I've had enough." (Bird 22)

The making of a "hero" is rather more ambiguous in Bird's understated narrative than it is in the commercial video version.[44] The ideology of valour informing this and the other episodes finally works to eclipse Bird's darker narrative of self-estrangement and exile at the end of *And We Go On*. As he stands with his fellow soldiers at the rail of a ship approaching Nova Scotia, Bird muses sadly in his memoir, "Ah – we were like prisoners. I had seen them standing together, staring over the wire to the field beyond, never speaking. And we were more or less prisoners of our thoughts" (Bird 171).

Of course, the omission of the sniper's nausea in the televisual text may also be rooted in generic differences between filmed and written history. "Film," as Robert Rosenstone puts it, "offers us history as the story of a closed, completed, and simple past. It provides no alternative possibilities to what we see happening on the screen, admits of no doubts, and promotes each historical assertion with the same degree of confidence" (55–56). It is really this failure to "open" the story to other choices that makes *For King and Empire* another species of history altogether. Not a word is said, for example, about the conscription crisis of 1917 that has poisoned to this day relations between Quebec and Canada, as we now ponder our choices in Afghanistan. Nor is much said about the role played by Canadian women in producing one-third of the shells fired from behind British lines, or in helping to make Canada a great industrial power. There is little room for aught but gratitude to the men who served, and to the mothers and wives who stayed behind to grieve.

There are nonetheless moments, as in Carolyn Papineau's letter to Colonel Agar Adamson in episode 4 responding to news of her son Talbot's death, when one can almost hear Andromache appealing to her husband Hektor, "Dearest, / your own great strength will be your death, and you have no pity / on your little son, nor on me, illstarred, who soon must be your widow" (*Iliad* 6. 406–8). Thanking Talbot's commanding officer for his words of condolence, Madame Papineau adds, "Nothing will ever console me for the loss of my boy" (27.45). We also hear the sober regrets of Mabel Adamson, whose husband had written to her every day of the war, but failed to adjust to the peace. Leaving Mabel two years after his return to her, Agar would later drink himself to death in England. "I had always hoped against hope that he would come back to me and lead a simpler life," Mabel writes quietly to her son after the funeral. "But it was not to be. And there is a blank in my life that will never be

filled" (VI 21.40–22.06). But these are not the stories on which a
45-minute episode can linger. The television show does what it can
do best – tell the "heroic" story behind each name it has picked out
on the monuments and headstones.

As Rosenstone notes, "Both dramatized works and documentaries use the special capabilities of the medium [of film] – the closeup
of the human face, the quick juxtaposition of disparate images, the
power of music and sound effect – to heighten and intensify the
feelings of the audience about the events depicted on the screen"
(56). It is precisely these capabilities of film that would appeal to
Ken Burns, the American filmmaker, for example, in explaining his
method in *The Civil War* (1990): "[W]e wanted you to believe you
were there ... there is not one shot, not one photograph of a battle
ever taken during the Civil War. There is not one moment in which
a photographer exposed a frame during a battle, and yet you will
swear that you saw battle photography ... You live inside those
photographs, experiencing a world as if it was real inside those photographs" (cited by Edgerton 311).

You are there. This is the fundamental principle to which the producers of *For King and Empire* adhere in their own quest to recover
the past on History Television. For they, too, want you to "live inside those photographs" that are ubiquitous in the series (amounting to one-sixth of all shots). Indeed, it is the intimacy of these
close-ups, as well as the dynamism of the camera panning across a
still image, bringing it to life, that draws us close to these men
whose hopes and fears engage us at a personal level. Here is a
method of "dramatizing the historical document" that differs little
from Ken Burns's assertion "that television can become a new Homeric mode. What other form would allow such powerful emotions
of the war to come forward, would allow you to follow the spear
carriers as well as the gods?" (Milius 43).

"THEIR NAME LIVETH FOREVERMORE"

At the level of ideology, *For King and Empire* has a deeper connection
still to Homer's *Iliad*. For what I call the discourse of the Name
shapes the series, not just the final episode in which the story of Canadian commemoration is told as part of a larger story of battlefield
clearances at the end of the war – this risky, painful work of gathering
unexploded ordnance and unburied corpses. Of the latter, 125,000

corpses were brought in for burial by the Imperial War Graves Commission between 1919 and 1921 (and these, Christie hastens to remind us, are only the Commonwealth dead). With so many burials comes reburial, of course, a great labour of moving thousands of lonely graves marked by wooden crosses into landscaped cemeteries that are kept to this day like "Edwardian gardens" (1 8.20). In the end, the War Graves Commission was to establish 956 cemeteries (CWGC 90) on three key principles: (1) "universality of treatment," that is to say, without distinction of rank or class; (2) the permanence of the name, or, in Christie's words, the principle that "every name was going to be remembered, which is why they have these cemeteries and the memorials to the missing"; and (3) the principle that "no bodies could be repatriated," meaning that every soldier was to lie in the field where he fell with his fallen comrades (VI 17.47–18.17). There were only a few successful instances of bodysnatching, as, for example, one Anna Durie of Toronto who in 1925 did manage to spirit the body of her son Lt William Durie out of France and home to Toronto, where he lies to this day beside the body of his mother.

Though given a proper burial, 110,000 of these bodies could not be identified (and 110,000 more were never found). In Commonwealth cemeteries such as Tyne Cot near Passchendaele, nearly 70 percent of the white headstones are inscribed with the words: "A Soldier of the Great War/ Known unto God." At nearby Poelcapelle Cemetery, Christie informs us, the number approaches 83 percent. At this point, the shot closes on a cemetery wall bearing a motto from Rudyard Kipling: "Their Name Liveth Forevermore" (45.25.) The irony is inescapable. Most of these Portland stones have no name. The anger of Achilles rises like bile in the throat.

But the story does not end in nameless headstones. For, in the shadow of a towering ziggurat on the Somme (where the second episode had ended), Christie says, "They decided, in an absolutely incredible decision, that every name of every soldier and sailor and airman who was killed in the war would be remembered, would be commemorated forevermore. And they decided to build memorials to the missing. This," glancing in the direction of the brick colossus filling the frame behind him, "was for all the British Empire. And we're now walking up to the Thiepval Memorial that commemorates 73,000, primarily British dead … Again, it lists the names of all the men who have no known grave, who vanished on these fields" (VI 27.00–27.30).

The fourth Act opens with a markedly different sort of remembrance, however: 80,000 veterans of the Canadian Corps gather in Toronto in August, 1934, "determined to remind the world of their service" at a time when "The sacrifice of the soldiers of the Great War is fast fading from memory" (30.58–31.10). A month later, another group of Great War veterans will gather at Nuremberg to "celebrate the success of one of their own in power for a year – Adolph Hitler" (32.27). The moral of the tale is clear: "As Adolph Hitler triumphs in Germany, Canadians squabble over the cost of building memorials to their Great War Veterans, and even to their greatest victories" (32.41). Those who forget history are condemned to repeat it. But the words of George Santayana will not be voiced for fear of descending into cliché. And yet we are made to realize the greater cost of forgetting; we see what happens if we don't remember.

And so we are brought back one final time to the Vimy Monument, where the third episode began and ended, to hear the narrative of its creation. A story popularized of late in Jane Urquhart's lyrical work of fiction, *The Stone Carvers* (2001), Christie's narrative focuses more narrowly on Walter Allward's determination to erect this "perfect" work of art that would mirror the unparalleled achievements of the Canadian Corps, as well as preserve the names of 11,285 Canadians still missing in France. After a segment in which we see King Edward VIII unveil the monument before a crowd of one hundred thousand on 26 July 1936, there is a dissolve to a two-shot of Christie with director Harvey Crossland, looking at the carved words of dedication to the missing. A following shot brings us to the base of the pedestal as Crossland kneels before a name that has leapt out of the thousands of letters carved in stone: "W. William Crossland. So that's all that's left of my grandfather. No known grave?" (39.45). Far more is left, of course – in this instance, a huge medal of bronze that Crossland hands to Christie, who says, "This is called the Next-of-Kin Plaque, or was known as the Dead Man's Penny. It was sent to families after the war, 1922, around then. Every family who lost somebody, they would get one of these plaques. And the plaques are unique in that they bear the name of the man who died. This is an individual commemoration of this particular individual, which is William Crossland. So this is unique to your grandfather." A whole society – made up as well of a later group of filmmakers – comes to take the place of the oral poet in order to ensure that the name of Achilles will live.

And so we arrive at a climactic story of grandfathers at the Vimy Monument – one that ultimately defines the ethos of *For King and Empire*. For it is the story of the Vimy Pilgrims, all six thousand strong, who sailed to Europe in 1936 for the public unveiling. "One of the men," Christie says quietly, standing on the pedestal of the monument, "was my grandfather. He had been here, obviously, in 1918 when he was wounded, and he came back to give a final statement, I guess, a final visit, to the people he had left behind. For him, it was a very big issue, and after he had died, we found in his drawer every piece of paper from the Vimy Pilgrimage, his special Vimy Pilgrimage Passport, he had the London Underground schedule for 1935, and he was a clerk at Bell Canada, so he wasn't making much money. So to save up that much money during the Great Depression to make this trip just shows how important this monument was to those Canadians" (35.58–36.42). The whole series comes into focus in this one shot. For all the "following shots" of Christie have made Vimy Pilgrims of us all. So, too, the technique of the dissolve, the editor's major device for linking shots in the series, stands revealed as a method of making the two eras one, of using the "nowness" of television to evoke the continuing presence of the past.

Not surprisingly, the final episode in the series ends with metadiscourse regarding the power of television to resurrect the dead, bringing them right into our living rooms. "I think what's odd about history, period," Christie says from the steps of yet another monument, "is that you're standing on the ground where so much took place before you. And you can certainly feel the shadows of the Great War. You know there's ghosts walking out there" (46.00–46.34). A colour shot of Christie on the battlefield dissolves in a faint cry of distant voices, as a final straight cut leads to archival footage of soldiers in a trench, munching on dry crusts of bread. One of them turns to look at the camera, then smiles and takes a few uncertain steps our way, before turning back. The shot holds on him for another 10 seconds as he stands in the trenches right "here" in our living rooms. And the screen fades to black. It is a remarkably fitting close to a program that has enabled us literally to see the "spectral images" that had haunted Siegfried Sassoon. But the program's ultimate achievement is to have put so many names of these dead on the lips of present men and women, to make their memory live again in our time.

HISTORY TELEVISION AND ORAL CULTURE

"It is time for the historian to accept the mainstream historical film as a new kind of history," Robert Rosenstone cajoles. "We must begin to think of history on film as closer to past forms of history, as a way of dealing with the past that is more like oral history, or history told by bards, or *griots* in Africa, or history contained in classic epics" (65). If this is true of history on film, it is doubly so of history on television. For, as John Fiske says, "Television's distinctive textual characteristics, quite different from those of literature or film, have derived from and are inserted into a popular culture in which orality plays a central role. Television is so often treated as an inferior cultural medium with inferior textual characteristics because our culture is one that validates the literary, or rather the literate, and consequently devalues the oral" (105).

Among the characteristics that television shares with oral culture are three of overpowering relevance to this discussion of "a new Homeric mode." First, television, like "oral culture," as Fiske says, "is active, participatory. Because the conventions are so well known and so closely related to the social situation of the community, all members of that community can participate more or less equally in the production and circulation of meanings: talk does not distinguish between producers and consumers" (Fiske 79). Producer and consumer are immediately joined in "the documentary look" of *For King and Empire* in its "call" to viewers to follow the host and see what he sees. In its repeated use of following shots and rapid dissolves between times, the televisual text most surely works to evoke that "participatory mystique" that Walter Ong regards as crucial in oral culture to the "fostering of a communal sense" (136).

The "nowness" of television is another telling link to the phenomenology of oral culture. In the third chapter on Homer in this book, we faced the paradox of an oral singer "watching" recalled events as if they were appearing at that moment on a wall in front of him (Rubin 59–60). The visual sense, one has to say, is fundamental to oral culture, much as it is to television, even producing a similar sense of presentness in both media. Similes also appear to serve as "a commentary on the scene which runs in the cinema of his mind's eye" (44), Elizabeth Minchin remarks of the Homeric poet, whose own performance necessarily mediates between the present audience and a past that he alone can "see." If performance is central to both oral poetry and television, then oral culture, in "its concentration on the present moment" (Ong 136), must likewise be shaped by audience response. Here, writ large, is the logic of taping television shows before a live audience.

In history television, however, it is the moment of viewing that puts producers and consumers in the same time zone, watching the same "film." Witnessing the historical event at *this* moment, in this medium, where the past inhabits our living space, we are not so very far from the oral singer and his audience who watch the past moving before their eyes. And so it is that the past on television acquires a new future, as it had in oral culture, where "a sense of the future that goes with an 'unwritten' text" (Fiske 106) works to govern the entire performance. This openness of the oral text to the future is especially telling in the *Iliad,* where the medium itself is called on to prove that it can preserve the past by anticipating the future. And this is what the televisual text also does best in *For King and Empire* through its invitation to viewers to participate in that past.

A third way in which television and oral culture overlap is by presenting us with "a direct, personalized address and its production of a textual or cultural *experience*" (Fiske 106). This experience is quite the opposite of "objective" history, with its separation of knower and known (Eric Havelock), or even its separation of the "photographic" object from itself (Walter Benjamin). By putting "the name" of Canada's Great War soldiers on the lips of ordinary Canadians, the producers and consumers of the show effect an "incorporation of the program into local culture" (79). For television history depends on getting popular audiences to talk about – even to put online – stories about their "grandfathers," posting their photos, letters, diaries, and medals as digital objects on the program's website. "Do you have a relative who fought in the Great War with the Canadian Expeditionary Force?" is the leading question posed in the website's "Archive" (www.kingandempire.com/archive.html; accessed 18 July 2007).

In the end, all this talk about a television program binds us together by creating continuity out of heterogeneity, unity out of diversity, in a way common to both television and oral culture. In John Fiske's view, "[A]n oral or folk culture provides the television viewer with a set of reading relations that are essentially participatory and active, and that recognize only minimal differentiation between performer and audience or producer and consumer" (80).

Hence the invitation to put a "relative" on the show's website. For such reasons, history on television may well approximate "history in the classic epics." For television opens a window on an ancient culture that has never really gone away. More to the point, the proliferation of history on television gives oral culture a new and modern channel in which the flow of popular experience carries farther than ever. Here is the crucial point about a Canadian folk memory of Vimy, first enunciated in 1923 by Arthur Meighen, the Opposition leader in the Commons: "The site of Vimy is beyond comparison, of the various battlefields of the war, the most closely associated in the hearts of the Canadian people with all that the war involved in story and in sacrifice" (cited by Hucker 285). If the battle at Vimy has displaced the memory of far greater achievements in the Last Hundred Days at the Battle of Amiens, at the Drocourt–Quéant Line, and finally at the Canal du Nord and Cambrai, it is because popular memory insists on seeing it that way. Indeed, it can be said that the popular memory of Vimy is ultimately concerned with another kind of truth than is written history,[45] and that television, with its unique properties, is best able to preserve, and even to extend, that popular memory.[46]

Sound Bytes in the Archive and the Museum

To anyone who has spent weeks or months in the silence of an archive, picking up fragile documents with white-gloved hands, it may be disconcerting to click on "World War I: 1914–1918," the website portal of the Dominion Institute's *The Memory Project* (www.thememoryproject.com/digital-archive/main.cfm) and be greeted by a voice in the Digital Archive, this new repository of veterans' stories and memorabilia. Even now, as I type these words on my iBook, I am listening to "Clare Laking, 27th Battery, Canadian Field Artillery," as the 104-year-old veteran reminisces about the Great War in a medium that brings his raspy voice right into my study. Of course, I am aware that Laking died since this interview was recorded, and that his virtual presence is really without precedent, his "apparition" being a product of new information technologies that digitize a voice and send it around the world at the click of a mouse.

In this gateway to the WWI Archive – its default point of entry – Clare Laking is nonetheless present to greet me and introduce himself by name. His recording lasts only 4 minutes 9 seconds, yet he speaks for himself after death in a way that Achilles never imagined. Entrusting his memory to a website (rather than to an oral poet), Clare Laking has had a potential worldwide audience ever since the Digital Archive was launched by the Dominion Institute on D-Day, 2003. His is a "living" voice of the First World War, enduring in a public forum (for as long, at least, as this website is maintained by a service group formed in 1997 with the sponsorship of the Government of Ontario and Canadian Heritage). Under current conditions, orally derived memories of the First World War are just as

likely to increase as to diminish, given the multiple and similar syn-
ergies created by History Television, the websites of *For King and
Empire* and *The Memory Project,* together with other virtual technologies. The voice of Clare Laking is just one of many gateways to
our current memory of the Great War, including a website user's ear
as a portal. With these thoughts in mind, I "rewind" and listen
again to the old warrior's story:

> My name is Charles Clarence Laking, but my dad's name was
> Charles, so my grandmother started calling me Clare, and it's
> stuck with me ever since. When I was 18 my father was abso-
> lutely against war, and they'd have recruiting meetings in differ-
> ent schools, and all that rot, and he'd get up, and he embarrassed
> me so much running everything down that they were doing, I told
> him I was going to enlist. He says: "You do, I'm through with
> ya." That made me pretty serious. So I did a carry-through, and
> went up to Guelph and enlisted.

How different our current cultural situation is now from that of
Jules Michelet, the great historian of the French Revolution, writing
forty years after the Terror, of the great "'catacombs of manuscripts' that made up the Archives Nationales in Paris," and again,
forty years after that, how these documents "desired no better than
to be restored to the light of day ... [And] as I breathed in their
dust, I saw them rise up" (cited by Steedman 10). Of course, it is
conceivable that Clare Laking also "desired no better" in his interview "than to be restored to the light of day." By voicing his memories in this digital recording, he haunts us with the knowledge that
Death and Silence are not synonymous.

By contrast, the dead of the French Revolution had some need of
Jules Michelet, writing in 1872–74, to be their spokesperson. He
seems to have been "the first," as Benedict Anderson put it, "self-
consciously to write *on behalf* of the dead" (197). But Michelet
could still take it as a matter of course that, "Oui, chaque mort
laisse un petit bien, sa mémoire, et demande qu'on la soigne. Pour
celui qui n'a pas d'amis, il faut que le magistrat y supplée. Car la
loi, la justice, est plus sûre que toutes nos tendresses oublieuses, nos
larmes si vite séchées. Cette magistrature, c'est l'Histoire" (cited by
Anderson 198) ["Yes, each of the dead leaves behind a small legacy,
his memory, and asks that it be cared for. For anyone who has no

friends, the magistrate must needs supply it. For the law, Justice, is more reliable than all our tender forgetfulness, our tears that are so quickly dried. That Magistrate is History" (my translation)].

Whereas Michelet needed to bury himself in the archive, breathing life into "their dust" (Steedman 10) – whether the dust of parchments and papers or the dust of the deceased is not made clear – a visitor to the Digital Archive is hardly through the portal when the dead man speaks. There is a sudden dip in Laking's voice as he comes to "all that rot"; but he quickly resumes his emphatic style as if recognizing that such sentiments may not be popular with audiences who fail to hear the discrepancy between "that rot" of patriotic rant and the battlefield shriek of whizzbangs. Insisting, "he embarrassed me so much," the old warrior communicates the defiance of a son disowned and that of a soldier still rejecting convention. Clare Laking needs no one to breathe life into his dust.

In a related way, it may be disconcerting to anyone visiting the new Canadian War Museum (2003) to hear loud strains of music beneath the entrance arch to Great War historian and curator Tim Cook's exhibit, "FOR CROWN AND COUNTRY: The South African and First World Wars 1885–1931." A brisk rendition in brass of "God Save Our Gracious Queen/King" is followed by "The Maple Leaf Forever" in marching tempo. The visitor to the exhibit is recruited to *feel* emotions of loyalty to Sovereign and Empire in this martial atmosphere approximating the typical experience of volunteers of 1899–1902 and 1914–18 who signed up for Canada's Expeditionary Force in *two* imperial wars. The music thus performs its own justification by situating the Great War in the wider context of the war for Empire. But it serves as well to shift the weight of museum-goers' experience from the object on view to the emotional response of the visitor. "Design and spectacle," as one theorist maintains, "the semiotics of display – appear increasingly as central elements of museum exhibition, sometimes pre-empting narrative order, as museums shift their emphasis from preservation and study to dramatic delivery" (Hein 5).

In this wider cultural "shift away from object centeredness to an emphasis on the promotion of experience" (Hein ix), there is a corresponding shift from objectivity to subjectivity, with grave implications for the "museum object." A traditional museumgoer, trusting in the "museum's presumed dedication to the 'real thing' – the authentic object that is prized and studied" (7), is more likely attracted to the "aura" of the museum object – its role as a survivor from times past with an "immediate" connection to events and personages. As an ambassador from another time, this object is what gives the museum its special cachet as a "time-machine" (Macdonald and Fyfe 9). But as a survivor from distant times, the object only ever speaks of its silent presence in our time; it cannot speak for itself. Most obviously, "[a]s museum workers point out ... the collection of rarities is worthless without additional documentation" (Hein 3). Museum objects are then not quite "mute. They signify within narrative systems" (31). Thereupon, the visitor is expected to move as a reader through the space of the traditional museum, decoding objects within a sign system of labels and storyboards provided by the author-curator.

While audio technologies have become a legitimate presence in the traditional museum, they are more often limited to headsets rented by the less literate, or at least more orally attuned, visitor. The net effect is the same: the curator's script is delivered to the "reader," allowing the "book" to be heard in private without disturbing other visitors. At the same time, a "postliterate"[47] viewer is evidently freed to "read" the object itself as a primary text while auditing a secondary text of institutional authority.

Digital multimedia and virtual technologies are another story, however, since "the relationships between material and digital objects" (Cameron and Kenderline 4) are often seen in the museum as foes. Most "existing discussions tend to be based on an opposition between the virtual and the material world; the virtual is thus interpreted either as a threat or as a radical process of democratization" (6). One way to subordinate new technologies to an "objective" representation of the past is to offer them as supplements to the printed text, so containing their revolutionary potential. "Despite claims to the contrary," Andrea Witcomb argues, "many multimedia stations continue to operate within traditional didactic frameworks. The problem is a similar one to that identified by Paul Carter in relation to the use of sound in museums. As he says, 'Conventionally, the spoken voice in museums and galleries is confined to the informative monologue heard by pushing a button or hiring a headset'" (36). The assumption seems to be that the traditional museum, like the archive, is a secular cathedral for citizens in a democratic society, a site of *silent veneration*. What is evidently taking place in institutional media of memory such as archives and museums thus amounts to "a conceptual revolution ... , one that calls into question the fundamental premises on which museums were grounded" (Hein viii).

THE MUSEOLOGICAL REVOLUTION

A number of theorists point to three key forces driving "the contemporary museological revolution" (Witcomb 37). The first of these, as Witcomb suggests, is the postmodern *mentalité*: "This is a revolution which has revealed the process of making meaning in exhibitions, a process which previously was made to appear neutral through a focus on the conventional world of objects" (37). Curators and museologists, in other words, are no more immune to the thought of Foucault and Derrida than are curators of the literary text. Hein remarks how, "[f]rom the perspective of some academic disciplines, the museum is a conservative agent of normalization, which, like survey courses and popular anthologies, objectifies things and reifies value. So viewed as legitimating authorities, museums are thought to be de facto dispensers of status, whose power to name and canonize demands deconstruction" (ix). More forcefully still, Fiona Cameron insists that "[t]he influences that have potentially liberated historical objects from the strict limitations of a materialist epistemology" are taking "the form of social and new history, products of the cultural turn in critical theory – the advent of poststructuralism and postmodernism and the rise of identity politics and social movements in the 1960s and 1970s. Theoretically speaking, historian Alun Munslow (2001) terms this new position as 'epistemic relativism,' one that views knowledge of the 'real' as derived through our ideas and concepts, including linguistic, spatial, cultural, and ideological compulsions" (53). The modern museum is changing, that is to say, because of several types of postmodern mentalités at work in it.

A second force driving "the museological revolution" is the everspreading power of popular culture. Hein states flatly, "A public weaned on television and computer screens has come to accept simulations as adequate indices of reality. Information *about* a phenomenon is routinely substitutable for the experience *of* it and even thought preferable where some aspects of that experience might be disagreeable" (11). A culture accustomed to seeing the "object" on electronic screens is less likely to be impressed by a static, monumental display, and could be drawn instead to more dynamic displays, whether in ever-changing camera angles or in digital simulation.[48] In fact, Hein says, "The display of static, inactive tools in glass cases bores people ... and attracts less attention than film loops and video demonstrations that explain and illustrate the operations that the older machine can perform" (9). Museum officials have no one to blame but themselves: the first generation of children to grow up with computers has also been weaned on "techniques developed by children's museums to attract and hold audiences" (35).

Theme parks are also forcing changes in museum culture because of "their capacity to mass produce and retail 'unique experiences' that are phenomenologically real" (80). Disney theme parks draw numbers that most museums can only envy in their virtual simulations of past history by means of virtual reality (VR) technologies. Heritage institutions that remain elitist, or that profess contempt for popular culture, are no longer even in the majority. All the same, "Virtual heritage is often labeled" by some museologists as "'edutainment,' and even the 'Disnification' of culture" (Cameron and Kenderline 11). But such disdain for popular culture, or even blind adherence to the standards of "high" culture, is likely to be self-defeating.

A third force driving the museological revolution is information technology itself, particularly in the way it dematerializes the object even as it helps to engage "an audience of 'doers' instead of 'viewers'" (Hein 34). Some museologists express anxiety about the digital object, much less about remote visitors in an online world of virtual viewing. "It is now possible," as Macdonald and Fyfe say with evident apprehension, "to visit museums such as the National Gallery, London, without leaving home and to dip in electronically to different collections around the world and effectively construct your own museum on screen" (2). Less alarmist is a far-seeing "Series Foreword" to Cameron and Kenderline's *Theorizing Digital Cultural Heritage*, in which David Thorburn and his associate editors graciously acknowledge the many "ways in which digital technologies have transformed the traditional museum, altering our understanding of such fundamental words as *indigenous, artifact, heritage, space, ecology, the past*" (ix–x). More sanguine still is one of their contributors, Andrea Witcomb, who cheerfully notes "the impact of multimedia technologies on museums" in order to tally up the many benefits amidst the losses:

For those who see it as a threat, the implications are a loss of aura and institutional authority, the loss of the ability to distinguish between the real and the copy, the death of the object, and a reduction of knowledge to information. For those who interpret it as a positive move, such losses are precisely what enable new democratic associations to emerge around museums. For them, the loss of institutional authority equates with the need for curators to become facilitators rather than figures of authority, an openness to popular culture, the recognition of multiple meanings, and the extension of the media sphere into the space of the museum. These are all interpreted as positive steps. (35)

Before such "steps" can be shown to be "positive," however, some assessment is necessary of the likely cultural outcome – or social epistemology – of these changes in the institutional mediation of memory. For an unresolved tension persists between the role of objects and the role of viewers in the "postliterate" museum. "Evidently subjectivity, as the ground of all experience," Hein concedes, "must occupy a preeminent place within the museum experience; but what, then, is the role of objects?" (x). At worst, "[a]ctual objects" can "seem superfluous to the experience of their reality, and it is conceivable that reality no longer needs anchorage in the world of physical things" (77).

At best, "[i]n redirecting interest from objects used as evidence to objects that evoke experience, museums" tend to reify "two contemporary cultural trends. We have noted the shift from object to experience that turns attention from real things to real subjective states. The second tendency, which merges with the first, valorizes emotive over cognitive meaning" (79). Under conditions of this sort, it may well be that "[t]he depersonalization and detachment that formerly defined objectivity and guaranteed its cognitive worth now strike people as both undesirable and impossible ... Since feeling, however, is notoriously subjective, its penetration of knowledge has the consequence of subjectifying cognition" (79). But how would it then be possible to untie the Gordian knot of "epistemic relativism," if it were truly impossible to "know" the object in itself?

In the longer term, this situation looks fairly ancient since it approximates cultural conditions that prevailed before Plato's banishment of the poet from the *Republic,* and before an analytic method based on writing "destroyed the immemorial habit of self-identification with the oral tradition" (Havelock 201). This is what

Eric Havelock means, in his reading of Plato's curriculum, by the phrase, "the separation of the Knower from the Known" (197) – the necessary ground of objectivity. All the values he associates with the new technology of writing – values of abstraction, analysis (breaking into parts), detachment, the power to generalize – all these are becoming unfashionable, if not impossible, in a world of electronic screens. And their opposites – values of concreteness, wholeness (or unity), involvement, and particularity – are also coming into vogue again as the "natural" view of the world. In other words, what seems to be driving this shift from cognition to experience are the very media that appear to be taking us back toward a form of oral culture. Which is why the traditional museum may well belong in ... the museum.

SOUNDINGS OF THE GREAT WAR

In this and two succeeding segments, I compare three types of war museum: the traditional (national) type, represented by le Musée de l'Infantérie in Montpellier, France; the postmodern (though still national) type represented by the Canadian War Museum in Ottawa; and the international type represented by l'Historial de la Grande Guerre in Péronne, close to the Somme and the battlefield of Amiens. I draw particular attention to, and conclusions from, the use or non-use of sound in each museum, as it latterly signifies the living "soul" of the "spectral image" as it now appears to us on electronic screens.

The Great War gallery in the Infantry Museum in Montpellier (visited on 5 April 2007) needs to be viewed in its context: an infantry museum qua *costume* museum. The museum collection focuses on uniforms from the late Middle Ages to the present, paying loving attention to the changing fashions of Empire from the Seven Years' War, through the Napoleonic Wars, to the conquest of North Africa. In context, the Great War gallery is a narrow room about the length of two railway boxcars. What one notices on entering is a movie screen on the far wall, lit by black-and-white images. But it is a silent film, composed of flickering, jerky images from a stationary camera panning in a continuous shot over the battlefield obscured by smoke. Human figures move in the speeded-up way of early film; and an occasional burst of sound from overhead speakers suggests the thump of distant artillery. The scene is remote in every sense of the word, so that a viewer can easily feel alienated – regretfully so after subtitles identify the scene as *Verdun vu par le cinéma des années.*

Along each wall flanking the small silver screen are the telltale signs of a static exhibit: glass cases holding the red pants and blue jackets of uniforms from 1914, together with new fashions from 1915, followed by the powder-blue greatcoat and blue puttees of Verdun in 1916. In the Verdun cabinet, there is a cardboard cutout of a *poilu* ("hairy" enlistee) in pale blue uniform. In other cabinets are collected a few French rifles (one labelled *Fusil 1915 CHAUCHAT*), as well as other items of trench life, such as spades and gas masks; a German MG08 machine gun, and various types of grenades, and even styles of boots. On the floor is a machine-gun "emplacement" – *La Mitrailleuse HOTCHKISS / M16* from 1914, and another rifle (*Mousqueton modèle 1916 avec sabre-baïonnette).* On a stretch of wall beyond the glass cabinets are photos of tanks, together with a maquette of a tank. On the opposite wall are a number of paintings by several war artists, bearing images of a shelled town, of troops winding through communications trenches, and of dead bodies beneath temporary crosses out in No Man's Land. There is even one image of "a heroic charge" over the top, and another of *"Le Général de Castelmane [qui] Distribue des Decorations" (29 avril 1917).* Two portraits are displayed, one of a *"Chasseur Alpin"* and another (in the sentimental tradition) of *"Mon Pauvre Vieux"* by Marcel Santi. The largest canvas is an image *"Sur la Route de Verdun" (le 25 janvier 1916),* a scene of transport carrying six men under canvas in the rear of a truck, with another vehicle in the background carrying six more indistinguishable shapes. It is the eve, one realizes, of the battle of Verdun, with all those sad *poilus* being carried off to the land of the dead (a million casualties would be suffered on both sides, 25 percent of them fatal).

Here, in all its strengths and weaknesses, is the ultra-traditional war museum that hallows the object above all – properly hallowed, it seems, by the sanctity of the defence of the homeland and the memories of two million French dead in the Great War. And yet, unless the viewer is already well versed in the history of this Offensive, it is unlikely to come alive. By any measure, the museum fails to communicate the terrible drama of the eight-month assault on

Verdun; worse still, the silent, flickering images become a tape loop running endlessly through the ninth circle of Hell. One might be relieved, but not particularly edified, when it is time to leave this gallery of hallowed relics.

There is another way, of course, in which this Infantry Museum can be seen. If it is true, as Martin Prösler suggests, that museums have their origin in "Camillo's 'Theatre of Memory'" (28) – that every museum is descended from the classical "art of memory" (see chapter 2) – then the very placement of these objects ought to speak with the considerable authority of classical rhetoric. The practice in ancient oral culture, in fact, was to "write" in the mind's eye every *thing or idea* one wanted to remember by setting it in a particular place in a familiar room, or rooms, or even complex of buildings. The museum, at its foundation, was evidently built on the classical art of memory, with a place for everything and everything in its place. The problem, of course, with such an "art" is that it still depends on the work of a viewer to call each space to mind, and after that to recall images for each assigned place. But these days we have machines to do that sort of thing for us. What is more, we have digital technologies to conjure up "places" that exist only in virtual space. In this new media world, a space is not a "place" so long as it is static; it has to speak and "move" if we ourselves are to be moved by it. One of the lasting legacies of film, as Erwin Panofsky would be the first to remark, was quite literally the "dynamization of space" (cited by Cavell 30). And no museum these days can afford to be without it, let alone use it in a way that fails to render space dynamic.

THE CANADIAN WAR MUSEUM

The Canadian War Museum in Ottawa (visited 26–27 June 2007), makes a more dynamic use of digital sound and video, from the martial music first heard at the entrance to the theatre near the exit screening a short film (in alternating French and English) on the legacy of the war. In the gallery itinerary of each year – most often marked by a turn in the corridor – a television monitor plays a mini-movie (about 3 minutes long) on a relevant topic. Walk by a photograph of Sam Hughes, the Minister of Militia, and you find text from 7 August 1912, to the effect that "Germany has to be taught a lesson." Then you step through a doorway under the framing legend, THE FIRST WORLD WAR 1914–1918, where, to your right, there is a padded bench where you can sit and watch a monitor play THE ROAD TO WAR (3:30 mins), narrated by Patrick Watson. There are maps, of course, and also a montage of newsreels giving a succinct and graphic account of why everyone is "Marching to War." So you move to the next monitor (appropriately black and white) playing silent pictures of men marching off to war. Nearby, school children (as well as bigger children) are encouraged to answer the question, "Do You Measure Up?" An interactive exhibit divides the short from the tall and the near- from the far-sighted, checking for flat feet, bad teeth, or anything else that would keep a volunteer at home. For many, a digital archive of "Attestation Papers" allows them to locate a family volunteer by name or regimental number or battalion, and to call up any number of the 600,000 enlistment papers of the era, papers bearing intimate details of the volunteer's body, such as "Mole left side back; Two scars right knee; One scar inside left foot." And then – look! It's his handwriting, the rounded letters like the hand of a child!

Around the bend, you suddenly find yourself at Ypres, almost as unprepared as the First Division had been on 22 April 1915, although you know you won't be gassed. In the midst of the guns and weaponry of a static exhibit, you stand before a gigantic painting (about 20' × 14') of a "heroic charge" over the top, that famous image painted by Richard Jack in 1917 of *The Second Battle of Ypres, 22 April to 25 May, 1915*. And then, as your pupils begin to dilate, you notice a smaller painting (perhaps 12' × 10') on a flanking wall to your right: *The First German Gas Attack at Ypres* (1918) by William Roberts. The scene is a whirl of red and green and yellow (French colonial troops) and khaki (Canadian troops) tumbling head over heels out of the picture toward you, looking like Milton's devils hurled out of Heaven, except that these are evidently the "good guys." Many of them writhe in terror, their bodies contorting in the final agonies of asphyxiation. Nearby, there is a rubber "gas hood" (introduced at the end of 1915, eight months too late for those poor devils in the painting), and a "small box respirator" (available at the end of 1916, just in time for Vimy). What the exhibit clearly asks you to do, after first catching your breath, is to make an aesthetic and moral choice. "Notice the heroic nature of Jack's subject matter," the placard under the first painting urges, "and compare it to Roberts' *The First German Gas Attack at*

Ypres." Over by the Roberts' painting, another placard says,
"Compare Roberts' approach to that of Richard Jack on the opposite wall. Do you think that Roberts' painting conveys the nature of
battle better than Jack's *The Second Battle of Ypres*?" Which is, of
course, a loaded question. And yet modern viewers do tend to
choose the Roberts' painting, not least because the writhing figures
tumble right out of the picture at you; you participate in the scene
in ways you cannot help, ways that do leave you helpless.

Around the next turn of the year, you are brought up short by a
42-inch flatscreen monitor, amidst headlines of WAR NEWS HITS
HOME. Under a narrow cone of sound in the ceiling, you suddenly
hear what that housewife in her blue taffeta dress is thinking at her
kitchen table. As if she has caught you watching her reading her
newspaper, she sets it down and starts talking, her elbows on the
table: "It's just beyond comprehension, I tell you," she looks *right
at you* as she speaks. "So many young men dead ... Their poor
grieving wives and sweethearts ... God bless them." And then, as
you are interpellated into her space and time, she invites you to
share the prejudices of the era. "Of course, we have our enemies
here too, you know who I mean. Lock 'em all up." It's like you've
entered a time warp, wondering if you'd be guilty of the discrimi-
nations that besmirch this kindly woman addressing you in both
official languages. Her comments are aimed as steadily as a sniper's
rifle; and you are forced to face the worst about yourself, or else to
pull free. There is no other way about it; this virtual presence compels you to choose.

You do pull away to stand before a blown-up photo of Nick
Olinyk, a Slavic man interned as an enemy alien who offers another
view of this "freedom-loving" country: "We get up at 5 o'clock in
the morning and work till 10 o'clock at night. Such conditions we
have here in Canada, I will never forget." Nor are you allowed to
forget where you have come from, a modern, "progressive" country
that would lock up Galicians for the crime of being "Austrian" in
the Great War. In all probability, of course, Nick Olinyk would not
have come to Canada had he been free of the Austrian enemy, had
he enjoyed the luxury of a Ukrainian homeland. Still, Nick Olinyk
could have avoided internment if he had done what a fellow Ukrainian immigrant did. Filip Konowal, vc, "A Canadian War Hero,"
is honoured in an adjacent exhibit for his bravery at Hill 70 in August 1917.

The first thing you see, stepping into the space of 1917, is a silver replica of Billy Bishop's Nieuport 17, a full-size flying machine of the type flown by the greatest surviving Allied ace (72 kills). In a brilliant use of limited space, Bishop's Nieuport 17 "flies" above a small theatre (18 seats), which is endlessly screening "Vimy Ridge: The Soldier's Story," a digital video and sound montage of veterans' memories of Vimy. Bishop, who was awarded a Victoria Cross for his combat skills in the air above the battlefield, continues to enjoy pride of "place" in the "sky" of the gallery. Meanwhile, you sit below, listening to an oral collage recalling the terrors as well as the joys of that famous victory. The voice of Patrick Watson once again relays the voices that have now gone to their eternal reward – to be remembered in perpetuity by their fellow citizens.

Outside the Vimy theatre stands "The Great Killer" that wreaked so much havoc on the Ridge, an 8-inch Howitzer that would launch a 90 kg shell up to 11 km distant. Here, the storyboard reminds you, "Artillery fire inflicted approximately 60% of all wounds in World War I." On the opposite side of the gallery is a captured German 77 mm gun with its muzzle blown off – a deliberate act of sabotage, it would seem, to render the gun inoperable. And beyond its splayed barrel you see a temporary grave marker (a wooden cross with its unmistakable "aura" of the battle) that once marked the remains of Lt Norman Pawley of the 44th (Manitoba) Battalion, killed on the final day, 12 April 1917, in the assault on the Pimple. Along the wall to your right you see what remains of the wrecked airframe of William Barker's Sopwith Snipe, crash-landed on 27 October 1918 after Barker had shot down 4 more enemy aircraft. Like Pawley a Manitoban, Barker is celebrated on the nearby panel for feats of daring that would make him Canada's most decorated veteran. A nearby monitor plays "Knights of the Sky," and you watch 2 minutes 30 seconds of footage of dogfights, the video clip narrated once again by Patrick Watson, with actors quoting the words of pilots.

What remains to be told of 1917, however, requires a separate, darkened room to make you feel the utter desolation of Passchendaele. As you round the bend, you enter a blasted landscape of mud and charred stumps and shell craters brimming with water, where you can barely tell the difference between the "stinking diarrhea of war" (Will Bird) on the floor, and the mud-churned horizon of a photo-diorama on the wall. As you step onto the duckboards, you pass the top of a gun-carriage wheel sunk in the mud, then the

barrel of a Lewis gun, with remnants of a haversack floating in a
scummy pond between a blackened stump and the remains of a
Vickers gun. But you are not prepared for human remains (a flat-
tened statue of bronze) lying face down in the mud, helmet slightly
askew, trampled deep by attacking troops who had to go over. Several high school boys come by you on the duckboards, and one of
them goes out of his way to step on the trampled back, as if he has
to find out what it was like. But it is his experience that matters, after all, not that "object" in the mud. Still, you wish he would stop
and pick up one of the handsets to listen to the audiotapes of "THE
FACE OF BATTLE," with actors speaking the words of "soldiers in
the nightmare world of the trenches."

As you leave the comfortable chair, you also leave the gloom of
Passchendaele to enter the bright and hopeful lights of 1918, where
the massive German offensive of March–April 1918 is finally
stopped, and the Canadians and Australians retaliate on 8 August
to finally break through in the largest Allied gain in four years of
war. "August 8th was the black day of the German Army," General
Ludendorf announces ruefully in black-letter text on the storyboard. By now, there is something almost perfunctory, a reflex of
modesty, perhaps, in the exhibit; these displays that represent the
deciding battles in the Last Hundred Days are hardly bigger than a
supermarket aisle display.

In "Breaking the Drocourt–Quéant Line," tactical maps demon-
strate the Canadian advance through a maze of reinforced trenches
east of Arras. And a monitor plays a tape loop in black-and-white
of the men and tanks and machine guns heading into action. But it
takes no more than a minute, and then it starts over again, as if it
too is weary of the dreary repetition of war. Thankfully, no gloating
is permitted, apart from one sentence fragment attributed to General Ferdinand Foch, the Supreme Commander of the Allied Forces,
speaking of Canadians as "[t]he ram with which we will break up
the last resistance of the German army." One last "aisle display"
represents "Crashing the Canal du Nord," where tactical maps
display the many risks involved in the bold plan adopted by Lt-
General Arthur Currie, Commander of the Canadian Corps. There
is a maquette of a partly dry Canal as well, the site where Canadian
engineers built bridges to forestall any attempt to flood them out.
On 9 October 1918, Cambrai, the storyboard says, was duly

captured by Canadians. One could wish for more emphasis on the stupendous rate of casualties in the Last Hundred Days (amounting to nearly a third of all Canadian casualties in the war). After a nod in the direction of Valenciennes, then Mons on 10–11 November 1918, the war is mercifully brought to a close on Armistice Day.

Around the last bend, George Varley's 1918 painting *For What?* challenges you to explain the significance of that fore-grounded body lying in a wheelbarrow, as if curled in a fetal position, while two men stare at you out of the muddy red landscape (blood-soaked, you suppose, unless it's meant to be alien, even Martian, in its terrible desolation), as if to say, "You see these crosses? Garbage, it's all garbage, you know." The barrow says as much, too, as if tipping of its own accord toward you to dump its load. What was it all for? "Was the War Pointless?" another storyboard challenges you from above the exit: "60,000 dead; 172,000 wounded" of the 420,000 Canadians who went overseas. Was it worth it? These "9 million battlefield dead; 20 million wounded; 3 new world powers: USA, USSR, Japan; 4 empires destroyed: Russia; Austro-Hungary, Germany, Turkey; 15 countries created"? Does such scorekeeping even begin to explain? You sit on a padded bench, watching a final film narrated by Patrick Watson telling you that one of the legacies of the war was Canadian "independence," though "at a terrible price." And yet, "Despite the costs, Canadians are determined to remember."

Obviously, the Canadian War Museum is a twenty-first-century instance of that nineteenth-century staple, the national museum,[49] intended to be "a space in which national culture and history were constructed, expressing the difference between one nation and all the others, a distinction all the more necessary since their state structures were broadly similar" (Prösler 34). Canada's proud military history is used to underwrite our national story of origins, a rather odd history of fighting Germans on French and Belgian soil to gain our independence from Britain (implicitly conceded in our role as a signatory to the Treaty of Versailles in 1919, though our true independence was not formally ratified until 1931 in the Statute of Westminster, a British Act of Parliament). At best, *For What?* begs a larger question: Why the Nation? At worst, it threatens to cut off discussion in much the same way that other questions are begged in the foyer outside the gallery. "When is war necessary?" a signboard asks. The photo beside it is of Hitler addressing the masses at Nuremberg. "Who would you miss?" An accompanying photo responds with the faces of a husband, a brother, a father, a son, condemned to the trenches. "Where were You?" another sign calls. Beside it, you see a photo of the fall of the Berlin Wall.

One question, however, is not rhetorical; it demands genuine reflection and self-examination: "WHAT WILL YOU DO?" a sign buttonholes you, literally to remind you: "History is not just the story you read. It is the one you write. It is the one you remember or denounce or relate to others. It is not predetermined. Every action, every decision, however small, is relevant to its course. History is filled with horror, and replete with hope. You shape the balance." And you see at last that you are the ulterior subject of the museum, or, rather, that your subjectivity is the ground of its display. For *how* you remember is the key to the future, at least as much as *what* you remember. And the *how* is evidently shaped by the way you are interpellated in these displays, either to recognize, or else to resist, the call to history. You are thus situated within a network of voices inviting participation and dialogue, not to mention empathy and vicariousness – all hallmarks of an oral culture – and you see at last why the Knower can no longer be separated from the Known, or why, in the memorable saying of John Donne, "No man is an *Iland,* intire of it selfe; every man is a peece of the *Continent,* a part of the *maine"* (243). For there really is no separate vantage point any more, no position of independence or true objectivity, where a subject is able to separate his or her subjectivity from the *experience* of the object.

L'HISTORIAL DE LA GRANDE GUERRE

To the political left of my spectrum of museum types is l'Historial de la Grande Guerre (visited 25 May 2006). Opened to the public in 1992 and located in the medieval Château de Péronne in the Department of the Somme in Picardy, the Historial announces its internationalist intentions (more openly, at least, than the Canadian War Museum), to offer "an international view of a conflict that was the first to involve so many civilian populations. The presentation of the collection, inclining more to social than to military history, is centred around the individual. It encourages constant comparisons among the different belligerent countries while making a clear distinction between life at the front and behind the lines" (www. historial.org/us/home_b.htm; accessed 26 July 2007).

Toward this goal of focusing on the individual (past rather than present individuals, it would appear), "[t]he centre of the rooms is devoted to life at the front, the central focus of peoples at war. The soldiers of different nationalities are represented by mannequins dressed in their uniforms, with their weapons and personal belongings. These bodies, lying in pits of white marble embedded in the museum floor, evoke the trenches that filled the entire area of the Somme, but also the shared suffering of the combatants." My digital photographs of the museum reveal a typical display of weapons. And yet these weapons are laid out on the floor together, not pointing at one another but all facing one direction, as if allied in a common cause. A British Vickers Machine Gun (1912) is flanked by a German Maxime gun (MG08) on one side, and a French St-Etiénne machine gun (1907) on the other. Perhaps the uniformed mannequins, at least, are not allowed to fraternize, maintaining separate positions in marble pits about the floor. At the exit, however, the political lesson is clear: a scrap heap of rusting steel helmets is piled together, a German *helm* occupying the foreground, with a French helmet in the middle, and a British "bowler" in the background. Such grim levelling in death points to the inevitable erosion of national causes and even of identity. All those national symbols of *Pickelhaube* and *Minnenwerfer, poilu* and *Mitrailleuse, Tommie* and *Lewis Gun* spread out upon that open floor are now reduced to this: a rusting heap of old armour riddled with bullet holes. This exit "poll" is a more powerful statement of "What For?" than even Varley's picture by that name.

At the same time, the openness of the two central rooms devoted to 1914–16 and 1916–18 labours to overcome the difficulty of a static Front with inflexible front lines. A low platform on which the uniform and instruments of a British Red Cross Nurse are displayed is placed in open space, letting "her" take her chances with the "lads" in the trenches (although no female mannequin is there to represent a female body). The same is true of a French display of hospital uniforms; after 90 years, an unmistakable levelling has come to occupy the "field." This levelling intention is also heard between the lines of the website description: "With the seeming inevitability of the road to war, a descending ramp takes visitors slowly but steadily into Room 2, where they are confronted with a striking mise-en-scène: fallen soldiers from all the warring countries lying in shallow pits of white marble. Embedded in the museum floor, these pits allude to the

trenches that covered the entire territory of the Somme, but also to
the sufferings common to all combatants." Doubtless, "[t]he presentation begins very formally, with the stiffly disposed uniforms and
standard gear marking the outset of the war. But the display becomes
more lively with the introduction of personal effects evoking the daily
lives of the soldiers as they settled into a war, that notwithstanding
first illusions, promised to be long."

Meanwhile, "[a]round the edges of the exhibition spaces, three-
tiered wall cases are devoted to the civil populations of France,
Germany and Great Britain." A social history of all three nations
(and occasionally their colonies) appears in the context of a new
Europe, the exhibit aiming at images of commonality among the
three major powers. "Reflecting the attitudes and mentalities of the
different belligerents, this presentation allows a comparative reading
of objects from daily life, imbued at once with patriotic faith and
with the omnipresence of death." A French poster, entitled "Com-
pagnie Algérienne," shows an Algerian man in puttees and fez kissing
wife and child goodbye under the stone arch of a souk. How normal,
how very natural, is the representation of this scene! Meanwhile, a
British poster depicts an unnatural monster: a little German child
with red lips and flowing blond hair, the heir of Prussianism be-
decked with the gifts of Christmas morn: a Pickelhaube on her head;
a sabre in her right hand; a toy Mauser over her left shoulder; a web
belt to cinch her nightgown; and a toy drum hanging from her belt. If
there is a German war poster of a British girl sporting the regalia of
Empire, I have failed to locate it. But propaganda cuts both ways,
and there could be such an image among the "25,000 civil and military quotidian objects" in the museum's collection.

More interesting is a truly unforgettable image of daily life in the
German trenches which were never as comfortable as Allied troops
liked to think. Here, headlined in 60-point black type, is a notice
guaranteed to make you rethink the hazards of war:

CHATS

L'Autorité allemand nous prie d'informer le public de son désir
d'acheter les chats. Les propriétaires qui voudraient vendre leur
chats, pouvent s'addresser à la Gendarmerie où il leur sera payé
de 5 à 4 Mk. par bête.

Gosselies, le 11 mai 1918.

[CATS

The German Authority begs to inform the public of its desire to purchase cats. Owners wishing to sell their cats can address themselves to the Gendarmerie where they will be paid from 5 to 4 Marks per animal.] (my translation)

This goes some distance toward levelling life in the trenches, not to mention in the towns and villages of occupied France, where even the family pet may be called on to confront the pestilence of war. The animal lover is reminded of other creatures, besides horses and mules, forced to suffer the depredations of war. Levelling of the combatants is one thing; the social levelling of animals down to the state of humans is another matter entirely.

There are reminders, too, of those on the margins for whom there would be no social levelling, unless in death. A poster from unoccupied France announces "Arrêté: portant interdiction de vendre des boissons alcoolisées aux Travailleurs Tunisiens" ["Bylaw: It is forbidden by decree to sell alcoholic beverages to Tunisian workers"]. Another display recalls the armies of Chinese workers recruited for transport and grave digging (100,000 by the British; 38,000 by the French), most dying eventually of dysentery, respiratory illness, or Spanish influenza. At the time, the field was not at all level for "guest" workers in France, perhaps less so than now. The Historial thus makes good on its social contract to focus on the fate of individuals, including colonials, in the midst of a world war.

The itinerary of the museum is likewise aimed at "an open-ended visit": "Trilingual signage, video monitors and historical and geographical maps allow visitors to orientate themselves throughout the itinerary, which has deliberately been left open ended. Making their way between the walls and the centre of the galleries, the visitors determine the order of their own visit." So why does it feel that something is still missing in the midst of this well-intentioned openness? There are even sixty video monitors to "present silent archival film footage documenting life at the front and behind the lines." Although the website indicates that these monitors "bring the objects displayed to life and permit a more intimate relationship between visitor and image," you realize that what is ultimately excluded from each room is *sound*. Indeed, all of the flickering images on those 12-inch video monitors continue to go about their ghostly business in utter silence. Here is a museum literally ruled by the silence of objects or their images, where the "experience" of the visitor is designed to be balanced, impartial, objective. This is not to deny that the Historial lives up to its claim: "The museum's design favours sobriety over spectacular staging. Intended to stimulate the mind as well as the eye, it invites visitors to use their intelligence and sensitivity in order to develop a coherent approach to the architecture, the museography and the collection." Yet was the Great War fought by the deaf? Even artillery gunners did not all go deaf at once, did they? So why not stimulate the "ear," as well as the "eye" and "mind"?

The answer should be obvious by now. The fear of spectacle, the suspicion of drama, the doubt of sound – these are all part of a long tradition of turning cathedrals into museums, of converting the "sacred" object into a silent text. Regressing to the space of noisy medieval libraries where a rabble of scribes and monks sounded out manuscripts in a busy scholarly hum is not an option. Europe, after all, is the home of the book, a whole universe of print, where reading aloud was mercifully replaced by the cogito, by the interiorization of thought. To return to that noisy world in a postliterate museum would be to disrespect the silence of the dead, to pander to the unwashed and unread.

And yet those spectral images moving in silence on 60 video monitors are quite as dead as the headless mannequins on the floor. They move about in a dream world of soundless inconsequence; there is no "report" from those big guns as they fire, no growl of motors, no clank of steel, as those primitive tanks pitch up and over a great heap of mud. Because they make no sound, those men of yore and their objects begin to look insubstantial, almost negligible. You want to believe that they are still here in our present; but their reticence has really sidelined them from virtual presence.

To exclude sound bytes from the museum is in fact to swim against the tide of popular culture, or (harder yet) to beat against the current of modern technology. For history in the "postliterate" museum has been moving for some time now toward a final rendezvous with oral culture. One cannot help but applaud the Historial's display in the Post-War Room of a small statue of Achilles breaking his sword over his knee – a powerful mock-up (1919) by the German sculptor Georg Marschall (1871–1956) for a proposed German War Monument. While Marschall's figure is an enduring (and endearing) testament to the tragic legacy of Homeric culture, the digital current of contemporary culture is sweeping us toward new forms of oral memory, even toward a new "medievalism," which the museology of an object-centred exhibit fails to realize, despite the spectacular medieval surroundings of the Château de Péronne.

For all its internationalism and laudable social intentions, the Historial puts its exclusive emphasis on past individuals, not on present viewers, as the virtual witnesses of past lives. And so the museum falls well short of breathing life into its historical subject. From its socially motivated levelling of combatants spread about on the open floors to the politically motivated open-endedness in its physical itinerary, the Historial aims at bringing a new Europe to life. And yet, by cherishing a bookish tradition of "objectivity," it stops short of making the viewer's subjectivity the ground of its display. The Historial, when all is said and done, remains a literate museum in a postliterate age.

ORIGINAL AND COPY

To return at this point to the Digital Archive of *The Memory Project* is to see what is truly revolutionary in its display of virtual documents and digital objects. Doubtless the war medals exhibited in 14 of 82 accessions (31 July 2007) from Great War veterans have lost their "aura"; we cannot touch them, or get a sense of their material connection to the past through our handling of them. And yet these "digital objects" are virtually present to us across time and space, since they are now capable of infinite replication and limitless observation. Instead of being "handled" by one or two persons at a time – in a museum they would in fact be under glass, their "aura" limited in any event to the fact of *our* presence to them – they here appear in digital form as the One that is a type of the Many, a virtual instance of the Platonic *idea* manifested as the *eidolon*. Similarly, the virtual documents on display, such as Attestation and Discharge papers from the Canadian Expeditionary Force, or pages of an open diary, are multiplied to infinity. Of less concern is the matter of their "aura," since for several decades now we have been accustomed, even in the archives, to working on photocopies to spare wear and tear on the originals.

What is ultimately at stake, however, in this digital proliferation of objects is the whole question of copy and original, a recurring subject of Plato's dialogues. As Stephen G. Nichols claims, the idea of the original "artifact as a unified whole, an organic unity" (138) is based on print technology, on a notion of the book as a "limited edition," or a self-bounded entity complete in itself. By contrast, he calls the illuminated manuscript of the Middle Ages a "mobile text" (140), a "copy that would intentionally differ from its model" (141) and so compose a new "original," since it presented "a surrogate that alters the original." As Nichols maintains, "*This means that the concept of surrogacy, of copy in the stead of a fixed original, ruled the manuscript culture of the Middle Ages*" (140).

Indeed, "the medieval manuscript space – perceived by scribes as a performative space" may serve as an analogue of cyberspace that values copies over originals. For the copy in medieval culture was also elevated "to the status of a unique artifact ... because it responds to and registers varying cultural forces that pull it in other directions" (141). As Nichols explains, "The instability of the literary texts in manuscripts allowed them to adapt and respond to evolving cultural possibilities from one context to another. It helped them adapt to new cultural situations, and it was the cultural reality of such evolving contexts that the manuscript matrix modeled so effectively." What is more likely entailed in the "evolving cultural possibilities" of oral-manuscript culture is the genuine flexibility of orally shaped thought to revise traditions in response to changing social needs and realities.

So what are these "new cultural situations" in our time that tend to favour "digital surrogacy" (139) over the original, the "true," the "real," the authentic object? As I have argued, our culture is now acclimatized to knowing the world through electronic "windows," of forming its views of persons and objects on the basis of their virtual presence. But it is the near ubiquity of the Internet that makes a material object or person confined to a single location somehow less "real" or present than a digital surrogate that can be everywhere at once. As Peter Walsh says in connection with the postliterate art museum, "Once, art historians said 'it's not in my books or slide library, thus it must not be important.' Now, their students tend to say 'It's not on the Internet. It must not exist'" (30).

It hardly matters any more whether we hold a printed photograph of Clare Laking on his enlistment in the army in 1917, or whether we view digital photographs of him in the Digital Archive. For this profound change in the technology of photographic imaging has completely overtaken the paper album, displacing images of family and friends and recent vacations to the hard drives of home computers, and even to virtual postings on the websites of Facebook, MySpace, YouTube, or Kodak EasyShare. The new social facts are these: we tend to congregate these days in virtual space, and we share stories and photos in ways that make older forms of socializing look quaint, if not claustrophobic. "I appear on the Internet; therefore I am." Here is a new cybernetic Cartesianism that has little to do with its seventeenth-century print original. For the copy *has* become the new original, and it now speaks for us in ways that we have barely begun to realize.

THE ARCHIVE AS FAMILY ALBUM

The Canadian Archival Information Network (CAIN), "a publicly funded agency" launched in 2001, was created "to transform the archival landscape for both researchers and archivists" by tearing down the walls of archive reading rooms and opening every archive "across Canada to all Canadians" (Millar 182). Two years later a stepchild of CAIN, the Digital Archive of *The Memory Project* was launched to create an archive without walls of veterans' experiences in both World Wars, in the Korean conflict, and in several decades of UN peacekeeping. This new environment of archiving in Canada has helped to promote more than just online descriptions of archival holdings; it has helped to "naturalize" the existence of digital objects and virtual presences.

Terry Cook, my esteemed colleague at St. Paul's College, University of Manitoba, tells a fascinating "postmodern story from Canada" (169) of our unique social and political approach to archives as a matter of federal policy:

> Canada alone of First World nations has developed at the national level the total archives approach, where almost all public archives in the country – national, provincial, territorial, municipal, university, and regional – acquire as part of their mandate, within one archival institution, a total archive of roughly equal extents of both public, government, or sponsoring institution records and related private-sector records and take into their archives the total record in every recording medium (including film, television, paintings, and sound recordings, which in many

countries are divided among several other repositories). In effect, the separated European and American and Australian public archives and historical manuscript traditions are combined inside one institution. Although there are many reasons why total archives evolved in Canada since the nineteenth century, this integration of the public and private reflects the same wider vision of archives I've just mentioned, one sanctioned in and reflective of society at large, of the total historical human experience, rather than limited to a view of archivists solely as the custodian of official state records. (Cook 175)

The Memory Project has been conceived within this framework of a "total archives approach," most notably in the way that it is both public (the soldier as servant of the nation) and private (the family as heir and custodian of the soldier's memory). In keeping with the mandate of "total archives," even at this voluntary level, it represents all but two (i.e., 7 of 9) of the Great War provinces – Saskatchewan and New Brunswick not yet (31 July 2007) being represented in accessions – although a vast majority (56 of 82) of accessions are from Ontario, followed by 10 from Manitoba. Each branch of the service is also represented, although here, too, the Army makes up the overwhelming majority (72 of 82), while 4 are from the Royal Flying Corps, 4 are from the Volunteer [Home] Service Force, and 2 from the Merchant Navy.

In its display of public documents such as Attestation and Discharge papers, as well as of artifacts derived from other media, the Digital Archive evidently conforms to the norm of multiple media in the "total archives approach." Photography might be expected to dominate over other media from 1914–18, since it was the most "personal" of all media forms in that era; in fact, 62 of 82 displays do contain at least one photo (some as many as 5). The medium of lithography is also represented in 11 postcards; handwriting is ubiquitous in posted letters and diaries. Even so, the most popular medium proves to be sound recording (73 of 82, thus making sound more dominant than photos). Print appears as well in transcripts of all 73 sound recordings. Here, in one institutional medium, can be found a wide variety of media carrying a wealth of historical information, including some "digital objects" that would otherwise belong in a museum – e.g., regimental badges (6), as well as other regimental insignia (2 pins, several shoulder patches and "flashes").

Even from this breakdown, it is apparent how far the Digital Archive has moved from what one archivist still regards as a "documentary heritage," or "documentary memory" of the nation (Millar 183, 190). To click on multiple entries in the archive of World War I, however, is to be struck by the overwhelming desire of family members to give *voice* to the soldier's experience. (Clare Laking was the only surviving veteran of the First World War to speak for himself in *The Memory Project;* the other voices are almost always those of a daughter or a son, or a grandchild or great-grandchild of the deceased soldier.) So why is *sound* the dominant medium in the Digital Archive, and not sight? Is it because, as the Canadian philosopher John Ralston Saul claims, "ours is an essentially oral culture" (221)? Or is it because, in the vastness of this territory stretching over six time zones, the only "natural" way to carry on a national conversation has been on radio (thanks to the creation of the Canadian Broadcasting Corporation in 1936, the same year Vimy was unveiled), or on television (again, CBC-TV was first to air in 1952)?[50] Whether we are by essence or necessity an oral culture, the Digital Archive underscores our lasting cultural bias toward speech.

Here, then, is one representative "voice" from the Digital Archive telling a war story in a mode that goes back at least as far as Homer:

> My name is Mollie Lancey [her maiden name is voiced, but omitted in the transcript] Lavelle. I am the only daughter of Albert William Lancey. His number, I'm almost positive, was 9575. He was a member of the Toronto Regiment, 1st Battalion, "C" Company. He fought the whole world war battles at Ypres, Somme and Vimy. He entered as just an ordinary soldier and he became a Sergeant [...]
>
> My father told us a few tales of the war. They were all about the good friends that he had and how wonderful the people were to them. He was married in 1917 to my mother, who was English, and he had returned from France just for the wedding. He was married on June the 30th, 1917 and I have a wonderful picture of their wedding, with the Colonel giving him what looks like a present of money or something, and all the men standing around with big smiles on their faces. It's a wonderful picture. He had to go back to France, and he was there when I was born on January the 24th, 1919. And he came home from France when I was three weeks old. They came to Canada in September 1919

and arrived in Halifax with all the other soldiers, and were inter-
rogated there. Then they came up to Toronto, where he resided
for the rest of his life.

While Mollie Lavelle does not share her "wonderful picture" by
posting it on the website, she does tell us about it in an unsupported
sound recording of family history, including the story of her own
birth as the daughter of a soldier and a war bride. She thus brings
us into her family circle through a speech-act that, like a stone
dropped into water, or like a radio wave, spreads in ever-widening
circles to encompass the effects of a global war that would bring
new families together across continents. Gathering us into her virtual community by inviting us to listen, Mollie Lavelle does what
Homeric poetry did for the peoples of Magna Graeca: she tells a
story that unites far-flung communities through an expression of a
common history with deeply shared values.

What are the values of *sound* that appear to make it our preferred
medium in an otherwise video age? Walter Ong claims that it is
"the unique relationship of sound to interiority when sound is compared to the rest of the senses" (71) that makes it a powerful agent
of collective identity. "Sight isolates, sound incorporates it" (72), he
declares with epigrammatic force. "Whereas sight situates the observer outside what he views, at a distance, sound pours into the
hearer ... I am at the center of my auditory world, which envelopes
me, establishing me at a kind of core of sensation and existence ...
You can immerse yourself in hearing, in sound. There is no way to
immerse yourself similarly in sight." For that reason, he views
sound as "a unifying sense," a bonding agent that results in "har-
mony, a putting together." By such means, individuals in an oral
culture bond together in communities whose extent is bounded by
the reach of shared history and oral technology (in the Homeric
world, this reach had extended from the Ionian coast of Turkey to
the Mediterranean coast of France). Axiomatically, "[p]rimary orality fosters personality structures that in certain ways are more communal and externalized, and less introspective than those common
among literates. Oral communication unites people in groups. Writing and reading are solitary activities that throw the psyche back on
itself" (Ong 69). To the extent that we participate in Mollie's story,
we are then "incorporated" into a "family circle" that likely extends much farther than she knows.

Another story handed down by the son of a Quebec veteran helps to illustrate how the isolating effects of war can be overcome through oral communication, since our empathy for the veteran helplessly suffering is what allows us to identify with his own speechless empathy:

> My name is Malcolm Fraser. As far as my father is concerned, he enlisted when he was seventeen in the 73rd Battalion of the Black Watch, and he served at Lens, Passchendaele, and Cambrai. He talked very, very little about the war ...
> He did have one memory of the 73rds first attack at Vimy Ridge, which was a March trench raid, and the 73rd got beaten up very very [the second "very" is voiced but absent from the transcript] badly. Later in the night when they were back at their start point, they could hear soldiers shouting, "Help, 73rd! Help, 73rd!" They were all tied up in the wire and the 73rd couldn't get to them, and I know that bothered my father immensely.

In repeating a story his father had told him only in part, Malcolm Fraser makes inferences from what had been left out; the body language of the haunted soldier reveals more than he can say. And yet we feel his helpless empathy in the very silences and occlusions of the story; the father's empathy for the men of the 73rd becomes the son's empathy for the father becomes our empathy for them both, extending in an unbroken line of community.

In part, this is the ground of Plato's hostility to oral poetry, his repugnance to its "pathological emotions, the unbridled and fluctuating sentiments with which we feel but never think," since its power necessarily consists in "the active personal identification by which the audience sympathises with the performance" (Havelock 26). In this view, "The Greek ego in order to achieve that kind of cultural experience which after Plato became possible and then normal must stop identifying itself successively with a whole series of polymorphic vivid narrative situations; must stop re-enacting the whole scale of the emotions, of challenge, and of love, and hate and fear and despair and joy, in which the characters of epic become involved. It must stop splitting itself up into an endless series of moods" (200), must give up its longing, that is to say, to identify simultaneously with old, grieving Priam *and* the young, grudging Achilles.

Another descendant, more than a generation removed from the soldier, preserves a line of oral storytellers unbroken in the Digital Archive by identifying with the differing experiences of two soldiers, as in this story from Bill Strange of Kingston:

> My mother's maiden name was Eleanor Snelgrove, and she lived with her family in Toronto. She had two older brothers who served in the Great War, 1914 to 1918. One brother, Charles Reginald Snelgrove, went overseas with the Canadian Expeditionary Force and was stationed in Siberia. And we have a lovely photograph of him wearing his heavy fur cap and fur-collared jacket – I assume part of the uniform that he wore in Siberia. The other brother, John Cecil Snelgrove, served with the 75th Battalion – a Toronto battalion, I believe – and he served in Europe. And [this "and" is not in the transcript] he sent home to his mother in a letter one time (I'm not sure of the year) a poppy that he had picked on a field. And [not in transcript][51] He said, "I can't believe that this is growing where there are so many shell holes, and I didn't know what to do with it so I'm putting it in a letter and I'm sending it to you."
>
> These were my two uncles on my mother's side, neither of whom did I know. One died before I was born, and the other one just after I was born.

Although he never met either man, Bill Strange puts himself in the place of each uncle, imagining one in terms of a romantic image got from sight, while cloaking the other in a tragic emotion derived from sound. In either case, the grandnephew identifies with both his veteran uncles; in the brief space of 1 minute and 41 seconds, he manages to communicate that identification to any careful auditor. What he says is fairly simple: Here are my two great-uncles who served in the First World War. But the effect of putting the photos online, so that we can also admire the man dressed in Siberian fur, and then gaze as well at the medals of the other uncle, is to place us and them both within a network of persons and events, enabled by this network of new technologies forming the digital basis of "imagined nations" (D. Williams 2003) across time and space.

Something in the structure of this digital network is likewise reminiscent of oral memory, in the way a user comes to occupy a position analogous to that of the oral poet. The Homeric repertoire, one recalls, was not just an encyclopedia of oral tales or a dictionary of metrical phrases, but an ongoing series of functional choices. "Borrowing a poetic term from the bard himself, we might emphasise that the 'pathways' (*oimai*) of oral traditional epic are important not chiefly in and of themselves but rather because of where they lead" (Foley, "What's in a Sign?" 10). In an intriguing footnote, Foley sees a similarity "between oral tradition and the Internet, which are alike in their dependence on pathways (as opposed to the Alexandrian Library, the prototype resource of objects)." Since "digital objects" are not really objects like codices and scrolls in the Alexandrian Library, but are rather like the "memory cues" of oral scripts (see chapter 4), the listener in the Digital Archive is that much closer to the position of the Homeric poet, taking one hyperlinked "pathway" rather than another, so that the route is not likely to be the same on any given passage. In fact, there is no one route through the Digital Archive. A user can sort by artefact, if that is the "pathway" chosen, or listen to sound recordings; or the user can sort through an archive of photos, medals, and Attestation papers. One can also sort by branch of service, or by province of origin, to get a "take" on a particular type of story. But a user can also click at random, proceeding by chance. The point, as Foley reminds us, is not what any given pathway suggests in itself, but rather where these pathways collectively lead.

Where they lead on this journey through the maze is to a written document read aloud by a proud grandnephew, a letter that, expressing serious reservations about the power of words to convey the experience, still leads further than the soldier might have imagined into contemporary understanding. I refer to the written words of John Cannon Stothers (quite a long letter, reproduced in part), which a relative takes it upon himself to read in the here and now of the Digital Archive as the memory of then and there:

France, February 1918

Dear Mother,

I wrote you after coming out of the line. And since that time, I've been busy here and there without being able to do much writing. In fact, after sixteen days of strenuous line work, nine of them in the front line continuously, a fellow feels like letting things slide. To provide against giving you information of value to the enemy, I'm not dating this letter. I suppose to let you know

that we did a trip some time during [not "in" as in transcript]
February will hardly stall the censor ...

I might say that walking into a barrage of enemy artillery fire
on the way to a working party near the front line had an effect
not exactly exhilarating, but rather electrifying. The speed with
which we covered the duck boards in that trench was about as
exciting as the farmers' trot at Dungannen Fair. Old Dick Horn
was playing 'the Old Soldier' and couldn't keep up, but when the
shells started bursting in our immediate neighbourhood, we all
got our heads down and sped along as though shod with seven
league boots, and tradition has it that Dick Horn won by a nose.
He showed a burst of speed that has seldom been equaled. I
doubt if it was ever beaten, and five minutes before that he
couldn't see and was continually getting out of touch. Speaking
personally, I never was so glad in my life as when the Corporal in
front was suddenly gifted with a glimmer of intelligence and
dived into a deep sap. We weren't long in reaching the bottom of
it, where we could listen to the burst of shells in comparative
safety. So much for that, and it has suffered in the telling.

While John Cannon Stothers regrets the seeming gap between the
letter and the event, he could not foresee how easily the gap is now
crossed by Internet users whose movie experience of diving into
shell craters makes his dive immediately intelligible. We sense that
we have been with him in that shell crater before; and we will not
leave him alone again.

What should we take from all these "soundings" in the archive and
museum? For one thing, the copy may replace, and even supersede,
the original, not only in the case of digital objects, but in a relay of
voices down the generations as we listen to Bill, who heard it from
Mother who got it from her soldier-father. For another thing, listeners may replace, or take the place of, distant relatives in sharing
contents of their family album and in hearing the oral stories that
go with them. What is most telling in this digital version of an institutional medium like the archives is its extension of the boundaries
of the family, handing on our cultural heritage as an expression of a
national, and, one hopes, human family, where ancient foes may be
united in the never-ending sound waves spreading out from the
event. For a third thing, we need to remember that, as listeners and

viewers, we are voluntary witnesses to the event, a volunteer "army" of witnesses who choose, like the original volunteers of 1914–17, to make ourselves part of a mass movement. In this way, at least, we do keep faith with "spectral images" of the past, to the point of keeping faith "with us who die," as John McCrae first called on us to do in "In Flanders Fields."

Is it possible, in this context of oral culture, to finally understand the hold that McCrae's "flawed" poem has had over the imagination of so many generations in Commonwealth countries? Far from being an "ironic" form of pastoral that fell disastrously short of its goal, as Paul Fussell chose to read it, "In Flanders Fields" continues to be read today as the oral expression of a "postliterate," rather than a pre-literate, culture. For its dramatic situation, as anyone can see, is that of dead men still speaking to the living in a way that is now made literal by the Digital Archive:

> We are the dead. Short days ago
> We lived, felt dawn, saw sunset glow,
> Loved, and were loved, and now we lie
>   In Flanders fields.

Presumably, that is why someone has left those poppies on the brass memorial plaque of the poem I keep in my digital album of the monument erected by the Canadian Battlefields Memorials Commission at the site of the work's composition (near McCrae's surgical dressing station on the banks of the Canal de l'Yser). As I study this image taken on a visit to the battlefields of the Western Front in May 2006, I find myself astonished by the presence of those red poppies; I hadn't noticed, or maybe hadn't stopped to think about them at the time, and had later forgotten that they were even there. Yet here they are in my digital photo: some kindly visitor was evidently moved to remember the poet, as well as the dead who go on speaking in his poem, by placing this ever-eloquent flower of Remembrance at both upper corners of the plaque.

Lest We Forget. How could I forget the very first poem I learned as a child? At this distance in time, at the end of writing a long book, I now see something else I failed to see those many years ago – that the "foe" is not what we took "him" to be. "Take up our quarrel with the foe" is rather a challenge, to those who will listen, not to let the horror and the anguish of 1914–18 be covered in the sands of time, not, above all else, to let our "loved" ones be swallowed up in oblivion. For the "foe," I now know, is our own experience of mortality; it is time and death and forgetfulness itself. And so I feel in my bones why a sporting franchise *comme les Habitants,* the Montréal Canadiens, with its legendary tradition of victory, should have painted those English words (of all things!) as the team Commandment on the Home team's dressing room wall in this greatest of all hockey franchises: "To you from failing hands we throw / The torch; be yours to hold it high." It is truly the voice of one generation speaking to another about the obligation to recall the past, to remember those who came before and what they mean to the living. It is nothing less than the voice of a great tradition enfolding the listener into its sacred dictate: *If ye break faith with us who die.* For here is the crux, the frightening moment of hesitation, in the recitation of the Lord's Prayer, just before the affirmation of "For Thine is the Kingdom." Still, these words ring every bit as true – *If ye break faith* – as on that day they were written. "If ye break faith" with the living word speaking here and now, what will remain of those dead, yet still speaking, voices? What will there be left to speak of in all those millions of names carved in Portland stone throughout the lower regions of Picardy and Pas de Calais and Flanders? No wonder that these voices say, with the sudden, overwhelming force of conviction, that "We shall not sleep, though poppies grow / In Flander's fields."

Conclusion

The Great War is now almost as far from us in time as the Battle of Waterloo was from those who fought the Battle of the Marne. And yet, a century later, our collective memory of pain and pride on the Western Front continues in Allied nations to inspire novels, plays, and films to an extent that a veteran of Napoleon's retreat from Moscow would surely envy.[52] Recent British cultural production (of which the enduring masterpiece has to be Pat Barker's *Regeneration* trilogy) bears witness to this powerful memory.[53] In Canada, too, we are still witnessing an efflorescence of Great War literature to rival our wealth of combatant writings from the interwar years, both in quality and in quantity.[54] Among Canadian Great War novels published since Timothy Findley's *The Wars* (1977), the following should repay reading: Robert MacNeil, *Burden of Desire* (1992), a flawed (if refreshingly un-Virgilian) reprise of the Halifax Harbour explosion; Kevin Major's *No Man's Land* (1995), a novel about the Newfoundland Regiment at Beaumont-Hamel on the First of July 1916; Jack Hodgins' *Broken Ground* (1998), a novel about veteran resettlement on Vancouver Island, at the heart of which lurks a traumatic memory of a deserter's execution; Joseph Boyden's *Three Day Road* (2005), a novel about two Ojibway-Cree snipers and the mystery surrounding the one who went missing before the other returned to James Bay after the war; and perhaps the most accomplished of these, Jane Urquhart's *The Stone Carvers* (2001), a richly embroidered and moving story of the creation of the Vimy Monument as a purgation of personal and national grief.

Canadian dramatists have also been bringing the Great War to centre stage in recent years, following the popular success of John

Gray's *Billy Bishop Goes to War* (1978), an irreverent and contro-
versial musical about Canada's best-known Royal Flying Corps ace.
Wendy Lill's *Fighting Days* (1985) stages the estrangement of Francis
Marion Beynon, author of the pacifist novel *Aleta Dey* (1919),
from Nellie McClung, her friend and mentor, whose patriotic works
Next of Kin: Those Who Wait and Wonder (1917), and *Three
Times and Out: told by Private Simmons* (1918) illuminate their
quarrel. Since 2000, several notable plays about the Great War have
been produced: *Mary's Wedding* (2000), Stephen Massicotte's
touching story of an Alberta woman who lost her lover on
30 March 1918 in a cavalry charge at the Battle of Moreuil Wood;
Unity (1918), Kevin Kerr's Governor General's Award-winning
drama (2001) about returning soldiers during the influenza epidemic of 1918; *Soldier's Heart* (2002), David French's play about a
traumatized survivor of Beaumont-Hamel; and *The Lost Boys*
(2001), the brilliant one-hander by R. H. Thomson (discussed in
chapter 8), clearly the most ambitious of these.[55]

So how to account for such a vigorous persistence of the Great
War in our cultural memory? Must we link it to "the birth of the
nation," our national myth of origins that Canadians might otherwise lack? (The "national" explanation doesn't begin to account
for the strength of the British need to reimagine the Great War, not
with a myth of origins reaching back to the Conquest, and even to
the myth of Arthur.[56]) Our own memory of the Western Front, by
contrast, cuts against the grain of our contemporary myth of Canada
as a peacekeeper, a myth that ignores the historical reality of our
military traditions – a reality that clearly weakens the "national"
explanation for our memory of the Western Front.

What about the Great War as a post-Christian version of Dante's
Inferno, an image of the worst the human spirit can endure and still
survive, in a setting that could well be captioned, "Abandon hope all
ye who enter here"? Probably not, for we have endured worse since.
"In the 1939–45 conflict, more than half of the approximately
50 million people who died directly as a result of hostilities were civilians" (Winter 9): not least among their number are the dead of
the Holocaust; of the London Blitz; of the firebombings of Tokyo,
Dresden, and Hamburg; of the nuclear destruction of Hiroshima
and Nagasaki. These are worse. Even the trials of Canadian troops
in Italy (1943–45), or in the Battles of Normandy and the Scheldt,
were not less than the sufferings of our troops in Flanders, the

Somme, or the Last Hundred Days. Nor should one forget the prisoners of war in the Japanese theatre after the fall of Hong Kong, who likely endured something quite as hellish as Hell itself. The photographs of emaciated survivors of those years are indistinguishable from the Nazi death camp survivors: you see it in their eyes as well as in their skeletal physiques. And yet the Second World War has not stirred the same kind of imaginative response that we find in Great War literature. Why should this be? Because of the way Hollywood and American interests have since laid "claim" to the Second World War, making the First World War a less expensive venue for written memories? Or because the Great War was really not a clear point of rupture?

Jay Winter chooses the latter answer: "The nuclear bombardment of Hiroshima and Nagasaki was new. So was the extermination of the Jews of Europe, an act with affinities to earlier mass atrocities, but which transcended them in method, character, and scale. Both of these catastrophes raised the possibility that the limits of language had been reached; perhaps there was no way adequately to express the hideousness and scale of the cruelties of the 1939–45 war" (9). At another level, however, it may be too easy to say with Winter that, "before the Death Camps, and the thermonuclear cloud, most men and women were still able to reach back into their 'traditional' cultural heritage to express amazement and anger, bewilderment and compassion, in the face of war and the losses it brought in its wake" (9–10). For the language of "modern" writers of the Great War suggests that the limits of an older language had already been reached.[57]

Indeed, the Great War feels "epochal" in a way that the Second World War still does not – though it ought, ending as it did in the opening of the Death Camps and in the apocalyptic image of nuclear holocaust. But our sense of epochal rupture in those years has as much to do with our experience of media as of horror – since the Great War fundamentally reshaped our experience of time. Our memory of that conflict seems to have been conditioned by two related factors – the growth of cinema as a new mode of information in the decades leading up to the Great War, and new forms of "cinematic memory" that were transferable to prose and poetry, as well as representations on film after that war – both serving to open a window on time itself, refiguring our human relation to temporality. This may go some distance to explaining the conundrum that the Great War continues to be associated with epochal change, since our cultural patterns of adaptation to a new form of memory were first established in the Great War era.

At the end of my Introduction, I suggested, in words borrowed from Hayden White, that nothing is "more real for human beings than the experience of temporality – and nothing more fateful, either for individuals or for whole civilizations" (180). At an underlying level, I have tried to show how cinema – and the "cinematic memory" it created of the Great War – burned a disturbing sense of the collapse of time into our collective memory. In the Great War era, we first began to see how the past might invade the present, and how this would take many forms, including prose and poetry. Novels such as *All Quiet on the Western Front* (1928), *Generals Die in Bed* (1930), and *The Memoirs of George Sherston* (1928–36), together with such poems as "Dulce et Decorum Est," created a new "allegory of temporality," or a new view of time, in which the past becomes a province of the present. "Cinematic memory," then, is not merely an effect of form or technique, but a deep-seated change in our view of time, of how we are necessarily implicated in it. The hold of these works on the popular imagination in the interwar years and ever since, suggests that the congruence of a "War to end all wars" and our "cinematic memory" of it was what truly opened a new window on time itself, marking the moment when the past would henceforth become a species of the present.

At the same time, I argue that it was in print genres – specifically poetry and the novel – that cinematic memory became both "natural" and "universal," no longer limited just to film. But, if poets and novelists could adapt a static medium like print to the laws of "motion pictures," it would follow that the so-called "second law of media" – the law of obsolescence – is really no law at all. It was Marshall McLuhan who, taking media to be "extensions of man," claimed, in work completed after his death by his son Eric, that any human sense favoured by a new medium will be enhanced, while any sense favoured by an older medium will be "pushed aside or obsolesced by the new 'organ'" (McLuhan and McLuhan 99). Evidently, film did not push print aside, as "Gutenberg technology" had done to "the scriptoria and scholasticism of the Middle Ages" (100). Rather, as Elizabeth Eisenstein shows with far more historical rigour, "book production had already left the monasteries in the course of the twelfth century, when lay stationers began to handle book provisions for university faculties and the mendicant orders" (*Agent* 12). For a century after Gutenberg, the printed book continued, at least on its surface, to resemble the codex manuscript. What was changing, according to Eisenstein, were the processes of production and reception that would lead to social and political revolution (51 ff).

Books, one has to remember, are not like buggy whips (any more than questions are like laws); and books were obviously not rendered obsolete by the *cinématographe*. Rather, in the crucible of the Great War, a number of writers felt a need to adapt their writing to cinema, evoking in their prose and poetry a cinematic epistemology that was all the more powerful for being fixed in print. Rather than deeming it a "law" of evolution (it is more like historical experience), I claim that new media, like other changes in our environment, necessarily trigger adaptive behaviours. And those who adapt are better able to survive, if in mutated form.[58]

In our century of multiple transitions from print to film to television to digital modes of information, we are still witnessing the adaptation of "memory" to this series of new environments. And yet, in evolutionary terms, this is not more than "local" history, a period so brief that it would be unwise to make generalizations about it without some form of historical "control." Such a period of media change, with its signs of a deep mutation in cultural memory, does exist, of course, at the beginning of Western writing. Here, Homer plays the part I assign to Remarque and Harrison, to Owen and Sassoon, since his poetry set the pattern for adaptation to new forms of cultural memory. At this level, what the *Iliad* preserves are the shaping effects of writing on the older form of oral memory, a record of the means by which a traditional poet, without other technical resources, could absorb the new technology by outflanking, or even incorporating, its effects into his own medium. The written sign, in other words, conditions the world of Homer's *Iliad* from its outset, since the oral medium sets out to prove its capacity to absorb its own negation, to make Achilleus be a devil's advocate, forcing Homer to "write" orally, whether or not the ancient poet dictated or composed orally as he wrote. Achilleus draws the whole poem into the shadow of writing by demanding that his memory be "fixed," as it were, in enduring form. This imperative to absorb the norms of written "fixities," while defending the integrity of the older cultural system, is what makes the *Iliad* such a remarkable and enduring expression of oral memory. At the very least, the oral poet challenges the "law of obsolescence" by preserving the memory of Achilleus into the new age of writing.

In my ensuing discussion of "imperial memory" – both in Virgil's *Aeneid* and in Hugh MacLennan's Virgilian novel of the Great War, *Barometer Rising* (1941) – I argue that a new relation to time, implicit in writing itself, would shape Roman memory in the *Aeneid* (*c.* 29–19 BCE), particularly in the "script" that calls on Augustus to "remember" a past that has not yet happened. This "script of empire" – "Roman, remember, these are your arts / To rule earth's people by imposing the habit of peace, / By sparing the humble and warring down the proud" – invents an "immemorial" tradition replete with Sybilline prophecies and a Father-god *reading* what is written in "the mystic rolls of Fate," not to preserve but to found the history that it names. Writing history in the future tense, Virgil calls on Augustus to become the sort of ruler who will fulfill this destiny, just as Aeneas will become the prototype of Augustus through his trials. By returning to the mythic past for an image of his "hero" in the making, Virgil is then able to script a future course for what Augustus will in fact do: make a show of conservatism in the many innovations that will transform the Roman Republic out of recognition.

The Virgilian model returns us to the Great War in a Canadian novel structured on "classical memory" to make the Halifax Harbour explosion of 1917 a reprise of burning Troy. By "remembering Virgil" in the way that he "remembers" the Great War, Hugh MacLennan effectively appoints himself architect of a *pax Canadiana,* envisioning his country as the "keystone" (208) of a trans-Atlantic arch that spans two English-speaking empires, one centred in London, the other in Washington. In true Virgilian fashion, the Latin scholar cloaks imperial ambition in the garments of the peacemaker even as he dons the robes of the Sibyl. By avoiding any modern, "cinematic memory" of the soldier-poets writing a decade before him, MacLennan is able to preserve a form of classical memory that locates the future in the ancient past, and that upholds "follow the ancients" as a rule of life.

This is the reverse, of course, of the sort of cinematic memory found in Owen, Remarque, Harrison, and Owen, where there is no hope of going back once the past is ever-present, and the future is obscured by two new factors: the immediacy of the visual image,

and the presentness of viewing. What is more, the ontological doubling of the subject on film alters more than temporal relations; the
cinematic subject, as in Sassoon's *The Memoirs of George Sherston*,
looks for a way to reconcile contradictory roles as an actor and observer, or warrior-poet. Sassoon does so by making the soldier a
camera-eye, recording "raw" footage, and the writer a sort of film-
editor, shaping the filmic structures of memory on the cutting-room
floor. These two moments of primary and secondary viewing are
the mechanism by which he envisions himself as "some epic poet a
hundred years hence" (*Infantry* 117), looking back from the future
in a cinematic mode of remembering that can free him from temporal constraints. By means of ontological doubling (spatial *and* temporal), cinema thus leads toward the transcendence of time.

Such transcendence is the implicit subject of Timothy Findley's
The Wars (1977), where an archival narrator looks back from a
point sixty years in the future to remember a deserter who, in admi-
ration of Sassoon, becomes the "hero" who does "the thing that no
one else would even dare to think of doing" (10). In the story of
Robert Ross, the war protestor does not write "A Soldier's Declaration" to challenge the sincerity of his country's "war aims," but
deserts to save some horses in the Canadian Field Artillery. Even as
Robert Ross becomes a Sassoon-like hero of the future, the archival-
narrator seeks, by means of "photographic memory," to distance
him from his own era's "mad" (10, 202) fidelity to Empire, a faith
that lionizes General Wolfe, who *grew up and got your country
for us* (120). In this version of "photographic memory," there is
an obvious challenge to imperial hegemony, but also a more subtle
challenge to the Virgilian myth of Empire, insofar as the hero makes
himself the willing servant of another kind of future. What emerges
from this "photographic memory" of Robert Ross, at least in terms
of Findley's own comments on his creative process, is a version of
cinematic memory in which the "hero" comes riding down the
light-rays into our more "enlightened" time. In studying photographic memory *after* cinematic memory, I suggest that Findley in-
clines to the latter, and that the stopping of time in a still image
signifies "dead" history for him.

A second chapter on photographic memory in *The Lost Boys* turns
a corner in this argument about cinematic memory, since it restores
sound as a player in the shift between epochs. The reception of film
in its early years is not always a story of unbridled enthusiasm or

even anxious wonder. There were notable dissenters, like Maxim Gorky, who "said that he was disturbed and depressed by the depiction of a gray and irrelevant world: 'Last night I was in the Kingdom of Shadows. If you only knew how strange it is to be there. It is a world without sound, without colour ... It is not life but its shadow, it is not motion but its soundless spectre'" (cited by Barsam 24). While the epistemology of cinema corresponds to the epistemology of relativity in Einstein's revolutionary theory of time, and while Einstein himself appears in photographic projections on the set of R. H. Thomson's play about five brothers lost in the Great War, what the playwright attempts in his use of multimedia is something of an answer to dissenters like Gorky who felt they had landed in Hades by stepping into the cinema hall.

The brilliance of Thomson's play inheres in his use of sound (or multi-directional modes of aural remembering), to offset the uni-directional movement of film light, where the past is still able to "invade" the present. For film-light from the past never reaches us with any more weight or gravity than starlight; the past in this "photo-play" remains over "there," even when the photograph changes back into a beam of light. Because light only travels in one direction, we remain downstream of the light source; we can no more return to that source than the past can be transmitted in its full weight to us on a beam of light. What *The Lost Boys* suggests, in its multimedia projection of the photo-image back into its light-source, is that any past time that invades the present in "cinematic memory" is likely to be relativized. The past written in light is then a form to which we must lend our own weight in a continuing pro-cess of identification with the time-bound image.

If "photographic memory" works in *The Lost Boys* to restore the past to itself, the actor's identification with his "lost" uncles does not mean "identity" with any one of them. Rather, the actor comes up against hard limits in his quest to recover the past, such as in his inability to fill in gaps, or to say what was left unsaid in George's letters. In the end, the actor admits that he can only ever be *here*, in his own time, although he can see the time of the "lost boys" across the curve of spacetime. But it is in the weight of his own body, par-ticularly in the immediacy of his dance with the "stars," that he does remember the "lost boys." At the same time, it is the presence (or "gravity") of a live audience to the actor's presence that works to reconstitute the body of oral community.

Television, while creating an "electronic memory" of the Great War, also creates another type of orality. As the disembodied voice of history in the television series *For King and Empire* (2001), R. H. Thomson disappears from view as an actor; his body no longer "grounds" us in our immediate presence to him. At the same time, the on-screen host Norm Christie "calls" us to follow him in a mode of oral address that is also underwritten by the ideology of "live" television. The institutional practices of television, together with the "camera of Now" and the host's "presentness" in our time of viewing, much less our living space, encourage the fiction that we witness a live performance, in which the "live" host conducts us on a pilgrimage to the past.

The beginnings of "live" television did displace cinema as a medium where silent images of the past came to invade the present. Cinema was reduced to an art form by "live" television, with its non-electronic camera henceforth exiled from "the world's presence" (Cavell 131). But the "camera of Then," defined by black-and-white footage of the Great War, is quickly absorbed on History Television by the colour "camera of Now." Through colour-fades to black and white, television henceforth invades film, entering the past, as it were, to bring back "news" shots of the battlefield. Two modes of address – the voice-over of the invisible narrator of history, and the "live" commentary of the series' host – are then joined in two distinct forms of camera work that merge, interpellating the audience in the moment of viewing into a scene of "what is going on" rather than of "what has been." Unlike the silent images of film that used to invade the present, the vocal, coloured images of television now begin to invade the past.

The "documentary look" of television relies nonetheless on a system of glances to construct "the social space" (Caughie 342) of the historical document to be dramatized. In surprising ways, the television documentary gives temporal priority to the image, to a point where it seems to generate the written word, as in Christie's "live" shot from Vimy towards the slag-heaps at Lens, and then a colour-fade to black-and-white, as if we are looking at an old photo of the scene, out of which emerges the voice-over of an actor describing the scene contained in the soldier's letter. The temporal direction of the shot (colour to black-and-white, now to then), as well as the generative power of the image to authorize the written word, lays bare the temporal bias of "live" television – that the medium can turn the clock back in ways that cinema cannot do. Now we invade the past, rather than awaiting its invasion of us, by answering the oral-visual "call" to follow the host through chalk tunnels under the city of Arras, only to find ourselves following a "camera of Now" up to the "camera of Then," where Canadian troops are waiting in these tunnels at the end of August, 1918, just before the assault on the Drocourt-Quéant line. And the point of entry to the "tunnel" of 1918 is the "voice" of Canon Frederick Scott "speaking" about what follows.

What History Television depends on is not so much "flow" – a continuous stream of images – as it is the segmented series of *regularities* wherein the ideology of "live" TV is writ large. Contrary to the evidence of our senses, we see how black-and-white archival footage becomes "news" that a videographer has "gathered" all day, just in time for our evening viewing. Among other "regularities" are the regular relay from voice to voice (from host to narrator to soldier-eyewitness, and back to the host who, for example, kneels in a cemetery by the grave marker of one of the witnesses); the regular relay of images from then and now in sequences that literally take us down the well of memory; and the structural regularity of building to a dramatic climax in each of five acts, before a break to commercial. Each of these formal regularities contributes to a dramatic structure that provides a genuine experience of participating in the action (not its reconstruction). The drama is not restricted to the outcome of the historical event, but literally expands the action in ways to make us feel contemporary with it.

Because the medium, with its ideology of "liveness," communicates a sense of immediacy – these events are happening here and now in my living room – the host's motivated errors can be too easily forgotten (the first Canadian to die in the Great War did not fall on the Western Front, but in a British naval battle two months earlier off the coast of Chile). Indeed, a "folk memory" is more suited to a medium that, by virtue of its immediacy, prefers stories of individuals to more "objective" forms of analysis. The bias of the medium, in fact, is to make you feel that *You are there,* from the first "call" of the "following shot" to walk in the steps of the on-screen host, to subsequent forms of editing that allow you to "live inside those photographs." It is for such reasons that History Television presents us with "a new Homeric mode."

What I call the "discourse of the Name" also helps to uncover Homeric dimensions in this form of history. Throughout the six episodes, at regular intervals, we follow our host into a cemetery that is intimately connected to the action we have just "witnessed." We are *here*, at the gravesite of a "hero" whose valour and whose suffering have left a visible impression. And we read the names on the crosses, or the names of the missing in white marble on the Vimy Monument, looking over the director's shoulder as he kneels, his fingers tracing his grandfather's name in the stone. And we sense that the call we have answered is to join (however belatedly) those Vimy Pilgrims who journeyed across the Atlantic to attend the christening of the Vimy Memorial in 1936. At the same time, it is also the call of Achilleus to ensure that his name will not be forgotten.

In other ways, history on television opens a window on an ancient oral culture that persists in spite of all. (We are reminded that old media are not "obsolesced" by new media so much as they are forced to adapt to each new mode.) As John Fiske suggests, television, like oral culture, "is active, participatory" (79), leaving no distinction between producers and consumers, and no "higher" authorities who are the "official" keepers of the historical record. Rather, viewers are asked to become producers themselves, to add their family members' names and stories and memorabilia to the digital archive of the series' website. As Walter Ong insists, it is this "participatory mystique" (136) of oral culture that is the real source of its ability to foster the communal sense.

The "nowness" of television also contributes to this oral epistemology with its sense of a poet performing for a live audience what he "sees" in the cinema of his mind's eye. And an audience that is "here" in this space where the past also moves again before its eyes, is that much more aware of its power to shape events. For an "oral text" that cannot be fixed is necessarily open to the future, to the needs of future audiences; as a living tradition, it will be open to change. Likewise, in its more personalized form of address, History Television revives older forms of relations between performers and audiences, suggesting another form of "truth" from written history, the truth of the shared memories and common bonds that are the basis of a living community. To this extent, *For King and Empire* brings us quite close to our historical beginnings in an oral memory of a figure daring us to forget his name.

If a "cinematic memory" of the Great War opened a new window on time, digital technologies tend to "recall" that event as a prototype for an ongoing adaptation of "time" and "memory" to changing media. Signs of an emergent form of this "digital memory" are evident in institutional media such as the digital archive and the interactive war museum. In "Sound Bytes in the Archive and Museum," I make a case for the resurgence of sound as a prime consequence of "live" television, as it appears, for example, in *The Memory Project*, a unique website created and maintained by the Dominion Institute since 2003 as part of its "educational programme, designed to connect veterans and students online and in classrooms across the country." In digitized form, voices of the dead reach us in a way that were only ever metaphorical for the Great War poet: "We are the dead. Short days ago we lived, / Felt dawn, saw sunset glow." Now the dead can speak for themselves in a way that was unthinkable in the traditional archive. It is as if these "dead," together with their photos, medals, regimental pins, and Attestation papers, reach out to us from cyberspace – a new Platonic Idea appearing in the world as *eidola,* or material copies. The copy, as in medieval manuscripts, becomes more pertinent than the original, recalling how "mobile texts" of the Middle Ages were open to the changing realities and social needs of ever-changing times. Since it is websites like *Facebook* and *MySpace* that have created this new social space where people congregate, sites like *The Memory Project* can then be "naturalized" as a new form of social memory.

Although the last of the Great War combatants has died, many of their descendants are determined to let their words speak for themselves, whether posting such words in the actual letters and diaries of the soldier, or performing them aloud, or even recalling tales passed down orally within families. With the exception of one old veteran (104 years old at the time of recording) who tells his own story, it is the descendants of Great War veterans who must give the dead a voice with which to speak on the website of *The Memory Project*. An oral "line" of tradition is thus established, welcoming visitors into the "family" circle and altering print-formed notions of community. Of equal import, the design of the website and the nature of digital networks create multiple "pathways" for a visitor to traverse, whether through "voice" or a sequence of documents or virtual artefacts. Such pathways recall the "*oimai*" (or "pathways") of oral memory that enabled an ancient singer to traverse corridors of remembrance in a variety of ways. This "oral" bias of digital networks may then help to revive networks of oral memory that are more responsive to the needs of an immediate audience, and are able to mediate in various ways between a fluid past and an ever-changing present.

Something similar is evident in the "museological revolution" that has begun to exalt a visitor's experience above the "aura" of the object, substituting video displays and digital multimedia for the unique presence of authentic artefacts. An ingrained suspicion of sound in the museum – likely related to the "authority" of the printed word – is giving way to something far more telling than headset rentals. In interactive museums, high-definition flatscreens appear around every corner, offering a surround-sound display that enables a visitor to "live" the experience of the historical moment. Bookish notions of the museum as a secular cathedral where relics are venerated in silence are currently giving way to what some curators dismiss as "edutainment."

Even so, powerful social and technological forces are behind this "museological revolution," not least of which are the postmodern *mentalité* (itself a reflex of electronic communications), the pervasive influence of popular culture, and the early conditioning of museum-goers, a generation reared largely on television, computer screens, and virtual reality technologies, who "know" the world best through animated forms. It is these modes of information that are undermining the traditional museum, lessening the "aura" of objects and the "authority" of curators, while at the same time expanding the range of meanings and the dynamic use of space that makes it seem we could step back in time. Indeed, we are witnessing a deep shift from print-formed notions of "objectivity" – valuing detachment, abstraction, analysis, and generalization – to more "oral" values of subjectivity favouring involvement, concreteness, wholeness, and particularity.

In three types of war museum, I find signs of these differing values according to the degree that interactive or static displays are the norm: (1) in the traditional type of national museum in the Infantry Museum in Montpellier, France; (2) in the interactive type of national gallery in the Canadian War Museum in Ottawa; (3) and in the static type of international gallery in l'Historial de la Grande Guerre on the Somme. The first is ultra-traditional in its display of objects for silent veneration, including a silent-film display of images of the Verdun Offensive. The third, despite its post-national attempt at the levelling of social and political differences in the Great War, or at the reconfiguration of a united Europe in this shared museum space, remains an exhibit that encourages silent veneration of the object in a space shared by sixty black-and-white monitors (with 12-inch screens) constantly running a loop of silent images of the war on the Western Front. The second type, despite its investment in the national story, accomplishes something very different by its use of computer monitors and televisual histories and flatscreen monitors that buttonhole and challenge the viewer to rise above the prejudices of the past. A more dialogical engagement with voices and faces from the past emerges from this subjective experience, giving a greater sense of involvement in the debates, the sorrows, and the apprehensions of the Great War era.

A hybrid form of experience is also enabled by the strategic deployment of artefacts, both from the battlefield and from the home front, in which one still feels the "aura" of things from that time, such as the wrecked airframe of a plane that William Barker crash-landed near the end of the war, or an exact replica of Billy Bishop's Nieuport 17 that "flies" on steel suspension cables above the Battle of Vimy Ridge today, which is to say above the 18-seat Vimy Theatre where the battle rages on. But in the space between the "object" above and the collage of voices and images below, a truly interactive space appears – at bottom the "space" of a viewer interacting with the static "object" and images of dynamic "subjects" who "live" in this space. At every turn, the viewer is called on to make aesthetic and moral choices, such as which is more "true" of Canadians resisting gas at Second Ypres: the grand, heroic image painted by Richard Jack, or the grotesque image painted by William Roberts? In scene after scene, and "year" after "year," the visitor is interpellated in much the same manner as he or she is by the "electronic memory" of History Television. And the "call" is both a sound and a gesture.

In the end, these newer forms of memory could put us in danger of losing our memory of the Great War altogether, dooming us to forget what "really" happened, much as the oral memory of the Greeks had made a hash of chronology, "recalling" a Troy destroyed by Mycenae some two hundred years after the fall of the latter. Even so, is it necessarily "narcissistic" to privilege our subjective experience over the historical reality? Or is it the case rather that we now live with plural forms of memory that neither replace, nor "obsolesce," older forms of memory? History on television or in the interactive museum may be taking us back toward Homeric memory, but the difference in our cultural situation today is that the "oral" poet is not our one and only medium.

It must be obvious to anyone who reflects for a moment that the contemporary revival of ancient ways of knowing does not spell the end of written history, any more than these ways are mere "supplements" to the written record. Each form of memory is distinct, and each presents a unique window on our human experience of time. Even books like this still have to compete, at whatever disadvantage, with cinematic, photographic, and digital forms of memory. What is intriguing in this trend toward multiple ways of knowing and remembering is how consonant it is with the emerging trend toward "multiple 'selves'" and social "multiphrenia" (Deibert 181, 186) that are likewise a consequence of the shift from print-formed notions of the Cartesian ego to multi-media that "naturalize" more plural forms of identity. Would it not be possible to be enriched, rather than threatened, by such plural forms of memory, much as we are enriched and challenged by plural forms of identity?[59]

Whether one regards this media-induced "multiphrenia" as a threat, a challenge, or a liberating possibility, one still needs to grasp how cultural forms of memory have been changing now for more than a century. And, at the leading edge of this historic shift, the Great War looms as large as ever, both for its own sake as a great and enduring cultural tragedy, and for its forward-reaching echo of the time when we first began to remember in new ways.

Notes

1 This is the reverse of Marshall McLuhan's approach in *Understanding Media,* where the new medium is "an environment" that "reprocesses the old one as radically as TV is reprocessing the film" (the truism that TV as a form absorbs film as its "content"). For McLuhan, "the 'content' of TV is the movie," just as the content of Plato's writing is the older "oral dialogue" of Socrates (ix). For whatever reason, McLuhan failed to see how a new media "environment" is likely to be the content of an older medium; or if he did see it, he never developed a method for exposing the new "content" in the older "form."

2 Elizabeth Eisenstein nonetheless reminds us that, "After their original functions were outmoded, ancient memory arts acquired an occult significance and received a new lease on life in printed form" (*Printing Revolution* 36).

3 The "Official History of the Canadian Army in the First World War," Colonel G. W. L. Nicholson's *Canadian Expeditionary Force 1914–1919,* is remarkably discreet about the capture of Canadian troops in the Second Battle of Ypres, mentioning only in passing that "two companies of the 7th Battalion were overrun 500 yards north-east of St. Julien, the majority being taken prisoner" (75). Nor does the St-Julien monument of "the Brooding Soldier" (Vance 67), erected after the war by the Canadian Battlefields Memorials Commission, refer to the "shame" of surrender, but only to "the first German gas attacks the 22–24 April 1915" where "2000 fell and lie buried nearby." The French plaque on the opposite face of the column is noticeably more "heroic" (as is the case with each of the eight monuments erected by the CBMC, a topic worthy of further study). The St-Julien text reads: "Ici les 22–24 avril 1915 dix-huit mille Canadiens du flanc gauche britannique resisterent victorieusement aux

premières attaques de gaz des Allemandes; 2000 d'entre eux glorieuse-
ment tombés reposent près de cette colonne" (from text in my photo).

4 "[S]tudents of memory today hold that past experience is necessarily –
both psychologically and neurologically – *constructed* anew in each
memory event or act of recall. Memories, then, are constructed, and
memory itself, moreover, is plural. Despite the traditional notion of
memory as a single mental faculty varying only in strength and accessi-
bility, memory is not, Larry R. Squire reminds us, 'a single faculty but
consists of different systems that depend on different brain structures
and connections'" (Eakin 107). See my discussion of the plurality of
memory in "Making Stories, Making Selves: 'Alternate Versions' in
The Stone Diaries," *Canadian Literature* 186 (Autumn 2005): 10–28.

5 The reader of *Imagined Nations: Reflections on Media in Canadian
Fiction* (2003) is invited to consider my reprise of this scene as a movement from questions of space (what Innis called the "spatial bias" of
print) in my earlier work on the nation as a mediated construct, to
questions of time (what Innis saw as the "temporal bias" of oral media, including radio) in this present study of "memory" and new conceptions of temporality.

6 Richard Lattimore's translation of the *Iliad* is used throughout. His use
of Greek spellings for names such as Achilleus is also observed wherever the subject is Homeric poetry or the oral culture of ancient Greece.
Outside of chapter 3, however, where the subject is the trope of name
and fame, together with its enduring importance in Western culture,
the Greek Achilleus becomes the Latinized Achilles.

7 The spatial implications of this scene of reading are discussed at the beginning of my *Imagined Nations: Reflections on Media in Canadian
Fiction* (5–6).

8 Here, the name "Achilles" refers to the Latinized version of a figure
who, for Virgil, was an egotist ready to sacrifice whole societies in order to preserve his fame.

9 For an illuminating discussion of the cognitive, social, cultural, intellec-
tual and political differences between scribal and print cultures, see
Elizabeth Eisenstein, *The Printing Press as an Agent of Change*
(Cambridge: Cambridge University Press, 1979), 9–159.

10 Virgil's script still figures prominently in the recently unveiled Valiants
Memorial of the National Capital Commission where, on the wall of the
Sappers' Stairway on Confederation Square in Ottawa, under nine busts
and five statues of fourteen valiant women and men (including General
Sir Arthur Currie, Commander of the Canadian Corps 1917–18), are

inscribed these words from *Aeneid* 9.447: "Nulla Dies Umquam Memori Vos Eximet Aevo" ("No day will ever erase you from the memory of time").

11 "Early British war films included *Men of the Moment, Termonde in Ruins,* and *Strand War Series,* and *The Great European War* (all 1914) ... Other British war films include C. M. Hepworth's *Men of the Moment* (1915), *Ready, Aye Ready* (1915), *Germany's Army and Navy* (1914), *Lord Kitchener's New Army,* George Pearson's *The Great European War* (1914), *Backbone of England* (1914), and an especially popular film, *What We Are Fighting For* (1918)" (Barsam 35–6).

12 In Will Bird's *And We Go On* (1930), a cavalry charge by "the Royal Canadian Dragoons, the Fort Garry Horse and the Strathconas," is viewed by troops of the 42nd Battalion held in support on the first day of the Battle of Amiens (8 August 1918) as "one of the finest spectacles of the whole war," before it is explicitly likened by Bird, a clear-eyed survivor of more than two years of war, to watching cinema: "Killing began as if it were a grand movie scene ... We had more thrills. More horses came into view, pulling a battery of heavy guns. They thundered by us and over the wide plateau, swinging about and into action with astounding speed" (reprint *Ghosts* 100).

13 Here, the pot could be guilty of calling the kettle black. Modris Eksteins cites evidence that Remarque "first saw front-line action in Flanders in June 1917," but that a leg wound suffered on 31 July 1917 kept him in hospital in Duisburg until October 1918 (the time of Paul Baümer's death). "The leg wound which hospitalized Remarque," avers a certain Peter Kropp, claiming to have spent a year in hospital with him and to be the original of the character Kropp, "was self-inflicted, the product of a *Heimatschuss*. While many of the allegations of Remarque's critics and opponents were malicious and prompted by envy, opportunism, and political intent, there do appear to be grounds for suspecting that Remarque's war experience was not as extensive as his successful novel, and particularly the promotional effort surrounding it, implied" (348).

14 Emil Marius Requark (pseudonym of Max Joseph Wolff), *Vor Troja nichts Neues.* Berlin: Brunnen-Verlag, 1930.

15 The Germans, belatedly recognizing the value of cinema, did not begin to produce propaganda films for some time. One of the first of these was *Behind the Fighting Lines of the German Army* (1915). Richard Barsam (37) notes as well that, "Alarmed by the growing number of effective anti-German propaganda films made by the Americans, British,

and French, the German government realized that such films would also make a vital contribution to the war effort" (36). It may well be, given his extremely limited experience at the Front, that Remarque recalled this film as his earliest "memory" of the Western Front, at once a homely and a "natural" scene with which to open his novel.

16 Kevin Brownlow helpfully recalls how "the Austrians were first among the Central Powers to entrust moving picture coverage to the army. Soldiers, they realized, could take pictures no one else could achieve. In 1917 the Picture and Film Board (BUFA – Bild und Filmamt) was founded in Germany, responsible not only for producing instructional films and newsreels but also for maintaining front-line cinemas. BUFA followed the Austrian example" (84–5).

17 Following the lead of Andreas Huyssen, John Urry locates a "crisis of temporality" in the recent "'electronification' of memory" (63), and not in the prior epistemology of film.

18 More convincing is Will Bird's (1930) account of the assembly point of the Canadian Army Corps at Gentelles Wood on 7 August 1918, where total silence and secrecy seem to be the rule, where platoon leaders and even company commanders are kept in the dark about the pending attack: "It had turned cold and the men were impatient to get moving, but as we were leaving the wood a great rustle of movement stilled them. It was something we had not heard before. All at once no one was speaking or whispering. Thousands of men were moving by us as quietly as possible, and the only thing audible was the soft sound of men jostling in the dark, the swish of feet in grass. There was something in the night that seemed pregnant with sudden violence, as if at any time some crashing chaos might envelop the entire landscape" (*And We*; reprint *Ghosts* 96).

19 Indeed, this was my premise in an earlier draft of this chapter, where I took Sassoon to be the antithesis of the Greek warrior, since his "fame" was literally in his own hand – on paper, at least, in the pen and ink that were supposed to preserve his "memory."

20 See my discussion of Walter Pater's aestheticism as articulated in his concept of "getting as many pulsations as possible into the given time" in *Confessional Fictions: A Portrait of the Artist in the Canadian Novel* (14–17, 31).

21 The original document is preserved in the Imperial War Museum in London.

22 Among the former were Thomas Hardy, Arnold Bennett, H. G. Wells, and Bertrand Russell; among the journalists were C. K. Ogden (editor

of the pacifist *Cambridge Magazine),* H. W. Massingham (editor of the liberal weekly *The Nation),* J. A. Spender (editor of the liberal *Westminster Gazette),* and the liberal journalist Harold Cox; most notable among the parliamentarians was H. B. Lees-Smith, who would raise a question in the House of Commons about Sassoon's "treatment" for "shell-shock" (*Diaries* 174).

23 The version printed in the *Times* on 31 July 1917 contains at least seventeen textual variants from the version in the *Diaries* (173–4), likely as a result of reportorial transcription.

24 One recalls Kevin Brownlow's report of "military euphemisms of the battlefield" (46) as a "picture-show," so linking Sassoon's "show" to the usual "fascination with pictures."

25 See the discussion of Augustine's doubled self in William C. Spengemann, *The Forms of Autobiography: Episodes in the History of a Literary Genre* (New Haven: Yale University Press, 1980), 1–7.

26 Joan M. Schwartz argues similarly that "the defining moments in both the history of modern archives and the history of photography can be traced to the same two-year period in France, 1839–41," because "the nineteenth-century epistemological assumptions upon which both archival practices and photographic practices rested" (61, 63) were in fact identical.

27 Historians themselves have often been resistant to accepting photographic documents as evidence, most likely because "light writing" undercuts the authority of a verbal epistemology, in effect privileging an "effortless" competition against word-writing.

28 See my discussion of Gabrielle Roy's revision of this Proustian trope in *Confessional Fictions: A Portrait of the Artist in the Canadian Novel,* chapter 8, "Imagism and Spatial Form in *The Road Past Altamont*" (174–90).

29 Einstein's remarkable deductions were based on his decade-long meditation on the problem of light – how could it be no more than a "wave" if there was no medium (the discredited idea of "ether") to carry it through space; how could its speed be relative (as Newton saw it) if its velocity was not altered by the motion of its source? From his second postulate, proclaiming "the *uniform propagation of light in every uniformly moving reference system, with the same constant speed c,*" Einstein deduced that time "is not an absolute quantity, nor is simultaneity something absolute" (Lanczos, 78, 39).

30 As Peter Kosso points out, "This does not mean that time is *the* fourth dimension. Time is not a physical, spatial dimension, and it is still very

different from the three spatial dimensions. For example, we are free to move in any direction in space, left or right, up or down. But the dimension of time is, for some reason, more restrictive. Things can only go forward in time" (56).

31 Renamed *Lancette Arts Journal* in January 2008.

32 One recalls Wilfred Owen's trenchant reservation about silent film: "[I]t is positively painful to me not to hear speech; worse than the case of a deaf man at a proper Shakespeare play; for all the finer play of mouth, eye, fingers, and so on, is utterly imperceptible, and so are the slower motions of the limbs spoiled, and their majesty lost, in the convulsed, rattling-hustle of the Cinema. Certainly, the old impression of driving through an electric hailstorm on a Chinese-cracker is not now so easily got, as of old; but, still, I cannot enthuse over the things as Leslie does. His infatuation would speedily vanish if he knew 'the real thing'. Which, poor fellow, he hankers to do" (162).

33 I am grateful for this point to my friend and colleague, Dr. Robert Smith, of the Theatre program at the University of Manitoba. His incisive commentary has helped at several turns to improve the argument of this chapter.

34 In fact, almost one million Austrian pines were planted in Vimy Memorial Park. In assessing "The Meaning and Significance of the Vimy Monument" (in Hayes et al.), Jacqueline Hucker calls it "an understandable (albeit incorrect) belief dating from the earliest years that a tree was planted for every Canadian who died on the ridge" (287).

35 A neologism used in screen theory, interpellate (Fr. *interpeller*, to call out to) here refers to those visual modes of address in television (camera angles, point-of-view shots, "glances" of presenters, etc.) that work in "the same way as direct verbal address to construct an intimate, explicit viewing relationship" (Fiske 53–4). Viewers who are "hailed" or interpellated into a scene thus "adopt the subject position proposed" (53) by the visual discourse, accepting its ideological assumptions while "repressing any discomforting contradictions" (55) in the program and in themselves.

36 Jonathan Vance makes it clear that the Stratford memorial is *atypical* of Canadian memorials (*Death* 28), with its greater visual impact than the more common cairns and steles. One could also argue that the logic of association conjures up the "other" Stratford of memory, lending an aura of Shakespeare's history plays to History Television.

37 Tyne Cot, the largest Commonwealth cemetery in the world, is located on ground fought over in the Third Battle of Ypres, 31 July to

10 November 1917, not the Second Battle of Ypres in which the Canadians were engaged from 22 April to 25 May 1915 (Nicholson 554–5). Passchendaele, taken by the Canadian Corps in the dreadful fighting of 26 October to 10 November 1917, surely marks a victory by men who no longer thought of themselves as being "British" in the way they had in April 1915. Nonetheless, to mark the national distance covered from Second Ypres to Vimy Ridge, probably Essex Farm Cemetery, situated on the banks of the Ypres–Yser Canal (adjacent to McCrae's field surgery in concrete bunkers), would be more appropriate, if less visually compelling.

38 Gary Sheffield ends his "Vimy Ridge and the Battle of Arras: A British Perspective" (in Hayes et al.) with an appropriate reminder: "Canadian nationalism has led to an exaggerated sense of the importance of the capture of Vimy Ridge and the British elements of the force that fought in the battle have been airbrushed out of popular memory" (27). His measured reappraisal is based on three key factors: "the Imperial nature of the force that captured Vimy" (17); a grossly inflated sense of the strategic significance of this victory (it was nothing like a turning point in the war); and the general blindness of historians to "the significance of the wider Battle of Arras" (17).

39 Here, one is reminded of how R. H. Thomson conjures the "presence" of the "lost boys" just around the curve of "spacetime" because of the "unmediated" presence of an actor-narrator. Gravity is what was missing from the Special Theory of Relativity; and it is the gravitas of this actor's body that "proves" the General Theory of Relativity in a way that television "light" could never do. See above, pp. 183, 198–202.

40 In his "Vimy Ridge: The Battlefield Before the Canadians, 1914–1916" (in Hayes et al., eds), Michael Boire recalls that, to the French in June 1915, Vimy Ridge "had become a metaphor for frustration, butchery and failure." At the same time, he shows in careful detail how "French blood and bravery were fundamental ingredients of the Canadian success at Vimy Ridge. It was an Allied victory, in the best sense" (56, 60).

41 "On November 1, 1914, Canada lost her first men at sea when four young midshipmen went down with the HMS *Good Hope* at the Battle of Coronel off the west coast of Chile" (Veteran Affairs Canada website). In all, German forces under the command of Vice-Admiral von Spee sent two Royal Navy armoured cruisers down, with the loss of 1,654 officers and men (G. Bennett 33–4, 180). Lance-Cpl Bellinger is the first Canadian to die in the Great War only if "memory" is limited

to the Western Front. Apart from a deep cultural bias in this "memory," there is television's visual bias to consider, since "peaceful fields" have a greater formal value than undifferentiated seascapes.

42 Christie cannot be alluding here to the sinister Fritz Haber (no relation), vilified in *The Lost Boys* (23) as the inventor of chlorine gas, literally months after Franz's death.

43 It is worth noting that, as the publisher of CEF Books, which has reprinted and holds all rights to the memoirs of Canon Frederick Scott and Will Bird as well as to the other "voices" heard in the series, Christie and his television series evidently serve to generate publicity for book sales that benefit the copyright holders.

44 In episode 1, "Baptism of Fire," the camera pans in admiring close-up over Richard Jack's 1917 painting, *The Second Battle of Ypres, 22 April to 25 May, 1915*. The heroic cast of Jack's painting is put in a rather different light by William Roberts's 1918 painting, *The First German Gas Attack at Ypres*. These two opposing views of the glory and horror of war are mounted on adjacent walls of the Canadian War Museum in Ottawa. Roberts's image of Algerians and Canadians twisting and convulsing in asphyxiation is not shown in this (or any) episode of *For King and Empire*.

45 Albeit with differing emphasis, Mark Osborne Humphries comes to a similar conclusion in "'Old Wine in New Bottles': A Comparison of British and Canadian Preparations for the Battle of Arras" (in Hayes et al., eds): "This idea that the Canadian Corps began to come into its own at Vimy Ridge has taken hold in the popular memory and has even been extended to suggest that Canada's national identity was born at Vimy Ridge. This interpretation, while spiritually satisfying, is problematic because it rests on the premise that the paths of the Canadian Corps and the British Army diverged in the months before Vimy Ridge. During the Great War, however, the Canadian Corps was but one part of the [British Expeditionary Force]" (66).

46 Jonathan Vance, in "Battle Verse: Poetry and Nationalism after Vimy Ridge" (in Geoffrey Hayes et al.), offers two good reasons for the "special appeal of Vimy Ridge" in the popular memory of Canadians: "its ability to bring together the religious and the nationalist" (265). An accident of timing lent to the victory of Easter Monday, 1917, the religious symbolism of resurrection: "Once the battle was identified with the celebration of the rebirth of Christ, it was only a small step to connect Vimy Ridge with the birth of a nation" (271). In this vein, as Vance wittily observes, "The spiritual and the secular meshed so

completely that the poet could not but help be drawn to it. Besides, Vimy Ridge was much easier to rhyme than Drocourt–Quéant" (266).

47 Robert Rosenstone distinguishes "postliterate" from "illiterate" on the basis of the dominant mode of information in contemporary culture: "Film is a disturbing symbol of an increasingly postliterate world (in which people can read but won't)" (50).

48 I confess my own partiality for a digital flatscreen display of the work of Paul Cézanne in the woods outside his atelier (2007) in Aix-en-Provence, a stunning succession of high-definition images of his paintings that seem to merge and emerge out of each other in a magical arrangement more revealing of his artistry than the "real thing" glimpsed in the canvases and brushes, the palettes and plaster casts, and other instruments that Cézanne once had to hand inside the high-ceilinged atelier. For me, the aura had fled; Cézanne was not to be found in these old objects but in the moving images outdoors.

49 At this point, it should be noted that the World War I gallery represents but one part of our military past. It needs to be situated within the larger architectural narrative, as a sign explains en route to the LeBreton Gallery of military vehicles: "Canadian War Museum architect Raymond Moriyama designed Regeneration Hall as an architectural representation of the power of hope, even amid the instability of war. Soaring to a height of 24.5 metres, the Hall's angled walls, and indeed the entire Museum, align with Parliament Hill. From the glass section to your left, a precise but fleeting view of the Peace Tower reflects the connection between past and present, war and peace. As you descend the stairs, losing sight of 'peace,' the allegorical statue of hope [Allward's plaster cast for the Vimy Monument] comes into view, silhouetted in the window at the far end of the hall."

50 See my discussion in *Imagined Nations: Reflections on Media in Canadian Fiction*, particularly chapter 3, "The Mode of Communication" (42–73), and chapter 4, "Orality and Print" (77–102).

51 This "additive" syntax (Ong 37), so typical of oral culture, is characteristically erased from the printed transcript, further highlighting old tensions between orality and literacy.

52 Honoré de Balzac's story "Adieu" (1830) is one of the enduring pieces of French literature about the dreadful events surrounding "Le Passage de la Bérésina." A decade after "Adieu," Stendhal's (Marie-Henri Beyle's) *The Charterhouse at Parma* (1839) painted a broader canvas of the Napoleonic era. The broadest canvas of all, of course, and one of the landmarks of Russian literature, is Leo Tolstoy's *War and Peace*

(1865-69). Among the visual arts, Édouard Détaille's *Le Rêve* (1888) evokes a brooding fantasy of Napoleonic glory in the wake of the Franco-Prussian War. Aside from this late nineteenth-century revanchist image (an immense canvas occupying its own wall of Le Musée d'Orsay in Paris), there is little a century after Waterloo to suggest the dominance of "Napoleonic memory" until the Battle of the Marne revived *les images d'Epinal*.

53 The following novels are only a few examples of British cultural production on the subject of the Great War both before and after Pat Barker's trilogy (1991–95): Susan Hill, *Strange Meeting* (1971; reprinted 1991); John Masters, *The Ravi Lancers* (1972); Michael Foreman, *War Game* (1993); Ben Elton, *The First Casualty* (2005).

54 Will Bird's combatant memoir *And We Go On* (1930), later reissued as *Ghosts Have Warm Hands* (1968), is to my mind the best single memoir of the Western Front. Bird's prodigious output of poetry, fiction, magazine and newspaper articles, trench collections, and travel guides to the Western Front was amplified in the interwar years by other memoirs and novels of combatants: J. H. Pedley, *Only This: A War Retrospective* (1927); Peregrine Acland, *All Else is Folly* (1929); Philip Child, *God's Sparrows* (1937); and C. Y. Harrison, *Generals Die in Bed* (1930). Memoirs of Canadian nursing sisters, only recently published, include *The War Diary of Claire Gass* (2000) and Katherine Wilson-Simmie, *Lights Out* (1981). From the home front in those years, the following are still worth reading: Lucy Maud Montgomery's patriotic novel *Rilla of Ingleside* (1920); and Francis Marion Beynon's pacifist novel, *Aleta Dey* (1919).

55 Monique Dumontet is writing her Ph.D. dissertation under my supervision at the University of Manitoba on Canadian Great War writings of the interwar years. Her literary study covers a number of themes, including "the anti-war canon," "'the Old Lie' and the Big Lie," "balanced texts of the interwar period," "gender and the home front," "gender at war," and "the birth of a nation."

56 One could conjecture that it is a "national" reaction formation against political and economic integration into the EU, but the Battle of Britain (1940), in which the nation stood "alone" (with the Empire) against Europe, would better serve that function.

57 The *locus classicus* for this sense of limits reached in language after the Great War is Frederick Henry's remark in Ernest Hemingway's *A Farewell to Arms* (1929): "I was always embarrassed by the words sacred, glorious, and sacrifice and the expression in vain ... I had seen nothing

sacred, and the things that were glorious had no glory and the sacrifices were like the stockyards at Chicago if nothing was done with the meat except to bury it ... Abstract words such as glory, honor, courage, or hallow were obscene beside the concrete names of villages, the numbers of roads, the names of rivers, the numbers of regiments and the dates" (184–5).

58 The novels of William Faulkner, like the poetry of the Imagists (including Eliot's "Prufrock" and *The Wasteland*), together with Joyce's *Ulysses,* have yet to be read at any length as mutations informed by a cinematic epistemology, although Ying Kong, one of my students, has already published such a reappraisal of Imagism. The whole history of literary Modernism has yet to be written, in other words, as a branch of film history.

59 See my discussion of these twin issues of "multiphrenia" and multiple identities in my *Imagined Nations: Reflections on Media in Canadian Fiction,* especially pp. 223–26.

RE PAGE 130. That *Generals Die in Bed* (1930) took the hybrid form of "prose cinema" and that the mental habits of its soldier-narrator, and likely its author, were shaped by film have become almost incontestable, given the historical researches of McGill University's Dr Peter Webb, who not only drew my attention to the following facts but very generously provided me with materials he had unearthed in archives and estate papers.

The first document is a 3×5 index card from the papers of Harrison's deceased niece Judith Rossner, the author of the novel *Looking for Mr. Goodbar,* with the notation "Harrison managed a motion picture theatre in Montreal after the war." While Dr Webb doubts that the handwriting is Rossner's, the information was evidently in her keeping and was attested to by a parenthetical reference to "N.Y. Graphic Louis Sobol's column Aug 15, 1930."

The second document is a typewritten, legal memorandum of five pages, detailing the "Similarities between 'Meet Me on the Barricades' and 'The Secret Life of Walter Mitty'" (p. 1), in which "the author" of the novel, "Mr. Harrison," claims to have "suffered a very real and conscious loss due to the making of the 'Mitty' motion picture" and seeks damages from James Thurber, the author of the "Mitty" story, inasmuch as "the making of the 'Mitty' picture has destroyed the film rights of 'Meet Me On The Barricades' " (p. 5). While the authorship of this memorandum is also unattributed, the lawsuit is mentioned by

Burton Bernstein in his biography *Thurber* (New York: Dodd Mead & Company, 1975): "Charles Yale Harrison, the author of a novel calleds *Meet Me on the Barricades*, directed the attention of Thurber and his lawyer to the alleged similarity between his book and 'Mitty' ... [T]he Harrison claim—'a time-consuming nuisance,' in the words of Thurber's lawyer—dragged on and proved to be rather expensive in legal fees" (313), although Thurber's stout denials, and his adamant refusal to submit to arbitration, eventually led to the suit being dropped.

A third document, a poster for the release of the documentary film *First Houses* (1936), "Sponsored by the New York Housing Authority," credits "Charles Yale Harrison" as the screenwriter, making it all the more likely that the author of *Generals Die in Bed* began his career as a print-cinematographer in his fictional memoir of the Great War.

DW: 27 January 2011

Works Cited

Aitken, Johan. "'Long Live the Dead': An Interview with Timothy Findley." *Journal of Canadian Fiction* 33 (1982): 79–93.

Anderson, Benedict. *Imagined Communities: Reflections on the Origin and Spread of Nationalism.* 1983. Rev. ed. London & New York: Verso, 1991.

Anonymous. "User Comments." Online review of *For King and Empire* (2001). Available: http://www.imdb.com/title/tt0308270/ (accessed 12 January 2007).

Arnason, David. "Canadian Nationalism in Search of a Form: Hugh MacLennan's *Barometer Rising.*" *Journal of Canadian Fiction* 1, no. 4 (Fall 1972): 68–71.

Auden, W. H. *Collected Poems.* Edited by Edward Mendelson. London: Faber & Faber, 1976.

Bal, Mieke. "*Light Writing:* Portraiture in a Post-Traumatic Age." *Mosaic* 37, no. 4 (December 2004): 1–19.

Barker, Christine R., and R. W. Last. *Erich Maria Remarque.* London: Oswald Wolff, 1979.

Barker, Pat. *The Eye in the Door.* 1993. New York: Dutton, 1994.

– *Regeneration.* 1991. New York: Plume, 1993.

Barsam, Richard M. *Nonfiction Film: A Critical History.* 1973. Rev. ed. Bloomington & Indianapolis: Indiana University Press, 1992.

Barthes, Roland. *Camera Lucida: Reflections on Photography.* Translated by Richard Howard. New York: Hill & Wang, 1981.

Benjamin, Walter. "Excavation and Memory." *Selected Writings, Vol. 2: 1927–1934.* Translated by Rodney Livingstone et al. Edited by Michael Jennings et al., 576. Cambridge, Mass: Belknap Press, 1999.

– *Illuminations.* Edited by Hannah Arendt. Translated by Harry Zohn. New York: Shocken Books, 1968.

- "Little History of Photography." *Selected Writings, Vol. 2: 1927–1934*, 507–30.

Bennett, C. E., trans. *Horace: The Odes and Epodes*. London: Heinemann, 1927.

Bennett, Geoffrey Martin. *Coronel and the Falklands*. New York: Macmillan, 1962.

Bird, Will R. *And We Go On*. 1930. Reprinted as *Ghosts Have Warm Hands*. Ottawa: Clark, Irwin & Co., 1968.

Blouin, Francis X. Jr, and William G. Rosenberg. *Archives, Documentation, and Institutions of Social Memory: Essays from the Sawyer Seminar*. Ann Arbor: University of Michigan Press, 2006.

Boire, Michael. "Vimy Ridge: The Battlefield Before the Canadians, 1914–1916." In Hayes et al., eds, 51–61.

Bowra, C. M. *From Virgil to Milton*. London: Macmillan, 1961.

Bowser, Eileen. *The Transformation of the Cinema 1907–1915*. Vol. 2 of *History of the American Cinema*. New York: Charles Scribner's Sons, 1990.

Brownlow, Kevin. *The War, the West, and the Wilderness*. New York: Alfred A. Knopf, 1979.

Cadava, Eduardo. *Words of Light: Theses on the Photography of History*. Princeton: Princeton University Press, 1997.

Cameron, Elspeth. *Hugh MacLennan: A Writer's Life*. Toronto: University of Toronto Press, 1981.

Cameron, Fiona. "Beyond the Cult of the Replicant: Museums and Historical Digital Objects – Traditional Concerns, New Discourses." In Cameron and Kenderline, eds, 49–75.

Cameron, Fiona, and Sarah Kenderline, eds. *Theorizing Digital Cultural Heritage: A Critical Discourse*. Cambridge, Mass. & London: MIT Press, 2007.

Caughie, John. "Progressive Television and Documentary Drama." In *Popular Television and Film*, edited by T. Bennett et al., 327–52. London: British Film Institute/Open University, 1981.

Cavell, Stanley. *The World Viewed: Reflections on the Ontology of Film*. Enlarged Edition. Cambridge, MA & London: Harvard University Press, 1979.

Christie, Norm. *For King & Empire. Vol VII, The Canadians at Amiens, August 1918*. Ottawa: CEF Books, 1999.

- Host. *For King & Empire*. Breakthrough Films, 2001. DVD (6´ 60).

Coates, Donna. "Myrmidons to Insubordinates: Australian, New Zealand, and Canadian Women's Fictional Responses to the Great War." In Quinn and Trout, eds, 113–42.

Cobley, Evelyn. "Postmodernist War Fiction: Findley's *The Wars.*" *Canadian Literature* 147 (Winter 1995): 98–124.

– *Representing War: Form and Ideology in First World War Narratives.* Toronto: University of Toronto Press, 1993.

Cockburn, Robert H. *The Novels of Hugh MacLennan.* Montreal: Harvest House, 1969.

Cohen, Debra Rae. "Encoded Enclosures: The Wartime Novels of Stella Benson." In Quinn and Trout, eds, 37–54.

Commonwealth War Graves Commission [CWGC]. *Cemeteries and Memorials in Belgium & Northern France.* London: Commonwealth War Graves Commission, 2004.

Connolly, Kevin. "*The Lost Boys.*" Online review. Available: http://www.eyeweekly.com/eye/issue_02.14.02/arts/onstage.php (accessed 1 August 2007).

Cook, Terry. "Remembering the Future: Appraisal of Records and the Role of Archives in Constructing Social Memory." In Blouin and Rosenberg, eds, 169–81.

Coulbourn, John. "*The Lost Boys* come home." Online review. Available: http://jam.canoe.ca/Theatre/Reviews/L/The_Lost_Boys (accessed 1 August 2007).

Deibert, Ronald J. *Parchment, Printing, and Hypermedia: Communication in World Order Transformation.* New York: Columbia University Press, 1997.

Derrida, Jacques. "Structure, Sign, and Play in the Discourse of the Human Sciences." In *The Languages of Criticism and the Sciences of Man: The Structuralist Controversy,* edited by Richard Macksey and Eugenio Donato, 247–72. Baltimore & London: Johns Hopkins University Press, 1970.

Doane, Mary Ann. "Information, Crisis, Catastrophe." In Landy, ed., 269–85.

Dominion Institute. *The Memory Project.* Internet website. 2003. Available: http://www.thememoryproject.com (accessed 10 January 2007).

Donne, John. *Sermons on the Psalms & Gospels.* Ed. Evelyn M. Simpson. Berkeley & Los Angeles: University of California Press, 1967.

Downing, Taylor. "'History on Television': The Making of *Cold War,* 1998." In Landy, ed., 294–302.

Dryden, John, trans. *Virgil's Aeneid.* Vol. 13. *The Harvard Classics.* Edited by Charles W. Eliot LLD. New York: P. F. Collier & Son, 1909.

Eakin, Paul John. *How Our Lives Become Stories: Making Selves.* Ithaca: Cornell University Press, 1999.

Edgerton, Gary. "Ken Burn's Rebirth of a Nation: Television, Narrative, and Popular History." In Landy, ed., 303–15.

Egremont, Max. *Siegfried Sassoon: A Life*. New York: Farrar, Straus and Giroux, 2005.

Einstein, Albert. "Autobiographical Notes." Translated by Paul Arthur Schilpp. In Schilpp, ed., 3–95.

Eisenstein, Elizabeth. *The Printing Press as an Agent of Change*. Cambridge: Cambridge University Press, 1979.

– *The Printing Revolution in Early Modern Europe*. Cambridge & New York: Cambridge University Press, 1983.

Eksteins, Modris. "*All Quiet on the Western Front* and the Fate of a War." *Journal of Contemporary History* 15, no. 2 (April 1980): 345–66.

Feuer, Jane. "The Concept of Live Television: Ontology vs. Ideology." In *Regarding Television*, edited by E. A. Kaplan, 12–22. Los Angeles: American Film Institute, 1983.

Findley, Timothy. "Alice Drops Her Cigarette on the Floor ... (William Whitehead looking over Timothy Findley's Shoulder)." *Canadian Literature* 91 (Winter 1981): 10–21.

– *The Wars*. 1977. Toronto: Penguin Canada, 1996.

Fiske, John. *Television Culture*. London & New York: Routledge, 1994.

Fitzgerald, Robert, trans. *Aeneid: Virgil*. New York: Vintage, 1985.

Foley, John Miles. *Homer's Traditional Art*. University Park, PA: Pennsylvania State University Press, 1999.

– "What's in A Sign?" In Mackay, ed., 1–27.

For King and Empire: Canada's Soldiers in the Great War. Directed by Peter Williamson and Harvey Crossland. Host: Norm Christie. Toronto: Breakthrough Films, 2001.

Episode 1: *Baptism by Fire: The Canadians at Ypres – 1915*.
Episode 2: *Slaughter and Sacrifice: The Canadians at the Somme – 1916*.
Episode 3: *Storming the Ridge: The Canadians at Vimy – 1917*.
Episode 4: *Slaughter in the Mud: The Canadians at Passchendaele – 1917*.
Episode 5: *Masters of War: Canadians in the Last 100 Days – 1918*.
Episode 6: *Shadows of the Great War*.

Frank, Philipp. *Einstein: His Life and Times*. Translated by George Rosen. New York: Alfred A. Knopf, 1947.

Fussell, Paul. *The Great War and Modern Memory*. New York & London: Oxford University Press, 1975.

Fölsing, Albrecht. *Albert Einstein: A Biography*. Translated by Ewald Osers. New York: Viking, 1997.

Gelernter, Mark. *Sources of Architectural Form: A Critical History of Western Design Theory*. Manchester & New York: Manchester University Press, 1995.

Gilbert, Martin. *The Battle of the Somme: The Heroism and Horror of War.* Toronto: McClelland & Stewart, 2006.

Goetsch, Paul, ed. *Hugh MacLennan.* Toronto: McGraw-Hill Ryerson, 1973.

Greenberg, Joel. "*The Lost Boys.*" Online review, n.d. Available: http://www.aislesay.com/ONT-LOSTBOYS.html (accessed 1 August 2007).

Griffin, Jasper. *Virgil.* 1986. London: Bristol Classical Press, 2001.

Gurval, Robert Alan. *Actium and Augustus: The Politics and Emotions of Civil War.* Ann Arbor: University of Michigan Press, 1995.

Hamilton, Edith and Huntington Cairns, eds. "Phaedrus." *The Collected Dialogues of Plato: including the Letters.* Translated by Lane Cooper et al. Princeton, N.J.: Princeton University Press, 1963.

Harrison, Charles Yale. *Generals Die in Bed.* 1930. Hamilton: Potlatch Publications, 1975.

Hart-Davis, Rupert, ed. *Siegfried Sassoon: Diaries 1915–1918.* London: Faber & Faber, 1983.

Havelock, Eric A. *Preface to Plato.* Oxford: Basil Blackwell, 1963.

Hawking, Stephen. *A Brief History of Time: From the Big Bang to Black Holes.* New York: Bantam, 1988.

Hayes, Geoffrey, Andrew Iarocci, and Mike Bechthold, eds. *Vimy Ridge: A Canadian Reassessment.* Waterloo: Wilfrid Laurier University Press, 2007.

Hazan, Susan. "A Crisis of Authority: New Lamps for Old." In Cameron and Kenderline, eds, 133–47.

Heath, Stephen, and Gillian Skirrow. "Television: a world in action," *Screen* 18, no. 2 (Summer 1977): 7–59.

Hein, Hilde S. *The Museum in Transition: A Philosophical Perspective.* Washington & London: Smithsonian Institution Press, 2000.

Hemingway, Ernest. *A Farewell to Arms.* 1929. New York: Scribner's, 1957.

Hibberd, Dominic. *Wilfred Owen: A New Biography.* London: Weidenfeld & Nicolson, 2002.

Hoile, Christopher. "Missing in Action." Online review of *The Lost Boys.* 2002. Available: http://www.stage-door.org/reviews/misc2002a.htm (accessed 1 August 2007).

Homer. *Iliad.* Translated by Richmond Lattimore. 1951. Chicago & London: Phoenix Edition, 1961.

Hopkins, Chris. "Beyond Fiction? The Example of *Winged Warfare* (1918)." In Quinn and Trout, eds, 9–23.

Horrall, Andrew. *Popular Culture in London c. 1890–1918: The Transformation of Entertainment.* Manchester & New York: Manchester University Press, 2001.

Hucker, Jacqueline. "'After the Agony in Stony Places': The Meaning and Significance of the Vimy Monument." In Hayes et al., eds, 279–90.

Hudson, Christopher. "Silent Suffering." Feature article on Geoffrey Malin's 1916 film *The Battle of the Somme*. *The Sunday Times*. 8 October 2006. Available: http://www.timesonline.co.uk/tol/life_and_style/article 655526.ece (accessed 12 February 2008).

Hulcoop, John. "'Look! Listen! Mark My Words!' Paying Attention to Timothy Findley's Fictions." *Canadian Literature* 91 (Winter 1981): 22–47.

Humphries, Mark Osborne. "'Old Wine in New Bottles': A Comparison of British and Canadian Preparations for the Battle of Arras." In Hayes et al., eds, 65–85.

Huyssen, Andreas. *Twilight Memories: Marking Time in a Culture of Amnesia*. New York & London: Routledge, 1995.

Jakobson, Roman, and Morris Halle. *Fundamentals of Language*. 2nd rev. ed. The Hague and Paris: Mouton, 1971.

Kaplan, Jon. "Lost Chance." Online review of *The Lost Boys*. n. d. Available: http://www.nowtoronto.com/issues/2002-02-14/stage_theatrereviews6.php (accessed 1 August 2007).

Klovan, Peter. 'Bright and Good': Findley's *The Wars*.' *Canadian Literature* 91 (Winter 1981): 58–69.

Kohlhaas, Alidë. *The Lost Boys*. Online review. March 2002. Available: http://www.lancetteer.com/Archives_Theater_LostBoys.htm (accessed 1 August 2007).

Kong, Ying. "Cinematic Techniques in Modernist Poetry," *Literature / Film Quarterly* 33, no. 1 (Jan 2005): 28–40.

Kosso, Peter. *Appearance and Reality: An Introduction to the Philosophy of Physics*. New York: Oxford, 1998.

Kröller, Eva-Marie. "The Exploding Frame: Uses of Photography in Timothy Findley's *The Wars*." *JCS* 16, no. 3/4 (Fall–Winter) 1981: 68–74.

Kullmann, Wolfgang. "Homer and Historical Memory." In Mackay, ed., 95–113.

Lanczos, Cornelius. *The Einstein Decade (1905–1915)*. New York: Academic Press, 1974.

Landy, Marcia, ed. *The Historical Film: History and Memory in Media*. New Brunswick: N.J.: Rutgers University Press, 2001.

Lattimore, Richmond, trans. *The Iliad of Homer*. 1951. Chicago & London: University of Chicago Press, 1967.

Lessing, Gotthold Ephraim. *Laocoon: An Essay upon the Limits of Painting and Poetry*. Translated by Ellen Frothingham. New York: Noonday, 1957.

Lucas, Alec. *Hugh MacLennan*. Toronto: McClelland & Stewart, 1970.

MacDonald, Laura. *Curse of the Narrows*. New York: Walker & Co., 2005.

Macdonald, Sharon, and Gordon Fyfe, eds. *Theorizing Museums: Representing Identity and Diversity in a Changing World*. Oxford: Blackwell Publishers, 1996.

Mackay, E. Anne, ed. *Signs of Orality: The Oral Tradition and its Influence in the Greek & Roman World*. Mnemosyne Bibliotheca Classica Batava Series. Leiden, Boston, Köln: Brill, 1999.

MacLennan, Hugh. *Barometer Rising*. 1941. Toronto: McClelland & Stewart, 1982.

– "Canada for Canadians." *Vogue* (15 May 1947): 136.

– "Postscript on Odysseus." *Canadian Literature* 13 (Summer 1962): 86–7.

MacMechan, Archibald. "The Halifax Disaster." In *The Halifax Explosion December 6, 1917*, edited by Graham Metson. Toronto: McGraw-Hill Ryerson, 1978.

Matsuda, Matt K. *The Memory of the Modern*. New York & Oxford: Oxford University Press, 1996.

McLuhan, Eric, and Marshall McLuhan. *Laws of Media: The New Science*. Toronto: University of Toronto Press, 1988.

McLuhan, Marshall. *Understanding Media: The Extensions of Man*. 2nd ed. Toronto: Signet Editions, 1966.

McPherson, Hugo. "The Novels of Hugh MacLennan." In Goetsch, ed., 23–33.

Melville, A. D., trans. *Ovid: Metamorphoses*. New York: Oxford University Press, 1986.

Milius, John. "Reliving the War Between Brothers." *New York Times*, 16 September 1990: Sec. 2, pp. 1, 43.

Millar, Laura. "Creating a National Information System in a Federal Environment: Some thoughts on the Canadian Archival Information Network." In Blouin and Rosenberg, eds, 182–92.

Minchin, Elizabeth. "Describing and Narrating in Homer's *Iliad*." In Mackay, ed., 49–64.

– "Similes in Homer: Image, Mind's Eye, and Memory." In *Speaking Volumes: Orality & Literacy in the Greek & Roman World*, edited by Janet Watson, 25–52. Leiden, Boston, Köln: Brill, 2001.

New, W. H. "The Storm and After: Imagery and Symbolism in Hugh MacLennan's *Barometer Rising*." *Queen's Quarterly* 74, no. 2 (Summer 1967): 302–13.

Nichols, Stephen G. "An Artifact by Any Other Name: Digital Surrogates of Medieval Manuscripts." In Blouin and Rosenberg, eds, 134–43.

Nicholson, Col. G. W. L. *Canadian Expeditionary Force 1914–1919: Official History of the Canadian Army in the First World War*. 2nd rev. ed. Ottawa: R. Duhamel, Queen's Printer, 1964.

Ong, Walter J. *Orality and Literacy: The Technologizing of the Word*. London & New York: Methuen, 1982.

Otis, Brooks. *Virgil: A Study in Civilized Poetry*. Oxford: Clarendon Press, 1964.

Owen, Harold and John Bell, eds. *Wilfred Owen: Collected Letters*. London: Oxford University Press, 1967.

Owen, Wilfred. *The Poems of Wilfred Owen*. Edited and with an introduction by Edmund Blunden. London: Chatto & Windus, 1931.

Page, T. E., ed. *The Aeneid of Virgil*. 2 vols. London: Macmillan, 1951, 1964.

Paivio, Allan. *Mental Representations: A Dual Coding Approach*. New York: Oxford University Press, 1986.

Phillips, Terry. "The Self in Conflict: May Sinclair and the Great War." In Quinn and Trout, eds, 55–66.

Pratt, George C. *Spellbound in Darkness: A History of the Silent Film*. 1966. Rev. ed. Greenwich, Conn.: New York Graphic Society, 1973.

Prösler, Martin. "Museums and Globalization." In Macdonald and Fyfe, eds, 21–44.

Quinn, Patrick J. and Steven Trout, eds. *The Literature of the Great War Reconsidered: Beyond Modern Memory*. New York: Palgrave, 2001.

Quinn, Patrick J. and Steven Trout. Introduction to *The Literature of the Great War Reconsidered*.

Reichenbach, Hans. "The Philosophical Significance of the Theory of Relativity." In Schilpp, ed., 289–311.

Remarque, Erich Maria. *All Quiet on the Western Front*. 1928. Translated by A. W. Wheen. New York: Ballantine Books, 1982.

Ricou, Laurie. "Obscured by Violence: Timothy Findley's *The Wars*.' In *Violence in the Canadian Novel since 1960. Violence dans le roman canadien depuis 1960*, edited by Terry Goldie and Virginia Harger-Grinling, 125–37. St. John's: Memorial University Press, n.d.

Rosenstone, Robert A. "The Historical Film: Looking at the Past in a Postliterate Age." In Landy, ed., 50–66.

Rubin, David C. *Memory in Oral Traditions: The Cognitive Psychology of Epic, Ballads, and Counting-Out Rhymes*. New York & Oxford: Oxford University Press, 1995.

Russo, John Paul. *The Future Without a Past: The Humanities in a Technological Society*. Columbia & London: University of Missouri Press, 2005.

Sale, Mary. "The Oral-Formulaic Theory Today." In *Speaking Volumes: Orality & Literacy in the Greek & Roman World*, edited by Janet Watson, 53–80. Leiden, Boston, Köln: Brill, 2001.

Samuel, Raphael. *Theatres of Memory*. London & New York: Verso, 1994.

Sassoon, Siegfried. *Collected Poems 1908–1956.* London: Faber & Faber, 1961.

– *Diaries 1915–1918.* Edited by Rupert Hart-Davis. London: Faber & Faber, 1983.

– *Memoirs of an Infantry Officer.* London: Faber & Faber, 1930.

– *Picture Show.* Cambridge: Cambridge University Press, 1919. Rep. New York: E. P. Dutton & Co., 1920. Online edition: Bartleby.com, 1999. Available www.bartleby.com/137/1.html (21 February 2008).

– *Sherston's Progress.* London: Faber & Faber, 1936.

– *Siegfried's Journey: 1916–1920.* London: Faber & Faber, 1945.

Saul, John Ralston. *Reflections of a Siamese Twin: Canada at the End of the Twentieth Century.* Toronto: Penguin Canada, 1998.

Schilpp, Paul Arthur, ed. *Albert Einstein: Philosopher-Scientist.* New York: Tudor, 1951.

Schwartz, Joan M. "'Records of Simple Truth and Precision': Photography, Archives, and the Illusion of Control." In Blouin and Rosenberg, eds, 61–83.

Scott, Canon Frederick George. *The Great War as I Saw It.* 2nd ed. Vancouver: Clark & Stuart Co., Ltd, 1934.

Sheffield, Gary. "Vimy Ridge and the Battle of Arras: A British Perspective." In Hayes et al., eds, 15–29.

Sorlin, Pierre. "How to Look at an 'Historical' Film." *The Historical Film.* In Landy, ed., 25–49.

Spengemann, William C. *The Forms of Autobiography: Episodes in the History of a Literary Genre.* New Haven: Yale University Press, 1980.

Stallworthy, Jon. *Wilfred Owen.* London: Oxford University Press, 1974.

Steedman, Carolyn. "'Something She Called a Fever': Michelet, Derrida and Dust (Or in the Archives with Michelet and Derrida)." In Blouin and Rosenberg, eds, 4–19.

Stray, Christopher. *The Living Word: W. H. D. Rouse and the Crisis of Classics in Edwardian England.* London: Bristol Classical Press, 1992.

Thomson, R. H. *The Lost Boys: Letters From The Sons In Two Acts, 1914–1923.* Toronto: Playwrights Canada Press, 2001.

Thorburn, David, et al. "Series Foreword." In Cameron and Kenderline, ix–x.

Thorpe, Michael. *Siegfried Sassoon: A Critical Study.* London: Oxford University Press, 1966.

Urquhart, Jane. *The Stone Carvers.* Toronto: McClelland & Stewart, 2001.

Urry, John. "How Societies Remember the Past." In Macdonald and Fyfe, eds, 45–65.

Vance, Jonathan F. "Battle Verse: Poetry and Nationalism after Vimy Ridge." In Hayes et al., eds, 265–77.

– Death So Noble: Memory, Meaning, and the First World War. Vancouver: UBC Press, 1997.

Veterans Affairs Canada. "Canadians in Other Campaigns." Web page. Available: http://www.vac-acc.gc.ca/remembers/sub.cfm?source=history/firstwar/canada/Canada18 (accessed 21 February 2008).

Walsh, Peter. "Rise and Fall of the Post-Photographic Museum: Technology and the Transformation of Art." In Cameron and Kenderline, eds, 19–34.

White, Hayden. The Content of the Form: Narrative Discourse and Historical Representation. Baltimore & London: The Johns Hopkins University Press, 1987.

Wilkinson, Glenn R. "Literary Images of Vicarious Warfare: British Newspapers and the Origin of the First World War, 1899–1914." In Quinn and Trout, eds, 24–34.

Williams, David. Confessional Fictions: A Portrait of the Artist in the Canadian Novel. Toronto & Buffalo: University of Toronto Press, 1991.

– Imagined Nations: Reflections on Media in Canadian Fiction. Montréal & London: McGill-Queen's University Press, 2003.

Williams, Raymond. Television: Technology and Cultural Form. New York: Shocken Books, 1975.

Wilson, Jean Moorcroft. Siegfried Sassoon: The Making of a War Poet. New York: Routledge, 1999.

Winter, Jay. Sites of Memory, Sites of Mourning: The Great War in European Cultural History. Cambridge: Cambridge University Press, 1995.

Winterer, Caroline. The Culture of Classicism: Ancient Greece and Rome in American Intellectual Life, 1780–1910. Baltimore & London: Johns Hopkins University Press, 2002.

Witcomb, Andrea. "The Materiality of Virtual Technologies: A New Approach to Thinking about the Impact of Multimedia in Museums." In Cameron and Kenderline, eds, 35–48.

Woodcock, George. "A Nation's Odyssey." Canadian Literature 10 (Autumn 1961): 7–18.

– Hugh MacLennan. Toronto: Copp Clark, 1969.

Yates, Frances A. The Art of Memory. Chicago: University of Chicago Press, 1966.

York, Lorraine M. 'The Other Side of Dailiness': Photography in the Works of Alice Munro, Timothy Findley, Michael Ondaatje, Margaret Laurence. Toronto: ECW Press, 1988.

Index

Access Network, 45

Acland, Peregrine, *All Else is Folly*, 294n

Actian Apollo, 92

Actium: battle of, 76, 77, 92, 97–8; and *Aeneid*, 98; in poetry before *Aeneid*, 98

Ad Herennium, 34

Adamson, Agar, 212, 220, 222, 228–9

Adamson, Mabel, 229

Aeneid, 20, 48, 72–100 *passim*, 105, 106, 274, 287n; and civil war, 73, 77, 79, 96; Juno as counter-Fate, 89, 90, 96; Jupiter as reader in, 48, 72–3; narrative structure of, 93; quoted in *Barometer Rising*, 78, 86; and Valiants Memorial, 286–7n; and written memory, 11–12, 48, 72–3, 75–6, 274. *See also* Virgil

Afghanistan war, 229

Aitken, Johan, 161–2, 181

Alexandrian Library, 265

Algerian troops, 22, 254

All Quiet on the Western Front 4, 8, 25, 29–31, 39, 121–8, 161, 272; compared with *Generals Die in Bed*, 31, 129, 132; German parody of, 123, 287n. *See also* Remarque, E. M.

Allward, Walter, 24, 226, 231, 293n

American Civil War, 103, 212

Amiens: battle of, 25, 134, 136–7, 236, 244, 287n

ancients and moderns, 6, 104

Anderson, Benedict, 172, 238

Apollinaire, Guillaume, 4

Aquinas, Thomas, 9–10, 34

Archives Nationales, Paris, 238

Arnason, David, 85, 93

Arras, 25, 214, 218, 278; battle of, 140, 152, 291–2n

Auden, W. H., 75–6, 78; "Secondary Epic," 75, 97

Augustine, St, 155, 289n

Augustus, 73, 76–7, 87–8, 94, 96–7, 174; at Actium, 92, 98–9; triple triumph of, 98

Australian Imperial Forces, 250

Australian national myth, 20

Baghdad, 76

Bakker, Egbert, 72

Bal, Mieke, 166

Balzac, Honoré de, 293 n.
Barbusse, Henri, 4
Barker, William, 249, 282
Barker, Christine R., 30–1, 121, 123–4
Barker, Pat, 29, 39, 269, 294 n; *Eye in the Door*, 28, 155–6; *Regeneration*, 145
Barsam, Richard M., 8, 108, 110, 114, 116, 287 n
Barthes, Roland, 43, 172–4, 177, 181, 210
Bartholomew, Theo, 138
Batoche: battle of, 26
Battalion, 1st (Western Ontario), 261
Battalion, 14th (Royal Montreal), 119
Battalion, 44th (Manitoba), 249
Battalion, 73rd (Black Watch), 263
Battalion, 75th (Toronto Scottish), 264
Battalion, 78th (Winnipeg Grenadiers), 225
Battle of the Somme, The, 13–14, 39, 112–13, 114, 116, 118; and Newfoundland Regiment, 113, 115, 269; screening in rest areas, 113, 116
battlefield clearances, 3, 230
Beaumont-Hamel, 115, 269–70
Becker, John Harold, 228
Beckmann, Max, 4
Bellinger, Lance-Cpl H. G., 221, 291 n
Benjamin, Walter, 1, 165, 167, 170–2, 173, 174–5, 176–7, 178, 179–80, 235; "Little History of Photography," 172, 174, 176; "On Some Motifs in Baudelaire,"
180; "Theses on the Concept of History," 165; "The Work of Art in an Age of Mechanical Reproduction," 177;
Bennett, Arnold, 288 n
Benson, Stella, 19
Berlin Wall: fall of, 252
Bernhardt, Sarah, 116, 117
Beynon, Francis Marion, 270; *Aleta Day*, 270, 294 n
Bird, Will, 212, 215, 222, 228–9, 249, 287 n, 294 n; *And We Go On*, 215, 227–8, 229, 287 n, 294 n; *Ghosts Have Warm Hands*, 228, 294 n
Bishop, Billy, 249, 270, 282; *Winged Warfare*, 19
Blunden, Edmund, 27; *Undertones of War*, 27, 29
Boer War. *See* South African War
Boire, Michael, 291 n
Bottomley, Horatio, 22
Boulogne, 157, 161
Bowra, C. M., 75
Bowser, Elizabeth, 117
Boyden, Joseph: *Three Day Road*, 269
Bracco, Rosa Maria, 21, 28
Britain: battle of, 294 n
British India, 76
British War Office, 111–13
Brock, Gen. Isaac, 24
Brownlow, Kevin, 111, 288–9 n
Brutus, Lucius Junius, 77
BUFA, Bild und Filmamt, 288 n
Bunyan, John, 6; *The Pilgrim's Progress*, 6, 27
Burns, Ken, 43–4, 47, 212, 230; *The Civil War*, 43, 44, 230
Byng, Gen. Julian, 222–3

Cadava, Eduardo, 165, 167–8,
    170–1, 173, 175, 177–8, 180
Calinescu, Matei, 104
Cambrai: battle of, 236, 251–2, 263
Cambridge: "Tripos," 104
Cameron, Elspeth, 83, 99, 103
Cameron, Fiona, 240–1, 242
Camillo, Giulio, 10, 35, 246
Canadian 1st Division, 214, 247
Canadian 3rd Division, 25
Canadian 4th Division, 224
Canadian Archival Information
    Network (CAIN), 259
Canadian Battlefields Memorials
    Commission (CBMC), 267, 285n
Canadian Broadcasting Corpora-
    tion: creation of, 261
Canadian conscription crisis, 229
Canadian Corps, the, 134, 209,
    214, 215, 223, 225, 232, 250,
    286n, 291–2n; 1934 reunion of,
    232; in Last Hundred Days, 25,
    226, 236, 250–1, 271; libel
    against, 25
Canadian drama: and Great War,
    269–70
Canadian Expeditionary Force
    (CEF): in Boer War, 239; numbers
    of dead, 225; numbers served in,
    225
Canadian Legion, 23
Canadian national myth, 20–1,
    25–6, 270
Canadian Nursing Sisters, 137,
    294n
Canadian War Museum, 12, 239,
    244, 246–52, 281, 291n
Canadian women: in war industry,
    229
Canal de l'Yser, 22, 267, 291n

Canal du Nord, battle of, 236, 250
Carroll, Lewis, 153
Carter, Paul, 240
Cartier, Jacques, 24
Catiline, 99
Cato the Elder, 95
Caughie, John, 212–13, 277
Cavell, Stanley, 188, 209, 246, 277
Central Powers, 22, 288n
Cézanne, Paul, 293n
Channel ports, 22
Chaplin, Charlie, 117, 184, 194
Chapman, Guy, 18
Child, Philip: God's Sparrows,
    294n
Chinese workers, 255
Christie, Norm, 12, 38, 45, 47,
    137, 206–7, 213–16, 218, 219–
    22, 225–6, 231–3, 277, 292n;
    For King and Empire, 12, 32, 38,
    45, 183, 205–36, 238, 277, 279,
    291n; as historian, 137; as pub-
    lisher of CEF books, 292n; as
    publisher of guidebooks, 38
Cicero, 9
Cinema: as actualité, 32, 39, 108–
    9, 110–11, 113–14, 118, 120,
    181; and anti-classicism, 107;
    and British propaganda, 111–12;
    before Great War, 6, 107, 115–
    16, 290n; early history of, 108–
    14; effects on language, 111–12;
    Griffith's transformation of, 117;
    invention of, 30, 40, 108–9; and
    oral culture, 43, 60, 234, 246; re-
    lation to relativity theory, 41,
    183, 184, 187–8, 201; return of
    dead in, 3, 5, 6; screenings in
    British sector, 111–12; screenings
    in French sector, 111; and social

class, 114; venues in Britain (1916), 113; West's Picture Palace, Reading, 115

cinematic epistemology, 7, 39–40; collapse of boundaries, 5, 30, 109–10, 114, 128, 131, 138, 149, 271; in Great War writing, 8, 31, 109, 111, 118–37, 144–57; immediacy of image, 5, 8, 30, 31–2, 35, 108–10, 114, 118, 120, 121, 129, 137–8, 147–8, 150–1; invasive power of image, 8, 31, 109, 111, 146, 148; in Modernist works, 295n; ontology of doubling, 8, 40, 149, 153–7, 275; past-progressive-present tense of, 5, 7–8, 30, 41, 44, 109, 150; presentness of viewing, 5, 8, 30, 110, 118, 138, 275; and relativity, 183–8; telescoping of time, 29, 30, 32, 109, 126, 132, 147

cinematic memory, 103–57; and modernist presentism, 35, 137; as new window on time, 271–2, 280

classical memory, 12, 48, 53–100; in Barometer Rising, 72ff, 274; as inner writing, 10, 34, 36

classical studies, 97, 103–5, 107, 122

Coates, Donna, 20

Cobley, Evelyn, 125, 131, 163–4

Cockburn, Robert H., 86, 96

Cohen, Debra Rae, 19

Commonwealth War Graves Commission, 24, 231

Conboy, Martin, 190

Connolly, Kevin, 183–4

Cook, Terry, 259–60

Cook, Tim, 239

Coronel: battle of, 291n.

Coulborn, John, 182

Cox, Harold, 289n

Craiglockhart Hospital, 67, 106, 117, 142, 156

Crossland, Harvey, 213–14, 232

Crossland, W. William, 232

Currie, Lt-Gen. Arthur, 25, 222, 250, 286n

Daguerre, Louis, 41, 172

Daily Show, The, 211

Dante, Inferno, 34, 270

Darfur, 136

Death of General Wolfe, The, 175

Defoe, Daniel, 124

Deibert, Ronald J., 283

Derrida, Jacques, 164, 241

Détaille, Édouard: Le Rêve, 193, 294n

Digital Archive, the, 12, 46–7, 237–41, 257–66, 279

digital media, 11, 12, 35

digital objects, 46, 235, 240–1, 257, 259–60, 265–6

Disney theme parks, 242

Dix, Otto, 4

Doane, Mary Ann, 42, 43–4, 210, 211–12

Dominion Institute, the, 11–12, 38, 46, 237, 280

Donne, John, 252

Dos Passos, John, 31

Downing, Taylor, 44

Dresden fire-bombing, 270

Drocourt–Quéant Line, 214, 227, 236, 250, 278, 293n

Dryden, John: translation of Virgil, 72

Dumontet, Monique, 294n

Durie, Anna, 231

Durie, Lt William, 231

Eakin, Paul John, 38, 286n
EasyShare, Kodak, 259
Edelman, Gerald, 38
Edison, Thomas, 108, 110, 186
education reform, 103–7
Edward VIII, 232
Egremont, Max, 138
Einstein, Albert, 12, 41, 183–4,
    194; American visit of 1931, 184;
    appearance in *The Lost Boys*,
    188–9, 191, 195, 197–8, 276;
    "Autobiographical Notes," 185;
    General Theory of Relativity, 41,
    198, 200; *On the Electrodynam-
    ics of Moving Bodies*, 186;
    Special Theory of Relativity, 41,
    185, 187, 289n
Eisenstein, Elizabeth, 272–3, 285n,
    287n
Eksteins, Modris, 287n
electronic memory, 11–12, 45, 205–
    68; crisis of temporality, 128,
    288n; and cultural amnesia, 36–7;
Eliot, Charles, 103
Eliot, T. S., 18, 103, 295n; *The
    Waste Land*, 18
Elton, Ben: *The First Casualty*,
    294n
Embarkation Parade, 207–8
empire, discourse of, 20; British, 7,
    12, 72, 91–2, 231, 274; Byzantine,
    76; French, 4, 193, 244, 293n;
    German, 30; Roman, 10, 12, 48,
    73–8, 86, 88, 97–100, 123
Englander, David, 21, 28

Facebook, 259, 280
Faulkner, William, 295n
Feuer, Jane, 210–11
Fichte, J. G., 122

film history; and oral epic, 46, 2
    34; as story of individuals, 44–5;
    and written history, 39, 43–4,
    226–30
film propaganda: *Advance of the
    Tanks* 112; Austrian, 288n; *The
    Battle of Ancre*,112; *The Battle of
    the Somme* 112ff; British, 112;
    French, 3–6; German, 124, 288n;
    St Quentin, 112
Findley, Timothy, 12, 32, 40–1,
    161ff; "Alice", 162; comments
    on photography, 161–2; and tele-
    vision writing, 162; *The Wars*,
    12, 32, 40–1, 161–81, 182, 269,
    275
Fiske, John, 43, 206, 208–9, 210–
    11, 213–14, 217, 234–5, 279,
    290n
Fitzgerald, F. Scott, 23
Fludd, Robert, 35
Foch, Ferdinand, 250
Foley, John Miles, 47, 53–4, 56–7,
    61–2, 72, 75, 265
folk memory, 217, 236, 278
Fölsing, Albrecht, 187–8
For King and Empire, 205–36:
    "Canadians in the Last 100
    Days–1918," 209; "The Canadi-
    ans at Passchendaele–1917,"
    209; "The Canadians at the
    Somme–1916," 205; "The Cana-
    dians at Vimy–1917," 205, 209,
    216–26; "The Canadians at
    Ypres–1915," 205, 226; dis-
    course of the Name, 222, 230–3,
    279; "The Maple Leaf Forever,"
    207, 226; and oral memory,
    234–6; photos in, 208, 210, 212,
    217–18, 220–1, 224–5, 230, 235;

"Shadows of the Great War," 209, 233; system of looks, 212–16; use of letters in, 212, 217, 235; use of paintings in, 217–18, 292n; website of, 45, 235–6, 279
Foreman, Michael: *War Game*, 294n
Foucault, Michel, 241
Fox, Talbot, 171
Franco–Prussian War, 30, 104, 294n
Frank, Philipp, 186
Fraser, Donald, 218–19, 222, 228
Fraser, Malcolm, 263
French, David: *Soldier's Heart*, 270
French Revolution, 238
Freud, Sigmund, 176, 180
Frye, Northrop, 26–7
Fussell, Paul, 6–7, 17–9, 20–3, 26–32, 139, 148–9, 153, 267
Fyfe, Gordon, 240, 242

Galicians: internment, 248
Galilei, Galileo, 197
Gance, Abel, *J'accuse*, 3–6
gas warfare, 22–3, 31, 106, 118, 119–20, 178, 184, 191, 194–5, 205, 247, 282; box respirator, 22, 118–19, 120, 247
Gass, Claire: war diary, 294n
Gentelles Wood, 288n
George, David Lloyd, 13, 113
German offensive: March–April 1918, 250
German romanticism, 122
Gibson, William, 125
Givenchy Wood, 225
Givenchy-en-Gohelle Cemetery, 225
Globe Theatre: as memory system, 35

Goethe, J. W., 123
Gombrich, Ernst, 36
Goody, Jack, 64
Gorky, Maxim, 116, 276
Graves, Robert, 146: *Goodbye to All That*, 6, 25, 27
Gray, John: *Billy Bishop Goes to War*, 270
Greek tragedy, 13–14, 80, 87, 114
Greenberg, Joel, 183, 190–1
Griffin, Jasper, 73, 76–7, 87–9, 95
Griffith, D. W., 117: *Birth of a Nation*, 31
Gunston, Leslie, 117
Gurval, Robert Alan, 76, 78, 97–9
Gutenberg, Johannes, 272

Haber, Franz, 222, 292n
Haber, Fritz, 194–5, 292n
Haig, Douglas, 114
Halbwachs, Maurice, 64
Halifax explosion, 12, 48, 78–9, 80, 83, 85–6, 93–4, 96, 269
Hamburg, firebombing of, 270
Hansard, 141
Hardy, Thomas, 86, 288n; *The Dynasts*, 144
Harrison, Charles Yale: and battle of Amiens, 25, 136–7, 288n; *Generals Die in Bed*, 7, 25, 39, 128–37, 294n; and Remarque E. M., 8, 25, 39, 129, 273–4
Havelock, Eric, 33, 54–8, 62–4, 68, 235, 243–4, 263
Hawking, Stephen, 186, 188, 200
Heath, Stephen, 206, 216–17, 219–29
Hegel, G. W. F., 122
Hein, Hilde S., 239, 241–3
Heller, Joseph, 17

Helmer, Lt Alexis, 22
Hemingway, Ernest, 294–5 n
Hill 70, 248
Hill, David Octavius, 174
Hindenburg Tunnel, 152
Hiroshima, 82, 270–1
Historial de la Grande Guerre, 13,
244, 252–7, 281
historical film, 38; conventions of,
44–5; relation to oral culture, 46,
234
History Television, 11, 12, 42, 45,
183, 205–36, 238, 277–9, 282,
290 n; modes of address, 207–8
History, first chairs of, 172
Hitler, Adolph, 232, 251–2
HMS *Good Hope*, 291 n
Hodgins, Jack; *Broken Ground*,
269
Hoile, Christopher, 183, 190–2,
197, 201
Holocaust, 270
Homer, 11, 43–4, 45–8, 49, 53–71,
74, 77–81, 87, 98, 114, 228, 234,
261–5; Bellerophontes' Tablet,
53–4, 57, 67, 71; Catalogue of
Ships, 62–3; *Odyssey*, 48, 54, 74,
79–81, 86–7, 96–7. *See also Iliad*
Hong Kong, fall of, 271
Honour Roll: cult of, 24, 207
Hopkins, Chris, 19
Horace, 66–7, 98, 106; *Epode* 9,
98; *Odes*, 39, 66, 105–6, 107
Hucker, Jacqueline, 215, 290 n
Hudson, Christopher, 14, 112–14,
117
Hughes, Sam, 25, 246
Hulcoop, John, 162
Humphries, Mark Osborne, 292 n
Husserl, Edmund, 173

Huyssen, Andreas, 26, 35–8, 42,
44, 128, 288 n
hypertext: and medieval manuscript
space, 258

Iliad, 46–9, 53–71, 87, 93, 229–30,
235, 273, 286 n; challenge to cultural system, 65, 68, 70, 273–4;
custom-law in, 55–8, 64, 68; history in, 55, 62–4, 67; and law of
obsolescence, 48, 274; as tribal
encyclopedia, 55, 71, 265; compared with Virgil, 77, 86–7, 88,
94; written communications in,
53–4. *See also* Homer
images d'Epinal, 4, 294 n
Imagist poets: and cinema, 295 n
Imperial War Graves Commission,
24, 231. *See also* Commonwealth
War Graves Commission
Imperial War Museum, 112, 288 n
industrialism: and modern war, 28–
9, 105, 228; in wartime Canada,
229

Jack, Richard, 247–8, 282; *Second
Battle of Ypres*, 248, 292 n
Jakobson, Roman, 117
Janson, Astrid, 190
Jones, David: *In Parenthesis*, 27
Jonson, Ben, 6, 17
Joyce, James, 79; *Ulysses*, 18, 79,
295 n
Jünger, Ernst, 178, 224

Kaiser Wilhelm Institute, Berlin,
194
Kant, Immanuel, 122
Kaplan, Jon, 183
Keats, John, 117

Kenderline, Sarah, 240, 242
Kerr, Kevin: *Unity*, 270
Kilback, Paul, 217, 222
Kipling, Rudyard, 20, 23, 231
Knowledge Network, 45
Kohlhaas, Alidë, 191, 197
Kong, Ying, 295n
Konowal, Filip, VC, 248
Korean War, 6, 259
Koselleck, Reinhart, 42
Kosso, Peter, 198, 200–1, 289n
Kracauer, Siegfried, 171, 173
Kröller, Eva-Marie, 162–3
Kullmann, Wolfgang, 55, 62–4, 67

La Salle, Sieur de, 24
La Targette French Military Cemetery, 219
La Vérendyre, Sieur de, 24
Laking, Clare, 237–8, 258, 261; enlistment photo, 258
Lancey, Albert William, 261
Lanczos, Cornelius, 184, 201, 289n
Langemarck German Cemetery, 221–2
Lankester, E. R., 104–5
Lavelle, Mollie, 261–2
lay stationers, 272–3
Lees-Smith, H. B., 141, 289n
Lens, 218–19, 263, 277
Lersch, Heinrich, 4
Lessing, G. E., 193
Levy, Ira, 205
Lill, Wendy: *Fighting Days*, 270
Linear B script, 55, 62
Lipsett, Maj-Gen. L. J., 25
literate memory: contrasted with oral memory, 9, 75–6; prescriptive power of, 77
Little Mother, 22

Llandovery Castle (hospital ship), 135–7
Loeb Classical Library, 105
London Blitz, 270
Lower Canada College, 99
Lucas, Alec, 79
Ludendorf, Gen. Erich von, 250
Lumière, Louis and Auguste, 30, 40, 108, 188; as brand name, 188; *Catalogue Général des Vues Positives*, 111; early exhibitions, 108, 153; first film, 108; invention of cinématographe, 108; quit filmmaking, 110–11; reception in Russia, 116

MacDonald, Laura, 82
Macdonald, Sharon, 240–1
Macdonell, Sir Archibald, 25
MacLennan, Dr Sam, 83
MacLennan, Hugh, 78–9, 83; *Barometer Rising*, 12, 48, 78–100; as a child, 83; as a classicist, 80, 96–7, 99, 103, 105; and Hardy, 86; later novels, 86; and letter to Woodcock, 80–1; and *pax Canadiana*, 48, 78, 100, 274; and radio play on Augustus, 99; as teacher, 78, 99; and *Ulysses*, 79–80; as Virgilian "architect," 81, 93, 274
MacMechan, Archibald, 81–2
MacNeil, Robert: *Burden of Desire*, 269
Major, Kevin: *No Man's Land*, 269
Malins, Geoffrey, 112–13; *The Battle of the Somme*, 112–14; *How I Filmed the War*, 112
Manchester Regiment, 150
Marne: battle of, 4, 269, 294n

Marschall, Georg: "Achilles Break-
  ing his Sword," 256–7
Marsh, Eddie, 139–40
Massicotte, Stephen: Mary's Wed-
  ding, 270
Massingham, H. W., 289n
Masters, John: The Ravi Lancers,
  294n
Matsuda, Matt K., 30, 34, 39–40,
  104, 107, 109, 121, 123, 125–6,
  131–2, 134, 147–8, 153
Matthews, Brander: "The Kineto-
  scope of Time," 186
McClung, Nellie, 270
McCrae, John, 13, 21–3, 26; al-
  luded to in Barometer Rising, 78;
  "In Flanders Fields", 13, 21, 23,
  267–8; surgical dressing station
  of, 267, 291n
McDowell, John, 112
McLuhan, Eric, 272
McLuhan, Marshall, 9, 272, 285n;
  law of obsolescence, 48, 272, 274
medieval memory: as Gothic architecture, 10, 34; as inner writing, 34
Meighen, Arthur, 236
Méliès, Georges, 30; cinematic sto-
  rytelling, 110–11
Meliorist myth, 17
memory: altered by media, 38–9;
  cinematic, 6–8, 11, 32, 35, 39–
  41, 103–5; electronic, 11–12,
  205–68; history of, 9, 11–13, 34–
  5, 47, 49; as inner writing, 10,
  34, 36; as medium, 1, 9, 47; as
  neural network, 38; oral, 9–10,
  46–9, 53–71, 75, 77, 257, 264,
  273–4, 279–80, 281–2; photographic, 12, 161–81, 182, 275–6;
  physiology of, 37; plurality of,

286n; research on subjects, 59;
  and site of viewing, 110; written,
  11–12, 48, 72–3, 75–8
Memory Project, the, 11, 12, 32,
  38, 42, 46–7, 237–9, 257–66,
  280; democratic character of, 47,
  267; digitized Attestation papers
  in, 46, 247, 265, 280; digitized
  diaries in, 46, 260, 280; and loss
  of aura, 243; and medieval texts,
  257–8; and oral pathways, 47,
  265, 280; and relay of voices,
  266; return of dead, 280; and social memory, 211, 280; and total
  archives approach, 259–60; volunteer character of, 47, 267
Menin Gate, the, 23
Mercer, Maj-Gen. Malcolm, 25
Michelet, Jules, 238–9
Milestone, Lewis: adaptation of All
  Quiet on the Western Front, 4,
  31, 121
Milius, John, 230
Millar, Laura, 259, 261
Milton, John, 247
Minchin, Elizabeth, 60–1, 65, 74,
  234
Mnemosyne, 36, 47
modern memory: and anti-
  classicism, 105–7, 118, 121–3,
  141; and breaking of time, 30;
  and Great War cinema, 31–2,
  108–14, 118–21; and ironic
  mode, 7, 18, 26–7, 32; as sever-
  ance from past, 26
Mons: battle of 1914, 25; battle of
  1918, 251
Mont St Eloi, 218
Montgomery, L. M.; Rilla of Ingleside, 294n

Montreal Canadiens: and "In Flanders Fields," 268

Moreuil Wood: battle of, 270

Morgan, Duncan: soundscape of *The Lost Boys*, 190

Moriyama, Raymond, 293 n

Mount Sorrel: battle of, 25

Munslow, Alun, 241

Musée de l'Infantérie, Montpellier, 244–6, 281

Musée d'Orsay, 193, 294 n

museum exhibition: aura of objects, 240, 243, 257; and classical memory, 246; fear of spectacle, 256; narrative systems of, 240; and silent film, 244–5, 255–6, 281; and silent veneration, 240, 281–2; and sound, 239–40, 244, 246–8, 250–2; static display, 241–2, 245–6, 247–8, 281; and theme parks, 242; and virtual technologies, 240, 242–4

Mycenae, 55, 62–4, 282

MySpace, 259, 280

Nagasaki, 82, 270–1

Napoleon, 269

Napoleonic Wars, 4, 193, 244, 269, 293 n

National Gallery, London, 242

Neuville St Vaast, 218, 220–1

New, W. H., 85

Newbolt, Sir Henry, 22

Newfoundland Regiment, 113, 115, 269

newspapers and periodicals: *Bradford Pioneer*, 141; *Evening News* (Port Hope , Ont.), 25; *Manchester Guardian*, 141; *Montreal Star*, 129; *New York Times*, 7;

pre-war, 20, 114; *Le Progrès*, 153; *Punch*, 22, 194; *Le Radical*, 108–9; *Scribner's Magazine*, 186; *Stage Door*, 183; *Times* (London), 105, 112, 114, 289 n

Newtonian physics, 185, 187, 289 n

Next-of-Kin Plaque, 232

Nichols, Stephen G., 258

Nicholson, Col. G. W. L., 137, 285 n, 291 n

Niepce, Joseph Nicéphore, 41, 172

Normandy: battle of, 270

North African Wars, 244

Nuremberg, 232, 252

Oedipus Rex, 80

Ogden, C. K., 288–9 n

Olinyk, Nick, 248

Olympic games, origin of, 63

Ong, Walter J., 64, 234–5, 262, 279

oral culture: as automated technology, 58; in Canada, 261; and custom-law, 55, 58, 64; and digital networks, 264–5, 280–1; and dual coding, 60; duration of, 64; and forgetting, 64; formulaic constraints of, 57, 59–60, 61, 74–5; and formulas, 56–8, 61, 67–9; contrast to history, 55, 62–4, 67; and homeostasis, 64; and hyperlinked pathways, 47, 75, 265, 280; as inner film, 60, 234, 246, 279; and knowledge structures, 59, 74; as literacy, 10, 34, 36; contrast to literate conception, 72, 75, 77; metrical transmission of, 55–6, 71; oral memory, 10–11, 46–9; participatory mystique of, 12, 234, 279; pathways (*oimai*), 47, 75, 265, 280; relation to television, 12, 42–3, 44–5, 234–6, 277, 279, 282, 290n; relation to virtual technologies, 240; as serial recall, 60; and threat of writing, 33, 48, 54, 71; values of sound, 262

Otis, Brooks, 86–90, 91, 93–4, 96

Owen, Colin, 115

Owen, Susan, 106, 115, 116, 117

Owen, Wilfred, 4, 6, 7, 8, 20, 22, 31, 39, 105–7, 115–21; ambivalence toward cinema, 115–18; anti-classicism of, 105–7; "Arms and the Boy," 105; and Charlie Chaplin, 117; cinematic techniques of, 118–21; *Collected Letters*, 115, 117; "Dulce et Decorum Est," 22, 31–2, 39, 106–8, 118, 121, 147, 272; gas letter, 118; and Keats, 117; *Poems*, 106; "Preface," 106; and Romantics, 6, 107; meets Sassoon, 117; on "Somme Pictures," 115, 117–18; University College, Reading, 107; and Virgil, 105–6

Oxford University, 103, 105, 107

Paardeberg: battle of, 26

Page, T. E., 105

Paivio, Allan, 60

Panofsky, Erwin, 246

Papineau, Carolyn, 229

Papineau, Talbot, 229

Parry, Milman, 62

Passchendaele: battle of, 26, 99, 198–9, 209, 226, 227, 231, 249–50, 263, 291n

Pater, Walter, 140, 288n

Pawley, Lt Norman, 249

Phillips, Terry, 19–20

photography, 12, 32, 41, 161–81; absence of future tense, 173–4; aorist tense of, 173–4; as distancing agent, 41; interruptive force of, 161, 165–8, 171; invention of, 12, 41, 172; pictorial arts, past tense of, 8; relation to history, 162, 172–3, 289n; reproducibility of, 166, 170, 174–5; structure of delay, 162, 176–7, 180; temporal discontinuity of, 168, 170

Plato, 33, 36, 113, 285n; antipathy to oral poetry, 57–8, 243–4; and inner writing, 36; original and copy, 258; *Phaedrus*, 33, 36; *Republic*, 243; written epistemology of, 33

Platonic idea: and cybernetic programme, 257, 280

Ploughman, Max: *A Subaltern on the Somme*, 29

Poelcapelle Cemetery, 231

poppies: flower of Remembrance, 22–3, 134; on McCrae memorial, 267–8

Pound, Ezra, 18, 81

Poussin, Nicolas: *Les bergers d'Arcadie*, 131

Princess Patricia's Canadian Light Infantry (PPCLI) 183, 191, 194, 200, 212, 220, 221

Princeton University, 78

Propertius, Sextus, 98

Prösler, Martin, 246, 251

Proust, Marcel, 18, 190, 192, 289n; *À la recherche du temps perdu*, 184

Quigley, Hugh: *Passchendaele and the Somme*, 29

Quinn, Patrick J., 19
Quintilian, 9

Reichenbach, Hans, 185
Reid, Gilbert, 217, 222
Remarque, E. M., 4, 7, 8, 30, 123,
  129, 273, 274, 287n; limited ex-
  perience at Front, 39, 287n. See
  also All Quiet on the Western
  Front; Wolff, Max Joseph
Remembrance Day, 226; in
  Naicam, Saskatchewan, 23
Renaissance memory, 10–11, 35
Requark, Emil Marius. See Wolff,
  Max Joseph
Ribot Commission, 104
Ricou, Laurie, 164, 179
Ridley College, 24
Rivers, Dr. W. H. R., 27, 154–5
Roberts, William, 248; First Ger-
  man Gas Attack at Ypres, 247,
  282, 292n
Roman Republic, 93, 98, 274
Roosevelt, Theodore, 110
Rosenstone, Robert A., 38, 43, 44,
  227, 229–30, 234, 293n
Rouault, Georges, 4
Rouse, W. H. D., 104–5
Roy, Gabrielle, 289n
Royal Montreal Regiment, 129
Royal Welch Fusiliers, 139
Rubin, David C., 59–60, 69, 74–5,
  234
Russell, Bertrand, 288n
Russo, John Paul, 36
Rwanda, 136

Sale, Mary, 62, 69
Samuel, Raphael, 226
Santayana, George, 232

Santi, Marcel, 245
Saskatchewan Communications
  Network, 45, 226
Sassoon, Siegfried, 6–9, 17, 27, 40,
  105, 107, 138–57; and Achilles,
  67, 139, 140–1, 288n; leaves
  Cambridge, 107; at Craiglockhart
  Hospital, 67, 117, 142, 156;
  Counter-Attack, 67, 139, 156; Diaries, 139, 140–2, 144, 151, 154,
  156, 161; "Everyone Sang," 138;
  "Falling Asleep," 138; Memoirs of
  a Fox–Hunting Man, 29, 139,
  153; Memoirs of an Infantry Officer, 40, 139, 142–3, 144, 148–9,
  150–7, 275; Memoirs of George
  Sherston, 27, 39, 139, 148–9, 153,
  161, 272, 275; The Old Huntsman, 139; Picture Show, 39, 138;
  "Picture-Show," 138–9, 144,
  289n; Sherston's Progress, 6, 27,
  139, 148, 154–7; Siegfried's Journey, 139, 143, 146, 150, 156; as
  soldier-poet, 39, 140–1, 143–4,
  147, 151, 153, 154–5, 157, 275;
  "A Soldier's Declaration," 141,
  155, 275; meets Wilfred Owen,
  117; and Whitman, 144
Saul, John Ralston, 261
Scheldt: battle of the, 270
Schnack, Anton, 4
Schwartz, Joan M., 289n
Scott, Canon Frederick, 212, 214–
  15, 222–3, 278; The Great War
  As I Saw It, 214, 227; Homeric
  discourse on fame, 227
scripts: cybernetic, 74; as knowledge structures, 74
Second World War, 6, 17, 48, 83,
  164, 271; and language, 271

Seven Years' War, 244

Shakespeare, William, 35, 116, 290n; history plays of, 208

Sheffield, Gary, 226–7, 291n

Sherriff, R. C.: *Journey's End*, 29

Simonides of Ceos, 10, 33, 35

Sinclair, May, 19

Skirrow, Gillian, 206, 216–17, 219–20

Smither, Roger, 112

Snelgrove, Charles Reginald, 264

Snelgrove, John Cecil: 75th Battalion, 264

Socrates, 33, 285n

Somme Offensive, the, 13, 18, 112–13, 114, 149, 151–2, 218, 227; Canadian casualties in, 218; Hawthorne Redoubt, 112

Somme River, 131, 205

Sorlin, Pierre, 45, 107

South African (Boer) War, 110, 239

South Uist, 60

Spanish–American War 110

Spanish Civil War 6

Spanish influenza epidemic, 255, 270

Spee, Vice-Admiral von, 291n

Spencer, Stanley, 4

Spender, J. A., 289n

Spengemann, William C., 289

Squire, Larry R., 286n

Srebernica, 136

Statute of Westminster, 251

Steedman, Carolyn, 238–9

Stendhal: *The Charterhouse of Parma*, 293n

Stevenson, Frances, 13, 113–14

St-Julien, Flanders, 23, 205, 285n

Stothers, John Cannon, 265–6

Strange, Bill, 264

Stratford War Memorial, 206, 209, 290n

television, 10, 11, 12, 37, 42–5, 47, 125, 132, 162, 183–4, 185, 205–36, 241, 246, 259, 261, 273; displacement of cinema, 209, 277; documentary look, 211–16, 234, 277; electronic scanning, 209; as flow, 208, 210–12, 278; as flow and regularity, 216–22, 278; ideology of liveness, 12, 42–3, 44, 210–11, 277; institutional practices of, 211, 277; and oral culture, 234–6, 277; participatory mystique of, 12, 234, 279; presentness of, 207, 209–10, 234; as segmentation, 208; system of looks, 212–13, 216; taping before live audience, 211, 235; textual characteristics of, 234

television editing: eye-line match, 212; field/reverse-field, 212; two-shot, 212, 232

televisual history; and call to follow, 45, 206–7, 214–15, 220–1, 225, 233, 234, 277–9; and folk memory, 236, 278; vs history on film, 206–7, 234; modes of address, 44, 207, 235, 277, 277; and narration, 217–18; 222, 277–8; sound as binding agent, 207–8; time shifter, 206; vs written history, 226–30; yesterday-today structure of, 206. *See also* Thomson, R. H.

Thiepval Memorial, 231

Thomson, R. H., 12, 41–2, 45; as actor, 182; *The Lost Boys*, 12, 41–2, 182–202, 205, 270, 275–6,

292n; compared to Proust, 190, 192; relation to *The Wars*, 41, 182; as television narrator, 205, 208, 277
Thorburn, David, 242
Thorpe, Michael, 139
Tokyo, fire-bombing of, 270
Tolstoy, Leo, 293n
Tonight Show, The, 211
total archives, 259–60
Trojan War, 11, 48, 55, 64, 74, 99, 123
Trout, Steven, 19
Tunisian workers, 255
TV Ontario, 226
Tyne Cot Cemetery, 209, 231, 290–1n

UN peacekeeping, 259; Canada's role in, 270
Universal Pictures, 121
Urquhart, Jane: *The Stone Carvers*, 232, 269
Urry, John, 126–7, 211, 288n

Valcartier, QC, 24
Valenciennes: battle of, 251
Valiants Memorial: National Capital Commission, 286–7n
Vance, Jonathan, 20–1, 23–6, 28, 223, 285n, 290n, 292n
Varley, George, 253; "For What?", 251
Verdun: battle of, 245–6, 282
Versailles: Treaty of, 251
Vietnam war, 7, 18, 40, 164, 170
Vimy Memorial Park, 205, 225; tree planting in, 290n
Vimy Monument, 24, 206, 214, 225, 232–3, 269, 279, 290n,

293n; Spirit of Canada, 226; unveiling of, 24, 233
Vimy Pilgrimage 24, 233, 279
Vimy Ridge: capture of, 206, 209, 215, 219, 223–7, 249, 263, 282, 291n, 292n; Black Watch at, 263; British attacks on (1916), 205; British elements in battle (1917), 216; Canadian attack on, 206, 250, 271; creeping barrage, 216; French attacks on (1915), 205, 291n; German casualties at, 220; German prisoners taken, 225; Grange Subway, 215; Hill 145, 224; Pimple, the, 215–16, 224, 225, 249
Virgil, 11–12, 72–100 *passim*; Aeneas: as Augustan prototype, 96, 274; as architect of empire, 12, 20, 48, 73, 76, 78, 88, 97, 123, 274–5; contrasted to Homer, 77, 86–8, 94, 98; "Second Eclogue," 20
virtual heritage, 242
virtual objects: and democratization, 257; as supplements to print, 257–8 ; as virtual presences, 241
Voormezeele Cemetery, 221
Vor Troja Nichts Neues, 123, 287n

Walsh, Peter, 258
war cemeteries; British Commonwealth, 24, 209, 221, 224–5, 231, 278; French, 219–20; German, 221–2
war painting: Canadian, 217, 218, 224, 247–8, 251, 292n; French, 190, 193, 245
Waterloo, battle of, 4, 269, 294n

Watson, Patrick, 247, 249, 251
Watt, Ian, 64
Waugh, Evelyn, 18
Wells, H. G., 105, 288n
West, Benjamin: *The Death of General Wolfe*, 175
Wheeler, Cpl Victor, 216, 222, 228
White, Hayden, 13, 272; allegories of temporality, 13–14; history and tragic form, 14
Whitehead, William, 161
Whitman, Walt, 144
Wilkinson, Glenn R., 20
Will, George, 44
Williams, David: *Confessional Fictions*, 288n, 289n; *Imagined Nations*, 11, 264, 286n, 293n, 295n
Williams, Raymond, 208, 211, 217
Williamson, Peter, 205

Wilson-Simmie, Katherine: *Lights Out*, 294n
Winter, Jay, 3–6, 7, 19, 270, 271
Winterer, Caroline, 103–4
Witcomb, Andrea, 240–1, 242
Wolfe, Gen. James, 24, 174, 275
Wolff, Max Joseph (pseud. Requark, Emil Marius), 287n
women's war fiction, 19–20, 269–70, 294n
Woodcock, George, 48, 79–80, 86; MacLennan correspondence, 80–1; on MacLennan's faults, 86

Yates, Frances A., 9–11, 33–5
York, Lorraine M., 163
YouTube, 259
Ypres: First Battle of, 221–2; Second Battle of, 22, 282, 291n; Third Battle of, 290–1n

McGill-Queen's Studies in the History of Ideas
(*Continued*)

50 Social and Political Bonds
A Mosaic of Contrast and
Convergence
F.M. Barnard

51 Archives and the Event
of God
The Impact of Michel
Foucault on Philosophical
Theology
David Galston

52 Between the Queen
and the Cabby
Olympe de Gouges's
Rights of Woman
John R. Cole

53 Nature and Nurture in
French Social Sciences,
1859–1914 and Beyond
Martin S. Staum

54 Public Passion
Rethinking the Grounds
for Political Justice
Rebecca Kingston